BOLLINGEN SERIES XXXIII · 3

HUGO VON HOFMANNSTHAL

SELECTED
PLAYS
and
LIBRETTI

Edited and introduced
by MICHAEL HAMBURGER

BOLLINGEN SERIES XXXIII · 3

PANTHEON BOOKS

*Translated from the German texts in the following volumes
of the* Gesammelte Werke *of Hugo von Hofmannsthal,
edited by Herbert Steiner and published by S. Fischer Verlag, Frankfurt a/M, Germany:* Dramen II (*1954*), III
(*1957*), IV (*1958*), Lustspiele I (*1959*), II (*1954*), IV
(*1956*).

LIBRARY OF CONGRESS CATALOGUE CARD NO. 63–10309

MANUFACTURED IN THE UNITED STATES OF AMERICA
BY KINGSPORT PRESS, INC., KINGSPORT, TENN.
DESIGNED BY ANDOR BRAUN

Translators

MICHAEL HAMBURGER
CHRISTOPHER HOLME
CHRISTOPHER MIDDLETON
WILLA MUIR
ALFRED SCHWARZ
VERNON WATKINS
NORA WYDENBRUCK

Contents

Introduction

I

THOUGH NOT quite twenty-six years old at the turn of the century, Hofmannsthal had not only come to the end of one distinct phase, the lyrical, but laid the foundations for the dramatic works of his maturity. His early (1893) adaptation of the *Alcestis* of Euripides can be regarded as the first of his strictly dramatic works, and it anticipated his rather different concern with ancient Greek myths during the early years of the new century. The extant sketches, of the same year, for a great mystical and apocalyptic drama based on the life of Alexander the Great touch on certain themes that he was to develop thirty years later in *The Tower*. At least one completed work, *Der Abenteurer und die Sängerin* (1898), had almost succeeded in making the difficult transition from a drama mainly of monologue to one of delicate interplay both of character and motif. Together with *The Marriage of Zobeide,* this play was first performed on the regular stage in March 1899. Hofmannsthal called both plays "theatre in verse," as distinct from his earlier "lyrical dramas," and their performance in the Burgtheater, Vienna, and the Deutsches Theater, Berlin, marked the beginning of his involvement in "theatre business" proper.

Hofmannsthal's need for active involvement generally towards the end of his "pre-existence" has already been discussed in my introduction to the *Poems and Verse Plays*. Yet the peculiar cultural divisions of the time, and the kind of reputation that Hofmannsthal's poetry had won, made the step puzzling—if not positively shocking—to quite a number of his admirers. Nietzsche, whose influence on German intellectuals was pervasive and decisive at this period, had condemned the theatre as "mass art." Stefan George and his Circle upheld Nietzsche's condemnation with a rigour and solemnity that might well have made Nietzsche laugh. Though one of Hofmannsthal's early playlets had appeared in George's *Blätter für die Kunst,* it could pass as a poem in dialogue form and had the further distinction of being both unfinished and utterly unsuitable for the stage. When Hofmannsthal invited George to the first night of his little play *Die Frau im Fenster,* in 1898, he received no direct reply, but a hint after the event that the Circle would soon be making provision for private performances of dramatic works and that this might prove as attractive to Hofmannsthal as "a conventional, inevitably crude presentation on the common boards." George already suspected that it would not. But as a German he could not understand the claustrophobia that would have beset Hofmannsthal if he had acted on the hint.

It was soon after, in 1900, that Hofmannsthal first approached Richard Strauss. Their collaboration was not to begin until 1906, and it happened that at this very time George and the Circle were extending their hostility to the entire art of music. Opera and ballet, in any case, would have been disqualified for their impurities and associations with "mass art"; but now music itself was to be excluded from the civilizing arts, though the dance was saved from total interdiction by its sculptural and corporeal qualities. Much of Hofmannsthal's art as playwright and librettist remained rooted in the same symbolist aesthetic from which George's had sprung; but the externals of hated conventions—of

psychological comedy, for instance, with its seeming concession to the dominant naturalism—were more apparent to
George and his followers than Hofmannsthal's deeper commitment to an art of gesture, mask, and myth. By 1906 Hofmannsthal was beyond the Circle's pale; only its most independent member, Karl Wolfskehl, defied the Master by
keeping in touch with Hofmannsthal in later years.

These circumstances would be trivial if the misunderstanding had been confined to George and his disciples; but
with very few exceptions it was shared by prominent critics of
every school, and it is still apt to crop up in discussions of
Hofmannsthal's libretti. The recent publication in England and America of the correspondence between Richard
Strauss and Hofmannsthal prompted comments that recall
the most blatant misrepresentation of fifty years ago. "We
seem to be watching a Siamese cat working out a *modus
vivendi* with a Labrador," Mr. Edward Sackville-West aptly
remarked in his introduction to the correspondence; and
the personal incompatibility of the two men was even
more extreme than the letters reveal. Thus Mr. Sackville-
West wonders why Hofmannsthal was unwilling to meet the
composer more often than he did. Hofmannsthal's letters
to close friends make it clear that he was less devoted to
Strauss personally than to the work they did together; and
meticulously as he applied himself to anything that concerned the work, he had other commitments and could not
afford to waste time on unnecessary conversations. Count
Harry Kessler mentions in his diary that, after his last meeting with the two men in 1928, Hofmannsthal felt
obliged to apologize to Kessler in writing for the "nonsense"
talked by Strauss. Nor did Hofmannsthal have any illu-
sion about Strauss's merits as a composer; in a letter of
1914 to his friend Bodenhausen he writes that his hair stood

on end when Bodenhausen compared Strauss to Beethoven.

Strauss's much more cordial and uncomplicated relationship to Hofmannsthal, of which Hofmannsthal was well aware, led several reviewers of the correspondence to come down heavily on Strauss's side and ascribe Hofmannsthal's part in the collaboration to various sordid or neurotic motives. That the partnership was successful in many ways, despite or because of the personal incompatibility, should have made the critics think again and perhaps even go so far as to acquaint themselves with some of Hofmannsthal's non-operatic works. Had he proved less difficult and bizarre in his collaboration with Richard Strauss than in his independent works, his libretti would not be worth reprinting and reading for their own sake, and the precarious partnership would be less fascinating and less perplexing than it is. Hofmannsthal's part in the operas and ballets can be appreciated only in the light of his other works, from the early poetry to *The Tower*. A number of his libretti—*Ariadne auf Naxos, Die Frau ohne Schatten,* and *Die ägyptische Helena*—are sequels, in a more viable medium, to his early "lyrical dramas." Others are closely akin to the non-operatic plays of his mature years. Even in retrospect and in the light of Hofmannsthal's non-operatic works the collaboration appears in no way fortuitous, if only because one can think of no other composer of the time with whom he might have worked out a happier or smoother *modus vivendi*. In his review of the correspondence the music critic of *The Times* (London) complained that Hofmannsthal was a "dyed-in-the-wool reactionary" and that Strauss "abandoned his forward-looking traits at the behest of Hofmannsthal"—presumably because Hofmannsthal repeatedly implored Strauss to abstain from the "Wagnerian kind of erotic screaming . . . this shrieking of two creatures in heat" which he found repulsive, and because he preferred delicate *concertante* effects to mere orchestral volume. If Hofmannsthal's taste in music points to a reactionary disposition, so does the taste of Stravinsky, say, or Bartok, or Hindemith. Without various kinds of primitivism on the one hand and neo-classicism on the other, there would have been precious little "progress" in early twentieth-century music; and both, historically, are regressive trends. Stravinsky has said of his *Pulcinella* adaptation: "It was the epiphany through which all my later work became possible. It was a backward look, of course—the first of my love affairs in that direction—but it was a look in the mirror too." Hofmannsthal's development as a writer was largely a matter of such backward looks that were also "looks in the mirror"; and if he induced Strauss to take a few looks "in that direction," that was all to the good.

Of the distinguished poets of his time, few shared Hofmannsthal's peculiar need for a fusion of words with music, and of the composers that might have been more congenial to him in taste and temperament, none could respond as readily or constantly to this need as Richard Strauss. This simple circumstance explains why Hofmannsthal entered into a partnership which could exasperate him to the point of telling Strauss that it "antagonizes half the world, including even friends I value." These friends were persons towards whom Hofmannsthal could never have been guilty of such bluntness and seeming callousness, just as they would have been incapable of Strauss's injunctions to Hofmannsthal: "So get your Pegasus saddled," or "When composing your text don't think of the music at all—I'll see to that." Somehow or other the Siamese cat had to make an impression on the Labrador; no wonder he was reduced to grotesque and painful antics.

Yet the partnership produced a number of operatic masterpieces. As far as Hofmannsthal was concerned, it involved no sacrifice other than a personal one—and he took care to confine personal relations with Strauss to indispensable meetings. His insistence in the letters on the impersonal nature of the collaboration, which seems priggish at times and gratuitously offensive, rested on deeply held convictions relevant not only to the difference between the two men as men but also as artists. To withhold these convictions from Strauss, or to suspend them for the sake of an easy relationship, would have demanded a sacrifice of integrity. Once again mere hints were not taken; yet if Strauss could not grasp what the idea of impersonality meant to Hofmannsthal, he could not begin to grasp what the libretti were about. To this incomprehension on Strauss's part we owe some of the finest and most revealing letters in the correspondence.

Hofmannsthal's stress on the principle of impersonality in the arts seems to be contradicted by passages in which he calls attention to the importance of his own contribution to the operas and ballets. The particular kind of collaboration that Hofmannsthal wanted—"poetry-*cum*-music," not merely the provision of frames for musical compositions—demanded that Strauss should respond to the poetry and respect its quality. Hofmannsthal was always prepared to make concessions on musical or dramatic grounds—the second act of *The Cavalier of the Rose* is an outstanding instance—but he would not allow Strauss to forget that the two arts must be kept on an equal footing. Self-effacement was one thing, concessions to the composer's literary taste another. If there were occasions when Hofmannsthal had to bring home to Strauss not only that the other art existed in its own right but also that Strauss's librettist had won some distinction in that art, he was driven to the inconsistency by

Strauss's obtuseness and his own exasperation. Considering how long the association lasted, these occasions were rare; and they were counterbalanced by periods of mutual satisfaction and respect.

II

Hofmannsthal's need for "lyrical drama," or melodrama in the strictest sense—that is, for a medium in which words were fused with music—is closely connected with the "word-scepticism" expounded by the fictitious Lord Chandos of his justly famous Letter. That the so-called Chandos crisis was not confined to any one period of Hofmannsthal's life but was anticipated even in the works of that early poetic phase which it is often said to have terminated, was suggested in my introduction to Hofmannsthal's *Poems and Verse Plays*.

Hofmannsthal's experience of the inadequacy of words —already hinted at in his first verse play, *Gestern* (1891) —involved a whole complex of related matters. Above all, it was inseparable from his awareness of living in a civilization lacking in style, cohesion, and continuity. One of his very first prose pieces, published at the age of seventeen, contains this observation: "We have no generally valid tone in conversation because we have no society and no conversation, just as we have no style and no culture." Hofmannsthal's concern with total art grew out of this dissatisfaction. Art, in this early phase, was the means of creating dreams and illusions powerful enough to banish the barbarous realities of the age. Like much Symbolist doctrine, Hofmannsthal's was based on a stark dualism. Only a fusion of all the arts and their reduction to a common core of expression that was not self-expression alone, but gesture, ritual, and myth, could resist the fragmentation of culture.

Introduction

In his early essay on Paul Bourget, also published when he was seventeen, Hofmannsthal wrote that in an age of individualism, "no understanding is possible between two persons, no conversation, no connection between today and yesterday" (the theme of *Gestern,* written in the same year); "words lie, feelings lie, even our self-awareness lies." The essay shows the rather Nietzschean addiction at this time to strong sensations, the desire "to feel rushing, living blood: *à sentir sentir*"; but when Hofmannsthal writes, "if we can die of the body, we also owe to the body, to the senses, the foundation of all poetry," he is stating a belief which he was to modify, but never wholly renounce. The unity of body and mind is explicitly or implicitly upheld in all the works of his maturity; there are formulations of it in his novel *Andreas* and in his late play *The Tower.* This belief was one basis for Hofmannsthal's aesthetic of gesture. Indeed, the early essay opens up the whole complex of Hofmannsthal's most characteristic preoccupations; from his "word-scepticism"—clearly expressed here ten years before the Chandos Letter—to the questions of individuality and tradition.

Hofmannsthal's interest in the actor and the dancer goes back to the same early period. Both could transcend words, circumstance, and personal identity. Hofmannsthal put it like this in an early tribute to Eleonora Duse, the first of two such tributes written in 1892: "We do not know where the limits of her art might be. Not in individuality, since she has none, or any whatever." In a letter of the same year Hofmannsthal tells his friend that it makes no difference whether he knows Italian well, since Duse "acts the sense, not the words."

It is significant, too, that the so-called Chandos crisis should have been most clearly anticipated in another tribute

Introduction

to an actor, Hofmannsthal's review, in 1895, of a book on Friedrich Mitterwurzer. Here Hofmannsthal remarks:

For people are tired of listening to talk. They feel a deep disgust with words. For words have pushed themselves in front of things. Hearsay has swallowed the world. . . . We are in the grip of a horrible process in which thought is utterly stifled by concepts. Hardly anyone now is capable of being sure in his own mind about what he understands, what he does not understand, of saying what he feels and what he does not feel. This has awakened a desperate love for all those arts which are executed without speech: for music, for the dance, and all the skills of acrobats and jugglers.

Akin to these last is the clown Furlani who plays such an important, though concealed, part in Hofmannsthal's much later comedy *The Difficult Man*.

The actor, like the poet, is a *persona* in the original sense of the word, a mask or mouthpiece through which not one man but all humanity speaks. That is why Hofmannsthal was able to allow him an ideal and archetypal function which most of his predecessors and contemporaries reserved for the dancer; and that is why he could write in his late collection of aphorisms, the *Book of Friends*: "Between the fleeting fame of the actor and the allegedly lasting fame of the poet, there is but a small and specious difference." The full force of that casual remark comes home to one if he imagines how it would have been received by Stefan George, by one of his idolatrous followers, or even by one of Rilke's more devout lady admirers. (Rilke himself could have understood it, and understood that it was aimed not at poetry but at the cult of personalities.)

Hofmannsthal's poems on the deaths of actors are especially revealing in this connection. The earliest was written for the same actor, Mitterwurzer, after his death in 1897;

[xvii]

and it is the question of identity that makes these occasional poems relevant to Hofmannsthal's deepest and most constant concerns:

> *Er fiel: da fielen alle Puppen hin,*
> *In deren Adern er sein Lebensblut*
> *Gegossen hatte; lautlos starben sie,*
> *Und wo er lag, da lag ein Haufen Leichen,*
> *Wüst hingestreckt: das Knie von einem Säufer*
> *In eines Königs Aug gedrückt, Don Philipp*
> *Mit Caliban als Alp um seinen Hals,*
> *Und jeder tot.*
>
> *Da wussten wir, wer uns gestorben war:*
> *Der Zauberer, der grosse, grosse Gaukler!*
> *Und aus den Häusern traten wir heraus*
> *Und fingen an zu reden, wer er war.*
> *Wer aber war er, und wer war er nicht?*
>
> *Er kroch von einer Larve in die andre,*
> *Sprang aus des Vaters in des Sohnes Leib*
> *Und tauschte wie Gewänder die Gestalten.*

> (He fell: then all the puppets collapsed with him
> Into whose veins he'd poured his own life-blood.
> Now speechlessly they died; and where he lay
> There also stretched out a heap of corpses
> In wreck and ruin: knee of a drunkard
> Pressed into a king's eye; Don Philip
> With Caliban a nightmare round his neck,
> All of them dead.
>
> Then we knew whom death had taken from us:
> The sorcerer, the great great conjurer,
> And we came from our houses, gathered round
> And so began to talk of what he was.
> Who was he though, and who else was he not?

Introduction

He crept out of one mask into another,
Sprang from the father's into the son's body
And changed his shape as though it were his clothes.)

Much the same question is posed in the poem *On the Death of the Actor Hermann Müller* (1899), though here Hofmannsthal dwelt more poignantly on the dualism of real and assumed identity, of the dream projected on the stage and the reality from which even actors were not exempt:

> *Doch wenn das Spiel verlosch und sich der Vorhang*
> *Lautlos wie ein geschminktes Augenlid*
> *Vor die erstorbne Zauberhöhle legte*
> *Und er hinaustrat, da war eine Bühne*
> *So vor ihm aufgetan wie ein auf ewig*
> *Schlafloses aufgerissnes Aug, daran*
> *Kein Vorhang je mitleidig niedersinkt:*
> *Die fürchterliche Bühne Wirklichkeit.*
> *Da fielen der Verwandlung Künste alle*
> *Von ihm, und seine arme Seele ging*
> *Ganz hüllenlos und sah aus Kindesaugen.*

> (Yet when the play was fading, and the curtain
> Came down in silence like a painted eyelid
> Over the magic cavern emptied now of life,
> And he stepped out, a stage appeared before him
> Like a wide, sleepless eye for ever open
> On which no curtain mercifully falls,
> The terrifying stage, reality.
> Then all the arts of transformation dropped
> From him, and his poor soul walked quite unclothed
> And gazed from a child's eyes.)

True, this dualism did not detract from the actor's exemplary function, since it was one that Hofmannsthal himself experienced and rendered in all his earlier works.

Yet the Symbolist notion of "the stage as dream image" —the title of an essay by Hofmannsthal published in 1903—

[xix]

had to be reconciled with reality in some way, much as the ideal of impersonality had to be reconciled with what was valid in personality. The change is apparent in Hofmannsthal's later tributes to actors and in his later writings on the theatre. Hofmannsthal's own dramatic works of the transitional period bridge the gulf in several different ways. The essay on "the stage as dream image" recommends De Quincey, Poe, and Baudelaire as favourite authors of the perfect designer of stage décors; but Hofmannsthal jotted down the draft of a crucial passage of the essay on the back flyleaf of a volume containing Shakespeare's *Macbeth, Hamlet,* and *King Lear.* Hofmannsthal's modification of the Symbolist aesthetic owes a great deal to his study of Shakespeare, of the Greek dramatists whose works he adapted at this time, as well as of Calderón, Molière, and the whole repertory of classical, medieval, and modern drama. It was in his lecture on Shakespeare of 1905 that Hofmannsthal remarked on the "space between characters" that is "not a vacuum but a space mystically alive," and this became such an important element in his own art that he was to coin a new word, "allomatic," to describe the mysterious relationship.

Hofmannsthal began by celebrating the "truth of masks" and of that dream image which the stage opposes to the "terrifying stage, reality." So in his Prologue to the *Antigone* of Sophocles (1899):

> *Die Maske aber darf dich nicht verstören:*
> *es tragen die Geliebtesten der Menschen*
> *vor dir ein maskenhaft Gesicht:*
> *ein menschlich Aug erträgt nichts Wirkliches.*

> (You have no need to let my mask perturb you:
> even the dearest beings that you know,

Introduction

they only let you see the masks they wear:
the eye of man cannot bear that which is real.)

The masked Spirit of Antigone in this Prologue asserts
that only on the stage there is truth:

alles andre
ist Gleichnis und ein Spiel in einem Spiegel.

(all other things
are parables and playings in a mirror.)

But in 1903 Hofmannsthal began to write his *Jeder-*
mann, the first of his plays derived from medieval and Ba-
roque dramatic conventions that make the theatre an allegory of life. A passage in his *Vorspiel für ein Puppentheater*
(1906) marks the significance of the change: "From this
dream I rise and step over into that other dream which is
called human world and human life." In 1902 Hofmannsthal
had also begun that adaptation of Calderón's *Life Is a*
Dream which was to occupy him for the rest of his life,
gradually turning into his own most personally committed
play, *The Tower.* The dualism of dream and reality had become far less drastic and far more complex. If life was not as
real as it had once seemed, the stage did not need to be as
dreamlike as Hofmannsthal had believed; and if personality was not as individual as it had seemed, Hofmannsthal could now draw closer to the current realistic and social
drama. Even psychological comedy, he was soon to discover,
could include the wordless gesture, the mystery, and the myth.

In a third article on Eleonora Duse, written in 1903,
Hofmannsthal found it necessary to modify his earlier tributes to her. Duse had now become greater than the parts
she played; she had "suffered the afflictions of our
age like no one else, and in a magnificent way"; she had

acquired wisdom and become "the embodiment of an un-
namable tragic force." Here Hofmannsthal's personal
aquaintance with the actress—she was to play the title role in
his *Electra,* and Jocasta in his *Ödipus und die Sphinx*—may
seem to have involved him in a contradiction; but a diary
entry of 1904 points to an inherent paradox that bears
on the question of individuality and Hofmannsthal's
changing attitude to it. *"Paradox of the Actor:* Duse today can impersonate only herself, i.e., in every role she acts
the mature woman grown wonderful through love and
suffering; i.e., she now raises every role to the universal
plane." Personality, Hofmannsthal implies here and elsewhere
in his later work, becomes a positive value as soon as it embraces more than the merely individual and circumstantial.

The same change and the same paradox are evident in the
last of Hofmannsthal's poems in memory of actors, that written on the death of the great actor Josef Kainz, whom Hofmannsthal had known personally and who had also acted in
two of his plays. The manuscript of the poem in the
Vienna Nationalbibliothek is dated 2 October 1910. Like
the later Duse, and unlike the two other actors commemo-
rated in poems by Hofmannsthal, Kainz is seen not only as the
vehicle of transformations but as a personality equal to, or
greater than, the parts enacted; as

> *Ein Unverwandelter in viel Verwandlungen,*
> *Ein niebezauberter Bezauberer,*
> *Ein Ungerührter, der uns rührte, einer,*
> *Der fern war, da wir meinten, er sei nah . . .*
> *Und Bote eines namenlosen Herrn.*

> (One untransformed in many transformations,
>   A great enchanter never himself enchanted,
>   A man unmoved who moved us, one
>   Who, when we thought him near, was far from us . . .
>   Messenger to us of a nameless Lord.)

[xxii]

Introduction

The allusion to an unexplained mission indicates a kind of personality that is more than individuality. Kainz, in the same poem, becomes the "actor without a mask," and another passage dwells on an aspect of this kind of personality that Hofmannsthal also emphasized in other later writings:

> O wie das Leben um ihn rang und niemals
> Ihn ganz verstricken konnte ins Geheimnis
> Wollüstiger Verwandlung! Wie er blieb!
> Wie königlich er standhielt!

> (O how life clutched at him, and never yet
> Could quite ensnare him in the mystery of
> Voluptuous transformation! How he *stayed*!
> How royally he stood fast!)

Hofmannsthal's cult of the actor had its roots in his early intuition that the very word *self* is "little more than a metaphor," and that "we and the world are not different things." This intuition was the source of much of Hofmannsthal's early lyrical poetry and early lyrical drama, though even in these works he was looking for an ethical principle that would prevent this metaphorical self from simply evaporating and would govern its relationship to the here and now. Though the individual could never be autonomous or clearly circumscribed, true personality demanded a commitment not only to the flux of being—"to have genius is to participate in the unreason of the cosmos," Hofmannsthal noted towards the end of his life—but to some fixed point outside the self. This is the constancy or loyalty attributed to Kainz in the poem, though the actual commitment is not explained.

What Hofmannsthal attempted everywhere in his life and works was to combine both these commitments—to be loyal to certain conventions and institutions, yet to remain open to the mystery and the flux. As he wrote in his prologue of 1926 to Brecht's first play *Baal*, "We move within forms and

conventions without sacrificing the mystery of life to them,"
contrasting this attitude with that of the younger generation. In Brecht's play and its "crude inarticulate language"
Hofmannsthal saw "the end of individualism . . . that
child of the seventeenth century which the nineteenth fat-
tened up"; he both censured and welcomed them as an
expression of an amorphous energy, a chaos that might
engender a new age.

I do not wish to suggest that Hofmannsthal ever finally
unravelled this complex of problems and paradoxes. "The
shaped work settles the problem," he wrote, and the verb implies that problems are only "solved" in the abstract. Compar-
ing the mime and the dancer with the actor in his essay *On
Pantomime,* Hofmannsthal had written that the former must
be "lacking in individuality, which cannot be conveyed in any
medium other than language"; yet a diary entry of 1921 reads
as follows: "The individual is inexpressible. Whatever is expressed, immediately takes on a general aspect and ceases to
be individual in any strict sense. Language and individuality
are mutually exclusive." We are left with the paradox and the
mystery with which Hofmannsthal had been at grips for
thirty years, and with the inference that the individual is inexpressible in any medium whatever. This points to the core of
Hofmannsthal's own art—an art of "I"-suppression, Hermann Broch called it—and comes as close as I wish to come to
an explanation of Hofmannsthal's cult of the actor, his renunciation of lyrical poetry, and his resort to various mixed media.
In the same late prologue to Brecht's play the actor is characterized once more as "the amoeba among living creatures,
the indeterminate archetypal creature that lets the situation
prescribe whether it is to be animal or vegetable"; and "that
is why he is the symbolic man."

The actor's medium, like the poet's, is words, and both

actor and poet are subject to the limitations and responsibilities imposed by that medium; yet both also transcend them: the poet by his capacity to render the timeless moment and transform circumstance into myth, the actor by his capacity to render not the words, but the sense, in pure gesture. It is this latter aspect of the actor that accounts for Hofmannsthal's tendency to speak of actors and dancers as though their function were one and the same.

Hofmannsthal's dance libretti are less well known than his opera libretti, but he wrote quite a number of them—for the traditional ballet, for Diaghilev, and for the solo dancer Grete Wiesenthal, a close personal friend. Dance forms an important part of several of Hofmannsthal's dramatic works, beginning with the climax of his *Electra*. The first work that Hofmannsthal offered to Richard Strauss, in 1900, and well before Strauss's composition of *Electra,* was a ballet libretto, *Der Triumph der Zeit*. This was the first of a long succession of dance libretti and "pantomimes" no less various in setting and style than Hofmannsthal's plays and opera libretti; the last, *Achilles auf Skyros,* was written in 1925.

"Dance," Frank Kermode wrote, "is the most primitive, non-discursive art, offering a pre-scientific image of life, an intuitive truth. Thus it is the emblem of the Romantic image. Dance belongs to a period before the self and the world were divided, and so achieves naturally that 'original unity' which modern poetry can produce only by a great and exhausting effort of fusion." Hofmannsthal's earliest references to dance belong to the brief phase in which he combined a Nietzschean vitalism and primitivism with a taste for the latest refinements of "decadent" art. His second essay on Duse of 1892 speaks of artists as "raising the unconscious to our awareness in words that die away, in fugitive gestures, and immersing it in dionysian beauty." In the same year he praised Swinburne's poems as vessels filled with "darkly glowing, potent wine of life, pressed from grapes from which dionysian ecstasy and anguish and dance and madness well, mysteriously blended." This tribute draws on the international vocabulary of contemporary aestheticism; but even in later years dance retained its associations for Hofmannsthal with orgiastic ecstasy, anguish, and madness. Where he tried to render these in another medium—as in a whole succession of mythical dramas, of which *Pentheus, Leda und der Schwan,* and *Semiramis* are outstanding—he produced only drafts and fragments. Only "fugitive gestures," wordless and "nameless," could convey them.

Yet Hofmannsthal's essays and his dialogue *Fear*—a work closely akin to Paul Valéry's *L'Âme et la danse,* but written some fifteen years earlier—at least evoke such moments in words, in a rhythmic and vivid prose peculiar to his visions of primitive mysteries. So in his *Dialogue on Poems* of 1903, mainly a tribute to Stefan George's works, which contains this passage on the ancient wine press:

Those who press the grapes feel like gods. They feel as though Bacchus were right in their midst while they work by night. As though he were stamping beside them, his long robe gathered up to above the knee, in the red juice whose very vapour intoxicates. They are at once bathers and dancers: and it is the drunkenness of their dancing that makes their bath rise higher and higher. The new wine gushes from the press in streams; like little ships the wooden cups sway on the purple flood. . . . In the vapoury darkness, amid screams, amid swaying torchlight, and the splashing of the blood of the grapes, suddenly Aphrodite is born from the purple foam: Bacchus rose from the wine-press, wild as a leaping wave, and drenched a garment, so that it flowed down like a shining nakedness, and out of a girl he created the goddess around whose body desire and rapture flow.

Fear (1907) is a dialogue between two Greek dancing girls, Laidion and Hymnis. Its theme is Hofmannsthal's constant concern with the trammels of individuality and the casting off of those trammels in art. Laidion suggests to Hymnis that all their impersonations and transformations in the dance are incomplete because they can never wholly escape from personal desire, from hope, and its concomitant fear. Laidion is obsessed by the thought of a barbarian island community whose dancing is impersonal because it is an annual rite, not a professional skill. Its women are "virgins and have forgotten it, they are to become women and mothers and have forgotten it: to them everything is ineffable. And then they dance."

At this point in the dialogue words fail Laidion: "She begins to sway from the hips. Somehow one feels that she is not alone, that many of her kind are around her and that all are dancing at once under the eyes of their gods. They dance and circle as dusk falls: shadows detach themselves from the trees and sink down into the crowd of dancers, and out of the treetops rise great birds housing the departed spirits, and join the circle, and beneath them all the island vibrates like a boat filled with drunken people. . . ."

Laidion has only heard about the island from a sailor; and the element of doubt as to whether there really is, or ever has been, a place where women could be "happy without hope," that is, wholly divested of their personal desires and fears, is an ironic reflection on the literary cult of the dancer in Hofmannsthal's time. Yet clearly the dancer was less subject to those complications and paradoxes which beset Hofmannsthal's cult of the actor as "symbolic man." Hofmannsthal's essay on Oscar Wilde of 1905, itself the celebration of a myth, concludes with a quotation from the Persian that sums up the peculiar mystery which Hofmannsthal attributed to the dance: "He who knows the power of the dance of life fears not death. For he knows that love kills." Hofmannsthal's Electra alludes to the same mystery.

Hofmannsthal's essay *On Pantomime* (1911) is the most

comprehensive and illuminating of all his writings on the actor and the dancer, not least because it subsumes both figures and reduces both arts to their common element of gesture. "A pure gesture is like a pure thought that has been stripped even of the momentarily witty, the restrictedly individual, the grotesquely characteristic," Hofmannsthal writes, and goes on to distinguish all these accretions from true personality. In a letter to Carl Burckhardt of 1928 Hofmannsthal outlined the plan of a comedy never completed in which one character, a notorious liar, decides to become a dancer and "says he has chosen this profession because he adores the truth, and dancing is the only profession in which there is *nothing but* truth." This is the truth rendered in gesture, and only in gesture or in pre-articulate thought. The essay continues:

In pure thought, personality appears by virtue of its nobility and strength, though not in a way perceptible at once to everyone. So too in pure gestures the true personality comes to light, and the renunciation of individuality is more than amply compensated. We see a human body that moves in a rhythmic flow, in response to infinite modulations prescribed by an inner genius. It is a man like ourselves who moves before us, but more freely than we ever move, and yet the purity and freedom of his gestures convey exactly what we want to convey when, inhibited and spasmodically, we discharge our inner plenitude. But is it only the freedom of the body that delights us here? Does not the soul reveal itself here in a special way? Does it not discharge its inner plenitude as in music, but more immediately still, with greater concentration? Words arouse a sharper sympathy, but it is vicarious, as it were, intellectualized, generalized; music, a more intense sympathy, but it is vague, longingly digressing; that evoked by gesture is clear and all-embracing, vividly present, joy-giving. The language of words is seemingly individual, but in truth generic; that of the body is seemingly general, but in truth highly personal. Nor is it body that speaks to body, but the human whole that speaks to the whole.

Introduction

The painter, the sculptor, the architect, the composer, the juggler, and the clown—these are a few of the figures who would have to be related to those of the actor and the dancer to make this survey complete. Hofmannsthal's concern with style extended to crafts and pastimes, to furniture and utensils, to gardens—in which he saw a symbol of all art—and to the minutiae of social convention. His writings on the visual arts, including architecture, are as perceptive as those on literature, the theatre, and the dance, and as rich in those moments of vision which make his essays an essential part of his imaginative work.

Gesture supports, or takes over from, words at critical moments in Hofmannsthal's plays and opera libretti; and his "word-scepticism" pervades their motivation and dialogue. One instance is the Casanova-like figure Florindo in his comedy *Cristinas Heimreise,* of whom one could say that he makes love to women out of an extreme reluctance to talk to them. "Words are good," he says, "but there's something better." (He seizes her hand.) "I don't want to turn this thing into talk." The Captain, Florindo's opposite in other respects, shares the conviction that "with us, all that is finest and most beautiful lies between words." And there is a gloss on this comedy in Hofmannsthal's prose piece *Ways and Encounters* (1907), where he writes: "Not the embrace, it seems to me, but the encounter is the truly decisive erotic pantomime," because "the encounter promises more than the embrace can keep," and "at no moment sensuality is so soulful or soulfulness so sensual as in the encounter." This is Hofmannsthal's philosophy of gesture on another plane. The gesture celebrates a moment—and more than a whole lifetime can contain; it is fugitive and timeless. Such moments and gestures recur throughout his plays and libretti; and everywhere they are dialectically contrasted with that sense of continuity, that loyalty to a single moment of commitment which Florindo lacks and the Captain possesses, despite his adventurous past. Florindo is merely a "word-sceptic"; the Captain is a "word-mystic" as well.

The reference to music in the essay *On Pantomime* suggests that Hofmannsthal thought less well of, and had thought less deeply about, this art than about acting, dancing, or the visual arts; and it is true that Hofmannsthal was primarily what the Germans call an *Augenmensch,* a man more receptive to visual than to auditive impressions. In an early postcard to Marie Herzfeld, accepting an invitation to listen to piano music in her house, Hofmannsthal added: "But I know nothing at all about music, and don't like people who talk about it cleverly—evidently, because I can't do so myself." Since Hofmannsthal could talk very cleverly about literature and the visual arts even in his adolescence, this admission is of some interest. "I am really unmusical," he admitted to Strauss as late as 1923; but the correspondence itself and scattered references to music and composers elsewhere show that his taste and interest in music developed in later years.

The sympathy aroused by music, Hofmannsthal writes in the essay, is "vague, longingly digressing"; though he may have had Romantic music in mind here—and it was the heavily Romantic tendencies in Strauss's music of which he least approved—the remark is generally valid in that music is a progressive art, dependent on duration in time. What Hofmannsthal feared in his collaboration with Strauss is that the moment and the gesture might be lost in a continuum of sound (if not in a continuum of noise, such as the Wagnerian "erotic screaming" which Hofmannsthal found brutish and revolting). Nothing is more telling in this regard than Hofmannsthal's letter to Strauss of 1911 about the staging of

Ariadne auf Naxos, the most delicately lyrical of all his libretti:

Even if I think . . . only of the two groups, Ariadne-Bacchus, Zerbinetta and the four men—even then I must tell myself that they need a mysterious power higher than music alone in order to reveal their ultimate significance at all. The subtly conceived exiguity of this play, these two groups acting beside each other in the narrowest space, this most careful calculation of each gesture, each step, the whole like a concert and at the same time like a ballet—it will be lost, meaningless, a tattered rag, in incompetent hands; only in Reinhardt's, yours and mine can it grow into a singing flower, the incarnation of dance. *Love* is what it needs, enthusiasm, improvisation. . . .

The operative words here are *gesture, concert, ballet, singing flower, incarnation of dance, love,* and *improvisation.* Music, to Hofmannsthal, was one means of making up for the lyrical poetry he had renounced because it was at once too personal in origin and too difficult to reconcile with the social, conventional functions of language; but music was one means only, and not the most effective at that. It had one obvious advantage over the spoken word, even when combined with it in opera: "Song is marvellous because it tames what otherwise is nothing but the organ of our self-seeking, the human voice." But total, concerted art aimed at the realization of the timeless moment and the pure gesture, and their paradigm was the dance.

III

Electra, the first of Hofmannsthal's works to be set to music by Strauss, was written, published, and performed as a play several years before Strauss started work on the composition. But for this fact, which is sometimes overlooked, it might well seem as though Hofmannsthal had deliberately set out to provide Strauss with the kind of text best fitted to succeed Wilde's *Salomé*. Hofmannsthal's play, however, was one of a number on Greek subjects which he planned or executed at this period, the period of his Chandos Letter and his renunciation of lyrical poetry. It was followed by *Ödipus und die Sphinx* (1905) and an adaptation of the *Oedipus Rex* of Sophocles (1906). Hofmannsthal intended to complement *Electra* with a play devoted to Orestes, but abandoned this project, like other fascinating explorations of ancient myths preserved in sketches for a *Leda und der Schwan* (1900–1904), *Jupiter und Semele* (1901), and *Pentheus* (1904). These sketches are illuminating because they show how close Hofmannsthal came in these years to the chthonic regions rediscovered by Nietzsche and Bachofen, to Dionysian mysteries and magical cults. Hofmannsthal's concern, at the same time, with the new depth psychology does much to explain why he was defeated by several of these subjects. Thus Pentheus is described as a "mystic who is sometimes assailed by the horrifying suspicion that he may be a sceptic," much as Hofmannsthal was to describe his Lord Chandos as "a mystic without a mystique"; and there is a symbolic motif that turns out to be symbolic of the subconscious: "that Pentheus does not know his own palace: does not know the grotto, nor the subterranean ponds, nor yet the shaft that leads into the mountain by a trap door (it is near this that he stands later, crying into it: Mother, Mother!)." A similarly ambiguous symbolism had already crept into Hofmannsthal's earlier verse play *The Mine at Falun;* but the sketches openly allude to "pathology, criminal psychology," to "phallic exuberance" and to a "chthonic god" whom the women go out to worship. The supernatural is related to the bestial. In *Jupiter und Semele* Hofmannsthal is also concerned with a "mysterious Queen" figure, akin to that in *The Mine at Falun,* whom he had encountered in Mabel Collins' theosophical romance *The Idyll of the White Lotus;* significantly he identifies her with the Muse. The sketches for *Jupiter und Semele* contain this revealing dictum: "The true domain of the poet: the relation of mind to body, of idea to expression, of man to beast."

Electra, too, appears to have its being in this domain, to the exclusion of all those concerns which unify Hofmannsthal's works of earlier and later periods. One critic, the late E. M. Butler, described the play as a "Graeco-Freudian myth," and quoted an interesting passage in a book by Hofmannsthal's friend Hermann Bahr. In this book, exactly contemporary with Hofmannsthal's *Electra,* Bahr drew attention to the "hysteria" that beset the whole of Greek culture, and claimed that "tragedy, in fact, aims at nothing other than what those two physicians [Freud and Breuer] do: it reminds a people made ill by its culture of what it does not wish to be reminded of, the bad impulses which it conceals. . . ." Hofmannsthal's library does, in fact, contain first editions of Breuer's and Freud's *Studies in Hysteria* (1895) and of Freud's *The Interpretation of Dreams* (1900); yet to call *Electra* a "Graeco-Freudian myth" is to forget that poets have always had access to the domain in question, and that Freud, at the most, was one of Hofmannsthal's many diverse guides to it. E. M. Butler's distaste for Freudian psychology led her to a sweeping judgment on *Electra* generally: "Just as disturbing to Hofmannsthal's native genius was his preoccupation with Greek tragedy. It transformed him temporarily from a delicate, subtle poet who dealt in shades and pastel tints and lilting lyrics into a frenzied creator of turgid spiritual melodrama, whose findings remain extremely questionable, and against which one instinctively rebels." But

Introduction

Electra contains many subtleties and pastel tints that escaped E. M. Butler's attention in her concentration on its Freudian aspects. She draws attention to Electra's analysis of her mother's dreams and fantasies, but not to the supremely ironic function of this quasi-Freudian treatment in the play as a whole; and she shows no awareness of all the metaphysical and mystical strands—very much in evidence, too, in Hofmannsthal's "lilting lyrics"—that are interwoven with the imagery of "birth, copulation, and death."

Nor is *Electra* as remote from Hofmannsthal's earlier and later works as it may seem. The tendency at present is to follow Hofmannsthal himself in stressing its affinity with all those plays in which he tried to transcend the self-centered and introverted mysticism of his "pre-existence." In *Ad me Ipsum* he writes of "the way to life and to men through sacrifice: two myths: Alcestis and Oedipus. Sacrifice as self-renunciation." And again: "The way to the social as the way to one's higher self: the non-mystical way: (a) through the deed; (b) through the work; (c) through the child . . . (a): transformation in the course of action. To act is to give oneself up. The Alcestis and Oedipus theme sublimated in *Electra* (Electra in relation to the deed treated with irony, it's true. Electra–Hamlet.)" Though an authentic clue to the place of *Electra* in Hofmannsthal's work, his comments do not account for the peculiarly hectic and hysterical mood of the play. A recent critic, Professor William H. Rey, has described *Electra,* the earlier *Alcestis,* and the later *Ödipus und die Sphinx* as "not tragedies in the strictest sense" but rather "mystery plays that rest on the dialectic of the tragic and the mystical." There is a valuable insight here into Hofmannsthal's serious plays generally, but the description still seems to fit *Jedermann, The Salzburg Great Theatre of the World,* and *The Tower* better than

Electra. One reason, perhaps, is that Hofmannsthal's notion of individuality and personality is itself ambiguous, since Electra's self-sacrifice or self-renunciation on one level is her self-fulfilment on another. Hofmannsthal indicated this ambiguity both in his reference to his ironic treatment of Electra's deed, and in another retrospective comment on the work: "All my three plays on ancient subjects are concerned with the dissolution of the concept of individuality. In *Electra* the individual is dissolved in the empirical way, inasmuch as the very substance of its life blasts it from within, as water about to freeze will crack an earthenware jug. Electra is no longer Electra, just because she has dedicated herself entirely to being Electra."

To say that *Electra* sacrifices herself, therefore, is not enough; she sacrifices one part of herself, her reason and common humanity, to another; and one cannot get away from the fact that this other part includes not only her super-ego but her subconscious compulsions. Hofmannsthal may have had this in mind when he wrote that Electra's individuality is "dissolved in the empirical way." Surely this serves to distinguish Electra's mode of self-sacrifice from that of the Beggar, say, in the late mystery play, or from Sigismund's in *The Tower.*

Other references to Electra in his notebooks and in *Ad me Ipsum* bear out Hofmannsthal's awareness of the distinction. Thus he mentions that when he first conceived the plan in September 1901, he wanted to write a work as different as possible from Goethe's *Iphigenia,* a work of which no one could say, as Goethe said of his *Iphigenia,* that "it was damnably humane" (*"verteufelt human"*). Between Goethe's "humane" and Hofmannsthal's "barbaric" treatment of Greek myths there lay not only Freud but Bachofen, Erwin Rohde, and Nietzsche, whose first major work had taken up Schopenhauer's critique of the "principle of individuation." When, in 1926, Hofmannsthal remarked that "Electra's deed springs from a kind of possession," he clearly indicated the pathological aspects of Electra's sacrifice; and in another passage of *Ad me Ipsum,* he explained in psychological terms Electra's difficulties in executing her deed, by observing that "action presupposes a transition from the conscious to the unconscious."

Nevertheless there is one related theme in *Electra* which undoubtedly links the play to the whole of Hofmannsthal's works, both early and late. The figure of Chrysothemis, Electra's sister, is contrasted with the heroine not only in her shrinking from the deed and her hope of fulfilment in marriage and motherhood but also in the desire to forget the past rather than lay its ghost by re-enacting it. No pre-occupation of Hofmannsthal's was more constant than the one to which these contrasted attitudes point; and it is Electra's heroic fixation on a single event, a single commitment, and a single continuity that relates her to the principal characters of Hofmannsthal's other comic and serious plays. The contrast and dialectic run through all his works, from the early verse plays to *Ariadne auf Naxos* and *The Difficult Man.* By a process common to many of Hofmannsthal's plays, the antinomy is subject to variations which sometimes seem to invert it. Whereas in the comedies marriage is presented as the state in which men and women establish the necessary continuity, and the adventurer or libertine stands for the opposite way, Electra's fixation on her murdered father assumes the kind of significance that marriage has in circumstances less extreme, and in fact makes the very idea of marriage impossible and loathsome to her. It is Chrysothemis who corresponds to the adventurers and libertines of the comedies in her failure to establish a higher continuity. To entertain human hopes in

these particular circumstances, Electra suggests, is to be
bestial. Here, as elsewhere, one can only commend Hofmannsthal's subordination of an ideal of abstract consistency
to the psychological and imaginative demands of the specific
case. Sigismund is another instance of a Hofmannsthal
hero whose early circumstances place him both below and
above common humanity and commit him to a kind of tie
different from that between man and wife. It is not without
significance that Electra and Chrysothemis have been reduced to a status scarcely less brutish than that of Sigismund
in his tower. Of Orestes, too, we are told that "they gave him a
wretched place to live" and that he was to have been killed in
infancy, like Sigismund. The tower motif also appears in
Hofmannsthal's next Greek play, *Ödipus und die Sphinx*.
Oedipus says at one point:

> *Ich dachte, meinen Vater zu bitten um einen Turm,*
> *um ein Lager von Stroh und um schwere Ketten—*

> (I wished to beg my father for a tower,
> for a bed of straw and for heavy chains—)

And at another he speaks of a tower that "stands remote
amid mountain chasms." Sigismund, after all, only just
avoids parricide; and Oedipus, too, is obsessed by dreams
that blur the "frontier between sleep and waking . . . between death and life." Like Electra, he has a horror of the
sexual act as such, because he cannot dissociate it from an
early trauma connected with his parents.

The precedent of *Hamlet,* to which Hofmannsthal alludes, may well be more relevant to the psychological motivation of his *Electra* and *Ödipus* plays than any discovery by
Freud; and in any case the most characteristic thread in
Hofmannsthal's *Electra* is the relation to time, and hence to

personal identity, of the two sisters and of the mother. Clytemnestra, too, is self-estranged because she fails to connect the past with the present; but, unlike Chrysothemis, she doubts the very possibility of making the connection. If Electra resembles Hofmannsthal and his Lord Chandos in their "word-scepticism," Clytemnestra is equally sceptical of deeds. "Now it was before, and then it was past," she says of the murder of Agamemnon, and asks: "For am I still the same who has done the deed?" Here again she voices one of Hofmannsthal's first and last questions. Personal identity rests not on the cultivation of personality, but on loyalty to something that is not oneself. Electra has this kind of loyalty, Chrysothemis and Clytemnestra have not. Granted that this play is governed by a mystique less of the spirit than of the heart and blood, that it is set from beginning to end in a domain in which the bestial impinges on the human and superhuman, *Electra* is neither a freak nor an aberration in Hofmannsthal's work. Had Hofmannsthal succeeded in writing his projected Pentheus and Semiramis plays, to mention only two extraordinary works sketched out and abandoned at different periods of his life, *Electra* would hardly strike us as an isolated product of his imagination.

Electra's "word-scepticism" has been mentioned; but in Hofmannsthal's works "word-scepticism" always has its mystical corollary. "Hatred is nothing," she says,

> *er zehrt*
> *und zehrt sich selber auf, und Liebe ist*
> *noch weniger als Hass, sie greift nach allem*
> *und kann nichts fassen, ihre Hände sind*
> *wie Flammen, die nichts fassen, alles Denken*
> *ist nichts, und was aus einem Mund hervorkommt,*
> *ist ohnmächtige Luft, nur der ist selig,*
> *der seine Tat zu tuen kommt.*

[xxxviii]

Introduction

(it eats and eats
and consumes itself, and love is still less
than hatred, it reaches after everything
and cannot grasp anything, its hands
are like flames which grasp nothing, all thinking
is nothing, and what issues from the mouth
is a powerless breeze, only he is blessed
who is coming to do his deed!)

Here the deed itself transcends its very object and motivation. The end in which Electra finds her fulfilment and liberation quite literally "dissolves her individuality." The dance in which she celebrates her fulfilment and liberation is not only "nameless," in the sense of indescribable or indefinable often given to it by Hofmannsthal, but beyond words *and* reason. It is the pure gesture to which both words and deeds can only approximate and aspire.

In the operatic version Hofmannsthal slightly elaborated the concluding dialogue. A duet between Electra and Chrysothemis is interpolated immediately before the dance. This is dominated by imagery of darkness and light, death and life. Electra sings:

Ich war ein Schwarzer Leichnam
unter Lebenden, und diese Stunde
bin ich das Feuer des Lebens und meine Flamme
verbrennt die Finsternis der Welt.
Mein Gesicht muss weisser sein
als das weissglühende Gesicht des Monds.
Wenn einer auf mich sieht,
muss er den Tod empfangen oder muss
vergehen vor Lust.

(I was a black corpse
among the living and at this hour
I am the fire of life, and my flame
burns up the darkness of the world.

[xxxix]

My face must be whiter
than the whitely glowing face of the moon.
If someone looks upon me
he must be struck dead
or be consumed with joy.)

To Chrysothemis' words "Now our brother is here and love flows over us like oil and myrrh, love is all! Who can live without love?" Electra replies:

*Ai! Liebe tötet! aber keiner fährt dahin
und hat die Liebe nicht gekannt!*

(Ai! Love kills! But no one passes on
and has not known love!)

This affirmation does not contradict Electra's earlier assertion that love is "nothing" or suggest any agreement between the two sisters. What is oil and myrrh to Chrysothemis is fuel to Electra's flame; her love can be neither thwarted nor gratified, because it has no object but to consume itself and her.

The free verse of *Electra* constitutes an important advance on the iambic blank verse of the *Alcestis* and of Hofmannsthal's own transitional verse plays. In one of these, *Der Abenteurer und die Sängerin,* he had used a mixture of regular iambic verse and prose. The free verse line of *Electra,* which he was to adopt for his libretti of the next twenty years, proved as suitable for lyrical climaxes as for trivial conversation. It was supple, often close to colloquial speech and speech rhythm, yet stylized without being stilted. It is no exaggeration to say that in regular blank verse Hofmannsthal's Electra would have been unbearable; the natural and easy way in which she can fall into the Austrian vernacular of Hofmannsthal's time distinguishes her from many other *fin de siècle* heroines, such as Wilde's *Salomé,* and saves her from both preciousness and the neo-Shakespearean rhetoric satirized by Max Beerbohm. The diction of *Electra* is not obtrusively grand, exquisite, or memorable, but subservient to the wordless gesture: it exactly fits the theme. "In action, in deeds," Hofmannsthal said of the play, "the enigmas of language are resolved."

IV

From *Electra* to *The Salzburg Great Theatre of the World*—this leap in space, time, *ambiance,* and morality (both in the sense of manners and of ethical absolutes) calls for some agility on the reader's part. It may be as well to begin by quoting Hofmannsthal's short preface to the play, written for its publication as a book in 1922 and drawing on a note appended to it when it appeared earlier that year in Hofmannsthal's periodical *Neue Deutsche Beiträge:*

Everyone knows that there is a spiritual drama by Calderón called *The Great Theatre of the World.* From this play the whole pivotal metaphor has been borrowed: that the World erects a stage on which men enact the play of life in the roles allotted to them by God; also the title of this play and the names of the six characters who represent human life—and that is the whole extent of the borrowing. Yet these constituents do not belong to the great Catholic poet as his invention, but are part of that treasury of myths and allegories which the Middle Ages shaped and bequeathed to later centuries.

Hofmannsthal refrains from justifying his adaptation on dogmatic or ethical grounds. If an apology is implied in the preface, it is an apology for the principle of adaptation itself, not for the particular work adapted or for its dogmatic character; and Hofmannsthal did feel strongly about the question of borrowings from other writers. Here again his attitude involved a rejection of nineteenth-century individualism and of its highly developed sense of private property in the realms of art and ideas. In his *Book of Friends* Hofmannsthal included this definition of the writer from the preface to Lesage's *Gil Blas: "Un auteur est un homme qui trouve dans les livres tout ce qui lui trotte par la tête."* Had he wished to elaborate his defence against those who accused him of plagiarism, Hofmannsthal could have cited not only this older freedom to borrow and adapt, but the practice of many distinguished artists of his own time, including the most "modern" and original. As early as 1909 a hostile critic had written that Hofmannsthal was "fated to be a dilettante, a keeper of the museum of culture, as it were"; but this was before individualism had been shaken out of its smugness, and long before the more characteristically twentieth-century awareness of a *"musée imaginaire."*

Nevertheless, none of Hofmannsthal's works and activities more effectively antagonized the great majority of his former public and of the younger generation than his adaptations of *Everyman* and *El Gran Teatro del Mundo.* These plays were understood not as "myths" but as Christian tracts in dramatic form. Writing to Karl Kraus about the chances of having a play of her own put on, the poet Else Lasker-Schüler summed up the view common to most of the German *avant-garde* of the time: "Hofmannsthal of the tribe of teachers, I suppose, will object to it!" The same poet wrote a devastating account of Hofmannsthal's *Jedermann* in a letter to Herwarth Walden, editor of the Expressionist periodical *Die Aktion:*

For I've been to see Everyman or is it called All-Sorts? I think it is called All-Sorts for Everyman or Everyman for All-Sorts. Come in, ladies and gentlemen, to the giant Punch and Judy show. Where did it all come from? I think from the stables, Herwarth.

Introduction

. . . Just think, if he'd taken to sculpture, if he'd taken to patching up sculpture, and fixed two new arms to the Venus de Milo! What literary things hasn't he dug up: first, the Oedipus of Sophocles, nourished with Viennese blood; and then he turned Electra into a demure schoolmistress! He lacks imagination. . . . The performance of *Jedermann* is an unartistic act, a shameful one.

However violent in its animus, Else Lasker-Schüler's indictment deserves to be taken seriously both because of her charge that Hofmannsthal lacked imagination—and she was by no means alone in making it—and because of her suggestion elsewhere in the letter that Hofmannsthal and Reinhardt were guilty of cynicism and hypocrisy in staging *Jedermann:* "Life and death, sin and judgment, Heaven and Hell—all are degraded to a spectacle, like those elephants and Arab horses decorated with ribbons and trinkets, yet not even for the delight of children as in that case, but for the edification of a rich sensation-hungry public." This criticism came from a fervently, though unconventionally, religious woman; and it raises questions that will continue to arise in the minds of readers and spectators of both plays.

In two essays on his *Jedermann,* published in 1911 and 1912, Hofmannsthal gave his own account of his reasons for writing this play; and most of what he says there applies equally to *The Salzburg Great Theatre of the World.* Hofmannsthal considers his dramatic adaptations generally, and remarks of *Jedermann:* "When I brought the play *Jedermann* on to the stage, I think it was not so much to add something to the German repertory as to restitute something that should have been part of it by rights, and of which it was deprived only by a kind of historical accident." This explains why Hofmannsthal abandoned an early attempt to write his play in prose and resorted to the irregular rhymed couplet made familiar to the German public by the sixteenth-century play-wright Hans Sachs (as well as by Goethe's *Faust*). To any contemporary who did not share Hofmannsthal's belief that "the powerful imagination is conservative," this kind of "restitution" was bound to smack of antiquarianism. Hofmannsthal's answer in the essay was: "In our time far too much fuss is made about our time"; and he justified his choice of the subject by calling it "a human fable in Christian dress."

"More and more," the second essay elaborates this description, "the true core revealed itself to me as humanly absolute, not part of any particular period, nor even inextricably bound up with Christian dogma. . . . For we are at bay and in the dark, in a different way from medieval man, but no less so: we have a wide perspective on many things, we can see through some things, and yet our true spiritual power of seeing is feeble; much is at our command, yet we are not commanders; what we should possess possesses us; and that which more than anything is a means, money, by a demonic inversion becomes our primary end."

Hofmannsthal also wrote a note on *The Salzburg Great Theatre of the World* for inclusion in a brochure on the Salzburg Festival (1925). By this time the theories of the Austrian literary historian Professor Josef Nadler, and of the poet and critic Rudolf Borchardt had begun to influence Hofmannsthal's thinking on cultural matters. The emphasis now falls less on the "humanly absolute" aspects of the fable, as on a particular South German and Austrian theatrical tradition which Nadler believed Hofmannsthal to represent in his time. To Borchardt Hofmannsthal owed some of his ideas about a "conservative revolution" that would do away with the evils of capitalism but preserve what was best in traditional values. These late preoccupations of Hof-

mannsthal, which made an increasing claim on him after Austria's defeat in the war, the partition of the Empire, and the
Russian Revolution, were as controversial as any political
commitment and open to misunderstandings that tend to
arise wherever a primarily literary imagination impinges
on political issues; but Hofmannsthal's sincerity is not in
doubt. In all his works Hofmannsthal combined an extreme
eclecticism in the choice of media with a constant and highly
personal vision. What Else Lasker-Schüler regarded as a
concession on Hofmannsthal's part to an amorphous "sensation-hungry" public sprang from his dominant need to
merge his own individuality in impersonal conventions
and to relate himself to the past. Else Lasker-Schüler's own
works are individual in diction and form, and individualistic
in attitude to the point of eccentricity; but her religious
imagery reveals an eclecticism almost inescapable for any
writer with a liberal bourgeois background, and more akin to
Hofmannsthal's than she knew.

Hofmannsthal's interest in sociology, politics, and economics goes back to the beginning of the century and earlier, to his reading of works as diverse as *An Onlooker's Note-
book* (articles from the *Manchester Guardian*) and Georg
Simmel's *Philosophie des Geldes*, G. Lowes Dickinson's *A
Modern Symposium* and the curious *Welt-Eroberung durch
Heldenliebe* by Frederik van Eeden and Erich Gutkind.
Hofmannsthal's annotations and marginalia in these
books show that he envisaged a synthesis of socialist and
conservative thinking—socialist in economics, conservative in
all other regards. His political writings of the war years
show much the same outlook, despite a growing concern
with Austrian conditions, with Austria's past and Austria's future. It is in his writings and lectures in the post-war period
that Hofmannsthal seemed to come closest to a political

position well to the right of centre; but his cultural conservatism must not be confused with the economic conservatism of classes and groups. Just as Hofmannsthal added Mammon to the characters in *Jedermann* to give more scope to his own concern with modern acquisitiveness, so he invested the character of the Beggar in the later play with an importance derived from his own concern with the modern ideology of revolt. His inclusion of an Adversary and a Busybody serves to strengthen the same thread in the play.

If imagination is shown not in the invention of plots—and even the plot of Hofmannsthal's play is given an entirely new twist—but in the concealed presence everywhere "of the determining personality," Hofmannsthal's antiquarian re-creations are by no means unimaginative. Even his "word-scepticism" and "word-mysticism" make their appearance when World says: "He to whom fulness is given . . . his tongue is too heavy for speech." As for the Beggar's part in the play—both before and after his illumination—to dismiss it as "counter-revolutionary" or "reactionary," as critics continue to do, is to forget that Hofmannsthal was no ordinary conservative but the representative "of a society that does not exist."

In his lecture *The Poet in Our Time* (1906) Hofmannsthal had characterized the modern poet as living "Under the staircase, where all must pass him and no one pays any attention to him"; and in his copy of Simmel's *Philosophie des Geldes* Hofmannsthal had entered the words "the poet" against the Franciscan motto *"nihil habentes, omnia possedentes."* Hofmannsthal, therefore, was closely identified with the figure of the Beggar. His various writings and jottings on the problem of the modern "money nexus," to "get to the back of which," he noted, "may be the meaning of the moral and even religious revolution in which we seem to be involved," confirm that he added the weight of personal conviction to the Beggar's accusations in the play. When the Beggar says "that the world must be renewed," this, too, is Hofmannsthal's own conviction, and the renewal became the subject of his later play *The Tower*. That revolt is not enough, personal revenge and hatred—however justified—are not enough, is a moral that remains revolutionary even in our time.

Other interrelations in the play that had a special significance for Hofmannsthal are those between Beauty and the King and between Beauty, the Beggar, and Wisdom. Beauty, in the play, condemns the Beggar for his physical ugliness; and it is only towards the end of the play that the King realizes the difference between "seeming and being," paying tribute to Wisdom's power to fuse both into a "higher light." This is the neo-Platonism that helped Hofmannsthal himself to overcome the "introverted" mysticism of his youth and the autonomous aestheticism which his early works were once thought to exemplify.

V

The Tower, too, began as the free adaptation of a play by Calderón which Hofmannsthal undertook in 1902. Though even this early version anticipated some of the drastic changes which make Hofmannsthal's post-war play an entirely original work, he took over the trochaic verse from Calderón's play *Life Is a Dream,* and this proved a most unsatisfactory medium. At this time Hofmannsthal was drawn to the subject mainly because of its symbolic parallels with his own "pre-existence"; what attracted him, he wrote in a letter of 1904, was "to descend into the ultimate depths of the dubious cave kingdom 'I' and discover the no-longer-I or the world." This theme remained prominent in the later play, but the "world" presented in it had become incomparably more various and complex than that of the Spanish play or of Hofmannsthal's early adaptation. Even in this early adaptation Hofmannsthal had tried to work out a new interrelation of the subsidiary characters both with one another and with Sigismund, but the "almost insuperable difficulties" had defeated him.

Hofmannsthal returned to the subject in 1918, and completed one version of *The Tower* in 1925. The "almost insuperable difficulties" remained, and, as Hofmannsthal wrote in 1910 about his trochaic adaptation, these difficulties were not so much of an artistic as of an intellectual kind. If Hofmannsthal was never quite satisfied with the 1925 version of *The Tower*—and his complete re-working of the play in 1927 suggests that he was not satisfied—one reason is that it was more to him than a play; amongst other things it was his reckoning with the post-war world, a last attempt to embody the substance of his own life in a myth, and a kind of moral and spiritual testament.

The 1925 version of *The Tower* presents two main difficulties. One has to do with the interrelation of the main characters and of the political or ideological powers which they represent. The other has to do with the ultimate implications of Sigismund's life and death. Hofmannsthal himself found it difficult to comment on the significance of the different characters and factions.

The poet's starting-point is the figures themselves; they appear to him, but at the same time they appear to him as a configuration of destinies. Their destiny consists in existing together (the mystery of contemporaneousness). But by crossing one another's paths, they influence one another, not in a particular way, not dialectically, not even by their characters, as in Shakespeare, but by their total volume, like stars. They hardly speak to one another, but each really only speaks to himself. By turns they mean something to one another that exceeds human standards: thus to his father Sigismund means revolt, revolution; and to Sigismund the latter means all that demands reverence but also all that is oppressive, all that is frightening. . . . Thus beside the legitimate King there appear his spiritual adviser and, at the same time, the worldly, political side of the Church. Opposed to them, Olivier, the revolt of the underdog, the perennially ochlocratic element. Julian is the most difficult to define: he is worldly wisdom, the gifted individual's craving for power, but he is denied the grace of *kairos*—his endeavours are in vain, are frustrated—and yet again they are not: he too has a part in Sigismund's destiny. The Children's King, to me, is like a reborn Sigismund: hence the brotherly note between them, their rapid, wholly reciprocal understanding.

It is characteristic of Hofmannsthal that several of the subsidiary figures in the play combine traits borrowed from many disparate literary or historical persons. The important character of the Doctor, for instance—important because exemplary in his unselfish devotion to Sigismund, his wisdom, and his penetration—draws on Paracelsus and the alchemical tradition ("There are connections everywhere"), Kierkegaard ("a strong will . . . a strong faith: the two are one"), and on the modern psychologists and physicians who have based their practice on the assumption that body and psyche are interdependent. The Grand Almoner of the play recalls Dostoevski's Grand Inquisitor ("an old man, almost ninety, tall and erect, with a withered face and sunken eyes"), but also certain features of Father Zossima in the same novel and of historical ecclesiastics of the seventeenth century. Hofmannsthal's primary source for the character of Olivier was Grimmelshausen's novel of the Thirty Years' War, *Der abenteuerliche Simplicissimus,* in which there is a marauder and thief of that name; but the affinities of Hofmannsthal's Olivier extend from sixteenth- and seventeenth-century rebels to recent revolutionary leaders of the extreme Left and the extreme Right.

The most purely mythical figures in *The Tower* are the Children's King and the Gipsy. Neither appears in the later version of the play, which simplifies and clarifies the action in many respects. The relative merits of the two versions remain controversial, and they cannot be discussed in detail here; in a sense the two versions should be regarded as two distinct works, the first more dreamlike, mythical, and utopian, the second more outward-looking, more clear-cut, and more starkly tragic in its conclusion. That Hofmannsthal should have written these two very different versions of the play sheds some light on the struggles and uncertainties of his last years, his premonitions of upheavals even greater than those of the First World War, and his doubts as to the outcome. The Children's King is the embodiment of Hofmannsthal's hope that the new order would be ruled not by the Oliviers of this world, but by Sigismund's spiritual successors. Sigismund himself has to die in both versions for reasons to which the figure of the Gipsy offers one clue; but in the later version he is shot by Olivier's men, and Olivier himself remains triumphant at the end, having gained the upper hand over Julian, over the conservative nobility, and over Sigismund's followers among the commoners and the poor.

The political configuration is necessarily complex in both versions; it is its complexity that makes it both lifelike and widely relevant. Motives everywhere are mixed, and Hofmannsthal does not reduce them to a neat pattern in black and white. In the late version even Olivier appears less black, partly because his bragging in the first scene is omitted, and it is the other soldiers who praise his formidable qualities. Julian's role becomes no less ambiguous in itself, but his part

in the revolution is hinted at already in the first act when he is
seen giving a secret order to Olivier. The later acts show
clearly that Julian has tried to control all the various factions,
including the dissident nobles and high functionaries as well
as Olivier's mob, mainly by playing off one against the other.
At his instigation, members of Basilius' own Court and Cabinet force the King to abdicate in Sigismund's favour, only to
be dismissed in turn by Julian. Basilius himself is banished to
the Tower. It is Sigismund's refusal to play his part in Julian's machinations that leaves a power vacuum ultimately
filled by Olivier. All these complicated issues are presented
more briefly and succinctly in the 1927 version; and even the
outward motivation of the central tragedy, Sigismund's, is
more clearly defined. Yet some of the more mysterious motifs
that go back to Hofmannsthal's first concern with the subject are lost in this tidying up. The episode of the Gipsy and
her part in Sigismund's death are a case in point. Hofmannsthal's many drafts and notes for the play show that at one
time Sigismund was to die of the plague as soon as he settled
in one place; and elsewhere Hofmannsthal interpreted the
Gipsy's role as the "vengeance of the material, maternal, time-
bound." Though never made explicit anywhere in the play,
this motif can still be "intuited" in the 1925 version, but it has
no place in the more condensed and outwardly plausible plot
of the 1927 version. This motif links up with Sigismund's as-
ceticism everywhere in the play, with his remark, "But we
have nothing else that could be our mother but this sex, and
this is the substance of which the world is made," and with
the Gipsy's pregnancy, to which the remark alludes. In this
connection it is of some interest that Hofmannsthal read
Claudel while drafting *The Tower,* and marked certain passages in *La Ville* that develop a religious and mystical symbolism of motherhood. Sigismund's remark may well be an

adaptation of one such passage, marked by Hofmannsthal in 1919: *"A qui, dans l'étreinte sacrée, restituerons-nous qu'à l'épouse/La vie que nous devons à la mère."*

The implication could be that Sigismund's estrangement from the feminine element, identified in his remark and in Hofmannsthal's draft with matter (*materia*) itself, makes him incomplete and vulnerable. The earlier scene with the Peasant Woman, his foster mother, and Julian's claim that he was father and mother to Sigismund, support the implication, as does Sigismund's obsession with the sow that eats her newborn litter. If we remember Hofmannsthal's early preoccupation with Bachofen's "mother-right" and with the advantages of matriarchy—best exemplified in his special cult of the Empress Maria Theresia—as well as his wholly unpuritanical orientation in other works, the motif becomes far from insignificant. Indeed it becomes a key to Sigismund's personal, as distinct from political, tragedy.

It is nowhere suggested that Sigismund has incurred guilt in forsaking his "pre-existence" in the tower and assuming the active functions of ruler and military commander. These functions are thrust upon him, and he remains true to his past. Yet there is a certain inconsistency between his messianic aspirations and his resort, in the last act, to such traditional measures as the threatened hanging of twelve of his own Tartars as a warning to other incendiaries. This inconsistency between Sigismund's dreams and "the language of the world" points to the primary tragic factor which dominates the 1927 version, and which Hofmannsthal could only mitigate in the earlier version by the arrival of the utopian figure of the Children's King. The Children's King, however, and his community also differ from Sigismund in their happier relationship to nature and the material world. This brings us back once more to a deficiency in Sigismund, for which he is not to blame—a guilt like that in certain Greek tragedies, like original sin, or like the complexes and traumas of modern psychology in that it does not arise from a specific or deliberate transgression. That Hofmannsthal was no abstract moralist can also be seen in his treatment of Sigismund's physical attack on Basilius; this is justified not ethically but psychologically, and it follows inevitably from what we know of Sigismund's early confinement in the Tower and his battles with animals and vermin. Basilius, too, is an ambiguous figure. He seems only too well related to nature and to *materia* in every sense, but rather in the manner of Hofmannsthal's adventurer figures who are slaves to the moment. His Christian devotions are more conventional than real; that is why he is excessively dependent on his spiritual and worldly advisers. He resembles Julian, his political opponent, in being essentially vain and hollow; the Doctor's diagnosis of Julian's sickness and the Grand Almoner's of the King's are mutually complementary. Body and soul, Hofmannsthal insists everywhere, must be at one. In this way the characters of Julian and Basilius cast an oblique light on Sigismund's (and vice versa), but especially on Sigismund's ultimate failure to do justice to the material world and to time. The phantasmagoric episode with the Gipsy Woman serves to show that though familiarity has made Sigismund proof against the cruder mysteries of the "black" and bestial domains, his balance lacks this necessary, merely human, centre. His mission, therefore, is only partly fulfilled; he is an exemplary, but transitional, figure, and the new order has still to be established by his successors.

The distinction of *The Tower,* both in absolute sense and in the context of Hofmannsthal's work as a whole, need hardly be stressed again here. It is the one completed work of Hofmannsthal that fully engaged all his disparate faculties and energies—the mystical and the worldly, the visionary and the analytical, the adventurous and the conservative—and co-ordinated his many-sided experience within a single imaginative structure. Sigismund's emergence from the dream of pre-existence into a world torn apart by conflicting ambitions, interests, and vanities corresponded to the course of Hofmannsthal's own life; and Hofmannsthal was left with the knowledge that no existing society had any real use for what he had tried to give it. Yet he had been "here," and had done what he could.

Dramatically the earlier and richer version of *The Tower* almost exceeds the capacities of the stage as well as the capacities of most audiences. Yet in recent years it is the earlier version that has tempted producers, despite the technical difficulties. Though the play may never become popular or frequent on the stage, "the fascination of what's difficult" should save it from being finally banished to the printed page. In diction it is an effective and unique amalgam of poetic and vernacular, seventeenth-century and modern elements. A present-day reader may be struck by occasional similarities with the diction of Brecht, especially in his *Mother Courage*, which also draws on the characters and idiom of Grimmelshausen's novel; and the two dramatists have a great deal in common, not least the tendency to appropriate, fuse, and remould the most diverse material. Both were accused of plagiarism in their time; and both, for rather different reasons, were indifferent to the laws of private property in literature. Both needed to lose themselves in order to find themselves.

VI

Hofmannsthal's comedies represent the social side of his nature, his Austrian, as distinct from German, characteristics, his strongly developed historical sense, and his interest in manners both as a means of communication between individuals and as an indispensable defence of their ultimate privacy. Just as there are comic ingredients in *The Salzburg Great Theatre of the World* and in *The Tower*—the characters of the Peasant and of Anton are instances; and Calderón, like Shakespeare, provided a precedent for the mixture—there are tragic or mystical strands in the comedies. Easily though Hofmannsthal seemed to move in the social element, there were moments when it became transparent, when the necessary artifice of manners became an empty container and even his comic characters must face the abyss. Indeed, his great temptation as a writer of comedies was to conceal too much depth on the surface, too many intricate connections and metaphysical undertones. Like his magnificent fragment of a novel *Andreas,* the early comedy *Silvia im "Stern"* came to grief for that reason; and even *Cristinas Heimreise,* a work of the same period, only just supports the weight of its symbolism.

Here the discipline of collaboration proved a distinct advantage. The final version of *The Cavalier of the Rose* owes much of its success to the limitations of opera, to Strauss's insistence on a simple and conventionally comic plot, and his inability to cope with Hofmannsthal's psychological or metaphysical subtleties. Remarkably enough, this discipline and Hofmannsthal's drastic concessions to Strauss scarcely detracted from the literary merits of the libretto. The discarded second act, which has now been published in its original form, is dispensable to any reader of the play not principally concerned with Hofmannsthal's ideas or with his progress as a writer of comedies. Though Hofmannsthal wrote to Strauss that the finished work did not *wholly* satisfy him "as a fusion of word and music," the play as such is in no way inferior to his other comedies of this decade. Hofmannsthal could afford

to sacrifice quite a number of his peculiar subtleties and pro-
fundities without becoming trite or superficial.

Hofmannsthal himself wrote in 1927 that this "libretto
was the most untranslatable in the world" because its diction
is no mere pastiche of eighteenth-century Viennese but "the
imaginary language of the time." This applies to all Hofmannsthal's comedies (and to *The Tower,* whose diction and
setting are those of an *imaginary* seventeenth century). The
nineteenth-century setting of *Arabella* provided Hofmannsthal with yet another kind of linguistic raw material; since its
imaginative restyling was less thorough than in other works, a
neutral equivalent for its Viennese forms was more easily
available. It is *The Difficult Man* that most stubbornly defies
translation, for Hofmannsthal's highly stylized recasting of an
aristocratic idiom—itself with no counterpart in the usage of
any twentieth-century English social set—had to be repro-
duced in a colloquial prose that could take no subterfuge in
poetic licence. Yet the delicate balance between artifice and
realism would have been utterly upset if the translator had
resorted to a style reminiscent of Sheridan or the Restoration
dramatists, who did command an idiom at once precious and
earthy enough to correspond to the hyper-Viennese, hyper-
aristocratic style in this play.

The diction of *The Cavalier of the Rose* is more highly
wrought than that of *Arabella,* less so than that of *The Difficult Man.* As in *Electra,* Hofmannsthal was able to combine
natural speech rhythm with a poetic tautening and condens-
ing of language. In exactly the same way, the historical and
social milieu is treated naturalistically, yet with a concealed
layer of mythical and utopian allusion. One instance is the
very simple yet magical identification of the Princess with the
Empress whose name she bears, and in whose reign the action falls. By the simple device of calling the Princess Marie

Thérèse, Hofmannsthal associates her not only with his favourite Austrian monarch but with those matriarchal virtues which the Empress exemplified in his eyes. What these virtues were can be seen in Hofmannsthal's essay on Maria Theresia, published in 1917, and more clearly still in a series of jottings in his copy of La Bruyère's *Les Caractères* (probably the nucleus of his essay). Here Hofmannsthal notes Maria Theresia's naïveté and her strength—which he calls "mother-strength"—her characteristically Austrian outlook and her capacity to "educate by example"; the most significant remark of all points to Bachofen's characterization of matriarchal societies: "Men, among the Germans, lacking in instinct. Service has to take the place of honour. Marlborough." (Marlborough, it seems likely, is cited as an example of a man not lacking in instinct.)

There is no reason, of course, why any listener or reader should be aware of the precise associations I have traced here; but any reader or listener who is at all attentive to the whole work, and to the Princess's role in it, will sense the degree to which this figure dominates the action, educating by example, shaming Ochs not by snubbing him but by opposing her finer instincts to his crude and dishonourable conduct, and giving her blessing at the end to the union of two classes. On the surface *The Cavalier of the Rose* is a conventional comedy with farcical elements; but the infiltration of a concealed myth also turns it into a social allegory at once historical and utopian (because exemplary). Here the depths have been successfully concealed in the surface.

By the same imaginative fusion, the love affair between the Princess and Octavian has been cryptically mythologized; and it is a tribute to Hofmannsthal's tact to repeat that no one need be conscious of the submerged myth. It matters little whether we accept the opening love scene because it fits in

Introduction

with our ideas of eighteenth-century morals, because it is true to the emotional needs of this particular woman, evidently childless and close to middle age, or because it is part of the political and social allegory and tallies with the concealed myth of the matriarch. All these layers are inseparable. The grave undertones—Hofmannsthal's own recurrent question "What does the you mean, what you and I," and the related question of personal identity in time—help to define the peculiar tenderness of a love always on the verge of renunciation. "Easy is what we must be—holding and taking, holding and letting go"—this not only takes us back to the roots of Hofmannsthal's work, to the early poems and verse plays, but sums up the whole libretto, its lightness and its profundity; for these words apply not only to the Princess's love for Octavian and his for her, but to the allegory and to the myth. Hofmannsthal's ideal ruler knows that tradition embraces flux and change, that the old order must be made to merge gently in the new if continuity is to be maintained. (In the same way Sigismund in *The Tower* tells the Bannerets at the end that the old nobility will have to renounce their powers and privileges under the new dispensation.) The woman and lover of the first scene is in no way inconsistent with the Princess and matriarchal figure of the last: the quality of Marie Thérèse's love for Octavian prepares us for the delicacy and generosity of mind required for her final renunciation, her social mediation and the reminder to Ochs that his game, too, is up.

For his essay on Maria Theresia, Hofmannsthal chose an epigraph from the historian Adam Müller: "The State is an alliance of past generations with later ones, and vice versa." The relevance of this motto extends to Hofmannsthal's political attitude generally, to the role of the Princess in this libretto, and to an awareness of the past not only in society, but in each individual's life, that distinguished Hofmannsthal

[lviii]

and his characters. In her love for Octavian the Princess tries to link her own past with the present and the future, yet knows all the time that another will have to take her place. Sophie and Octavian, too, have a part in this counterpoint of past and present. Though they fall in love at first sight, their love has a prehistory, a pre-existence, as every truly decisive moment has in Hofmannsthal. Octavian tries to express this sense of prehistory in a reminiscence of his childhood. Sophie, more concretely, has prepared herself for the encounter by a girlishly snobbish study of Octavian's pedigree.

In all his comedies, if not in all his dramatic works, Hofmannsthal was more concerned with the relation between individuals—the "space between characters that is mystically alive" of his Shakespeare lecture, a space that could be filled by the dead or by something other than the persons in question—than with the individual's psychology. In his 1927 postscript to *The Cavalier of the Rose* he wrote that "Molière's comedies, too, rest not so much on the characters themselves as on the relations of the often very typical figures to one another." Nevertheless, in the discarded second act Hofmannsthal had done more to bring out Sophie's growth into an individual. At one point there Octavian says to her:

> *Erst muss Sie selber sich helfen!*
> *Dann hilf ich Ihr auch!*
> *Tu Sie das erste für mich,*
> *dann tu ich was für Sie.*

> (First you must help yourself
> then I will help you too.
> You do the first thing for me
> then I'll do something for you.)

This, perhaps, would have sounded too deliberately moralizing a note, and the Octavian of the final version is more gallant in his readiness to take Sophie as she is; but in the words of a perceptive critic, Franz Tumler, the lines serve to show that "members of the new society now being shaped must fulfil this harder demand to justify themselves as persons; they are entering an order whose values have ceased to be aristocratic." The old aristocratic order, the same critic says, placed all the stress not on the individual's character but on his rank: and it is true that Ochs's behaviour is justified in his own eyes by his rank alone, as he repeatedly makes clear. Because the Princess understands both codes, she can mediate between them in the last scene. Even then she does not appeal to Ochs's honour as an individual—far less to any puritanical code which no character in the play observes—but reminds him that this is his last chance to save his face as a man of the world. At the same time we know that a whole social class is being asked to retire decently; like the paralysed old nobleman with the symbolic name Greifenklau ("griffin's claw"), it has come to the end of its predatory reign. Yet an alliance of the old with the new has been effected.

A similar social allegory is contained in *Arabella,* though the texture of this work is thinner and less rich. The nobility, by now, has been well and truly displaced. Count Waldner and his family live in an hotel (based on the Ungarische Krone, an hotel near St. Stephen's Cathedral, Vienna, frequented by the country gentry on their visits to the capital even in Hofmannsthal's time) and can no more afford two marriageable daughters than their temporary quarters. Hofmannsthal's main difficulty here was that by the time he wrote the libretto even this historical phase was a thing of the past; his hope, before and during the war, that the Empire might be saved by a fuller integration of the non-German nationalities had been defeated by their secession. In *The Cavalier of*

Introduction

the Rose, Croatia is a remote region where the Marshal hunts bear and lynx; in *Arabella* it comes to Vienna in the person of Mandryka to save the fortunes of the Waldner family; but by 1927 it was part of a foreign nation, Yugoslavia, and the Waldners of the time were either coming to terms with the little Austrian Republic and their reduced status in it, or placing their hopes in its union with a larger, more prosperous, and more industrialized Germany. These realities cast their shadow on *Arabella;* though Hofmannsthal agreed with Novalis that after a lost war one should write comedies, *Arabella* lacks the mythical undertones of the pre-war work. Hofmannsthal's social utopia, by this time, lay at the far end of tragic processes; and all the waltzes of Vienna could not drown the rumble of that apocalypse which had been his theme in *The Tower.*

"The Prussian threatens to the left, the Russian to the right," Adelaide elaborates on Dominic's truly Austrian remark that "we are always poised on the edge of an abyss." Champagne, waltzes, and love, if not guardian angels, were still an effective remedy in 1860, but Hofmannsthal could not lend much conviction to them in 1928; and when Adelaide exclaims "O Vienna! City of scandal and intrigue!" a real and recurrent complaint of his own was also voiced by Hofmannsthal. Ochs's version of it in the earlier libretto is that of a country gentleman confronted with an alien code, and caught in the snares of newfangled institutions; in *Arabella* it is not Mandryka, the true stranger to Vienna, who makes it, but the more sophisticated Adelaide.

The symbolism of the glass of water (and its association with the healthy, primitive order represented by Mandryka and his forests) almost provides a substitute for the myth; but it is more deliberate, less organic, than the concealed

[lxi]

depths of *The Cavalier of the Rose*, just as the contrast between the characters of the two sisters is less subtly drawn
than in Hofmannsthal's earlier treatment of the subject in
his story *Lucidor*. Yet *Arabella* has other virtues, apart from
its merit as a libretto. Together with *The Cavalier of the Rose*
and *The Difficult Man* it can be read as part of a trilogy em-
bodying Austrian manners and Austrian history—always with
the proviso that Hofmannsthal's true domain was not the
realism but the symbolism of manners. Waldner's gambling,
Adelaide's selling of her jewellery and her trust in the fortune-
teller, Mandryka's wad of bank notes—the proceeds of his
sale of *real* estate—all such details are at once realistic and at
least as telling as the obvious symbolism of the glass of water.

As in other works, Hofmannsthal also conveys his distinctly Austrian and unpuritanical morality, though the prominence given to Arabella almost blurs Zdenka's more truly
heroic role. Arabella, of course, is more dignified and more
conventionally admirable; but it is relatively easy to be dignified when one knows that both the truth and convention
are on one's side. Hofmannsthal's true heroines, like Helen in
The Difficult Man and Zdenka in *Arabella,* take greater risks
and know that social conventions may have to be broken for
love's sake. As Arabella herself admits, it is Zdenka who has
"the kinder heart" and has taught her

> *dass wir nichts wollen dürfen, nichts verlangen,*
> *abwägen nicht und markten nicht und geizen nicht,*
> *nur geben und liebhaben immerfort!*

> (that we should not want anything, nor ask for anything,
> not calculate and not barter and not covet,
> only give and go on loving always.)

[lxii]

Introduction

In her lack of calculation Zdenka resembles not only Helen, but the most completely realized of all Hofmannsthal's comic figures, The Difficult Man himself.

If *The Tower* is the most daring of Hofmannsthal's non-operatic plays, *The Difficult Man* is the most nearly perfect. Beneath its unbroken surface it holds greater tensions, cross-currents, and whirlpools than any comparable work in the classical repertory. Indeed its classicism is deceptive; once again Hofmannsthal had set himself the task of creating a classical convention in a modern void. Much as the play owes to Molière, Goldoni, Marivaux, Sheridan, Lessing, and all those comic masterpieces which Hofmannsthal had assiduously studied and emulated, *The Difficult Man* has no precedent in Austrian literature and only a superficial affinity with foreign models. Even Molière in his *Misanthrope,* whose hero seems to foreshadow the individualism of a later age, did not span such distances. Hofmannsthal's Difficult Man is at once the representative of a society that Hofmannsthal had to invent for the purpose of his play, and a man beyond society for reasons that Hofmannsthal indicated in a letter about his play to Anton Wildgans in 1921:

You will find that in it I have hidden all that sprang from my own soul, all that was personally metaphysical, or as you like to call it, "confessional," under the irony of its figuration—as in *Cristina,* but in this case even under the double irony of its figuration in the social, preconditioned element. And yet this individual, metaphysical *core* is very strong, and I was afraid at times that it would break the shell.

It is the problem that has often tormented and oppressed me (already in *Death and the Fool*), most acutely in the *Letter of Lord Chandos,* which perhaps you know: How does the lonely individual come to commit himself to society through language, indeed, how does he come to be connected to it through language whether he likes it or not, inextricably? And also: how can the speaking man act, when to speak is to understand, and to understand is to be incapable of action—my personal, never-ceasing concern with the perennial antinomy between speaking and doing, knowing and living. . . .

The distance spanned by Hofmannsthal in this comedy is that between a society itself ideal because it has the consistency and style of a work of art, and a character who has experienced that almost mystical detachment from all human institutions, that extreme isolation, which Hofmannsthal knew to be a peculiarity of his own time. To span such a distance in a comedy that never ceases to be social called for consummate art. Even historically, the social world of *The Difficult Man* lies at one remove from any reality that an audience of 1921 might have taken to be their own. The time of the action is not specified, but Hofmannsthal wrote the play during the war and appears to have planned it as early as 1908. The actual conditions of the immediate post-war period, the defeat and dissolution of the Austrian Empire, the social revolution and economic straits, do not impinge on the setting. One thinks of Proust's world rather than that of any distinctly post-war writer, or, closer to Hofmannsthal in more than locality, of Robert Musil's retrospective novel *The Man without Qualities*. Yet neither recollection nor caricature accounts for the special *ambiance* of Hofmannsthal's twentieth-century aristocracy, and the reason is that Hofmannsthal had created this world as the representative of a society that did not exist, incorporating so many historical and national traits that no one need suspect him of creating an utopia.

One possible analogy is the Ireland of Synge and Synge's deceptive use of a diction which the uninitiated would call naturalistic, though in the later plays it is as much a distilla-

tion and stylization of colloquial usage as the language of Hofmannsthal's aristocrats. The precise character of Hofmannsthal's Austrian utopia—as distinct from the Germany
represented in the play by Neuhoff—is defined in Hofmannsthal's table entitled "Prussian and Austrian," of 1917,
drawn up when he had begun to have second thoughts about
the military alliance and its consequences:

As a whole

PRUSSIA	AUSTRIA
Created, an artificial structure, a country poor by nature, all in men and by men,	Grown, historical tissue, a country rich by nature, all from the outside: from nature and God,
hence: held together by a belief in the State,	held together by a love of home,
more virtue,	more piety,
more efficiency	more humanity

Social Structure

PRUSSIA	AUSTRIA
A loose social texture, the classes divided by cultural differences; but a precise machinery	A dense social texture, the classes unified by culture; the mechanics of the whole imprecise
The lesser nobility sharply distinct, consistent in itself	High nobility rich in types, politically inconsistent
Homogeneous officialdom: embodying *one* spirit. "Dominant" attitudes and customs	Heterogeneous officialdom: no prescribed way of thinking or feeling
The people: the most easily disciplined mass, unlimited authority (army; scientific social democracy)	The people: most independent mass, unlimited individualism
Supreme authority of the Crown	Supreme confidence in the Crown

Introduction

The Individual

THE PRUSSIAN	THE AUSTRIAN
Up to date in his views (cosmopolitan around 1800, liberal around 1848, now Bismarckian, almost without a memory for past phases)	Traditional in his views, stable almost for centuries
Lacks a sense of history	Possesses an instinct for history
Strength of abstractions	Little talent for abstractions
Incomparable in orderly execution	More quick on the uptake
Acts according to instructions	Acts according to fitness
Strength of dialectic	Rejection of dialectic
More skill in expression	More balance
More consequential	More ability to adapt himself to conditions
Self-reliance	Self-irony
Seemingly masculine	Seemingly immature
Makes everything functional	Gives a social twist to everything
Asserts and justifies himself	Prefers to keep things vague
Self-righteous, arrogant, hectoring	Shamefaced, vain, witty
Forces crises	Avoids crises
Fights for his rights	Lets things go
Incapable of entering into other people's thoughts	Enters into other people's thoughts to the point of losing his character
Willed character	Play-acting
Every individual bears a part of authority	Every individual bears a part of all humanity
Pushing	Pleasure-seeking
Preponderance of the occupational	Preponderance of the private
Extreme exaggeration	Irony to the point of self-destruction

Introduction

What is most striking about the scheme is that Austria has those instinctive and organic qualities which Bachofen had attributed to the matriarchal order, whereas Prussia is all "masculine" artifice and will. In drawing up the scheme and in his confrontation of Hans Karl and Helen with Theophilus Neuhoff, Hofmannsthal was aware of his own relations to men like Stefan George, who had once admonished Hofmannsthal for refusing to become his partner in a joint dictatorship over German literature. (To be more precise, Hofmannsthal had not refused, but had evaded the issue and gone his own way—in typically Austrian fashion.) At one time the play was to be called *The Man without Designs;* and the whole society which Hans Karl at once represents and avoids is characterized by its disapproval of anything that is too deliberate. Crescence has designs of a practical and maternal kind; but when these are thwarted by events, she is quite happy to let them go. Even Stani, a member of the younger generation who believes in steering a definite course, accepts the unpredictable with good grace. Clearly a nation or a class or an individual so purely Austrian in this regard could not survive for long; and both the play and the table show a sharp awareness of this danger. In the play the awareness takes the form of irony: faced with a man without designs, Helen, in the end, is forced to break her own code by reversing the conventional roles and proposing marriage to a man. To be wholly without designs is to be "like a child," as Helen says of Hans Karl, and to run the risk of self-destruction in a competitive world.

The Austrians, according to Hofmannsthal's table, reject every abstract dialectic. Although a great deal of theory is concealed in the play—Hofmannsthal's borrowings from Kierkegaard are one instance—a delicate interplay of characters and ironies takes the place of a deliberate dialectic, thesis, or moral. The implications of this interplay are almost inexhaustible because the work remains "open" in a way which almost suggests that its author, too, was a man without designs. Needless to say, this very openness was the product of Hofmannsthal's intricate art. There is scarcely a sentence in *The Difficult Man* that does not reveal some new aspect of a character or of a relationship between characters, adding to the significance of the whole. To disentangle this web and comment on the function of each thread in turn would require an essay at least as long as Professor Emil Staiger's brilliant and satisfying study of the play. Since this study is itself a highly organized work of art, no extract from it would amount to an interpretation of the play as a whole, and I shall attempt no such interpretation of my own. A few hints will have to suffice here.

Once again a symbolism of names points to some of the more obvious connections and antinomies. Two characters not quite at home in the social world of the play incorporate the particle *Neu* (new) in their names: Neuhoff, the German aristocrat, and Neugebauer, the secretary whose disapproval of his employer's sheltered life is intimated at one point. Both names also suggest a formerly rural order, as opposed to the combination of "old" with "town" in the surname of Helen and her father. Helen's Christian name needs no comment, but Hans Karl's surname may well indicate his role of lover (*buhlen,* to love; *Buhle,* lover)—which he performs so incompetently—and offer a clue to his inmost nature, a capacity for love, tenderness, and sympathy so great that it becomes a danger to him and to others, especially in conjunction with his extreme aversion to declarations, explanations, and confessions. How much of himself Hofmannsthal put into this bizarre and complicated character must be apparent to any perceptive reader.

Introduction

The name Vincent explains itself; a double irony—Vincent fails to conquer—connects the servant both with Neuhoff, the designing, deliberate, and self-assured German suitor who at once admires and despises the world into which he has intruded, and with a new social order impatient to displace the "degenerate" aristocracy of the play. His antipoles are Lukas and Agathe, whose names evoke Christian associations and an old master-servant relationship deeply rooted in the Austrian tradition. This Austrian tradition, in turn, derived from the Spanish. The roles of Anton in *The Tower* and of his prototype Clarin in Calderón's *Life Is a Dream* are more relevant to it than those of the servants in Molière's comedies. In Hofmannsthal, as in Spanish plays, a religious and mystical significance attaches to the relationship and to the notion of service generally, and the prominence of the relationship in works by Cervantes, Calderón, and Tirso de Molina was carried over into Austrian plays by Grillparzer, Raimund, and Nestroy. Hofmannsthal's later comedy *Der Unbestechliche* (1923) hinges on the relationship: here it is the incorruptible, but far from impeccable, servant Theodore—a symbolic name once more—who dominates the action and prevents his master from betraying the old values.

Antoinette's affinities, on the other hand, are French, eighteenth-century, rococo; but they extend to the Venetian figures of Hofmannsthal's early comedies and of his novel *Andreas,* to Zerbinetta in his *Ariadne auf Naxos,* and to all those of his characters who agree with Antoinette that "all beginnings are beautiful" and "the only thing that's real to me is what I have at any one moment." Yet by one of those reversals that prove Hofmannsthal an ironist rather than a dialectician, she can turn the tables on Hans Karl and present him as the faithless and fickle seducer; for though her memory is short on the whole, in this one instance she did commit herself—to the one man who, apart from her husband, had no designs on her. Hans Karl, it seems, had always wanted to lead her back to the only commitment that is valid in his eyes, her first and last commitment to her husband; but in doing so he comes up against the consequences of having no designs and no confidence in speech, "that indecent excess of self-esteem." Only religious love can presume to be impersonal; by practising altruism on Antoinette, Hans Karl has gone too far and precipitated something more serious, for once, than a mere muddle or misunderstanding. As for the outcome, Hofmannsthal wisely left the ends loose; but Antoinette's treatment of Neuhoff and her encounter with her transmogrified husband suggest that all may yet be well.

For all his seeming roughness, Hechingen himself has many facets. To Hans Karl he stands for a partly inarticulate decency, loyalty, and lovingness, a humility and self-effacement comparable to that of the clown Furlani. Hans Karl's nephew sees only the clownishness of Hechingen, since Stani lacks Hans Karl's mystical unworldliness. Furlani, too, has "no purpose whatever," and his performance, like Hechingen's company, delights Hans Karl "much more than the wittiest talk of anybody on earth." Hans Karl's friendship for Hechingen is illuminated by the reply of a very different Austrian writer, Kafka, to the remark that a certain acquaintance was stupid. "To be stupid is human. Many clever people are not wise, and therefore in the last resort not even clever. They are merely inhuman out of fear of their own meaningless vulgarity." This meaningless vulgarity, of course, is represented in Hofmannsthal's play by the Famous Man, as well as by Neuhoff. The true antinomy everywhere in the play is not one between cleverness and stupidity, but between delicacy of feeling and a scheming vanity. The ultimate bond between Hechingen and Antoinette is that both have this delicacy of feeling, however differently it is manifested.

Hofmannsthal's counterpoint of ironies in this play includes both Neuhoff and the Famous Man, no less than Neugebauer. Their points of view are by no means to be discounted as purely negative or antagonistic. For all his partial self-identification with Hans Karl, Hofmannsthal's attitude to him necessarily involved a corresponding measure of self-irony. Neuhoff's strictures on Hans Karl and on the Viennese aristocracy always contain a substantial grain of truth, as well as reflecting Neuhoff's own resentment and frustration. As for the Famous Man, Hofmannsthal was far from wishing to justify either Edine's stupidity or the indifference of other characters to new developments in learning and art —contrasted here with Neuhoff's German reverence for "culture." Hofmannsthal was too conscious of another irony, that of his own situation in Austria. The notorious cultural conservatism of the Austrians prevented his own work from being recognized and understood; this very play was first performed in Germany. Hofmannsthal's place in Austrian society would have been not unlike the Famous Man's if Hofmannsthal had allowed personal vanity and snobbery to determine his attitudes.

As it was, he remained the Difficult Man and representative of a society that did not exist, using social, historical, and literary conventions as a frame for intimate enigma variations. Sigismund and Hans Karl define their range: the disinherited prince in his tower, carried from the dream of pre-existence into active life, struggling with it for the dream's sake, defeated; and the seemingly mundane man, seemingly at home and at ease in his social world, but secretly a perfectionist no less than Sigismund, ruled by a mystical absolute as a lover and a friend, opposing a necessity rooted in pre-existence to the improvisations, accidents, and machinations of active life. Ultimately, therefore, *The Difficult Man* is as difficult and mysterious a work as *The Tower;* and it is in its trivialities that Hofmannsthal attained the utmost refinement of his art.

MICHAEL HAMBURGER

A Note on "The Tower"

THE LONGEST and much the most important single piece in the present collection is the difficult and little-known *The Tower;* and to this strange play I wish to call special attention. I doubt whether this play can be called a "success," but if not, it is at least a failure grander and more impressive than many successes. In a postscript to an edition of the German text of the play,[1] Herr Gerhard Meyer-Sichting tells us that the poet spent nearly ten years—from 1918 to 1927, the last years of his life—in writing and rewriting this play. *The Tower* is written in prose; but here also I speak of Hofmannsthal as "the poet," for the play is essentially poetic drama. I do not know whether it has ever been presented on the stage; but the latter part, with the episodes of the Gipsy and the King of the Children, becomes so phantasmagoric that one can only imagine its representation in terms of a dream-film such as Jean Cocteau might devise. The plot is suggested by that of Calderón's *Life Is a Dream;* but Calderón's play is for Hofmannsthal hardly more than a point of departure; two plays could hardly be more different in spirit and intention than these of the Spaniard and the Austrian. Hofmannsthal was well practised in the craft of the theatre, and if *The Tower* is unplayable, we must attribute this not to failure of

---

[1] *Der Turm* (Frankfurt a/M: S. Fischer Verlag, 1952).

skill but to the fact that what the author wished here to express exceeded the limits within which the man of the theatre must work. For the surface meaning, the real or apparent reason for human behaviour which must be immediately apprehensible by the audience if a play is to hold their interest, Hofmannsthal cares less and less as the play proceeds. He seems to have loaded this play, in symbolism which perhaps has more than one level of significance, with all the burden of his feelings about the catastrophe of the Europe to which he belonged, the Europe which went down in the wreck of empires between 1914 and 1918. As Herr Meyer-Sichting justly says, there is much in the play which cannot be "understood," but only "intuited." [2] The play expresses not only the author's suffering during those years that remained to him, but also his ultimate Christian hope. I find it interesting to compare the message of *The Tower,* so far as I have succeeded in grasping it, with that of the masterly essay which Paul Valéry wrote in 1919, called *La Crise de l'esprit:* an essay which, because so much of its prophecy has already come to pass, is more terrifying since the second World War than it was at the date of its first publication. Both men were poets; both had their formation and first practised their art in the world before 1914; both lived on—the French poet eighteen years after the death of the Austrian—into a waning civilization. Perhaps the hope of the one and the despair of the other were each in its own realm justified.

T. S. ELIOT

[2] He is speaking specifically of the episodes of the Gipsy and the King of the Children. His words are: "beide Vorgänge sollten nicht 'gedeutet' werden. Man kann sie nur ahnen, nicht 'verstehen.' " I give the quotation in full, as my "intuit" is a rather free translation of *ahnen.*

ELECTRA

A Tragedy in One Act
freely rendered after Sophocles

Translated by

ALFRED SCHWARZ

CLYTEMNESTRA

ELECTRA

CHRYSOTHEMIS ⎫
⎬ *her daughters*
⎭

AEGISTHUS

ORESTES

THE TUTOR OF ORESTES

THE CONFIDANTE

THE TRAINBEARER

A YOUNG SERVANT

AN OLD SERVANT

THE COOK

WOMEN SERVANTS

THEIR MATRON

The inner courtyard, bounded by the rear wall of the pal-
ace and low buildings in which the servants live. Women
Servants at the well, left front. Among them Matron Over-
seers.

FIRST SERVANT

lifting her water pitcher

What's become of Electra?

SECOND SERVANT

Why, it's her hour,
her time of day when she howls for her father
so that the walls resound.

Electra comes running from the hallway, which is already
growing dark. All turn to look at her. Electra bounds back
like an animal into its hiding place, holding one arm in
front of her face.

FIRST SERVANT

Did you see how she looked at us?

SECOND SERVANT

Spiteful
like a wild cat.

THIRD SERVANT

Not long ago she lay there
and groaned—

[5]

Hugo von Hofmannsthal

FIRST SERVANT

Always when the sun goes down
she lies there and groans.

THIRD SERVANT

And two of us went by
and came too close to her—

FIRST SERVANT

She cannot bear it
if you look at her.

THIRD SERVANT

Yes, we came
too close to her. She spit like a cat
at us. "Off with you, flies!" she yelled. "Off!"

FOURTH SERVANT

"Blowflies, off with you!"

THIRD SERVANT

"Don't settle on my wounds!"
and struck at us with a whisk.

FOURTH SERVANT

"Off with you,
blowflies, begone!"

THIRD SERVANT

"I won't have you glut
on the sweets of my pain; nor relish the foam
of my writhing lips."

[6]

FOURTH SERVANT

"Begone, crawl away
and hide," she yelled after us. "Eat fat things
and sweet things and creep into bed with your men," she
    cried,
and this one here—

THIRD SERVANT

I didn't mince my words—

FOURTH SERVANT

                        She answered her!

THIRD SERVANT

I did: "When you are hungry," I answered her,
"you also eat," and she sprang to her feet and shot
horrible looks at us; she stretched her fingers
like claws at us and screamed: "I'm feeding,"
she screamed, "I'm feeding a vulture in my body."

SECOND SERVANT

And you?

THIRD SERVANT

    "That's why you always squat," I told her,
"where the smell of carrion holds you and scrape
for an ancient corpse!"

SECOND SERVANT

                And what did she say
to that?

Hugo von Hofmannsthal

THIRD SERVANT

She broke into howls and threw herself
in her corner.

They have finished drawing water from the well.

FIRST SERVANT

That the queen allows
such a demon foot-loose to play her tricks
all through the house.

SECOND SERVANT

And her own child, too!

FIRST SERVANT

If she were mine, I'd keep her—by God, I would!—
under lock and key.

FOURTH SERVANT

Are they not harsh enough
with her? Do they not set her bowl of food
down among the dogs?

Softly

Haven't you ever seen
the master beat her?

FIFTH SERVANT

a very young girl, with a trembling excited voice

I will throw myself
down before her and I will kiss her feet.
Is she not a royal child and suffers
such disgrace! I will anoint her feet
and dry them with my hair.

[8]

Electra

MATRON

Inside with you!

Pushes her.

FIFTH SERVANT

There is nothing in the world that is nobler
than she. She lies in rags stretched out
on the threshold, but there is no one,

Shouting

there is no one in this house who can endure
her look!

MATRON

Inside!

Pushes her through the low open door on the left, front.

FIFTH SERVANT *caught in the door*

None of you is worthy
to breathe the air which she is breathing! Oh,
if I could see you strangled, see you all
in a dark shed hanging by your necks,
for what you have done to Electra!

MATRON

slams the door shut and stands with her back against it

Do you hear? what we
have done to Electra! who pushed her bowl from our
table, when she was told to eat with us,
who spat at our feet and called us bitches.

[9]

Hugo von Hofmannsthal

FIRST SERVANT

What? She said: *no* dog can be degraded
to do what we were trained to do: to wash
with water and with more and more fresh-drawn
water the everlasting blood of murder
off the floors—

THIRD SERVANT

And sweep the shame, she said,
the shame which renews itself by day and night
into the corners . . .

FIRST SERVANT

Our body, so she cries,
bristles with the filth which we are forced to serve!

They carry their pitchers into the house, left.

MATRON

who has opened the door for them

And when she sees us with our children, she screams:
nothing can be so accursed, nothing,
as children which, like animals, slithering about
in blood on the stairs, we have conceived and borne
here in this house. Does she say these things
or not?

THE SERVANTS *from inside*

Yes! yes!

ONE OF THEM *from inside*

They are beating me!

The Matron goes inside. The door closes.

[10]

Electra

Electra comes out of the house. She is alone with the patches of red light which fall like bloodstains from the branches of the fig tree obliquely across the ground and upon the walls.

ELECTRA

Alone! Ah! all alone. My father is gone,
driven away, down into his cold pit.

Towards the ground

Where are you, father? do you not have
the strength to lift up your face towards me?
It is the time, it is our time!
It is the hour in which they butchered you,
your wife and he that sleeps with her
in one bed, your royal bed.
They struck you in the bath, your blood
ran over your eyes, and the bath
steamed with your blood; then he seized you,
the coward, by your shoulders, dragged you
out of the room, head first, the feet
trailing behind: your eyes, wide open,
stared fixedly into the house.
And thus you come again, setting one foot
before the other, and suddenly you stand there,
with wide-open eyes and around your forehead
a royal wreath of purple which feeds
upon the open wound of your head.
                              Father!
I want to see you, leave me not alone today!
Even if only like yesterday, like a shadow,
there by the wall show yourself to your child!
Father! Your day will come! From the stars

all time comes rushing down, so will the blood
from a hundred throats rush down upon your grave!
As from upturned jugs it will flow
from the shackled murderers, and roundabout
like marble jugs will be the naked bodies
of all their helpers, of men and women,
and in one flood, in a swelling stream,
their life's life will rush out of them—
and we will slaughter the steeds for you
which are in the house, we will drive them together
before your grave, and they will sense their death
beforehand and neigh into the wind of death
and die, and we will slaughter the dogs for you
because they are the brood and the brood of the brood
of those who have hunted with you, of those
who licked your feet, to whom you flung
morsels of meat, therefore their blood
must go down to do you service, and we,
your blood, your son Orestes and your daughters,
we three, when all this is done and purple tents
have been raised by the haze of the blood
which the sun sucks upward to itself, then
we, your blood, will dance around your grave:
and above the dead men I will lift my knee
high in the air, step by step, and they
who will see me dance, yes, even they
who will see my shadow only from afar
dancing so, they will say: for a great king
this royal pageantry is being held
by his flesh and blood, and happy is he
who has children that dance such royal dances
of victory around his noble grave!

Electra

CHRYSOTHEMIS

the younger sister, stands in the doorway of the house. She looks fearfully at Electra, calls softly

Electra!

Electra starts like a sleepwalker who hears his name called. She staggers. Her eyes look about as if they did not at once discern anything. Her face is contorted as she sees the frightened face of her sister.

Chrysothemis stands pressed to the door.

ELECTRA

Ah, that face!

CHRYSOTHEMIS

Is my face so hateful to you?

ELECTRA

What do you want? Speak up, pour out your speech,
then go and let me be!

Chrysothemis raises her hands as if warding off a blow

           Why do *you* lift your hands?
Thus, father lifted both his hands,
then the axe fell and split his flesh.
What do you want, daughter of my mother?

CHRYSOTHEMIS

They are plotting something dreadful.

ELECTRA

The two women?

[13]

Hugo von Hofmannsthal

CHRYSOTHEMIS

Who?

ELECTRA

Why, my mother
and that other woman, aye, that milksop,
Aegisthus, that brave murderer, he
who does heroic deeds only in bed.
Well, what are they plotting?

CHRYSOTHEMIS

They will throw you
into a dungeon where you cannot see
the light of sun and moon.

Electra laughs

They will do it,
I know, I heard it.

ELECTRA

I feel as if *I* had heard it.
Was it not at table, and over the last dish?
Then he likes to raise his voice and boast,
I think it helps his digestion.

CHRYSOTHEMIS

Not at table.
Not to boast. He and she, alone
they talk of it.

ELECTRA

Alone? Then how could you
have heard it?

[14]

Electra

CHRYSOTHEMIS

At the door, Electra.

ELECTRA

Open no doors in this house! Faugh!
Choked breathing, faugh! and the death-rattle
of strangled men, there's nothing else here
in all these rooms. No, leave alone the door
behind which you hear a groan: for they're not always
killing, sometimes they are alone together!
Open no doors! Do not sneak about.
Sit on the ground like me and wish for
death and judgment upon her and him.

CHRYSOTHEMIS

I cannot sit and stare into the dark
like you. As though I had a fire inside me,
I am driven constantly about this house,
I cannot bear to stay in any room,
I must be running from door to door, oh!
upstairs and down again, as if a voice
were calling me, and when I come, an empty
room stares at me. I am so afraid,
my knees are trembling by day and night,
my throat is choked, I cannot even weep,
all has turned to stone! Sister, have pity!

ELECTRA

On whom?

CHRYSOTHEMIS

It is you who rivet me to the ground
with iron bolts. If it were not for you,

[15]

they would let us out. But for your smouldering hatred,
your sleepless and ungovernable mind,
at which they tremble, they would let us out
of this prison, sister! I want to get out!
I do not want to sleep here every night
until I die! Before I die I also
want to live! I want to bring forth children
before my body withers, and were it a peasant
to whom they give me, I will bear him children,
and warm them with my body in the cold nights
when gales beat down the shack! But this
I cannot endure any longer, loitering here
with household servants, yet not their equal,
shut in by day and night with my mortal terror!
Are you listening? Speak to me, sister!

ELECTRA

Poor

creature!

CHRYSOTHEMIS

Have pity on yourself and me. Who profits
by this anguish? Our father perhaps?
Our father is dead. Our brother is not
coming home. You can see that he will not come.
With knives each passing day carves his mark
on your face and mine, and outside, the sun rises
and sets, and women whom I have known slender
are heavy with blessing, and toil on their way
to the well and scarcely lift the pail, and all
at once they are delivered of their weight
and come to the well again and they themselves
flow with sweet drink, and, suckling, a new life

[16]

Electra

clings to them, and the children grow—
but we sit always here on our perch
like fettered birds, turning our heads
to left and right, and no one comes, no brother,
no messenger from our brother, not even
a messenger's messenger, nothing! Better dead
than live and yet not live. No, I am
a woman and I desire a woman's fate.

ELECTRA

                                Fie,
the woman who thinks of it, who calls it by name!
To be the cave the murderer enjoys
after the murder; to play the beast giving
pleasure to the fouler beast. Ah, with one
she sleeps, presses her breasts on his two eyes
and beckons to the other who creeps from behind
the bed with axe and net.

CHRYSOTHEMIS

            You are horrible!

ELECTRA

Why horrible? Are you such a woman?
You only want to become one.

CHRYSOTHEMIS

                        Can you not
forget? My head is always confused. I can
remember nothing from today until tomorrow.
Sometimes I lie there, and then I am what I was
before, and cannot understand that I am
no longer young. What, what has become of it all?
For it is not water which is rushing by,

[17]

and it is not yarn which is rolling off,
rolling off the spool; it is I, I!
I would pray that a god might kindle a light
in my breast, that I might find myself again
inside myself! If I were gone from here,
how quickly I would forget all bad dreams—

ELECTRA

Forget? What! Am I a beast? Forget?
The brute beast falls asleep, the half-devoured
prey still dangling from the lip, the brute forgets
and begins to chew while death already sits
on it and throttles it; the beast forgets
what crept out of its body, and stills its hunger
with its own child—I am no beast, *I cannot
forget!*

CHRYSOTHEMIS

Oh, must my soul forever eat
of this food which it loathes, which it
so loathes! to smell it only makes it
shudder; never, never should it have
touched it; never, never should it have
known that such a gruesome thing exists,
never known! never seen with eyes! never heard!
Such dreadful things are not for the heart
of man! When it comes, when it shows
itself, one must flee from the houses, flee
into the vineyards, flee into the mountains!
and if it climb the mountains, one must again
come down and creep away into the houses:
never must one abide with it, never
remain in one house with it! I must get out!

[18]

Electra

I want to conceive and bear children who know
nothing of this; I will wash my body
in every water; I will plunge deep down
into every water; I will wash each
part of me; the hollows of my eyes
I will wash clean—they must not be frightened
when they look into their mother's eyes!

ELECTRA *scornfully*

When they look into their mother's eyes!
And how do you look into father's eyes?

CHRYSOTHEMIS

Stop it!

ELECTRA

May your children, when you have them,
do to you as you have done to your father!

Chrysothemis bursts into tears

What are you wailing for? Be off! In with you!
There is your place. I hear a noise inside.
Are they perhaps preparing your wedding feast
for you? I hear them run. The whole house
is up. They labour in childbirth or
they murder. When they have no corpses
to sleep upon, they must needs murder!

CHRYSOTHEMIS

Stop it. All that is past. Stop!

ELECTRA

Past? In there it is beginning again!
Do you think I do not know the sound as they

drag dead men down the stairs, as they whisper
and wring out linen full of blood?

CHRYSOTHEMIS

Sister!
Go away from here.

ELECTRA

This time I want to be present!
Not like that other time. This time I am strong.
I will throw myself upon her, I will snatch
the axe from her hand and swing it above her—

CHRYSOTHEMIS

Go away, hide yourself! that she may not see you.
Do not stand in her way this day; there is
death in her every look. She has been dreaming.

*Inside, the noise of numerous people approaching, coming
nearer*

Go away from here. They come through the corridor.
They are passing by here. She has been dreaming:
I don't know what, I heard it from the servants,
I don't know whether it is true, sister:
they say that she has dreamed of Orestes,
and that she cried out loud in her sleep
as one cries out who is being strangled.

ELECTRA

I! I!
I sent it to her. From out of my breast
I visited this dream upon her! I lie
and hear the steps of him who looks for her.

Electra

I hear him walk through the rooms, I hear him
raise the curtain from the bed: screaming
she escapes, but he is after her:
the hunt is on, down the stairs
through vaults, vaults upon vaults.
It is much darker than night, much quieter
and darker than the grave, she pants and staggers
in the darkness, but he is after her:
he waves the torch in his left, in his right the axe.
And I am like a dog upon her heels:
if she tries to run into a cave, I leap
at her from the side, thus we drive her on
until a wall blocks everything, and there,
in the deepest darkness, yet I see him well,
a shade, and yet limbs and yet the white
of one eye, there sits our father:
he does not heed it and yet it must be done:
in front of his feet we press her down,
and the axe falls!

*Torches and human figures fill the passageway to the left
of the door.*

CHRYSOTHEMIS

They are coming. She drives all the servants
with torches before her. They drag animals
behind them and the sacrificial knives. Sister,
when she trembles, she is most terrible; if only
this day, only this hour, go out of her way!

ELECTRA

I am in the mood to speak with my mother
as never before!

Hugo von Hofmannsthal

A hurried procession passes the glaringly lit-up windows, clanking and shuffling by: it is a tugging and dragging of animals, a muted scolding, a quickly stifled scream, the whistling sound of a whip, a recovering and staggering onward.

CHRYSOTHEMIS

I do not want to hear it.

Rushes out through the courtyard door.

The figure of Clytemnestra appears in the wide window. Her pale, puffed-up face in the glaring light of the torches appears even paler above the scarlet robe. She supports herself on the arm of a Confidante, who is dressed in dark violet, and on an ivory staff adorned with jewels. A yellow figure, with black hair which is combed straight back, resembling an Egyptian woman, with a smooth face, like an upright snake, carries her train. The queen is completely covered with jewels and charms. Her arms are covered with arm bands, her fingers bristle with rings. The lids of her eyes seem excessively large, and it appears to be a terrible effort for her to keep them open.

Electra stands rigidly upright, her face turned towards this window.

Clytemnestra opens her eyes suddenly, and trembling with anger she steps to the edge of the window and points with her staff at Electra.

CLYTEMNESTRA *at the window*

What do you want? Look, my women! Look, there!
How it rears up with swelling neck
and darts its tongue at me! And that

[22]

I let run free in my own house!
If she could kill me with her looks!
O gods, why do you thus bear down on me?
Why do you ravage me? Why must
my strength be lame inside me, why is
my living body like a waste field,
and this nettle growing out of me,
and I do not have the strength to weed!
Why does this happen to me, you eternal gods?

ELECTRA

Gods! But you are yourself a goddess!
You are what they are.

CLYTEMNESTRA

Did you hear? did you
understand what she speaks?

THE CONFIDANTE

That you are also
of the race of the gods.

THE TRAINBEARER *hissing*

She means it maliciously.

CLYTEMNESTRA

as her heavy eyelids shut

It sounds so familiar. And only as if
I had forgotten it, long long ago.
She knows me well. Yet one can never know
what she is plotting secretly.

*The Confidante and the Trainbearer whisper with one
another.*

[23]

Hugo von Hofmannsthal

ELECTRA

You are no longer yourself. These reptiles
always hang about you. What they hiss
into your ear tears your thinking forever
in two; and so you go about in a frenzy,
you are always as in a dream.

CLYTEMNESTRA

I will come down.
Let be, I wish to speak with her. She is
not loathsome today. She speaks like a physician.
The hours hold all things in their direction.
Each and every thing can first be frightful,
then turn its pleasant face towards us.

She leaves the window and appears in the door, the Confi-
dante at her side, the Trainbearer behind her, torches be-
hind them.

CLYTEMNESTRA *from the threshold*

Why do you call me a goddess? Do you speak so
out of spite? Take care. This day could be
the last day that you may see this light
and that you may breathe this free air.

ELECTRA

Truly, if you are not a goddess,
then where are gods! I know of nothing
in the world which makes me shudder except to think
that this body is the dark door through which
I crept into the light of this world.
Did I lie upon this lap, naked?
Did you lift me to these breasts?

[24]

Electra

Why, then I crept out of my father's grave
and played in swaddling clothes upon
my father's scaffold! Why, you are
a colossus from whose iron hands
I have never escaped. You keep a tight rein
on me. You tether me to what you will.
You have spewed out for me, like the sea,
a life, a father, brother and sister:
and swallowed down, like the sea,
a life, a father, brother and sister.
I know not how I should ever perish—
except of this, that you should perish too.

CLYTEMNESTRA

You do me such honour? Is there yet
something of piety left in you?

ELECTRA

Much! Much!
What weighs heavy on your heart also
touches mine. You see, it grieves me
to see Aegisthus, your husband, wearing
the old robes of my dead father, you know,
the former king. Indeed, it grieves my heart:
I think they do not suit him. I think
they are too wide around his chest.

THE CONFIDANTE

She says not
what she means.

THE TRAINBEARER

Each word is false.

[25]

Hugo von Hofmannsthal

CLYTEMNESTRA *angry*

I will not listen to you. What comes from you
is only the breath of Aegisthus. I will not
find fault with everything. If she speaks
to me what I am glad to hear, then I will listen
to what she speaks. What the truth is
no man can find out. No one on earth
knows the truth about things that are hidden.
Are there not some in the dungeons who say
that I am a murderess and that
Aegisthus is a common assassin?
And when I wake you in the night, do you
not each say something different? Do you not
cry that my eyelids are swollen and that
my liver is sick, and that everything
comes only from the sick liver, and you,
do you not whine into the other ear
that you have seen demons with long pointed
bills that suck my blood? Do you not show me
the marks on my flesh, and do I not
obey you and slaughter, slaughter, slaughter
victim upon victim? Do you not rip me to death
with your pleas and counterpleas? I do not want
to hear any longer: this is true and this a lie.
If anyone says pleasant things to me,
and were it my daughter, were it that one there,
I will loosen the covers from my soul and let
the soft breeze in wherever it may come,
as do the sick when in the evening, sitting
by the pond, they uncover to the cool breeze
their boils and all their festering parts, sitting
in the cool breeze of evening and thinking of nothing

[26]

Electra

except to find relief. So now will I
for once begin to look after myself.
Leave me alone with her.

*Impatiently she directs the Confidante and the Trainbearer
with her staff to go into the house. They disappear, hesitating at the door. Also the torches disappear, and only
from the inside of the house a faint light falls through the
corridor into the yard and touches now and then the figures of the two women.*

CLYTEMNESTRA *after a pause*

I do not have good nights. Have you
no remedy for dreams?

ELECTRA *moving closer*

Do you dream, Mother?

CLYTEMNESTRA

Have you no other words to comfort me?
Loosen your tongue. Yes, yes, I dream.
As one gets older, one dreams. Yet it can be
dispelled. Why are you standing there in the dark?
We need only make subservient to us
the powers that are scattered somewhere. There are
rites. There must be proper rites for everything.
How one pronounces a word, and a sentence,
much depends on that. Also on the hour.
And whether one is full, or fasting. Many a man
has perished because he stepped into the bath
at the wrong hour.

ELECTRA

Are you now thinking

of my father?

Hugo von Hofmannsthal

CLYTEMNESTRA

That is why I am covered
so with gems. For there dwells in each of them
a power, I am sure. One need only know
how to use it. If only you were willing,
you could say something that is of help to me.

ELECTRA

I, Mother, I?

CLYTEMNESTRA

Yes, you! For you are clever.
In your head there is great skill. You speak
of old events as if they had happened
yesterday. But I—I rot inside.
I think, but it all mounts up in me,
one thing on top of another. I open my mouth,
and Aegisthus screams, and what he screams fills me
with hatred; I want to rear up and be stronger
than his words—and I find nothing,
I find nothing! Suddenly I do not know
if he had said today what makes me tremble
with wrath, whether today or another time,
once long ago; then I am giddy, suddenly
I do not know any longer who I am,
and that is the horror of sinking alive
into chaos, and Aegisthus! Aegisthus,
he mocks me, and I find nothing, I do not find
the terrible things before which he would
have to be silent and, pale like myself, stare
into the fire. But you possess the words.
You could say much that would be of help to me.
Even though a word is nothing at all! For what is

[28]

a breath! And yet between night and day,
when I lie with open eyes, something there is
that creeps over me, it is no word, it is
no pain, it does not press, it does not strangle me,
it lets me lie there as I am and here
at my side lies Aegisthus, and there,
there is the curtain: everything looks at me
as if from eternity to eternity:
it is nothing, not even a nightmare, and yet
it is so terrible that my soul
wishes it were hanged and every limb
of mine yearns for death, and yet I live
and am not even sick: as you can see:
do I look sick? Is it then possible
to perish, alive, like a rotting carcass?
Can one waste away and not be sick?
Go to wrack, with waking senses, like a robe
eaten up by moths? And then I sleep
and dream, and dream! So that the marrow dissolves
in my bones, and stagger to my feet again,
and not the tenth part of the water clock
has run out, and that which grins at me underneath
the curtain is not yet the pale morning,
no, it is still the torch before the door,
which flickers frightfully like a living thing
and spies on my sleep.
I do not know who they are that do this
to me, and if they dwell above or somewhere
down below—when I see *you* standing there
as now, I think you must have a part in this.
But then, what are you? You do not even know
how to say one word when one listens to you.
Whom could it profit or harm at all

whether you live or not? Why do you stare
at me so? I will not allow you to look
at me so. But these dreams must have
an end. Whoever it may be that sends them:
any demon will let go of us
as soon as the right blood has flowed.

ELECTRA

Any demon!

CLYTEMNESTRA

And if I had to bleed every beast
that creeps and flies, and rise and go to sleep
in the steam of the blood, like the people
of the farthest Thule in the blood-red fog:
I will no longer dream.

ELECTRA

When the right
victim falls beneath the axe, you will
no longer dream.

CLYTEMNESTRA

stepping closer to her

You know then with which
consecrated beast—

ELECTRA

One that is not consecrated!

CLYTEMNESTRA

Which is tied up, inside?

[30]

Electra

ELECTRA

No! It runs free.

CLYTEMNESTRA *eagerly*

And what sort of rites?

ELECTRA

Wonderful rites,
and to be strictly performed.

CLYTEMNESTRA

Speak up!

ELECTRA

Can you not guess?

CLYTEMNESTRA

No, that is why I ask.
Say the name of the victim.

ELECTRA

A woman.

CLYTEMNESTRA *eagerly*

One of my serving women, speak!
A child? A young virgin? A woman
already known by man?

ELECTRA

Yes! Known!

That's it!

[31]

Hugo von Hofmannsthal

CLYTEMNESTRA

And how sacrificed? What hour?
And where?

ELECTRA

In any place, at any hour
of the day or the night.

CLYTEMNESTRA

Reveal the rites!
How would I perform them? I must myself—

ELECTRA

No.

This time you do not hunt with net and axe.

CLYTEMNESTRA

Who else? Who does it?

ELECTRA

A man.

CLYTEMNESTRA

Aegisthus?

ELECTRA

laughs

I said: a man!

CLYTEMNESTRA

Who? Answer me.
Someone from this house? Or must a stranger
come?

[32]

Electra

ELECTRA

gazing vacantly on the ground, absent-minded

Yes, yes, a stranger. But still
he is of this house.

CLYTEMNESTRA

Do not pose riddles for me.
Electra, listen to me. I am glad
that today I find you for once not stubborn.
When parents are harsh it is always the child
who forces them to be so. No strict word
is quite irrevocable, and the mother,
when she sleeps badly, thinks rather of her child
lying in the marriage bed than on a chain.

ELECTRA *in an undertone*

The opposite of the child: who would rather
think the mother dead than in her bed.

CLYTEMNESTRA

What are you mumbling? I say that no thing
is irrevocable. For do not all things
turn before our eyes and change like fog?
And *we,* we ourselves! And our deeds!
Deeds! We and deeds! What odd words!
For am I still the same who has done the deed?
And if so! Done, done! done! What a word
to throw in my teeth! There he stood
of whom you always talk, there he stood
and here stood I and there Aegisthus,
and from eye to eye our glances met:
so it had not happened yet! And then

[33]

your father's dying look altered
so slowly and horribly, but still
fastened to mine—and then it had happened:
there is no space between! Now it was
before, and then it was past—in between
I did nothing.

ELECTRA

No, the work that lay between
the axe had done alone.

CLYTEMNESTRA

How you thrust in
the words.

ELECTRA

Not so skilled nor so fast
as you the strokes of the axe.

CLYTEMNESTRA

I do not want
to hear of it. Be silent. If I met
your father today—as I am speaking here
to you, so could I speak with him. Maybe
I would shudder, but it may also be
that I could speak tenderly and weep
as when two old friends happen to meet.

ELECTRA *in an undertone*

Horrible, she speaks of the murder as if it were
a quarrel before supper.

Electra

CLYTEMNESTRA

Tell your sister
she should not flee before me like a frightened dog
into the darkness. Tell her to greet me
cheerfully, as is becoming, and answer me
calmly. Then I would truly have no cause
to hinder me from giving you and her
in marriage before the winter.

ELECTRA

And our brother?
Will you not let him come home, Mother?

CLYTEMNESTRA

I have forbidden you to speak of him.

ELECTRA

Then you fear him?

CLYTEMNESTRA

Who says that?

ELECTRA

Why, Mother,
you are trembling!

CLYTEMNESTRA

Who would fear
a feeble-minded boy?

ELECTRA

What?

Hugo von Hofmannsthal

CLYTEMNESTRA

They say,
he stammers, sprawls in the yard among the dogs
and cannot tell man and beast apart.

ELECTRA

The child was perfectly well.

CLYTEMNESTRA

They say they gave him
a wretched place to live and the barnyard
animals for company.

ELECTRA

Ah!

CLYTEMNESTRA

with lowered eyelids

I sent
much gold and yet more gold that they might
keep him like a royal child.

ELECTRA

You lie!
You sent the gold that they might strangle him.

CLYTEMNESTRA

Who tells you that?

ELECTRA

I see it in your eyes.
But by your trembling I also see that he
is still alive. That you think of nothing

[36]

by day and night except of him. That your heart
is withering for fear, because you know: he comes.

CLYTEMNESTRA

Do not lie. Anyone outside this house
does not concern me. I live here and I am
mistress. Servants I have enough to guard
the doors, and if I wish I will have three
armed guards sit with open eyes by day and night
before my room. I do not even hear
what you say. Nor do I know who he is
of whom you speak. I will never see him:
what is it to me to know if he is
alive or not? To say it quite plainly,
I have had enough of dreaming about him.
Dreams are unwholesome, they waste our strength,
and I wish to live and be the mistress here.
I do not want to have such fitful spells
as to stand here like a market woman
and to tell you of my nights. I am
as good as sick, and sick men gossip
of their ills, that is all. But I will
not be sick any longer. And in one way

She raises her staff threateningly towards Electra

or another I will force the right word
from your lips. Already you have betrayed
yourself saying you know the right victim
and also the rites that will help me. If you
will not speak being free, you will on the chain.
If not, being full, then you will speak from hunger.
One can get rid of dreams. He who suffers
from them and does not find the means to get

[37]

relief is only a fool. I will find out
who must bleed so I can sleep again.

ELECTRA

with a leap out of the darkness, coming steadily closer towards
her, rising up, more and more terrible

What must bleed? Your own neck must bleed
when the hunter has moved in for the kill!
He will knife his game: but only on the run!
Who'd slaughter a victim in sleep! He'll hunt you up,
he'll drive you through the house! If you go to the right,
there stands the bed! To the left, there foams the bath
like blood! The darkness and the torches cast
red-black death nets over you—

Clytemnestra, shaken with voiceless fear, tries to run into
the house. Electra hauls her by her dress to the front.
Clytemnestra draws back against the wall. Her eyes are
wide-open, the staff drops from her trembling hands

You want to cry out, but the air stifles
the unborn cry and lets it drop to the ground
silently; as if out of your senses, you offer
the nape of your neck, and you feel the sharp edge
plunging into the seat of life, but he
holds back the stroke: the rites have not yet been fulfilled.
He draws you by the tresses of your hair,
and all is silent, you hear your own heart
beating against your ribs: this space of time
—it spreads before you like a dark abyss
of years—this time is given to you
to guess how shipwrecked men feel
when the blackness of clouds and death corrodes

their useless cries; the time is given to you
to envy all those who are fettered with chains
to dungeon walls, who on the bottom of wells
cry out for death as for their deliverer—
for you, you lie imprisoned in your own
self as if it were the glowing hot belly
of a brazen beast—and, just as now,
you cannot cry out! And I stand next to you:
you cannot turn your eyes away from me,
for you are tortured with convulsive desire
to read one word upon my silent face,
you roll your eyes, you want to think
of anything, grinning you want to lure the gods
down from the cloudy skies of the night:
the gods are having supper! As at the time
when you slaughtered my father, they sit
at supper and are deaf to choking throats!
Only a half-mad god, Laughter, he staggers
in by the door: he thinks you are dallying
with Aegisthus at loving time; but
instantly he notes his error, laughs
his shrill laugh and is gone at once.
Then you also have enough. Your gall trickles
bitter drops into your heart, expiring
you want to recollect one word, to utter
only one word, any word, instead of
the tear of blood which even the beast
is not denied in death: but I stand there
before you, and then you read with a fixed
eye the monstrous word that is written
upon my face: for my face is mingled
of my father's features and of yours,
and so with my standing there in silence

I have utterly destroyed your last word;
hanged is your soul in the noose twisted
by yourself, the axe now whistles through the air,
and I stand there and see you die at last!
Then you will never dream again, then I need
dream no longer, and he who then is still
alive can shout with joy over his life!

They stand face to face, Electra in the wildest intoxication, Clytemnestra breathing harshly with fear. At this moment the hallway becomes bright, and the Confidante comes running out. She whispers something in Clytemnestra's ear; but at first she does not seem to understand. Gradually she collects herself. She beckons: lights! Servants with torches come out and stand behind Clytemnestra. She beckons: more lights! More women come out and take their stand behind her so that the courtyard becomes bright with lights and a red-yellow glare floods the walls. Now the features of Clytemnestra's face gradually change, and the tension of her terror gives way to an expression of evil triumph. She demands to hear the whispered message again and meanwhile does not let Electra for a moment out of her sight. Glutting herself with a savage joy, she stretches both hands menacingly against Electra. Then the Confidante picks up the staff for her, and Clytemnestra, leaning on both, hurriedly, eagerly, gathering up her robes on the steps, runs into the house. The servants with the lights rush behind her as if pursued.

ELECTRA *in the meantime*

What are they saying to her? why look, she is glad!
O my head! I can't think why. What gives such joy
to the woman?

[40]

Electra

Chrysothemis enters by the courtyard door, running, howling loudly like a wounded animal

ELECTRA

Chrysothemis! Quick, quick,
I need your help. Name something in this world
that can give one joy!

CHRYSOTHEMIS *shrieking*

Orestes! Orestes
is dead!

ELECTRA

warns her off; as if out of her senses

Be still!

CHRYSOTHEMIS *close by her*

Orestes is dead!

Electra moves her lips

CHRYSOTHEMIS

I came outside, they knew it already! They all
stood about, and all knew it, only we
did not.

ELECTRA

No one knows it.

CHRYSOTHEMIS

All know it!

[41]

Hugo von Hofmannsthal

ELECTRA

No one can know it: because it is not true.

Chrysothemis throws herself on the ground. Electra pulls
her up

It is not true! I tell you! I say to you,
it is not true!

CHRYSOTHEMIS

The strangers stood by the wall, the strangers
who are sent here to bring the message: two of them,
an old man and a young man. They had already
told it to everyone. All stood around them
in a circle and all knew it already.

ELECTRA

It is not true.

CHRYSOTHEMIS

Only we are not told!
No one thinks of us. Dead! Electra, dead!

A YOUNG MANSERVANT

comes hurrying out of the house, stumbles over the form
lying before the threshold

Make room here! Who's loafing here before a door?
Ah, I might have known! Ho there, stableboy! Hey!

THE COOK

comes through the door, right

What is the matter?

[42]

Electra

THE YOUNG MANSERVANT

I split my lungs calling
for a stableboy, and who crawls out of his hole—
the cook.

AN OLD SERVANT

with a dour face, appears at the courtyard door

What do you want at the stables?

THE YOUNG MANSERVANT

Saddle up,

as quick as you can! Do you hear?
A nag, a mule, or a cow for all I care,
but be quick about it!

AN OLD SERVANT

For whom?

THE YOUNG MANSERVANT

For the fellow
who tells you. Now he stands there and gapes! Quick,
for me! Right now! One, two! One, two! For I must
ride out in the fields and bring the master home,
because I have a message for him, great news,
important enough to ride one of your mares
to death.

The Old Servant disappears.

THE COOK

What sort of news? Say
a word or two!

[43]

Hugo von Hofmannsthal

THE YOUNG MANSERVANT

A word or two, my dear cook,
would probably be of no use to you. Besides,
it would be hard to sum up in one word
and plainly what I know and what I have to
report to the master: let you be satisfied
when you are told that a message has just arrived
here in the house of the utmost importance
—how long such an old bag of bones takes
to saddle a horse!—which, as a loyal servant
of this household ought to delight you: whether
you know what it is or not, all the same,
it has to delight you.

Roaring into the yard

A whip, you scoundrel! What,
do you think I'll ride him without a whip? You,
it's you keep me waiting, not I the nag!

To the Cook, on the point of leaving

Well, in a word: the young fellow Orestes,
the son of the house, who was always away
from home, and therefore as good as dead:
in short, this fellow, who after all has, so to speak,
been always dead, is now, so to speak, really dead!

Rushes off.

THE COOK

*In the direction of Electra and Chrysothemis, who lie there
pressed close to one another, like one body which is shaken
by the sobs of Chrysothemis and above which rises the
deathly pale silent face of Electra*

[44]

Electra

Eh! Now I have found it out! The dogs howl
with the full moon, and you howl because now
it is always new moon for you. The dogs are driven
away when they disturb the peace of the house.
Be on your guard, or it will happen to you.

Goes in again.

CHRYSOTHEMIS *halfway rising*

Perished in a foreign land! Dead! Buried
there away from home. Killed by his horses
and dragged along the ground! Ah, his face
unrecognizable, they say. We have never
seen it, his face! When we think of him,
we think of a child. And he was tall.
I wonder did he ask for us before
he died! I could not question them:
everybody stood around them. Electra,
we must go up and speak with these men.

ELECTRA *in an undertone*

Now it must be done by us.

CHRYSOTHEMIS

Electra,
let us go there: they are two, an old one
and one much younger; when they find out
that we are the sisters, his poor sisters,
they will tell us all.

ELECTRA

What good is it
to know more? That he is dead we know.

[45]

CHRYSOTHEMIS

Ah, to have brought us nothing, not even
a lock of hair, not one small lock of hair!
As if we were no longer among the living,
we two girls.

ELECTRA

Therefore we must now show
that we are.

CHRYSOTHEMIS

Electra?

ELECTRA

Yes, we!
We two must do it.

CHRYSOTHEMIS

Electra, what?

ELECTRA

It were best, today, and best, this night.

CHRYSOTHEMIS

What, sister?

ELECTRA

What? The work that has now
fallen to us, because he cannot come
and, yet, it must not remain undone.

CHRYSOTHEMIS

What work?

ELECTRA

Now you and I must go
and kill the woman and her spouse.

CHRYSOTHEMIS

Sister, do you speak of our mother?

ELECTRA

Of her. And also of him. It must be done
without delay.

Chrysothemis is speechless

ELECTRA

Keep still. There is nothing to say.
Nothing to consider except: how?
how we will do it.

CHRYSOTHEMIS

I?

ELECTRA

Yes, you and I.
Who else? Has our father other children
hidden somewhere in the house who could
come to our aid? No, as far as I know.

CHRYSOTHEMIS

We two must go and do this? We? We two?
With our two hands?

ELECTRA

That you may leave

to me.

[47]

CHRYSOTHEMIS

But even if a knife—

ELECTRA *contemptuously*

A knife!

CHRYSOTHEMIS

Or else an axe—

ELECTRA

An axe!
The axe! The axe with which our father—

CHRYSOTHEMIS

You?

O, horrid, you have it?

ELECTRA

I kept it
for our brother. Now we must swing it.

CHRYSOTHEMIS

You? These arms to slay Aegisthus?

ELECTRA

First him, then her; first her, then him, no matter.

CHRYSOTHEMIS

I am afraid. You are beside yourself.

ELECTRA

No one sleeps in their anteroom.

Electra

CHRYSOTHEMIS

Murder them in their sleep, and then live on!

ELECTRA

My concern is with him, and not with us.

CHRYSOTHEMIS

If only you came to your senses to see this madness!

ELECTRA

One who sleeps is a fettered victim. Did they
not sleep together, I could accomplish it
alone. But so, you must go along.

CHRYSOTHEMIS *warding her off*
Electra!

ELECTRA

You! For you are strong!

Close to her

How strong you are!
The virgin nights have made you strong.
Your hips, how slender and lithe they are!
You can twist yourself through every crevice,
pull yourself through a window! Let me feel
your arms: how cool and strong they are!
As you struggle against me, I feel what arms
they are. You could crush whatever you clasp
in your arms. You could press me, or a man,
against your cool firm breasts with your arms
and one would suffocate! Everywhere
there is such strength in you! It flows like cool

[49]

pent-up water from the rock. It streams down
with your hair upon your strong shoulders!

CHRYSOTHEMIS

Let me go!

ELECTRA

No: I will hold on to you!
With my wretched withered arms I will
embrace your body, the more you struggle
the firmer you tie the knot, and I will wind
myself around you, sink my roots
deep into you and implant my will
into your blood!

CHRYSOTHEMIS

Let me go!

Flees a few steps.

ELECTRA

wildly after her, seizes her by her robe

No!

CHRYSOTHEMIS

Electra!

Let me go!

ELECTRA

I will not let you go.
We must grow so close together that the knife
which would tear my body from yours would kill
us both at once, for now we are alone
in this world.

[50]

Electra

CHRYSOTHEMIS

Electra, listen to me.
You are so clever, help us to get away
from this house, set us free.

ELECTRA *without hearing her*

                You are full of strength,
your sinews are the sinews of a colt,
slender are your feet, easily I clasp them
with my arms as with a rope. I can feel
the warm blood through the coolness of your skin,
against my cheek I can feel the down
on your youthful arms. You are like fruit
on the day of its ripeness. From now on
I will be your sister as I have never
been your sister before! I will sit
in your chamber with you and will wait
for the bridegroom, I will anoint you
for him, and you shall dip yourself
in the fragrant bath like the young swan
and shelter your head at my breast
before he takes you, gleaming like a torch
through the veils, with his strong arms
into the wedding bed.

CHRYSOTHEMIS

closes her eyes

No, sister, no.
Do not speak such words in this house.

ELECTRA

Ah, yes! Far more than a sister I will be
to you from this day on: I will serve you

[51]

like your slave. When you lie in travail,
I will stand at your bed by day and night,
keep off the flies, and draw the cool water,
and when all at once a living thing
lies in the naked lap, frightening almost,
then I will lift it up for you, so high!
that his smile may fall from on high
into the deepest secret caverns
of your soul and the last icy horror
there may melt under this sun and you may
weep it out in heavy tears.

CHRYSOTHEMIS

Oh,
take me away! I die in this house!

ELECTRA *at her knees*

Your mouth is beautiful when it opens
to speak in anger! A dreadful cry
must spurt from your clean strong mouth,
dreadful like the cry of the goddess
of death, when someone lies like this
beneath you as I do now: when one awakens
suddenly and finds you like the goddess
of death above one's head! When one lies
bound beneath you and so looks up at you,
forced to look up at your slender body
with staring eyes, as shipwrecked sailors
look up at the cliff before they die.

CHRYSOTHEMIS

What are you saying?

Electra

ELECTRA *rising*

Before you escape
from this house and me, you must do it!

*Chrysothemis wants to speak. Electra covers her mouth with
her hand*

There is
no way out but this. I will not let you
go before you have sworn mouth to mouth
that you will do it.

CHRYSOTHEMIS

wrenches herself free

Let me go!

ELECTRA

seizes her again

Swear
that you will come tonight, when all is still,
to the foot of the stairs.

CHRYSOTHEMIS

Let me go!

ELECTRA

holds her by her robe

Child, do not resist!
Not one drop of blood will cling to your body:
quickly you shall slip out of the bloodstained robe
and with a clean body into the wedding shirt.

CHRYSOTHEMIS

Let me go!

Hugo von Hofmannsthal

ELECTRA

Do not be cowardly! The shuddering
fear which now you overcome will be repaid
with shudders of bliss night after night—

CHRYSOTHEMIS

I cannot!

ELECTRA

Say that you will come!

CHRYSOTHEMIS

I cannot!

ELECTRA

Look,

I lie before you, I am kissing your feet!

CHRYSOTHEMIS

escaping into the door of the house

I cannot!

ELECTRA *after her*

A curse on you!

To herself, with savage resolution

Well then alone!

*She begins digging eagerly near the wall of the house, to
the side of the doorsill, without making a sound, like an
animal. She pauses, looks around, digs again.*

*Orestes stands in the courtyard door, his figure set off in
black against the last gleam of light. He enters. Electra*

Electra

*looks at him. He turns slowly around so that his glance
falls on her. Electra starts up violently; she trembles.*

ELECTRA

What do you want, stranger? Why do you prowl
here at this dark hour, spying out
what others do! Maybe you have yourself
something in your mind that you would not want
others to discover. Then leave me to myself.
There is one thing I must do here. What is it to you!
Begone and let me burrow in the earth.
Do you hear when you are spoken to? Or does
your curiosity not let you go? I do not
bury anything, I am digging something up.
And not the dead bone of a little child
which I covered days ago. No, my fellow,
I gave no life, and so I need not smother
a life nor bury it. When the earth's body
will some day take something from my hands,
it will be what I came out of, not what came
out of me. I am digging something up:
as soon as you stand back from the light, I'll
have it and caress it and I'll kiss it as if it were
my dear brother and my dear son, all in one.

ORESTES

Have you then nothing on earth that is dear to you
since you want to scrape a thing out of the earth
and kiss it? Are you all alone?

ELECTRA

I am no mother, I have no mother,
I am no sister, I have no sister,

I lie before the door yet I am not
the watchdog, I speak and yet I do not answer,
live and do not live, have long hair and yet
feel nothing of what, they say, all women feel:
in short, I beg you, go and leave me! Leave me! Leave me!

ORESTES

I must wait here.

ELECTRA

Wait here?

A pause

ORESTES

But you belong here
to this house? You are one of the maidservants
of the house?

ELECTRA

Yes, I serve here in this house.
But you have no cause to meddle here. Be glad
and go.

ORESTES

I told you that I must wait here
until they call me.

ELECTRA

They, in there? You lie.
I know well enough the master is not home.
And she, what should she want with you?

Electra

ORESTES

I and one
who is with me, we have a message to bring
to the mistress.

Electra is silent

We have been sent to her
because we can bear witness that her son
Orestes died before our eyes.
For he was killed by his own horses.
I was as old as he and his companion
by day and night; the other one
who is with me, an old man, he was
our guardian and tutor.

ELECTRA

Did I yet have to
look upon you! Did you have to crawl
down here into my wretched corner,
herald of misery! Can you not trumpet
forth your message where it gives pleasure!
You live—and he, who was better than you
and nobler a thousand times, and a thousand times
as important that he should live—he is dead!
Your eye stares at me and his is jellied.
Your mouth opens and shuts and his is
crammed full of earth. Oh, that I could cram
yours with curses! Get out of my sight.

ORESTES

But what do you want with me? They receive it
with pleasure here in the house. Let the dead be dead.
Let Orestes be. Well now, Orestes

[57]

has died, and it all had to come
as it did come. He rejoiced too much
in his life, and the gods up there
cannot endure the ringing sound of joy,
they detest the vigorous beat of wings
before evening, quickly they reach
for an arrow and nail the living creature
to the dark tree of his hidden fate
which had long since somewhere secretly
grown for him. And so he had to die.

ELECTRA

How he speaks of dying, this young fellow!
As if he had tasted it and spewed it out
again. But I! But I! To lie here knowing
that the child will never come again,
that they in there are alive and rejoice,
that this brood lives in its cave and eats
and drinks and sleeps and multiplies
while the child lingers down below
in the pit of horror and does not dare
come near his father. And I up here,
alone! Living a lonely and horrible life
unlike even the beast in the forest.

ORESTES

But then,
who are you?

ELECTRA

What do you care who I am?
Did I ask who you were?

[58]

Electra

ORESTES

I cannot help thinking:
You must be related by blood to those
who died, Agamemnon and Orestes.

ELECTRA

Related? I am this blood! I am the brutishly
spilled blood of King Agamemnon!
Electra is my name.

ORESTES

No!

ELECTRA

He denies it.
He scoffs at me and takes my name from me.
Since I have no father and no brother
I am the laughingstock of boys! Whoever
comes along the way kicks me with his foot,
they leave me not even my name!

ORESTES

Electra must be
ten years younger than you. Electra is tall,
her eye is sad but gentle whereas yours
is full of blood and hatred. Electra dwells
apart from men, and her day is spent
with tending a grave. Two or three women
she has about her who serve her silently.
And animals steal timidly around her dwelling
and nestle against her robe when she goes by.

[59]

Hugo von Hofmannsthal

ELECTRA

claps her hands

Good! Good! Tell me more fine things
about Electra. I'll repeat them to her

With a choking voice

when I see her.

ORESTES

Then I see her? I really
see her? You?

Quickly

So they let you starve or—
have they been beating you?

ELECTRA

Who are you
that you ask so many questions?

ORESTES

Tell me!
Tell me! Speak!

ELECTRA

Both! Both! Both! Queens
do not prosper when they are fed with the refuse
of the table's trimmings, priestesses
are not made for leaping under the whip
and in such brief rags instead of flowing
garments. Leave my dress alone, do not
burrow in it with your eyes.

[60]

Electra

ORESTES

Electra!
What have they done with your nights!
Your eyes are frightful.

ELECTRA *sullenly*

Go into the house,
I have a sister there who keeps herself
for joyous feasts!

ORESTES

Electra, hear me.

ELECTRA

I do not want to know who you are, you shall not
come any closer to me. I want to see no one!

Crouches down, her face towards the wall.

ORESTES

Listen, I have no time. Listen. I may not
speak loudly. Listen to me: Orestes lives.

Electra spins around

ORESTES

Make no sound. If you stir, you will
betray him.

ELECTRA

Then he is free? Where is he?
Do you know, where? Is he hiding? He lies
imprisoned! Crouching somewhere in a corner,

he is waiting for his death! I have to
see him die, they have sent you in order
to torture me, to pull my soul high up
with a rope and dash it down again
onto the ground!

ORESTES

He is uninjured
as I.

ELECTRA

Then save him! Before they put him
to death. Can you not give him a sign?
I kiss your feet that you may give him
a sign. By your father's dead body
I entreat you to run as quickly as you can
and bring him away! The child must die
if he spends the night in this house.

ORESTES

By my father's dead body! The child came
to this house in order that still
this night they die who must die—

ELECTRA *struck by his tone*

Who
are you?

*The dour Old Servant rushes in from the yard without a
sound, throws himself down before Orestes, kisses his feet,
rises quickly, looking around him fearfully, and rushes out
again without making a sound.*

Electra

ELECTRA

hardly controlling herself

Who are you? I am afraid.

ORESTES *gently*

The dogs in the yard recognize me,
and my sister does not?

ELECTRA

cries out

Orestes!

ORESTES *feverishly*

If anyone in the house has heard you, he has
now my life in his hand.

ELECTRA

very softly, tremulously

Orestes!
No one is stirring. O let me see
your eyes! No, you shall not touch me!
Move away, I feel ashamed before you.
I do not know how you can look at me.
I am no more than the corpse of your sister,
my poor child. I know I make you shudder
with dread. And yet I was a king's daughter!
I think I was beautiful: when I blew out
the lamp in front of my mirror, I felt
with chaste wonder how my naked body
gleamed immaculate through the sultry night
like something divine. I felt how the thin beam

[63]

of the moon bathed in its white nakedness
as in a pond, and my hair was such hair
as makes men tremble; this hair is wiry, soiled,
dishonoured now! Do you understand that, brother!
These sweet feelings of wonder and awe I have
had to sacrifice to my father. When I
rejoiced in my own body, do you think
his sighs did not reach, his groans did not press
up to my bed? Jealous are the dead:
and he sent me hatred, hollow-eyed hatred
for my bridegroom. And I had to let the monster,
who breathes like a viper, come over me
into my sleepless bed, who forced me to know
all that goes on between man and woman. Alas,
the nights, those nights in which I understood!
My body was cold as ice and yet was charred,
consumed with fire inwardly. And when
at last I knew it all, then I was wise,
and the murderers—I mean mother and him
who is with her—could not endure
a single glance of mine!
Why do you look about so fearfully? Speak!
Speak to me! Why, your whole body shivers!

ORESTES

Let this body shiver. Do you think it would
not shiver far worse if it could guess
on what errand I shall be taking it?

ELECTRA

You are going to do it? Alone? You poor child.
Did you bring no friends with you?

[64]

ORESTES

Let it pass,
do not speak of it. My old tutor is
with me. But I am the one who will do it.

ELECTRA

I have never seen the gods, yet I know
they will be there with you to help you.

ORESTES

I do not know what the gods are like. I only
know they have imposed this deed on me,
and they will condemn me if I shrink back.

ELECTRA

You will do it!

ORESTES

Yes, yes. If only I did not
have to look first in my mother's eyes.

ELECTRA

Then look at me, what she has made of me.

He looks at her sadly

O child! child! You come, stealthily
you have come, you speak of yourself
as of a dead man, and you are alive!

ORESTES *softly*

Be careful!

[65]

Hugo von Hofmannsthal

ELECTRA

Who am I then that you cast
such loving glances at me? Look, I am
nothing at all. All that I was I have
had to surrender. Even my shame which is
sweeter than all, which like the milky
silvery haze around the moon envelops
every woman and which turns infamy away
from her and her soul! I have sacrificed
my shame, as if I had fallen into the hands
of bandits who have torn from my body
even the last garment! I am not
without my wedding night as the virgins are,
I have felt the agony of childbirth
and have brought nothing into the world,
and always I have been a prophetess
and have called forth nothing from me
and my body except curses and despair.
At night I did not sleep, I made my bed
in the tower, and I cried out in the yard
and whined with the dogs. I made myself hated
and I saw everything, everything
I have had to see like the watchman on top
of the tower, and day turned into night,
and night turned into day again, and I found
no delight in the sun and in the stars,
for everything was as nothing to me
for his sake, everything was but a token
to me, and every day was but a landmark
on the way!

ORESTES

O my sister.

Electra

ELECTRA

What is it?

ORESTES

Sister, does not our mother
resemble you?

ELECTRA *savagely*

Resemble me? No.
I do not want you to look her in the face.
When she is dead, then let us look together
at her face. Brother, she threw a white shirt
over our father's head, and then she struck
at the thing which stood before her, which was
helpless, which had no eyes and could not turn
its face towards her, which could not set
its arms free—do you hear me?—at this
she struck from above with the axe raised high.

ORESTES

Electra!

ELECTRA

Her face is the face
of her deeds.

ORESTES

I will do it,
I will do it quickly.

ELECTRA

Blessed is he
who may do a deed! The deed is like

a bed on which the soul may rest,
like a bed of balsam, to rest the soul
which is a wound, a blight, an ulcer,
and a flame!

*Orestes' Tutor stands in the courtyard door, a vigorous old
man with flashing eyes.*

ELECTRA

Brother, who is this man?

THE TUTOR *hurrying towards them*

Are you out of your wits that you do not restrain
your tongue where one breath, one sound, a mere nothing
may destroy us and our work—

ELECTRA

Who is that?

ORESTES

Do you not know him? If you love me, thank him.
Thank him that I exist. This is Electra.

ELECTRA

You! You! Oh, now it all is real! It all
ties together! Let me kiss your hands!
I know nothing of the gods, I do not know
what they are like, therefore I had rather
kiss your hands.

THE TUTOR

Hush, Electra, hush!

Electra

ELECTRA

No, I want to shout with joy over you
because you have steered him to this place.
When I was full of hate, I kept my silence
amply. Hatred is nothing, it eats and eats
and consumes itself, and love is still less
than hatred, it reaches after everything
and cannot grasp anything, its hands
are like flames which grasp nothing, all thinking
is nothing, and what issues from the mouth
is a powerless breeze, only he is blessed
who is coming to do his deed! And blessed
who may touch him and who digs up the axe
for him out of the earth and who holds the torch
for him and who opens the door for him, blessed
is he who may listen at the door.

THE TUTOR

seizes her roughly and presses his hand over her mouth

Be silent!

To Orestes in great haste

She is waiting inside. Her maids are looking
for you. There is no man in the house. Orestes!

Orestes draws himself up, overcoming his horror.

*The door of the house lights up, and a servant appears
with a torch, behind her the Confidante. Electra has leaped
to the rear; she stands in the dark. The Confidante bows
down in the direction of the two strangers, beckons to them
to follow her inside. The servant fastens the torch to an
iron ring in the door-jamb. Orestes and the Tutor go in.
Orestes closes his eyes for a moment, feeling giddy; the*

Tutor is close behind him; they exchange a quick glance. The door closes behind them.

ELECTRA

alone, in terrible suspense. She runs to and fro in a single straight line in front of the door, with lowered head, like a captive animal in its cage. Suddenly she stands still and says

I could not give him the axe!
They have gone, and I could not
give him the axe. There are no gods
in heaven!

Again a terrible moment of waiting. Then from inside the piercing cry of Clytemnestra.

ELECTRA

cries out like a demon

Once more, strike!

From inside a second cry.

From the living quarters, on the left, come Chrysothemis and a swarm of servants.

Electra stands at the door, with her back pressed against the door.

CHRYSOTHEMIS

Something must have happened.

ONE OF THE SERVANTS

She cries out
like that in her sleep.

SECOND SERVANT

There must be men inside.
I heard men's footsteps.

THIRD SERVANT

All the doors
are bolted.

FOURTH SERVANT

They are murderers!
There are murderers in the house!

FIRST SERVANT

cries out

Oh!

ALL OF THEM

What is it?

FIRST SERVANT

Don't you see, there at the door
stands one!

CHRYSOTHEMIS

It is Electra! Why, that is Electra!

SECOND SERVANT

Then why does she not speak?

CHRYSOTHEMIS

Electra,
why do you not speak?

[71]

FIRST SERVANT

I will go out
and bring the menfolk.

Runs out, right.

CHRYSOTHEMIS

Why don't you open the door
for us, Electra!

SEVERAL

Electra, let us into the house!

FIRST SERVANT

coming back through the courtyard door, crying

Get back!

All are terrified

Aegisthus! Back to our quarters! Quick!
Aegisthus is coming through the yard! If he should
find us and something has happened in the house,
he will have us killed.

ALL OF THEM

Quick, back! Quick inside!

They disappear into the house, left.

AEGISTHUS

at the entrance on the right

Is no one here to light my way? Will not one
of these villains stir? Can this race never
be taught discipline!

*Electra takes the torch from its ring, runs down the steps
to meet him, bows before him. Aegisthus is frightened of*

Electra

this dishevelled figure in the flickering light; he retreats before her

Who is this sinister woman?
I have forbidden that an unknown face
come near me!

Recognizes her, angrily

What, is it you?
Who bids you come to meet me?

ELECTRA

May I

not light your way?

AEGISTHUS

Well now, this news
concerns you above all. Where can I find
the strangers who bring this message to us
about Orestes?

ELECTRA

Inside. They found
a kind hostess, and they amuse themselves
with her.

AEGISTHUS

And they truly report that he
is dead, and bring such reports that there can be
no doubt?

ELECTRA

O my lord, they report it not merely
with words, no, but with actual tokens
which cannot possibly be doubted.

[73]

Hugo von Hofmannsthal

AEGISTHUS

What is that in your voice? And what
has come over you that you fawn
on me so? Why do you stagger
back and forth with your light!

ELECTRA

                    It is only
that I learned good sense at last and stick
to those who are the stronger. Will you
permit me to go before and light your way?

AEGISTHUS

Up to the door. What are you dancing for?
Watch the way.

ELECTRA

as she circles around him in a kind of weird dance, sud-
                    denly bowing very low

          Here! the steps,
lest you fall.

AEGISTHUS *at the house door*

          Why is there no light here?
Who are they over there?

ELECTRA

                    They are the men
who want to wait upon you in person, my lord.
And I who often annoyed you with my bold
immodest presence, now I will learn
at last to withdraw at the right moment.

[74]

Electra

AEGISTHUS

goes into the house. A short silence. Then noise inside. Immediately Aegisthus appears at the small window on the right, rips away the curtain, cries

Help! Murder! Help your master! Murder! Murder!
They are murdering me!

He is dragged away

Does no one hear me?
Does no one hear?

Again his face appears at the window.

ELECTRA

stretches to her full height

Agamemnon hears you!

AEGISTHUS

is being pulled away

Woe is me!

Electra stands facing the house, breathing furiously.

The women come running out wildly, Chrysothemis among them. As if out of their senses they rush towards the court-yard door. There they suddenly stop, turn back.

CHRYSOTHEMIS

Electra! Sister! Come with us! Do come
with us! Our brother is inside the house!
It is Orestes who has done it!

A confused din of voices, a commotion outside

Come!
He is standing in the antehall, and all are

[75]

gathered round him, they kiss his feet,
all who hated Aegisthus in their hearts
have flung themselves against the others,
everywhere, in every courtyard, lie
the dead, all who live are spattered with blood
and have wounds themselves, and yet their faces
beam, they all embrace—

*Increasing noise outside, the women have run out, Chry-
sothemis is alone, light is falling in from the outside*

—and shout for joy,
a thousand torches have been lit. Don't you hear;
well, can't you hear?

ELECTRA

crouching on the doorsill

Do I not hear? Can I
not hear the music? Why, it is coming
from inside me. The multitude who carry torches
and whose steps, whose endless myriad footsteps
make the earth resound with hollow rumbling
everywhere, they all are waiting for me:
I know very well that they are waiting for me,
because I must lead the dance, and I cannot;
the ocean, the enormous twentyfold ocean
buries my every limb with his weight, I cannot
raise myself!

CHRYSOTHEMIS

almost shouting from excitement

Don't you hear, they carry him,
they carry him on their hands, their faces

are quite changed, their eyes are glistening
and their old cheeks, with tears! They are
all weeping, can you not hear it? Ah!

She runs out.

Electra has risen. She comes striding down from the door-
sill. She has thrown back her head like a maenad. She
flings her knees up high, she stretches her arms out wide,
it is a nameless dance in which she strides forward.

CHRYSOTHEMIS

reappears at the door, behind her torches, a crowd of peo-
ple, faces of men and women

Electra!

ELECTRA

stops, looks at her fixedly

Be silent and dance. All must
approach! Here join behind me! I bear the burden
of happiness, and I dance before you.
For him who is happy as we, it behooves him to do
only this: to be silent and dance!

She takes a few more steps of the tensest triumph and col-
lapses.

CHRYSOTHEMIS

rushes to her. Electra lies rigid. Chrysothemis runs to the
door of the house, pounds on it

Orestes! Orestes!

Silence

Curtain

[77]

THE SALZBURG GREAT THEATRE OF THE WORLD

Translated by

VERNON WATKINS

MASTER

ANGEL

SECOND ANGEL

WORLD

BUSYBODY

DEATH

ADVERSARY

UNBORN SOULS

KING

BEAUTY

WISDOM

RICH MAN

FARMER

BEGGAR

Music. Holy men and women, Prophets and Sibyls, enter-
ing, look expectantly in ascending degrees towards the
palace of the Master.

Angel enters, and behind him World. Behind her Death
and Busybody follow. Death is dressed in black, with cloak,
white hat, and sword; Busybody wears the many-coloured
garb of a lackey, with a fan in his belt and a lute slung
round him.

WORLD

Where are you leading me?

ANGEL

points out a place to her

Wait here. Your people behind you. You are called.

WORLD

Who are those there?

ANGEL

Also called. Observe how I greet them.

Steps towards them, bows

Greetings to you, holy prophets, soothsaying women;
of your words each one shines through the ages.
The Lord is with you.

WORLD

I know you well. My mountains bore you and let you
stretch your hands to heaven, my deep caves were the true

[83]

place where you might conjure up the shades of the dead; you might greet me, too, beforehand.

PROPHETS *together*

You, World, you great miracle of seven days, we greet you.

WORLD

to the Sibyls, who preserve their silence

Are you women so proud? With your A O U you have called up many spirits and picked up a good deal of fame. But he to whom fulness is given, he neither cries A nor U and his tongue is too heavy for speech, but if he wished he might easily say more than you have been able to say. What brings us together in this place?

PROPHETS

The Will which can accomplish all it wills. We are summoned, and wait.

Fanfares

WORLD

That sounds like a great Lord. Is the Master coming now?

Looks round about her.

ANGEL

Be silent and wait.

Adversary steps cautiously forward; he wears the black costume of a man of learning.

WORLD

Is the Insinuator here too? That makes a remarkable gathering!

The Salzburg Great Theatre of the World

ANGEL

Where you are he is given the right of entry, just as he who stands behind you has this right. Quiet now.

Fanfares repeated. Prophets and Sibyls turn in awe towards the palace.

WORLD

Where does he come from? Around me I can see nothing.

ANGEL

Look upward, and when you see, fall on your knees.

Fanfares for the third time. It grows dark and becomes suddenly light again. The Master stands there in the cloak of stars. Prophets and Sibyls fall on their knees, their hands stretched out behind them. World also falls on her knees, as does the Angel and behind him Death and Busybody. To the right, Adversary presses into the curtains.

MASTER

directs his gaze upon World, not with severity.

WORLD *on her knees*

Master, what command have you for me, your handmaid?

MASTER

A feast and a spectacle I would have prepared for me. For this I order you to put up the stage. Rise and set about it.

WORLD *upon her feet*

You are the Creator of all four elements, uplifter of all the mountains, restrainer of all the seas. What can I create that might afford you variety, surprise, or delight? Or can I?

[85]

Shall I? Shall I hurl mountain over sea, sea over mountain, shall I tear the eternal rivers from their beds and fling them down in cataracts to the firm land? Will you have all the elements glowing? I have been a tame woman so long; let me loose from my chain again and I will give such a spectacle it will strike terror in the moon!

MASTER

What you propose would be to me no more than seeing a two-year-old child playing with straws. A choice and quite different piece of work I mean to watch, a lively, mysterious, free production. For such a play fit me out the stage.

WORLD *looking round*

Of what mystery does the Master speak?

BUSYBODY

Alchemy! Alchemy! That is his subject. He will make gold out of base materials.

ADVERSARY

He never repeats himself. I have never heard him talk about creation in such a way.

Angel steps up to him, as if to silence him.

MASTER

signs to the Angel to leave Adversary alone; then to World, kindly

Of Man I am speaking, your guest.

WORLD

Men? Will you take pleasure in beetles? Like ants they run here and there, forwards and backwards, build cities, found kingdoms, destroy it all again, leave no stone upon another. There is more reason in a swarm of wasps than in them.

MASTER

In that in which you do not understand them lies their greatness: for know that in my image I created them. You, though, are there to bear the feet of men. That is the most glorious thing that will be said of you.

ADVERSARY

What strange thing does he want? What is all that leading up to? I must hold myself in readiness. My books of reference, my compendiums!

Puts on his glasses

Avicenna is missing, Lucretius is not there—slovenly packing on the part of young Grassdevil, my librarian.

WORLD

Ho, Lord! Man is my piece of work, even though not the most important. Whatever worth he has, I gave it him. If he were well advised and stayed in his own bounds and kept his erratic thoughts in check, if he wanted nothing except to enjoy my glories, and would sink, where the breath went out of him, back into me, then it would be well with him, the millipede, the cursed one, who insists on climbing perpendicular walls.

ANGEL

Curb your unanointed mouth, painted, insolent being! Heathen woman! Has the Lord not drowned you once already, and when you were at your last gasp allowed a new world order to rise above you? Take care!

Hugo von Hofmannsthal

ONE OF THE PROPHETS

You flaunt your powers, World, because you still stand fast on your feet. Already the day is coming when you, too, will go down on your knees, when he who stands behind you will leap on your back and become your rider, and under him you will drive down into darkness.

World groans, hides her face.

Busybody hides himself.

ADVERSARY

coming a step nearer, removes his barret

I see, a high court is to be held here, and in this affair it goes hard with a poor woman who has a slow tongue. I beg leave to submit that she is entitled to a lawyer. I would be prepared, although the action is unknown to me, if such a role were allowed me, to step forward as legal representative of this woman; of course I should have to have a talk with her first, so that she might let me into the secrets of her affair. I am a Doctor of Logic, but also in matters of justice I have considerable experience.—

MASTER

without paying any attention to him, kindly as before

Enough. The conduct and activity of men is worthy of a play for me. For this I have invited these guests of mine. Now build us the stage and let the play begin.

WORLD

But I know nothing yet about it!

The Salzburg Great Theatre of the World

ANGEL

to World, at a sign from the Master

Call up now a crowd of unborn souls and clothe them with flesh; then He will give each one of them a destiny.

ADVERSARY

One question, if the Lord will allow it: how can a play delight him who decides it beforehand, entrance and exit, even to the dotting of an i?

A step nearer

There stands he who has said: Our works you alone work in us. There he stands, one of your prophets. He is to testify to me! Will the Lord amuse himself with puppets who hang on wires in his own hands?

MASTER

Choice is given them between good and bad: that is the situation in which I have placed them as creatures. Are you pretending that you do not know that? It has been your grazing-ground from the beginning! Whisperer from the time of Eve's apple, whisper to whom you will. I have not stopped their ears. That it may have power of choice, I have endowed the creature with a spark of the highest freedom.

World whispers softly with Busybody, who appears to explain something to her.

Master mounts the upper stage, his retinue behind him, there remains standing.

Angel steps out of the palace carrying an armful of scrolls; he presents them to the Master.

Hugo von Hofmannsthal

BUSYBODY

Now for clothes! Clothes are what make people, that is
what the gracious Lord wanted to say!

WORLD

I can produce those in a moment. I always have such things
ready, rooms and warehouses full of them. He who plays
the king will get his crown from me, and the peasant his
spade. Religious cowls are there and court dresses, shep-
herds' crooks and swords, gold-plated armour and beggars'
rags, patched in ten places.

*Baskets are brought in by attendants while she speaks, con-
taining crowns and suits of armour, mitres and bishops'
croziers, ladies' dresses and coifs, masks and fans*

Am I to dress them up, as they stand there, indiscrimi-
nately?

MASTER

from the upper stage, a scroll in his hand

To each one I assign a destiny. He will find that written in
the part I shall hand to him. As befits the part, so you are
to dress him.

WORLD

on Busybody's prompting

Then several will have short parts, Lord, and they will not
want to leave the stage. It will be hard to persuade them to
withdraw, if I know men!

MASTER

Well thought of; that is why I am appointing him who
stands behind you—

BUSYBODY

Hi, Death, Lord Chamberlain, Your Lordship is being addressed!

MASTER

Him I appoint Stage Manager. Whom you call away will come to me and leave the stage for good, and not mount it again; you are to take care of that for me.

Death bows, genuflects.

BUSYBODY *softly, to World*

Nobody will want to play a bad part, even if it's a long one!

WORLD

takes a step forward to the Master, who turns away

Master!

MASTER

turns once more to World

What is troubling you? Has not everything been said?

WORLD

No, Lord. They are, nevertheless, my children—you will allow me the word—and so I know them well. Each one considers himself the centre of all things; to accept a bad part consciously is something I cannot compel them to do. Each will fling down a thankless part at my feet and call me a wicked stepmother, a slave-driver, and all kinds of names.

MASTER

Who bids them know in advance what is a bad part and what a good?

WORLD

Anyone who looks into it will know that well, if he can read what is written. To order and procure much, to live masterfully and well, to boast, to allow others to feel your power: that is a good part. To suffer knocks and blows, to swallow rebukes, to humble oneself, to hold one's tongue when others speak: that is a bad part—so men have thought from the time of Adam.

MASTER

Then they have thought foolishly, and therefore you are to be their mistress and show them.

WORLD

How, then, when I do not know better myself?

MASTER

It is a game: does not the Word open your eyes to the plain truth? Make them understand it!

THE FIRST ANGEL

steps forward and speaks to World from the upper stage

Are you so hard of understanding? Ordering and obeying, lifting oneself up and humbling oneself, feasting and doing without, all this is done by those who take part in the play: it is done symbolically, though, and not in reality, and good or bad cannot be applied to the part but to the play, when the actions have been concluded; and one or several shall be called to the Master's table, not for the sake of his part, whether he has had a beggar's stick or a king's sword and sceptre in his hands, but for what he has made of it. But a bungler is one whom his Master looks on with disfavour, and there is no reparation afterwards where someone has wasted his part on the stage. Make all that clear to them in time, in so far as they are dear to you.

Turns to follow the Master. The curtain on the palace door is raised from the side by Angels.

BUSYBODY

runs after him

We have been told neither the name of the piece nor the theme, not even in the sketchiest way as with an impromptu play.

Master ascends into the palace, his followers behind him. Second Angel with the scrolls follows him in. Fanfares.

FIRST ANGEL

steps forward again

The name of the play I announce to you: "Do Right: Under God!"

VOICES *from above*

"Do Right: Under God!"

ANGEL

Have you heard it?

BUSYBODY

Yes, indeed, twice over. But we are still no wiser about it than before. Of how the action proceeds you have told us no word, not even, if I may be allowed to say so, one hint by which a thoughtful man might be guided.

Hugo von Hofmannsthal

ANGEL

a book in his hand, which another has handed him

In what I hold here in my hands, the book which you all
know, the core and meaning of your play is contained in a
single saying. Here is written: You shall love your neighbour as yourself, but your God, Him you shall love above
all.—This shows what the play is to contain, and it is the
same as what the title itself comprises: "Do Right: Under
God!"

Silence

BUSYBODY

The way he has mixed the title and plot together, that is
not at all silly, that would have done quite well for a
prologue, but he should have waited until the players had
dressed, until the lights had gone up and everything was
quite ready; now we are not so well on yet; the players
are only now turning up very slowly. And the distribution
of parts, too, will not go off without trouble.

*The Unborn Souls move up, range themselves, singing, in
two semicircles on the lower stage. They wear fawn-
coloured, cowl-like garments, each one like the next. Their
faces, too, resemble each other like masks, without any
distinguishing feature of sex, age, or person. As soon as they
have taken up their positions on the lower stage, with their
faces turned towards the palace, their singing stops. World,
Death, and Busybody have withdrawn into the proscenium.
Adversary has similarly settled himself in the proscenium
upon a descending step, taken his books out of his travel-
ling-bag, and arranged them in front of him. The Second Angel emerges from the palace door, carrying a bundle
of parchment scrolls in his arm.*

[94]

SECOND ANGEL

advancing to the rim of the upper stage

You bodiless souls, my eye can distinguish you, for this the Master taught me. So I call you up: you are chosen to play before him. Step forward, you (*he points to one of the Souls*) and receive the part of the King.

One of the Souls steps forward and receives the part from the hand of the Angel, who bows towards him from above. He unrolls it and inspects it. Others step close and look curiously into the scroll, over his shoulder.

SECOND ANGEL

pointing to another of the Souls

You, play Wisdom!

WORLD

steps closer, beckons to the attendants

Crown and mantle for him! The sword with the golden hilt! Wisdom is represented by a nun. A habit forward! A girdle!

SECOND ANGEL

signalling to a third Soul

You are the Farmer!

WORLD

Forward! Rough shoes for the Farmer, a rough costume, a spade! Forward!

SECOND ANGEL *as above*

You are to play Beauty.

[95]

Some of the attendants have brought several pieces of tapestry or silk damask, made up as curtains only the height of two men, but sufficiently broad to shut off the front stage. Three of them have tall, pronged poles in their hands, with which they prop the curtains so that the lower stage is completely curtained, but between the strips of curtain there is access for exit or entrance.

Busybody at the same time gives them instructions, fussily shows them the places where they have to stand.

WORLD

steps out through the curtain, but peers again through the folds to see how the dressing up is proceeding. Calls out at intervals

It will soon begin!

Musicians are heard tuning their instruments; World listens to them. Meanwhile agitation is heard on the stage. Out of this one strong voice emerges, which several times vehemently cries: "No!"

BUSYBODY

slips forward through the curtain, stupidly excited

A hitch has cropped up in there, which at least with me has never cropped up before.

WORLD

Where?

BUSYBODY

points behind him

There on the stage, in the distribution of parts. There! Take a look at that!

The Salzburg Great Theatre of the World

A Soul, the Beggar, steps hurriedly forward through the curtains. He carries a part in his hand. Behind him comes one of the attendants carrying a tattered piece of patchwork, the costume of the Beggar.

SOUL

steps up to World

There, take my part back. Another can play that, not I! Not I! *Not I!*

The theatre attendant follows him, and remains standing behind him.

WORLD

What is all this? Why do you scream: *Not I!*

SOUL

I am not playing the part. I am not putting on this costume.

Takes it from the attendant and throws it at the feet of World.

BUSYBODY

That's something unheard of. Or has a mistake been made there, perhaps?

Takes the part out of his hand, examines it.

Part: the Beggar. In brackets: an unhappy man.

Examines the costume, touching it cautiously

Costume of the Beggar. Altogether appropriate. Very beggarly. Then everything is in order. What does the player want? What is he complaining about? They are difficult people!

[97]

Hugo von Hofmannsthal

SOUL *to World*

I tell you no! Rather stay unborn! Be dead and remain so!

Holds the part out to her.

WORLD

takes the part, looks into it, gazes round her

Why is the unborn one so angry? Does anyone understand him?

BUSYBODY

It is the arbitrary way in which the parts are distributed: he cannot put up with it.

SOUL

Here!

Tears the part out of World's hand.

BUSYBODY

I am not going to have you using violence against the mistress of the play.

WORLD

Let him be. He may speak.

SOUL

holds the part out to her

Look here! Look there! Do you call that a life, that a life's beginning, that a youth?

He turns the pages of the part

That a man's lifetime! There: pain and need, need and pain, pain and need! Ridicule and scorn! Loneliness, horrible, a hell! There I am groaning in utter desolation. There I am lodging under a bridge, making my meals of whatever the rats have left. There I cry in anguish of heart, and they shrug their shoulders; then I bare my teeth in desperation. There, abandoned as no dog is, I pull myself up once more and live, still live, speak almost nothing more. Then I sing songs! Have you any idea what kind of songs those can be which my toothless mouth is then to sing?

WORLD

Well? What else?

SOUL

grabs the costume and holds it beneath her eyes

That is to be my costume! A tattered remnant, the habiliment of dishonour, stinking! In this I am to live and die. And the least of your animals, Woman, wears a soft, silken coat or a scaled vesture of gold and silver!

Flings the costume down again and treads on it.

WORLD

Are you so cowardly, human Soul? Out of my sight! I hate the sight of a cowardly creature. The least of my animals stands up boldly in the battle into which I have thrust him. And you will not take upon you the bad part, even in play? Get dressed, or I must call men to help you. For we must proceed.

BUSYBODY

Cowards make us sick. Have you never heard speak of a thing called courage? That was already known to the Romans.

WORLD

Call servants here; dress this one in his player's costume. It is time for us to begin.

Theatre attendant makes a signal; two others step forward. They seize the Soul, look as if they would put the costume on him.

SOUL

frees himself

Do you allow me to be insulted by your servant as a coward who will not accept the hard role? Know this, then: this miserable role I shall not play. And nor shall anyone else!

He crumples the part up in his hand.

ADVERSARY

Spoken like a man! I claim for this Soul the right to the natural equality of fate!

WORLD

signals to the attendants

Enough time has been wasted. Get the man dressed and out on to the stage. When he stands there he will come to terms with the play.

ADVERSARY

Intercedo! I object! I protest against assault. There has always been this complaint, that a blind, tyrannous power has ruled over men already in the womb: of two twins, both unborn, both innocent, Jacob favoured from the first, Esau rejected! Is that still to go on and is the same raving despotism to continue in our enlightened time?

Angel steps forward between the curtains.

[100]

SOUL

has torn himself away from the hands of the attendants;
cries out

No!

ADVERSARY

I see, his Lordship sends a messenger. Probably to propose
a compromise. It's the young man's turn to speak. We are
eager.

ANGEL

I am not speaking to you.—Why do you hold us up, in-
tractable Soul? The others are dressed. The Stage Master
is waiting to give the sign. Why do you snort like a horse
which the smith has had to throw? Speak to me.

Soul, still on his knees, looks up to him.

The theatre attendants have stepped back; one retains the
Beggar's costume in his hand.

ANGEL

bends over the Soul with a smile

Do you know, then, whether you have drawn Esau's lot
and not Jacob's? Your soul has an inborn fire which burns
upwards, pointing more to Jacob than to Esau. His flame
burned dark and smoky.

SOUL

rises

And even if I were Jacob: Esau should not be treated as he
is. I will not endure it. The role is cursed.

Tries to tear it up, cannot.

[101]

ANGEL

Stop. Men's hands do not tear any parchment that comes from there.—Hand me the scroll. I shall give it you again as soon as you control yourself.

SOUL

Never. That anyone should be condemned to live like that, it's unthinkable!

ANGEL

Intrepid Soul! I know: you shudder, not because you are to suffer for a short hour in a play; you shudder to recognize the darkness in which the children of Adam live.

SOUL

There are some in the play in whose hands power is placed, there are lords and slaves, privileged and unprivileged ones. Who portions it out? Fortune? I will not stand under the rod of a blind whore. I will not!

ANGEL

Your mouth speaks wildly, but in yourself, like a miner's lamp quietly shining in the deepest pit, burns the willingness to accept.

SOUL

You hold a bait to me, and something in me does indeed thrill towards it to swallow it.

ANGEL

Do you acknowledge that? Candid Soul!

SOUL

But I know when I have swallowed the crooked hook, then you will pull me away against the stream, and I will not!

Give me a part in which there is freedom, as much as one needs in order not to suffocate, or else leave me out of the play.

ANGEL

But whoever has freedom and is worthy of it asks: For what do I have freedom? and does not rest until he knows what fruit it will bring. Yet the fruit of freedom is one: to do right.

SOUL

Do not deceive me!—No. You do not deceive me. Have pity, then!

ANGEL

The act alone is creation above creation. To bear its perfume immediately to God is our service. Do you grasp, heroic Soul, your tremendous privilege? Will you, then, play the part of the Beggar?

He holds up the part.

SOUL

You say "act"? My soul thirsts for action. In this miserable part where would there be room for a single act?

ANGEL

Play the part, and its meaning will be revealed to you.

SOUL

I cannot. Leave me out. There are some this time without a part. I'll hide among those.

ANGEL

But you have got one. So you are chosen.

[103]

Hugo von Hofmannsthal

SOUL

struggles with himself

I have seen words in the part that should not properly come from any creature's mouth.

ANGEL

Have you read these words: My God, my God, why hast Thou forsaken me? And also these: Yet not mine, but Thy will be done?

Soul covers his face.

ANGEL

Take it upon you! Bend! How should the unutterable speak to you except through this shudder?

SOUL *kneeling*

Must I?

ANGEL

Bend into the clothes that are allotted to you.

SOUL

reaches for the part

I will. Dress me!

Beckons the attendant over to him, steps through the curtain; attendant follows him with the costume.

Angel steps through the curtain at another point.

World goes to the curtain, looks through a chink.

[104]

BUSYBODY

blows his nose

Until now I thought the whole thing would be a jolly piece of comedy, but it seems to me that if it goes on like this I shall be wearing out my handkerchief, as you might say. That is unexpected.

WORLD

at the curtain, turns towards the audience

A fine, powerful thing my play is going to be. They are dressed up for it out of my boxes. Their eyes sparkle with reserves of power, and they can hardly wait to begin the play of life. Let the music now start up! Blow, and tread the organ, and sing, so that all who look on from above may discern what I can do on my stage.

The symphony begins. World stands before the curtain and sings into it. The men who hold the curtain move apart from one another. Busybody leaps to the left, opens a folding chair, sets up, on a raised place, a throne for World. The lower stage becomes visible. It is empty, but on the left a rock stands, on the right a tree. Angels stand on the upper stage. World seats herself on her place in the proscenium. Death, on a sign from her, crosses diagonally and places himself on the right between the curtains. Adversary squats low down in the proscenium on the right. The symphony ends.

ANGEL

advances to the rim of the upper stage in the centre

People the play of life has called awake,
pay careful heed to every step you take.

You from the cradle's quietness
travel to your coffin's peace.
The Master from the lofty throne
looks down and weighs you punishment and boon.

BUSYBODY

Now we've had enough announcing and proclaiming; surely
they might now begin.

Fanfares, less powerful than at the arrival of the Master.

KING

enters from the left and strides to the middle of the stage

My steps drawn to this place, I enter;
here I remain: the Lord stands in the centre.
Look where I will, all things submit to me;
to rule is life, all else a fantasy.
The counties, hard to number, and their borders
receive magnificence and wealth from orders.
The mountains gaze, the rivers flash, and see
me sit in my inherited majesty.
Let heart in heart to me be consecrate,
and with the glory of a righteous state,
with intellect, with wisdom and with strength,
blest be my days and works. May I at length,
ruling as lion and eagle of the land,
keep the high high, low lowly, in my hand.

BUSYBODY

A fine speech! But fine speaking and good acting are two
very different things.

*Beauty enters from the left, Wisdom from the right. They
go very slowly towards each other.*

That one is very beautiful. She must be a lady of the court.
—And the other a nun! My goodness, so young!

KING

Two marvellous women, fine to see.
They must at once entrust themselves to me.
How blest to have it in my power
to draw such to me in their splendid flower!

BEAUTY

remains standing

O glorious world, unfolded pageantry,
how all things sparkle, glance, and laugh to me!
Alluring distance, magic neighbourhood
in which I stand as one enchanted would.
Round me this feast of gardens holds its breath,
and in the background a fine man goes forth;
though he were king and laws to all men gave,
if he steps near he soon becomes my slave.

BUSYBODY

Ah, she is too beautiful! Now she is looking at herself in
the glass. She's right!

BEAUTY

lowers the glass

Something like fear breathes on me from the glass;
should one then carry openly God's seal?

WISDOM

How could the joy of Earth look in the glass
and not a sigh of death across it steal?

Hugo von Hofmannsthal

BEAUTY

looks at her hand

But you, my hand, you wonderful creation,
you ivory hand, you flower, you magic sign,
what secret plot is yours, so flexibly
turning the key to make what earth-realms mine?

WISDOM

hides her hand

You, my own hand, open the quiet cell,
then quickly cross, my foot, the threshold peace loves well!

BEAUTY

Look up! The whole world's laughing to us both;
for us adorned, the silken tent of youth!
Dear one, look up!

WISDOM

Dear, let me go apace.
We two can never shelter in one place.

BEAUTY

No, stay with me, I fear to be alone.

WISDOM

There will be someone at your side quite soon!

BEAUTY

Stay, I implore! If I'm alone, no man must come my way.

WISDOM

I am drawn to be alone: in solitude to pray!

She takes one step to the left.

[108]

BUSYBODY

I find her dull. All the time praying! Praying! Such a young person!

BEAUTY

Men's eyes may look at me, for each eye laughs delight!

WISDOM

Me only one shall see, who sees even through the night.

King advances to Beauty.

BEAUTY

out of the corner of her eye

Power and exalted pride, how they adorn a man!

WISDOM

A man like other men: a weak head, with a crown!

Both bend their heads.

KING

Come to me, nameless one, you glorious being!
Where you approach, a royal palace there appears.
The works of Helen were not once for seeing;
they cast the burden of a thousand years,
are now again, today, are always here!
What once was beautiful again is near.
Here at my side with me you are to stay.
Do you think who has seen you ever goes away?
I ask not. To a king no worth has No,
nor is there need of Yes. It must be so.
That way! With me!

Hugo von Hofmannsthal

He leads her a few steps to the place on his left, then re-
turns, goes to Wisdom

　　　　　　But you, so wise, serene and mild,
take here upon my right your seat, you noble child.
And if we turn to pious thoughts, then throw
your light upon us with a lamp's soft glow.

WISDOM

Too near the whirlpool, in the midst of this world here.
I have made eternity my place, away from her.
Do you see the rock, the lovely solitude?
That way!

KING

　　　　To leave my city and my court for good?
Not gladly. But who comes? My powerful merchantman—

Rich Man has entered; he strides respectfully up to the
King.

BUSYBODY

That's the Rich Man! One can see that plainly. The fur
coat and the chains. Heavens! Ah, the Farmer is there, too.
Now only the Beggar is missing; then the whole quartet
would be together.

Farmer has entered immediately after the Rich Man from
the opposite side. He carries a scythe, besides an axe and a
spade. He goes at once to the tree, rests the axe and spade
against it, and sets about hammering, whetting his scythe.

KING

And there the peasantry, our honest subject, stands.

[110]

FARMER

Not too much gaping, that's a thing I shirk.
Give me a bit o' peace to get on with my work.

Withdraws behind the tree.

WISDOM

Wisdom may not be his, yet it is in his labour.

KING *to the Rich Man*

My greatly gifted man!

RICH MAN

   Would your Grace grant the favour
kindly to see how much I have improved the land?

KING

You are most honoured here. Beside me you must stand.
You have done much already.

RICH MAN

     Much more is being prepared
if you protect me more with this exalted sword.
The ruler's strong fame is assigned to you;
the realm's increaser, deep peace is your due.
Your lofty mind has bowed to the new age
and its great issues, with your patronage.
You have shown yourself a prince preferred
to others, adept, trusted with the watchword.
And in the initiate's robes you stand arrayed.
This new time's god is called commercial trade.
Rebuild your realm a temple for his sake,
tunnel the mountain, dam the mountain lake,

and let canals join stream and stream,
valley to valley, plain to sea;
for every hour more quickly goods are rolled
creates new wealth, is unmixed gold
raising in power your throne's felicity.
The neighbours, by such lofty strength subdued,
in their own tongues agree,
if not, then let that be which has to be,
for their enlightenment let yours obtrude!

FARMER

When a boom in things of the state is born
by a couple of ducats up goes corn.
Till now it's not been too bad.

WISDOM

O curse upon the world, O greed, vain seeking!

KING

I must esteem the mind that burns in you
related to my own mind as it is,
for it acknowledges no boundaries.
So am I, too: the word "enough" I do not know.

RICH MAN

Enough? That is an abject word and base,
used by the slothful to describe their sloth.
We have grown wings, ten wings within us both.
Cursed is the man who squats in his low place
with sloth and cowardice and the other wrongs.

FARMER

If a man didn't sit where he belongs
then you'd soon see what would . . .

KING

> Tried by me, proved worthy,
Treasurer already, be my Minister
And Chancellor, also: he must know new ways
who is to hold all forces taut, and tame
all to the greatness of a single aim.

Rich Man kisses his hand, kneeling; stands up again, remains silent, as if ashamed.

ADVERSARY

prompts him in a whisper

If that must be, then must your sword for me—

RICH MAN

If that must be, then must your sword for me—

ADVERSARY

Out of its sheath—

RICH MAN

picks it up

Out of its sheath flash forth—

KING

What's that you say? For you?

ADVERSARY *quickly*

For what we are worth!
For our own power and glory!

RICH MAN *strongly*

For our own power and glory!

[113]

Hugo von Hofmannsthal

KING

God protect them!

He draws his sword.

WISDOM

Think back: keep high the high, the lowly low!
Do you act on what you said?

BEAUTY

looks at herself in the glass

How splendidly lit up, in power's reflection
kindling, I see myself!

Farmer whets his scythe.

King thrusts his sword back in the sheath.

ANGEL

Mark well the play
in which you stand, and how its name first sounded.
The Lord is over you! Do not forget the action.

World plucks a few notes on the lute she holds in her lap.

KING

*beckons the Rich Man to take his place on his right, and
himself takes up his place in the centre.*

With an enlightened and a careful mind
I have rounded out my kingdom like a ring
and watch contentedly its blossoming.
Power upon the sword is founded;
within the golden palace beauty dwells;
prayer rises up from consecrated walls;

[114]

rightly the peasantry for us bears all the load,
stands firm on its true, bounded common sense
and will continue so.

FARMER

leaves off whetting his scythe

Aye, aye, I stand on my two feet quite fast!

WISDOM

Have pity, Lord, stay near till this be past!

BUSYBODY

They are all very contented! I like good-natured people. But
now I should like to know what has become of him who is
going to play the Beggar. If he came into such a happy company now he could hardly be vexatious.

Beggar comes slowly, with dragging step, from the right.

BUSYBODY

sees him while he is still far off

Ah, there he is, the Beggar! But they have got him up in a
most disreputable way!

*Beggar goes with bowed head, propped on a stick; he talks
to himself, appears to see nothing. He wanders round the
stage like a lost soul.*

BUSYBODY

What a ghastly hobble the man has! His feet must be stiff
with cold.

Wisdom leaves her place and advances to the Beggar.

Beggar mutters to himself.

Hugo von Hofmannsthal

WISDOM *at his back*

What is the trouble on your mind, strange man?
Come!

BEGGAR

stops with a jerk

There are people there: I must be gone.

WISDOM

steps in front of him

Come here. I'll put you up and see you fed.
Too long, I think, you have lain without a bed.

BEGGAR

without looking at her

Without a bed? Come the ninth year that way.

WISDOM

From where?

BEGGAR

I canna tell where I was yesterday,
and where today will take me I don't know.

WISDOM

You have endured necessity and woe.
Take that; look after yourself.

Hands him money out of a bag.

Beggar turns away.

[116]

The Salzburg Great Theatre of the World

WISDOM

Answer me!

BEGGAR

I shall not answer.

WISDOM

Take my gift away;
I am the goods' distributor, no more,
for it belongs to you and all the poor.

BEGGAR

I want to hear no bibble-babble,
need no compassion and no gabble;
I will be off!

He starts to go, but falls to brooding again.

WISDOM

Man carries in himself two kinds of pride:
too much good luck brings one and too much grief the other;
and He who reigns above condemns them both.

BEGGAR

without looking at her

I don't like your sermon. I want nothing from the world.

WISDOM

I stand not for the world, I stand for Him
who never stops yearning for you with love,
so that with tenfold iron about your heart
still from that heart you cannot fend Him off.

[117]

Hugo von Hofmannsthal

BEGGAR

looks at her seriously

Talk—woman's talk—I had a woman once;
there came no useless word out of her mouth—

He breaks off.

WISDOM

Is she then gone?

BEGGAR

Ask nothing. I'll not answer.

BUSYBODY

What did she die of? It can't have been so bad.

BEGGAR

Of chance she died. I was not home, it chanced,
and this stick, too, not there—

FARMER

looks up

His rambling makes no sense!

BEGGAR

There came a couple of foreign dogs that way across the
    border
that in a moment seized her life and ended it with murder.
The hut we lived in was burnt down, my wife, too, and the
    cow.
The smoke looked strangely peaceful as the blaze died down.
The children hid themselves in the wood

and the goats in a thicket forced their way,
so they were left alive that day.

FARMER

Ah, out there on the border! Life there's not fit for swine,
the folk a beggarly lot and a quite rotten wine.
I would not live there, not for all the world;
at the country's heart I have my seat.

He whets his scythe.

BEGGAR *staring, half aloud*

Why? Why?

WISDOM

Call on your inner light to help you.

BEGGAR

That light's gone out. Not yet that day
when they took my wife from me and killed her;
no, later, when I had to dig one grave for all my children.

BUSYBODY

They can't have all died at once!

BEGGAR

No, no. They did not all four die at once
of the shame-swallowing pestilence of hunger.
On Wednesday only two, on Thursday one,
on Sunday then the last: it was a quiet funeral,
relatives, bearers, and grave-diggers all
met in the selfsame person there. And you?

[119]

Did you that day pray earnestly? yes, you?
Sing sweetly and breathe smoking incense, too,
following tradition and its holy custom,
and round about you massive walls
and iron trellis-work before each vault,
only to keep it safe, only quite safe!
And others—others are fair game
and can sweat blood and wring their hands
and yet compel no sympathy!
Why?

WISDOM

    Since it had to be. To your defiant Why
the sapphire court of justice offers no reply.

She points upward.

BEGGAR

No: it had not to be! No! Do not lie.

He stamps his stick on the floor

To others nothing happened. He who was rich missed that.
He who could buy a horse
might race before the plague, escape its net.
Why? In what tablet is that law inscribed:
my flesh and blood was destined to the dung,
while others saw theirs leap and stay alive!
Where is that written, where? Where, that my brood
has been found worthy of untimely death,
for which the brood of others was too good?
Now then, open your mouth! Bring justice here
to judge this matter between me and you.
I cry here for my right!

WISDOM

Your cry is what the creature suffers,
but whom in an earthly court will you arraign?
Who from among ourselves has done you wrong?

King takes a step.

WISDOM

Here he comes forward whose hand bears the sceptre,
lay the legitimate grievance now before him,
but take care not to let a dark delusion
drive you beyond all bounds.

She goes towards her place.

KING

What does he want, this man? Why is he with us?

BEGGAR

Why? Not for your own good.

WISDOM *from her place*

Be moderate, man;
keep within bounds: anger is deadly sin.

KING

Which of mine do you accuse of what injustice?
With what do you charge whom? Answer! We have—

BEGGAR

You have, and I have not—that is the answer,
that is the strife and that what it's about.
You have the wife and have the child,
you have the house, the court and royal household, too,

[121]

you have the cows and have the field,
you have the clothes and besides these the shoe,
and have a warm, dark, easy blood in the flesh,
and have the time, yes, and the pastime, too,
you have the day and have as second day the night
with torches, candles, pomp, and glittering light.
You have the wine and lutes to play for you,
you have the substance and the shadow, too,
and have the whole Earth at your feet,
and the book, too, so rich in idle hours to read,
in which your world's flattered and parodied,
making what you enjoy the enjoyment's dream repeat.
All this you have, and whence? because you stole it,
building upon your brother's shameful ruin your throne.
Jacob, you sit in your inherited pillage,
and Esau comes, to fetch what is his own!

ADVERSARY

prompts, as he sees the Beggar pause

Nature gives you and me an equal right;
Nature knows no rich thief and no poor vagabond!

BEGGAR

without turning round

Shut up! I found my answer for myself:
I need no advocate.

ADVERSARY

That suits me fine.

BUSYBODY

Devil take him, how the ugly fellow bridles!

[122]

BEAUTY

*goes to the King, who has involuntarily raised his sword in
the sheath from the belt towards his breast*

My lord, it seems to me a wasted hour
to hear a blind harangue with horrid power
break loose like this from a distorted mouth.

ADVERSARY

draws himself up

Samson was blind and tore the house to pieces
in which the Philistine lay banqueting.

WISDOM

Strange man, have you no secret reckoning
other than this that your wild grief releases?

BEAUTY

See how with bestial gaze he fixes me.
Deliver me from that evil eye!

KING

lifts his cloak and hides her

My Chancellor!

RICH MAN

bends a knee

Lord, what is your gracious wish?

KING

It ill befits us in exalted company
to endure such brazen rage:

[123]

we expect homage when we mount the stage,
respectful recognition, tender, meek.
Signify to him, ours is not the office
from which we can degrade ourselves to brawl;
you, in our place, must answer him for all.
Should the day come when rank and order weakened,
then, as with flesh in which the heart has sickened,
so it would happen to the common lot
whose preservation we acquire from God.
Show that to him, rebuke him for his grievance;
you would not be the man we know you are
were eloquence and intellect not yours,
needed to turn the stubborn from his course.

RICH MAN

Yours to command.

KING

*King takes Beauty by the hand to lead her back. Beauty,
about to leave, turns her face full upon the Beggar.*

BEGGAR

now for the first time perceives Beauty in her entire power

       She! Is she also with you?
Is also this there, gift among all gifts,
one beam from which flies through the poorest heart,
turns night to day, what's base to glory lifts?
Is this included, too, in your estate?

WISDOM

You are blest if in the image you can know
above the shrine the refulgence of the Highest:
so I still hope.

BEGGAR

No, no, and three times No!
That is too much, that this life's very crown
in your thief's lodging-house should settle down.
What, does she cling to you? Enough embraces!
I'll break into your precincts, bring a new age on!

Throws the stick away

Down, Philistine! Here are Samson's naked hands!

King has led Beauty to her place, then stands in his own.

RICH MAN

goes up to the Beggar, measures him first with his eye

Pick up that stick, you will have need of it
unless you have had enough of barren wandering
and of this cudgel, snatched up in the wood,
and change it for a tool, some useful thing.

One step nearer

That I advise. You are, I think, a man;
my commerce is with men: I'm used to it.
There's this about an honest man: one can
often convince him straightway with an honest word.

BEGGAR

The gall is ours, the honey is your share.
Are you trying to smear my lips with honey's ooze?
What are you trying otherwise? Take care:
I've nothing now to lose.

RICH MAN

But much, I think, to gain,
just as we all, we working folk,

[125]

all of us here, and you, we are under the same yoke.
Perhaps, in the light of this, you'll think again.

BEGGAR *morose, sullen*

The world that exists must go, the world must now grow
    new,
and if it first must plunge beneath a sea of flames
and bloody deluge that it may be freed,
then it is blood and fire that we need.

RICH MAN

Order is what you need.

BEGGAR

          With that accursed word
don't come to me, for so you name the power
that grinds us into the ground.

RICH MAN

               Why does your speech not spurt
out of your eye that rolls to feel rage tower,
why not out of your fist so wildly swung?
Why do you trust it to the ungainly tongue?

BEGGAR

What?

RICH MAN

     Because that order is in your own flesh.
If you will let your wild lament bay there,
placing us all before the judge,
it is that order's stamp your tongue will bear.

The Salzburg Great Theatre of the World

Faces all red with rage, and stamping feet,
they are not themselves enough. And if your tongue is not
to stammer your protest even while producing it
and stifling the offspring make it a still birth,
then your mind's eye is bound to make an image
in a quite secret place for its own need,
a miraculous, pregnant sign, and so instruct the tongue
to shoot against us the sharp-outlined word.
Again: to create afresh the miracle of order,
the inner mind must first snatch the conception
out of a spirit-world which, like the sea of stars,
arches above, flashes, and shoots rays down;
for, if it strains not up to grasp such lights,
your speech falls lame; mere concepts make its measure.
What here you are snarling about lord and slave,
inheritance, disinheritance, right and wrong,
this did not thrive in your brain by itself;
you have drawn on order's thousand-year-old treasure.
So do I see you, Samson of our world,
our house's shaker at the pillar's station
conjuring up hell's fearful desolation,
you who against all order have rebelled:
with all your frenzy, your defiance of right,
you are still primeval order's parasite.
Tear order down, that holy dike of time,
tear that, and you dissolve the world in slime.

ADVERSARY

From slime, I understood, the world first came;
let it from slime rise up again,
even though in birth-pangs thirty-three years long,
but never more we'll let the windy flights
of your glib talkers cheat us of our rights.

Hugo von Hofmannsthal

RICH MAN

advancing half a step more

Tear down, destroy, uproot everything round about,
plunge your knife in our belly,
but know this, too: You have done not only evilly
and vilely, but in folly.
This sum entire, this worthy, ancient flesh,
incomprehensible, would you presume to gauge
on one look's daring in a single flash,
with your brief sense that hardly spans the stage?
Is it, then, as you think, a sum of mere possessions,
a treasure thieves have hoarded,
placed in strong walls and guarded
by ancient dragons of eternal wrong?
And can you not be awakened to a look
where it would strike you as a sum of forces
playing each through each, their fiery joy renewed
always towards aims inscrutably ordained,
and needing only your own force in the effort
for the fulfilment of its utmost end?
Does nothing bid you join this as a friend?

ADVERSARY

O you tangle of slyly twisted lies!

To the Beggar, suggestively

Now go for him, now cast it in his face!
We? Join? We go in the treadmill night and day
and see no fruit of our own misery
and see no end. Toil turns to drudgery,
days of dishonour, execrable pay:
drive all this home to him.

[128]

RICH MAN

I am waiting for it.

KING

You are being spoken to; you are permitted,
unfearing, to reply. Make yourself heard!

WISDOM

Answer. Share out that inner load. In the word
that flies out of your mouth God's breath is hidden.

BEGGAR

I will say nothing. This might well suit you,
that I should answer pat upon the cue.
Your cue means nothing to me. Be prepared:
in what begins now, speeches will be spared.

BUSYBODY *half audibly*

Heaven help us!

RICH MAN

If you're too dull, and that gives me distress,
to grasp the wonderful loom which can create us
out of earth-stuff a changing spirit-dress,
nothing indeed is left you but to hate us.
Then from our workrooms only go away;
we have no bed for you, unless you lie our way.

BEGGAR

Whether I go or do not go you'll see.

RICH MAN

Bring something forth, there must be some beginning;
out of the web some thread must be set spinning:
from nothing nothing comes!

Hugo von Hofmannsthal

Beggar is silent.

KING

turns away

An odious, wicked silence!
We turn from him—

Beggar laughs.

WISDOM

lifts her hands to God

Ward off the frightful deed
which in itself this silence holds compressed!

ADVERSARY

Like thunder now a Word! a manifesto!
A single, monstrous creed,
to blast us into the ground!

Beggar is silent.

ADVERSARY

Your pauses send a chill even down *my* spine!

Beggar takes a few paces sideways, as though about to go.

ADVERSARY

Now—now—the tension not yet high enough
to be delivered in a lightning stroke!
Not yet enough cloud gathered round your breast!
What? stay of execution? but no revoke!
For you the way out's utterly cut off.

*Beggar has come by slow steps to where the Farmer stands,
who is occupying himself with his scythe and behaves as if
he did not notice him.*

[130]

Rich Man takes one step after him.

Beggar turns to go.

Rich Man, with an expression of self-control, turns, too, to go back to his place. All look with suppressed anxiety at the Beggar, to see whether he will go or not.

Beggar goes very slowly, as if lost in heavy brooding.

BUSYBODY *half audibly*

Now then, is he going at last—or isn't he going? It was high time!

Beggar goes a few more steps, then stops, now at the side of the stage, in front of the Farmer.

FARMER

has before this hung his scythe on the tree and pulled out of his pocket a piece of bread and bacon and had his lunch, without apparently noticing the others. Now, as the Rich Man looks towards him, he hastily shoves the last fragment of bread and bacon into his mouth and again takes his scythe, lays it across his knee, and whets it. Nothing about him could betray whether he has heard the last speeches or not

My scythe's gone crooked, the edge is torn,
I must have hacked it into a thorn.
What's the man want with me?

Loudly

Why do you stand there, who are you?

BEGGAR

Who might *you* be, so I know whom to greet?

[131]

Hugo von Hofmannsthal

FARMER

gives the scythe a few more strokes

Me? Hm. A farmer. Don't yer know what that is?

He stands up and straightens himself before the Beggar

It's nothing but a bread-loaf on two feet.

After a pause

Why d'yer look round?

BEGGAR

The farm back there is yours?

FARMER

It's mine.

BEGGAR

The meadows there?

FARMER

Are mine.

BEGGAR

The strip of field?

FARMER

It's mine.

BEGGAR

And there

the other?

[132]

FARMER

Mine.

BEGGAR

That garden?

FARMER

Will you have done
with asking?

BEGGAR

But it costs you only a word.

FARMER

Ten words more to give you I choose.
The shirt on my back is spun o' my flax,
out of my leather are the shoes,
house and home, shed, walls, and fences stand
out of my wood, put up with my own hand.
So I live in the field between coppice and brook
on my own created handiwork.

WISDOM

Call you created what another to you leased,
do you forget through whom your handiwork increased?

BEGGAR

drinks in the air with raised head, to himself

O breath of meadow-grass beyond the brook!

FARMER

to himself, restlessly

I think he smells the chimney's sausage-smoke.

[133]

Hugo von Hofmannsthal

BEGGAR *after a pause*

There stay, and there be quiet and settled once again!
Would you have work for me?

FARMER

looks at him critically

Dunno, in the end you'll find hard work too big a strain—

BEGGAR

I'm not a stranger. From up there, two hours away,
I come, from beyond the wood.

FARMER

        Aha! Aye, I dare say.

BEGGAR

My father was a forester, and a keeper then;
he was struck dead by a tree, he was a weak, poor man.

FARMER

And well he might be that. They're penniless folk up there,
nor are they strong. A poor field you can quickly reap,
a thin goat quickly milk. They've never done a stroke;
no money in the bag, in the arm no sap, no sinew thrives;
so they roam out and then sleep home again, flat broke,
no rhyme or reason in their lives.

BEGGAR *darkly*

Farmer, would you have any work I asked you—in the
stable? in the field?

FARMER

brings out from behind the tree a long-handled axe, weighs it in his hand

I've eight kids of my own and I do the work myself.
If things hadn't been like that, there would have been no yield,
for then the master's strength were weaker than the field.

Beggar decides to go.

FARMER

the axe in his hand

A woodman I might need.

BEGGAR

remains standing

Is the wood also yours?

FARMER

The farm has been in timber now six hundred years.
Felling-right's mine, and grinding-right by the brook,
pasturing-right in the valley and the right to fish in the stream.

BEGGAR

You're stuck with rights just like a hedgehog, beyond doubt.
Whoever tried to take one from you—

FARMER

weighs the axe on his knees

He'd have his work cut out!

[135]

Hugo von Hofmannsthal

World strikes a chord on her lute.

Beggar again takes a step as though he wished to go.

FARMER

So you don't want to.

Makes as if to put the axe behind the tree

      With my wood I'm building a new shed,
want planks and timber. Just the right season now to go
 ahead.
There's nothing lacking in the wood, what's lacking is the
 man.

BEGGAR

Felling-right. No strung firewood, door and roof,
nothing to buy, all out of your own stuff,
nothing to buy, not cradles, not the marriage-bed,
no, nor the coffin——

FARMER

     Wood-buying? That's a lousy game!
Will you or not? I have no time.

Offers the axe to him

I give three talers' wage a year, a pair of shoes,
and wool for a coat thrown in on top of that.
The hut stands in the wood, dead leaves are free;
you'll find a pan inside, near it a pot of fat.

BEGGAR

holds the axe irresolutely in his hand

Get wood for the bed, and in the bed there will be others
 lying,

[136]

and in the wooden cradles another's children crying;
but the wood is beautiful, and there alone to be
is better than to stand there and squabble angrily.
Now, Farmer: if I stick it to the end
and chore for you in the wood with my two hands,
and keep your wood in order like a room,
will you give me, too, for a coffin half a dozen boards
out of your wood?

FARMER

You'll get them. Trust me.

BEGGAR

I accept.

I am drawn into the wood as by a cord.

FARMER

So you've got to go into the wood, it is your fate.
But stay. I've something else you must get straight
if you're to keep me order in the wood.
The scrub's a regular plague,
thrives in the forest soil, preys on it everywhere,
vile parasite it is, you must clear it out!
Understood? But wait! You must get this right and proper:
what are you, eh? A forest copper!
The very thing the dog is, here on the farm,
you are in the wood, the shadowy trees' alarm.
D'you understand?

Beggar wants to go away.

FARMER

Now wait. You surely can't be quite so pressed?
Wood-gathering's lately grown quite popular
and it's gone a bit too far.

[137]

There you must take a hand, they're mostly widows,
and children, too; don't shout there in the shadows;
no one gets anywhere by screaming at this rabble,
and no reporting, please, that only makes a fuss.
Just beat 'em up, chase 'em out, make 'em respect my wood
and hang round somewhere else, up to no good.—
D'you get me?

BEGGAR *to himself*

Now something's coming to me, yes, quite near.

FARMER

Ah, you're already making a scowling face
fit for the devil at the court of hell!
Are you so eager now to earn your place?
We'll stay together, then, and things will work out well.
If one nail always drives the other on,
something will come of it. Now look to your employment,
just look, and let your service give you real enjoyment—
What's up?

Leaps up.

BEGGAR

leaps to the centre, threatening them all

Yes, I must clean things up, that's understood,
as I'm entrusted to, but not just in the wood!

Swings the axe at them all

You thieves and swindlers all together leagued,
now mind your hides!

[138]

FARMER

leaps towards him

Hi, scoundrel, give me the axe out of your hand;
the law of the wild doesn't hold here in this land.

BEGGAR

What do you want, what's all the cry about?

FARMER

Give me that axe, you vagabond, and get out!
Jailbird!

BEGGAR

What? Who?

FARMER

What? Who?
I am the farmer, and you stand on my demesne.
Beat it, or I'll use house-right!

BEGGAR *sinisterly*

What, not another right?

FARMER

And lord's right, too, if you rebel, you menial rogue!

BEGGAR

lifting the axe powerfully

You thief, your rights are stolen, and now this moment
I call each home to me like a stray dog.

[139]

He whistles

Here now the first right comes. Felling-right now is mine.
D'you see now? Rights are lackeys to trust no longer
who always lend their service to the stronger.

ADVERSARY

On! what you want to do, do quickly, my dear son:
blood rightly shed's the source makes joys eternal run.

World has jumped up.

FARMER *in great fear*

Is no one there? Help! Help! Come quickly!

Tries to avoid him.

BEGGAR

Shut up, and quit the loud lament.
Prepare your soul for the last end.
Now comes the ancient struggle's lasting settlement.

Seizes him

Die in the ditch. Go forth in shame!
If I've had nothing, you shall have the same.

WISDOM

with arms lifted in terror, Rich Man, King, Beauty: all
four step forward simultaneously

Stop, murderer, stop!

ANGEL

Think who is watching you, think of the play's plot!

[140]

The Salzburg Great Theatre of the World

WISDOM

When you were a child, did Cain strike terror in you?
Do you desire his lot?

BEAUTY

goes up to the Beggar

Strike me! Destroy us all!

ALL TOGETHER

Strike hard, and in one instant make the whole world fall!

*Beggar, the axe raised high, with unseeing gaze, stands be-
fore them all menacingly.*

WORLD

Trumpets, come in!
My play's now risen to its highest climax.

A pause

WISDOM

Strike hard! We are ready for our end!
And, should it come with faces full of dread,
where is the terror we've not merited?

Throws herself on her knees, to God

But you, throned high above entangled fates,
you see how in the net of wrong beneath
we have secretly all, all, ensnared ourselves.
How easy for you to mend all with a breath,
with a beckoning finger put all this to rights;
but best you love from the exalted dais
an infinite willingness to let men play,
then, with an eagle eye piercing the wrangling voices,

[141]

to let your eagle's talon seize the prey.
You call forth with a sign the actor dreads
a sudden end to the play of your command,
without misgiving see us leave your stage,
and before our play has sunk into the shades,
still, to the last, see our uplifted hands.

*She remains for a moment with folded hands, then rises
and, standing, speaks to the others*

For now the time has come—are you apprised of this?—
that we must quit the stage and quickly must be gone.
There's a short moment granted all of us
leaving the play to find ourselves alone.
And he, grim envoy of the highest will,
given fearful power to summon us away,
his play is over, too, with all his threats to kill,
he leaves the stage with us by the same short-propped way.

*She speaks the following lines with her face turned up-
ward, her eye resolutely avoiding the Beggar. The Beggar
meanwhile goes up to her, the axe raised. The nearer he
comes to her, the firmer, in overcoming deepest fear, becomes her voice. The Beggar stands before her as if rooted
to the ground; his face changes violently. The raised hand
holding the axe falls. The Farmer lies near the tree, his face
hidden in his arm, like one dead, motionless.*

WISDOM

But you, that are the life above all living,
you marvellous judgment found at rest in things,
see me now lift my hands for him: forgive him,
when tremblingly before you now he brings,
tinctured most hideously with all our blood,
the semblance of the being, fateful still,

in which you stamped the mark of lofty will,
forgive him—in your play on him was laid,
of all its parts, the one that heaviest weighed.

BEGGAR *trembling*

Where is the tree?

WISDOM

What tree?

BEGGAR

That I like thunder struck,
that crashing buried you and me together?
But I—

WISDOM

And you?

BEGGAR

Woman? What happened? Where's the light?

WISDOM

What light?

BEGGAR

That broke from the tree's crest,
that spoke to me, and with a human voice!
Was this before? was it after? Woman—what arose,
that I did not strike you?—You were coming close—

WISDOM

Did a light then burst forth?—and—

Hugo von Hofmannsthal

ANGEL

Was that not the white
lightning of Saul and speaking Heaven's light?

BEGGAR

You raised your hands and prayed for me?

WISDOM

For you.

BEGGAR

Knowing me and my lot, the judgment due?

ANGEL

Was that not Isaac's lamb that radiant fell before you?

BEGGAR

O thou my God!

He kneels down, buries his face in his hands.

ANGEL

Soul, your impulse was towards deeds;
Wrongdoing was near, its dark web spun;
but gloriously the play proceeds:
deed, and not misdeed, now is done.

BEGGAR

Done?

WISDOM

Done!

[144]

BEGGAR

I struck the blow?

WISDOM

You did not strike!

ADVERSARY

A stroke, a dizzy fainting-fit
and, after all that, nothing come of it!

In a rage he flings his books to one side.

The glance of the Beggar, who, again upon his feet, looks about him like someone in a trance, meets the glance of Wisdom, who has again advanced to him two steps from her place. She smiles. He smiles, too. His face has a trans-figured expression.

WISDOM

Are you released from your recrimination
which made your brother clench his fists and groan,
while the soul yearned in your soul parched with passion
for those eternities which are its own?
Did you receive in sudden blaze of heaven
this, of all gifts the most inordinate,
and can you call your brothers now forgiven
their hollow credit in Earth's dull estate?

BEGGAR

What do I care what you have? I'm so full of joys,
I'll go to the wood; communing there I'll roam,
ringed with eternity's lightning, nor squander there, nor lose
Heaven's inner fullness on a single breath of time.

[145]

Hugo von Hofmannsthal

WISDOM

Does your converted mind pardon us now?

BEGGAR

How do I know who you are, or who I am, how?
As though from eternity
the wood's awaiting me
where I, an innocent child,
lay on a mossy stone.
To lie there and in joy
quicken to God alone!

WISDOM

O soul, you have suddenly come to the great end;
take root in the wood and blossom as a Christian.

Beggar has turned to go.

ADVERSARY

stepping sideways into his path

What, the hand crippled that once could judge upright!
And still Injustice, in the shameless light
basking as ever, spreads its peacock tail,
and you in the wood pursue a dreamer's trail!
For shame! O can a brain grasp this demented state?
Man's vigour wasted, that productive hate!
Do you not shudder to see yourself?

BEGGAR

brushing him off with his arm

I was put in their way,
as antagonist enrolled:

[146]

The Salzburg Great Theatre of the World

for this is God's play,
we call it the world.

ADVERSARY

Will you lick the foot that crushed you, like a coward?

BEGGAR

I am with God, in all things at their heart!
But in the play I am the Beggar, yes,
from whom I take my being and my shape.
What therefore should I want of these?
To learn my ways and sayings in their school?
I'd have to be a bungler and a fool.
If I stripped off that mantle where he stands
and struck the golden sword out of his hands,
usurp him straightway, see myself enthroned,
and sit there the fat breadth of all my days,
then sits Tom Fool on the throne, the leaf remains unturned,
and this world keeps its old, dishonoured ways.
What if I boast with gesturing airs of power
in place of them? There's small gain either way.
The world must be renewed, true and entire,
or this remains indeed a sorry puppet play.

He takes one step

I shall not lodge with them, I must away elsewhere;
for me the clock of stars has struck prodigious time.
Now I awake myself, my mind becomes a flare,
at midnight the dark wood shall catch from it like day:
I have heard now a word that long was lost to me;
It seems, now I have heard it, that I was then unborn,
such tender truth an angel's mouth then made me learn,
his theme was freedom and its quality.

[147]

I was not free—my soul—when under gloomy stress
I swung sharp iron over these;
all this I realized suddenly,
as one who stands within stained windows sees
the pictures in the glass. Freedom is always near,
but if you force your way to it, then at once it is far;
press close to it but gently, then again it is there
and upward sighs from you even to the heavenly stars.
It is concealed so well, no earthly name will show it:
it's an abyss above which it is grand to lean,
yet also yearning with the power to draw you in.
I'll go in the wild wood, completely there to know it;
I think it is from God, and if I stay alone,
through God it then will pierce into my very bone
and then on every path and way will go with me:
so keep away from me, and make my pathway free!

He goes slowly past him.

WISDOM

Go, and be a good spirit in the wood, and praise
God, the great Master, who directs all ways.
I bow before you!

Beggar turns right, to go off.

WISDOM

Stop, take your axe.

*She goes to where the axe lies, bends, picks it up and gives
it to him.*

BEGGAR

does not take it

It is not mine.

The Salzburg Great Theatre of the World

WISDOM

Take it and use it as yours.
So the Lord says: you must not waste in sloth your powers.
If my high wood shall fence you round,
hermit, you must keep it sound;
mild as the crook that lightens the shades' room,
take your axe out to meet heaven's early beam,
and let its full, calm stroke ring like a bell that says
autumn to the village and rich, peaceful days.

*Beggar fastens the axe on the cord that girds his waist and
goes slowly out.*

*Farmer, half hidden behind the tree, gazes after him until
he has disappeared.*

*Busybody raises himself on the tips of his toes so as to see
the departed one still as he goes into the wing, then heaves
an audible sigh of relief.*

*Wisdom has returned to her place; she folds her hands in
silent prayer. All five figures remain calmly in their places.
Farmer looks into the wings, as though into the wood into
which the Beggar has disappeared. He makes a satisfied face,
signifies in dumb show that he hears him chopping wood.*

A signal.

WORLD

takes up her lute, plays and sings after a short prelude

Time, my handmaid, fly away,
dress me at nightfall, dress me for day,
braid my hair, play round my shoe,
I am the mistress, the handmaid you.
Heya!

Hugo von Hofmannsthal

She plays more sombrely on the lute, her face darkens

But one day you will enter angrily,
the stars throw light deceptively,
the wind drive through the lofty hall,
the sun go out, the light grow pale,
the floor in death shine spectrally,
and then my mistress you shall be!
O grief!
And I your maid, dejected, weak,
O sad to speak!

Again more gaily and lightly

Fly away, time! that time is far!
Heya!

The light on the stage alters while she sings, as though approaching a gloomy evening.

BEAUTY

after a silence, as though waking out of a dream

Alas, what has befallen me?
I feel the change from heel to hair!

She looks at herself in the mirror, lowers it at once

Something disastrous, unforeseen,
has left its fearful imprint there!
Time like the wind has flown away,
I was a child but yesterday,
and it has wrought on me disgrace
and shamefully transformed my face.
Am I not, then, a youthful bride?
On my temples some grey wisp I spied!

Looks again into the mirror

[150]

The Salzburg Great Theatre of the World

O God! I see it now again quite clearly!
And what is the dark wicked line
on which the eyelashes decline?
The whole thing is indeed still there

She smiles at her image

and yet a wicked thing quite near;
if too intent I fixed my eyes thereon,
I should discern the mask of an old crone.

She lowers the mirror, looks furtively towards the King

He, too! The same and yet not as he was:
something now gaunt and furrowed in his face!

Looks towards the Farmer

And he! changed even in his mould!
How grey, how worn and dull, how quickly old!

*She leaves her place and takes a few steps to the left, steals
a glance at the Rich Man*

An eagle's look from brows of confidence.
Gone! but now lightly, like a passing glance,
or he will stare at me! and yet in going
I have seen enough to satisfy my knowing.

Crosses over to Wisdom

And you, how fair you are, what light your features throw,
where do they get this inner radiant glow,
where found you this no longer earthly smile,
what airs play round your forehead all the while?

Closer

And yet, even you, grown old, but like the precious stone
that, ageing, sheds the light it has drawn in!
Even you?

Hugo von Hofmannsthal

WISDOM

smiles, as though wakened out of a state of rapture

What did you say?

BEAUTY

standing in the centre, wrings her hands

O heart-consuming grief!
O single true disaster on the world,
by which the high joy of our being is galled!

WISDOM

What do you complain of?

BEAUTY

Time, the murderess, time!
Time with her robber's hand on us has chosen to fall,
and evilly abused both you and me and all!

*A roll of a kettledrum begins, and with it a rushing of wind.
The figures, as though waking out of rigidity, leave their
places and go in confusion, but like dreamers, talking each
to himself without noticing the others, and, as they go,
wring their hands, except for Wisdom, who keeps hers
folded.*

KING

Power is weakness: that strikes home
and cuts me through my marrow and bone.

RICH MAN

Rule and constraint I did not know,
yet there is something rules me now.

[152]

FARMER

I've always had my firm place here;
what's leading me a dance so queer?

WISDOM

In the storm's raging is thy sign;
pity the creature that is thine—

BEAUTY

O frailty, fear unresting, constant,
what will become of me this instant?

ALL

together, to the kettledrum's accompaniment

A fallow light, a hollow wind,
ah, we are creatures in the end!

The raging of the wind drops to complete silence.

*They all pause. Each finds himself at his place. They stand
motionless.*

*Busybody, as their dance-like confused wandering begins,
comes up inquisitively to join in, and becomes involuntarily
caught up in it, dancing with them to the end, only without opening his mouth. Now he wipes his forehead and
slips back to his place.*

The kettledrum also is silent.

ANGEL

*turns, as though reached by a signal, to the palace of the
Master and looks with reverence up to the balcony*

Here, waiting on your signal!

[153]

Hugo von Hofmannsthal

He hurries back, listens upward, hurries again to the fore-
ground, always on the upper stage, and from a distance calls
to Death, who has already become visible now and then at
the side of the upper stage

The play already soon will reach its end;
Now call the actors, one by one, away!

DEATH

advances from where he stands to the rim of the upper stage
and calls loudly

You who have the role of the King, step off!
The part you play is over: leave the stage!

He goes again to the side, where, however, he remains
visible.

King understands. Beauty and Rich Man both flinch.

Farmer, as if he had heard nothing, begins digging with his
spade.

Wisdom throws a radiant glance at the King.

KING

advances, looks upward, takes the crown from his head,
contemplates it

What? Such a shadow-play, so quickly gone,
that seemed so real, so full of pomp and thought!
My eye, whose signal they all hung upon,
itself soon lies with things that are cast out;
you crown that seemed a part of the head itself,
gently you now break free and keep your light.
O light, O noble light, light fixed above all seeming,
he who aspired to you, to him you were true being,

glorious existence, given the power of swaying
the sullen conflict of things self-obeying.
To whom do I give you up? In what thrice worthy hand
lay, as I go, this pledge, this spiritual bond?

He steps to Wisdom

Wise, holy woman for whom seeming gives no light
but seeming and being into a higher light unite,
this sign for me will you protect,
to hand it to the next Ruler Elect?

He makes as if to hand over the crown to Wisdom.

WORLD

rises suddenly and steps between them

To me, to me! You all are in my house;
I dress you and again take off the dress.
Give it to me and go. Now let it be!

*Takes the crown from the hand of the King. Sits down
again and holds the crown in her lap.*

DEATH

Go off! Delay can profit nothing.

KING

O Master of the drama, see me coming!

He goes

With awe and with knees quaking I must bring
before you now the player of a King.

Exit

[155]

Hugo von Hofmannsthal

BEAUTY

steps in terror from her place and wrings her hands

O, what has happened here? Where must he go?
How can it be that he must go away?
Who dares give orders to the mighty one?
What will become of me: he loved me so.
I was fair, in his gold rooms, through him alone.
Where, then, for me? What land will bring him back?
Where shall I go, abandoned thus?

RICH MAN

steps forward

To me!

BEAUTY

steps instinctively away from him to Wisdom.

RICH MAN

To me! Your place is at my side,
you, secretly assigned to me so long,
of all my treasures the most glorified!

BEAUTY *fearful, alarmed*

Ah me!

RICH MAN *more emphatically*

To me! What's happened that's so wrong?

BEAUTY

The powerful one who was the imperial lord
of me and you and of these all,

[156]

loved by the people, by his vassals honoured,
have you not seen? Do you not think it real?

RICH MAN

So in the end the mask was bound to fall!
To me! Now this arm holds you fast—for him;
for I am really what he did but seem.

Beauty recoils from him.

RICH MAN

follows her, they both come to the foreground

When bright he stood upon the golden wain
it was this hand that held the rein.
I was that power, the hundred-handed one;
I was and am alone what broke that wildness in.
Disdaining glamour, silent for the mob,
I turn the heavens round me like the globe.
There is no being in the abysmal night
could shun me, and no heaven-high towering form
that my force could not seize in flight,
no fortress that I could not take by storm.
Here came the gift to inherit the world's glory,

He points to his breast

here also you! The rest is fragmentary.

BEAUTY

O sister, help me if you can!
shield me from this appalling man!

WISDOM

This light that fearfully goes down to darkness,
can it not strike a warning in your soul?

[157]

Hugo von Hofmannsthal

RICH MAN

Fool, you who take great pride in loneliness
through which a dead light throws a sickly glare,
if you but knew the way of things out there
you would be clever; then to grasp truth whole,
you would discover in fear that you and yours,
subsisting in protective provinces,
were tolerated so by my broad mind,
that what is spirit, what lifts you above the beast,
is blossom of my doing, and owed to me.
Out of my way, there's nothing besides me!

DEATH

steps to the centre and speaks downward

You fair one, go now from the stage.
Your play is already at an end.

He remains after this standing in the same place.

BEAUTY

clinging to Wisdom in terror

At an end! My sorrow!
But let me be near you! Guard me! Not, not be lost entirely!

Rich Man draws back, stands as if numb.

WISDOM

*holding and supporting Beauty, almost unconscious, in her
arms*

Can you, then, Soul, be lost entirely?

BEAUTY

Fear!

[158]

The Salzburg Great Theatre of the World

WISDOM

Compose yourself. Seize on a powerful word;
it will carry you onward as wings bear a bird.

BEAUTY

What kind of word?

WISDOM

"I am with you."

BEAUTY

Do you speak with me?
Are you with me? It is I speaking with you!

Wisdom attempts to shake her free.

DEATH *to Wisdom*

Go off with her, your time is ended, too.

WISDOM

prepares to go, while supporting Beauty

I am going with you.

BEAUTY

With me! With me! Now forward!
Say now the word—say evermore the word!
With me! With me!

WORLD

stands up and goes to meet them;—to Beauty

Give me your looking-glass,
you will not need it there where you are going.

[159]

Hugo von Hofmannsthal

To Wisdom

And you your cross!

Beauty gives up the looking-glass, as though unconsciously;
they go.

WISDOM

remains standing, lifts her gaze to God

       Take it: those realms make shine
true being, there one needs no sign.

BEAUTY

You speak for us!

WISDOM

O you I dare not name, trembling below you,
give without bounds to me that I may know you.
I am the nothing and have need of all;
you, who are all, give to this nothingness
out of your all into its poor decease.
You did indeed not stint it when you cast
over the heavens the radiance of the stars;
your light the night with suns surpassed
in which a thousand suns reflected shone:
you who created me as well from night,
transfigure me, through no worth of my own,
but through what I am unworthy to requite.

BEAUTY

Amen.

They go.

[160]

DEATH

has climbed down from the upper stage to the lower one.
He appears to be looking for the Farmer, who crouches be-
hind his tree. But he also casts a long look at the Rich Man.
*   At last he lifts his hand to the Farmer and calls to him*

Time for your exit, you, your play is done.

Farmer behaves as if he did not hear.

DEATH *louder*

You there, retire!

FARMER

acts as if he did not refer to him, points into the wing

Ah, him you mean, that one in there in the wood,
you want to give him an order? That's your thought.
Well, he lives there, sometimes he's heard about;
one hears him felling, sometimes singing, too,
but I've not heard him now for quite a time.
The message, maybe I could give it him?
Do you want me to go in and fetch him out?

DEATH

shakes his head, comes nearer to him

I bring the message to each myself.

FARMER *alarmed, eagerly*
                    Yourself?
Aye, in the wood he gets so lost himself,
following the beasts, bent on their cure the while,
even arguing with them in the queerest style.—

[161]

Hugo von Hofmannsthal

Calls

Hi, you!—He surely can't have gone stone deaf!

DEATH

It's you I mean; go off, your work on Earth is over.

FARMER

Ah no, by no means! It's not over!
I have no time—

DEATH *powerfully*

Now is the time for this!
You must now leave the stage.

FARMER

Slowly now, just one after the other,
you've said. I have still work to do. There are plenty of idle
    fellows
who stand about. You look to those.

DEATH

You go now. Then the other.

FARMER

again looks in the direction of the Rich Man

I've no time.

RICH MAN

groans

O, not to fall a victim to this gaze,
Oh stand, stand upright! It will soon be sped.
Oh, once again! My selfhood, whither, whither?

[162]

Nothing! And now so heavy! Oh like a mount of lead!
My selfhood! Now so monstrous, to the stars it sprawls,
scatters, dissolves in distance horribly unfurled;
it shrinks now, dwindles fearfully and falls and falls,
falls like a stone, where to, then, from the world?
Where to? Where to, then, still?

He staggers, falls

O whirlpool without grace!
Enough! Enough! Enough! Enough! Enough!

He dries his forehead.

DEATH

goes up to the Farmer

Now! Farmer!

FARMER

Often there's a deal to do
before the snow comes, and I feel it on the way;
one must put leaves down—

DEATH

No, you must away!

FARMER

What? I have to go? You're right; this way I must be making
        tracks
and quickly load manure up on the racks.

DEATH

No, you must into your grave.

[163]

Hugo von Hofmannsthal

FARMER

Jesus! That slipped my mind,
my apples for cider-pressing, hedge to bind,
flax to hackle for the women—

DEATH

strongly, as he grasps him by the shoulder

The Farmer's act is over. Here it ends.

FARMER

wavers, despondently

I always thought at last there would be time
to have a rest, to sit about on the bench
that I might think on my Lord God a dram
and rouse repentance for my wickedness.
But now you tear me away. You leave a man no time.
Now I repent my unrepentingness.
I've worked a lot, and prayed not very much;
my part, for what it's worth, the Master take and judge!

He goes.

BUSYBODY

takes the spade from him

He has made his exit rather well, the Farmer.

DEATH *to the Rich Man*

Now away with you!

In the direction of the wings with stronger yet gentler voice

And you, come forth out of the forest;
retire through the grave's door like all the rest!

[164]

To the Rich Man

Still lingering there? Begone!

Rich Man, on the ground, groans heavily.

BEGGAR

comes out of the wing. He has grown a large white beard.
He scares a twittering bird away

Go off! Fly back into the wood! Quick! Quick!
Here is no rightful place for you to pick.
Here there are people!

DEATH

Here am I!

BEGGAR

But who are you?

Gazes at him, recognizes him, his face lights up

You!

He stretches his arms out

Are you taking me away now? in this instant?

Death nods.

Beggar kneels down, kisses the ground.

DEATH

What are you doing?

BEGGAR

I am kissing the dear ground
that is to take me in to narrow rest.

Hugo von Hofmannsthal

Sweet will it be, the seed-corn's rest,
then I rise up—

He stands up

in an instant dressed.

He turns to Death

I am old already, full of impatience, too;
come, then, with that great favour you must do.

DEATH *to the Rich Man*

Away with you first, you, as I commanded!

RICH MAN *on the ground*

O pit of ruin with no floor beneath,
O sea of anguish never sounded!

BEGGAR

approaches the Rich Man

You!

Bends over him

Come, my brother, come now; this is death.

RICH MAN

I am frightened! You!

Shudders back.

BEGGAR *in a friendly way*
Of what?

RICH MAN
Of the ghastly sight.

[166]

BEGGAR

Stop gnashing. Come! Use me for your support.

RICH MAN *painfully*

Who are you?

BEGGAR

Who but your brother!

RICH MAN

fearfully, uncomprehending

How? from whence

do you come to me?

BEGGAR

From my magnificence.

RICH MAN *full of fear*

From where?

BEGGAR

Oh, not so far from here.
Out of the wood there. I was lying on my dead leaves
when I was sternly called; so I prepared myself
and stepped forth from my luminous Canaan
and came into your deserts here
to see what might be asked of me.
What troubles you? What weighs upon your breast?
You, too, indeed are called! Brother, get up!
Do you not feel, like balm, the sweet behest?

[167]

Hugo von Hofmannsthal

RICH MAN

his teeth chattering

Great, little—powerful, nothing—powerful—nothing—
with you is power! Power I have always sought.
Was I so evil just because of that?

BEGGAR *strongly*

Power, glorious word! blest be the mouth given power
to utter this word now in this last hour.
Power be with you, with manly, strong regret,
even in your marrow to renew you, dying, yet!
Up now, and once again with eagle's eye
gather your strength above your destiny.
See through this trick, tear yourself from its rites:
one calls us off: they are putting out the lights;
now open the tightened hands, that we make known:
all was stage property; we kept nothing for our own.

Gently opens the Rich Man's hands

Now come, we'll go and sing with one another.
But come! Down there! We'll gain it and discover
the place where we as actors of the play
before our Master stand, all make-up wiped away.

*He takes him by the hand, they go off, the Beggar strikes
up a holy song.*

*Death goes across, places himself behind World. World has
before this already stood up.*

*Busybody has grabbed for himself the folding chair and
hung the lute round himself.*

*Angel, in the moment when the Beggar goes off with the
Rich Man, hurries into the palace of the Master.*

[168]

The Salzburg Great Theatre of the World

The stage is plunged in semidarkness.

WORLD

Quickly! Take from them everything that we have lent them! From the Farmer his rough shoes, from the nun even her hair-shirt, strip them all quickly, nothing is theirs! Maybe the play is going to begin again at once, then others must get into the same clothes: what do I care? Make haste!

Attendants at once jump forward, closing the curtain before the lower stage. On the one side World with her retinue, on the other the Adversary, who has in the meantime packed his books up and donned his barret, stand in the proscenium.

Music. After a short time the attendants jump back, open-ing the curtain. The lower stage now is quite empty, in a pale, greenish light. The tree and the rock have been cleared away.

One hears in the distance the "De Profundis" being sung. The Souls—formerly King, Rich Man, Farmer, Beggar, Wisdom, and Beauty, all in similar white shrouds—enter upon the lower stage, coming forward from the side, and indeed in two groups, three at a time. Only their faces dis-tinguish them from one another.

They step slowly up to each other, then remain standing, separated by some six paces.

The upper stage remains empty.

ONE SOUL
formerly the King

O terror!

Hugo von Hofmannsthal

ANOTHER SOUL

formerly Wisdom

O joy!

ANOTHER

formerly the Rich Man

O horrible fear! O judgment now near!

ANOTHER

formerly the Beggar

O yearning delight, O fast-growing light!

TWO

the Farmer and Beauty together

O waiting! O terror!

TWO OTHERS

Wisdom and the Beggar together

O lightning of day!

The Angel steps from the palace to the foremost rim of the upper stage.

WORLD

calls to her servants, pointing to the six Dead

Will you forever be flaunting a something, you dead? Then my green storm of decay will rush on you and whirl you miserable shadows away, till you are pulverized into a thousand nothings! Quickly!

A storm rises.

[170]

ANGEL

bids the storm be still; it dies down immediately

Go away, World, for your task is finished, and the Master is satisfied with you. But these are no longer subject to you: they are souls, indestructible, and what in them your eye takes for an expression of countenance, that is the seal of their spiritual being, with which He has sealed them. This your storms do not touch. You are dismissed.

World bows and withdraws.

ANGEL

But you who had to play the Beggar's role,
your act before your fellow-players all
has pleased our Master well.
Go in the Palace now, be thanked by Him,
and break with Him the bread that causes fear in Hell.

Beggar detaches himself from the others and comes forward.

ANGEL

Next to him, Wisdom, you came off best in the play,
only your part was the less onerous;
next to him be its prize and glory yours.

WISDOM

comes forward

And these here, helpless, shuddering where they stand,
lost almost, feeling hell and heaven at hand?

ANGEL

Creature of higher works, to them extend
something of your vigour with your hand.

[171]

Bound to you by the golden chain of grace,
here be, before the gate, their waiting place.

*As Beauty, the last in the chain, tries to stretch her free
hand out to the Rich Man also.*

ANGEL

Not to him!

WISDOM

Never to him? O do not speak the dreadful word!
Show him the cold, dark place of solitude,
but speak no Never!

ANGEL

*points to a place graded below them, where the Rich Man
kneels down; then to the others.*

Up! Into the Master's sight!
Prepare yourselves for unimagined light.

*He goes before them, all follow. Out of the palace step
flag-waving Angels. Angel strides in, Beggar and Wisdom
follow. Beauty, King, and Farmer kneel at the side of the
entrance, the Rich Man lower down, in darkness. Music
and singing.*

Curtain

THE TOWER

A Tragedy in Five Acts

[First Version]

Translated by

MICHAEL HAMBURGER

BASILIUS, *the King*

SIGISMUND, *his son*

JULIAN, *Governor of the Tower*

ANTON, *his servant*

BROTHER IGNATIUS, *a monk, formerly Grand Almoner*

OLIVIER, *a soldier*

THE CHILDREN'S KING

A DOCTOR

A YOUNG MONK

COUNT ADAM, *a royal chamberlain*

THE KING'S CONFESSOR

SIMON, *a Jew*

JERONIM THE CLERK ⎫
ARON THE TARTAR ⎬ *rebels*
INDRIK THE SMITH ⎭

A HORSEMAN

A CAVALRY BOY

A PEASANT WOMAN

A YOUNG GIPSY WOMAN

Bannerets, courtiers, chamberlains, pages, a steward, an equerry, soldiers, a man with a wooden leg, an old woman, a porter, a beggar, monks, rebels, generals, boys.

[175]

Hugo von Hofmannsthal

*The place: A kingdom of Poland, but more legendary than
historical.*

*The time: A past century, similar in atmosphere to the seven-
teenth.*

Act One

*In front of the tower. Outworks, partly masonry, partly
hewn out of the rock. Half-light between the walls, though
the sky is still bright.—Corporal Olivier and a few crippled
old soldiers, amongst them Pancras and Andrew.*

OLIVIER

calling out to the back

Recruit, come here! (*The recruit, a flaxen-haired farmer's
boy, comes running*) Jump to it, recruit. Go and get me a
light for my pipe. I want to smoke tobacco!

RECRUIT

Yes, sir.

About to run off.

OLIVIER

Very well, Corporal, sir, is what you say. And don't you forget it.

RECRUIT

Yes, sir.

OLIVIER

Ass! Filthy blockhead! *Bougre! Larron! Maledetta bestia.*
What is it you have to say?

[177]

Recruit gapes at him in terrified silence.

OLIVIER

Go and get the light. And make it lively!

RECRUIT

Yes, sir.

Runs off.

OLIVIER

I'll tan the hide off you one of these days!

ANDREW *after a pause*

Corporal, is it true you were a student once?

Olivier does not reply. Pause.

PANCRAS

So you're our new guard commander?

OLIVIER

What? You dare to put a direct question to me? You have the insolence to open your big mouth in my presence?

ANDREW

You've a sharp tongue in your head. People of your sort go far these days.

There is an intermittent sound of muffled banging.

OLIVIER

What son of a whore is that, chopping firewood in the cellar whilst I'm holding my inspection here? He is to stop it at once—I order him to. (*Recruit returns with a light. Olivier is about to light his pipe*) Which way is the wind blowing?

RECRUIT

Don't know, sir.

OLIVIER

In that case, animal, I'll nail your nostrils so far apart that twelve yards of string wouldn't put them together again. Stand between my pipe and the wind.

RECRUIT

Yes, sir.

OLIVIER

lights his pipe

I can't endure that damned knocking. They're to stop. Get along, recruit, at the double. It's my order: wood-chopping is to cease. It vexes me.

PANCRAS

No one is chopping wood. It's the one back there—the prisoner.

OLIVIER

You mean the prince who goes naked, with a wolfskin round his loins?

PANCRAS *looking round*

Say: the prisoner. Never let that other word pass your lips, or you'll find yourself in the provost's room.

[179]

OLIVIER

It takes two men to do that. The times are not such that a man like me can be punished.—What's the brute up to? Why does it bang about in its cage?

ANDREW

He's dug up a horse's bone, and when the toads and rats get too much for him, he lays about the vermin like a madman.

PANCRAS

They've tormented him ever since he was born, so he torments whatever he can lay his hands on.

OLIVIER

Listen! A bagpipe. And now it's broken off halfway through the tune. Do you hear something?

PANCRAS

What if we do? What does it matter?

OLIVIER

Now it's started again. And now it's quiet. Signals—that's what it is.

ANDREW

What makes you think so?

OLIVIER

Why, do you imagine I don't know the code of Jewish smugglers? It's a language all of its own. Now the bagpipe stops: that means, quick, run for it behind the alders, the sentry isn't looking. A one-horned cow: that means, you can get through here at the new moon. A girl who's singing: look out, there are fox-traps here.

PANCRAS

You certainly weren't born yesterday.

ANDREW

In that case we ought to patrol, since we're here to watch the frontier.

OLIVIER

Leave them alone. What they're smuggling suits me very well.

PANCRAS

What would that be?

OLIVIER

Arms, gunpowder, lead, halberds, pikes, quarterstaffs, axes. Up from Hungary, over from Bohemia, down from Lithuania.

PANCRAS

Damned Jews! Where do they unearth the stuff?

OLIVIER

They can sense what's afoot. They sense the bloodshed to come. They smell the roof-trees burning.

RECRUIT *secretively, anxiously*

A three-legged hare has been seen, a lean pig has appeared, a calf with glowing eyes is running through the streets.

[181]

OLIVIER

All will be against all. Not a house will remain standing. They'll sweep up what's left of the churches like so much dirt.

THE MAN WITH A WOODEN LEG

who has not spoken before

They will draw him up into the light, and the lowest shall be the highest, and he will be the poor men's king and ride on a white horse, and the sword and scales will be carried before him.

OLIVIER

Shut your mouth, Bohemian heretic. Throw a stone into the cage. I won't have this din.

THE MAN WITH A WOODEN LEG

Sword and scales will be carried before him.

OLIVIER

Throw a stone, recruit. Or the hangman will shave you with a wide razor.

RECRUIT *trembling*

A human head has grown out of the wolf's body. He stretches five-fingered hands and folds them like a man.

OLIVIER

Does the beast look as strange as that? I'll get into his cage and flay his hide. That should make a man sword-proof.

PANCRAS

Don't go. He stinks too.

The Tower

OLIVIER

Why, in beleaguered towns I've lain all night on rotten flesh as though it were my bedstead. Hand me a pike. I shall rouse him first. Quick, a pike! When I want something, it happens. Can you bear my glance?

He snatches Pancras' pike.

RECRUIT *crying out*

Look, a cockatrice flying! If it flies in your face, you're blind for ever. (*He points into the air*) When a human being begins to sweat blood, the serpents take pity; they hurl themselves into the air in a ball and give birth to an egg between them. That makes the blind see and the seeing blind.

Olivier wipes his eyes. The Recruit gently leads him aside, takes away his pike and lays it down; then he kneels down, his face turned to the wall in the background.

ANDREW

goes up to Olivier

I warn you, Corporal. Remember our instructions—the most emphatic of all.

OLIVIER

I've never heard of any.

ANDREW

There are ten prohibitions.

OLIVIER

Where would they come from? I spit on them.

[183]

ANDREW

Everyone here has to swear to them. Always keep at a distance of ten paces from the prisoner. Never speak one word to him, one word about him, on pain of death.

OLIVIER

I'd like to see the man who could put me under oath. He'd be spilling some red juice before he'd got very far.

PANCRAS

who has joined them

It's the Governor here who gave the orders, and we're all bound to obey him.

OLIVIER

Never seen the fellow. He can lick my shoes if he likes. Some creeping flunkey of a courtier. His sort will hang soon —every one of them. They're already greasing the rope for them.

ANDREW

He is a great lord. He's been given power over the prisoner and over us.

OLIVIER

An anointed rascal, that is what he is. He stinks of musk and civet, of balm and louse-ointment; and he washes his hands in a silver basin.

PANCRAS

He dispenses summary justice. He has been granted such power over our heads as a ship's captain has over his crew.

The Tower

OLIVIER

Just let him show it! Just let him try it on me! Here I stand!

ANDREW

He will have a man tied to a tree trunk on an icy winter day. Such power has been given to him.

OLIVIER

Such power indeed! Over old toothless beggars, perhaps, over marauders who've come down in the world and exchanged their muskets for begging bowls. Not over a man like me!

PANCRAS

You will see, Corporal.

OLIVIER

See? What shall I see?

PANCRAS

That supreme military power has been granted to him here, even if he does wash his hands in a silver basin.

OLIVIER

Granted to him? By whom? No one can confer supreme military power on another unless he has it himself. Perhaps it was given to him by this one here? (*He pulls out a coin and holds it up in front of Pancras' face*) He doesn't count. I wipe my shoes with *him*. I piss on *him*. (*He throws the coin over his shoulder contemptuously*) If my quarters here are not to my liking, if within a fortnight everyone here doesn't dance to my tune, there'll be trouble between me and your lousy courtier! Where is the fellow? I want to see him.

ANDREW

You'll never see him. When he has an order to give us, he has the alert blown three times by the bugler, and then he sends his servant—

OLIVIER

His servant, you say? To my martial person? His snotty-nosed servant? We shall see about that! Why, before a month is up I shall crack your courtier fellow on the head with his silver basin. I shall hang him, that's what I shall do, and grease my boots with the fat on his paunch.

PANCRAS

That's what I said. He has the alert sounded three times. Listen!

Three consecutive blasts of a horn. Anton appears on a wooden bridge above the outworks and makes to descend. The soldiers, except Olivier, withdraw. Olivier stands there as though he had not noticed Anton.

ANTON

approaching him from behind

Are you the new guard commander, sir? (*Olivier remains silent*) In the Governor's name! (*Olivier does not reply. Anton, close to him, at his back, salutes*) In the name, and by the order, of His Excellency! (*Salutes again. Olivier half turns to him, weighs him up with a contemptuous look from top to toe. Anton salutes again, very affably*) A very good day to the guard commander! (*Olivier knocks out his pipe, ignoring him. Anton salutes once more)* In the Governor's name: the guard commander will withdraw his men from here and occupy the approaches. But his men will turn their backs and yet not lose sight of anything. They will observe everything and hear nothing. What is about to happen here does not concern the commander, but I shall tell you, sir: the prisoner will be brought out for medical inspection. *(Olivier whistles some tune)* Did you understand me, sir? I beg you to execute the order. *(Olivier spits and walks away. Anton, following him with his eyes, salutes)* A most courteous gentleman. A most uncommonly courteous young gentleman! He would like to thank me, but is afraid of embarrassing me. A magnanimous, soldierly young gentleman. To be with him for a moment is worth an hour's discussion with another man. He must have taken a special liking to me, but he wouldn't show it for fear of weakening military discipline!

OLIVIER off-stage

Guard, form up! Guard, right turn!

Short drum-roll.

DOCTOR

entering the same way as Anton

Where is the patient?

ANTON

The prisoner is what you mean, sir. One moment, sir. I shall fetch the creature for you.

DOCTOR

Where is his room?

[187]

ANTON

What room?

DOCTOR

Well, the dungeon, then, the cell.

ANTON

points behind him

Back there!

DOCTOR

Where do you mean?

Turns round to look.

ANTON

In front of your nose, sir, if you'll pardon the expression.

DOCTOR

What I see is a small open cage, not fit for a dog.—You don't mean to tell me that he's in—or else a crime has been committed here that cries out to heaven! (*Anton shrugs his shoulders*) In there? Day and night?

ANTON

Summer and winter. In winter half a load of straw is chucked in for a treat.

DOCTOR

Since when?

ANTON

Four years ago. (*The Doctor is speechless*) Four years ago everything was tightened up. One night some great gentlemen came on horseback and conferred with the Governor. Since then he's been sleeping in the cage at night, has not been allowed out for exercise, has had a chain on his feet, and a great ball attached to it, that stinking wolfskin round his loins, whether it's summer or winter, has never seen the sun except for two hours in the dog days.

The muffled banging is heard again, as before.

DOCTOR

covers his eyes with his hand

How does he spend the day?

ANTON

shrugs his shoulders

Doing nothing. Like a lord or like a dog. When I push in his food, he's pleased. I always talk to him. (*In anxious haste*) Only as much as I have to, of course.

DOCTOR

I want to go to him. I want to see him.

ANTON

Certainly, if you can bear the—um—exhalation, sir.

DOCTOR *going nearer*

My eyes are adapting themselves. I see an animal crouching on the ground.

Steps back.

ANTON

That's the object in question.

[189]

DOCTOR

That!—Call him. Lead him out to me.

ANTON

looks round

I'm forbidden to speak to him in the presence of strangers.

DOCTOR

In the presence of his appointed physician it must be per-mitted. I assume the responsibility.

ANTON

Sigismund!—He doesn't reply. That means he's angry, and mustn't be provoked. Else he flies into a rage, goes quite mad. I know him well.—But he can hear me. I can see that by his eyes. Do you see them glare at us, sir?—Careful! He won't suffer anyone to go near him. Once he had a bit-ing bout with a fox which the guards threw over the bars to see what would happen—got his teeth stuck in the fox.

DOCTOR

Can't you call him? Coax him? Has he no sense?

ANTON

That one? Why, he knows Latin and can get through a fat book as though it were a side of bacon.—But sometimes a word sticks in his mouth, and he can't get it out. At other times he's just like you and me, sir. (*Approaches the cage, calling to him gently*) Come out, then, Sigismund. Who did you think it was? It's your Anton; your dear old Anton. Your Anton is going to open the door. (*He opens the door with a pike that has been leaning against the wall*) There, now I'm putting my stick away. (*He lays the pike on the ground*) Now I'm sitting on the ground. Now I'm sleeping. (*Softly, to the Doctor*) Be careful, sir. He mustn't be startled, or there'll be trouble.

DOCTOR

Why, is he armed?

ANTON

He always has a horse's bone by him. They must have buried the beast in that corner before he came.—At heart he's a good creature. Give him some medicine, sir, that will make him gentle again.

DOCTOR

With the weight of the whole world pressing down on him? There are connections everywhere.

ANTON

Ssh! He's stirring. He's looking at the open door. This is something new for him.—(*To the cage*) Shall I lie down? Then you'll lie down beside me? All snug and cosy?

Sigismund comes out of the cage, a large stone in one hand.

ANTON

beckons to him

There, sit down beside me.

SIGISMUND *parrotlike*

Sit down beside me.

[191]

Hugo von Hofmannsthal

ANTON

sitting on the ground

A gentleman has come to see you. (*Sigismund sees the Doctor and starts*) Don't be afraid. A good gentleman. A fine gentleman. What will the gentleman think of you? Put down that stone. He thinks you're a child. And yet you're twenty. (*Gets up, goes to him slowly, gently takes the stone out of his hand*) You must control yourself. I told him that you're my friend.—Just think, he knows your name!

DOCTOR

Sigismund, come to me!

Sigismund looks at him.

ANTON

You see? A good gentleman.—(*Softly*) Look at his eyes, sir. —(*Aloud*) The gentleman will help you. Better food! A blanket! But you must show him your best side. A child controls himself, even a dog controls himself. Do you remember? The dog called Tyras? (*To the Doctor, but Sigismund listens*) When he was a child he lived with country folk, good people; till he was fourteen. Romped about, jumped about, shot with a bow and arrow. That was a good life. (*Softly*) Don't stare at him; he can't bear a piercing glance —it makes him go rigid. (*Louder, without looking*) Now Sigismund is going to speak as well. We're all going to converse together. Speech is what draws people together. Dogs speak too. And so do sheep; they say "baa."

SIGISMUND

—speak too.

[192]

The Tower

ANTON

Sigismund is going to speak to his Tony. Because today, for once, speaking is allowed.

SIGISMUND

Speaking is allowed?

ANTON

I should say it is! It's commanded! Come forward now, anyone who wants to open the discussion! (*Slaps his knee*) Haccus, Maccus, Baccus—those are three sacred words! Prove their worth in any place! The seven planets with great speed will comfort us in all our need.—There are better times coming for you, too, Sigismund.

DOCTOR

without turning his eyes away from Sigismund

A monstrous crime! Unthinkably monstrous.

ANTON

Answer, then! What will the gentleman think? The gentleman has come a long way.

DOCTOR

goes closer to him

Would you like to live in a different place, Sigismund?

SIGISMUND

looks up at him, then turns his eyes away; then speaks to himself rapidly, like a child

Of beasts there are many kinds, and all of them make to attack me. I cry out: not too near! Wood lice, worms, toads, grasshoppers, vipers! They all want to attack me. I beat them to death, they're released, the hard black beetles come and bury them.

DOCTOR

A moving voice, still half a child's.—Get me a light, I must look into his eyes.

ANTON

I won't leave you alone with him, sir; it's against orders. (*Calls to the back*) A spill!

Doctor goes up to Sigismund, lays his hand on his forehead. A horn blast off-stage.

DOCTOR

What's that?

ANTON

It means that no one must come here, or he'll be shot at.

SIGISMUND *very rapidly*

Your hand is good, now help me here! Where have they put me? Am I in the world? Where is the world?

DOCTOR

The boundary between what's within and what's without has been blurred.

SIGISMUND

looks at him with understanding

When all's topsy-turvy, an angel blows his trumpet, all things fall into their place.—Lovely hand, skilful hand!

Gropes about in the cell, gropes under the stone, pulls out the crayfish! throws it into the pot, lights the fire, makes the crayfish turn a lovely red and the fishes a lovely blue!

ANTON

Say your little piece about the fishes.

SIGISMUND *rapidly*

Thus say the seven seals: that all the fishes shall roar, the angels shall weep and throw stones at one another, the little blades of grass shall grow teeth and all the towering fir trees—

ANTON

Whatever he's once heard haunts him. Forgets nothing.

DOCTOR

The whole world is only just enough to fill our minds when we look at it through the little peephole, secure in our own houses! But woe when the partition collapses!

A soldier enters with a lighted spill.

ANTON

There's the spill.

Hands it to the doctor.

DOCTOR

I must look into his eyes. (*Gently draws Sigismund, who is leaning against his knees, towards him and lights up his face from above*) None of the fixity of madness. Not a murderous eye, by God, only an immeasurable abyss. All soul and agony without end.

[195]

He hands back the spill. Anton puts it out with his foot.

SIGISMUND

Light is good. Goes in, makes the blood pure. Stars are light of that kind. There's a star in me. My soul is holy.

DOCTOR

A ray of light must have entered into him at some time and stirred up his deepest being. So the crime committed against him is twofold.

Julian, the Governor, attended by a soldier carrying a lantern, appears above on the wooden bridge, peers down.

ANTON

His Excellency has come in person. They are signalling from above. That means that the examination is ended.

DOCTOR

That is for me to decide. (*He feels Sigismund's pulse*) What do you give him to eat?

ANTON *softly*

The answer wouldn't please you, sir. Put in a word for him, sir. It isn't enough for a mangy cur.

DOCTOR

I have finished.

ANTON

Now Sigismund will be a good boy and go back in.

Sigismund twitches, kneels on the ground. Anton picks up his pike, pushes the dungeon door wide open. Sigismund remains on his knees, stretches out one hand.

[196]

The Tower

DOCTOR

covers his eyes

O man, O man!

Sigismund utters a mournful cry.

ANTON

Do you want them to come with staves and drive you back?

DOCTOR

I beg you to return to your place just one more day. I promise you that I shall do all I can. (*Sigismund rises and bows
to the Doctor, who says to himself:*) O more than dignity in
such degradation! This is a princely creature if ever there
was one on this earth.

Sigismund has gone back into the cage.

ANTON

who has locked the door from the outside

Permit me to lead the way, sir. You are expected up in the
tower without delay.

They go up.

SCENE II

A room in the tower; a larger and a smaller door.

Julian, Anton

JULIAN

Has Simon come in? Someone said he had seen him. Let
me know as soon as he appears.

[197]

Hugo von Hofmannsthal

ANTON

pointing behind him

The doctor.

JULIAN

Show him in. (*Anton opens the small door. The doctor enters, bows. Exit Anton*) I am much obliged to you, sir, for undertaking this strenuous journey.

DOCTOR

I am at Your Excellency's service.

JULIAN *after a short pause*

You have examined this person?

DOCTOR

With terror and amazement.

JULIAN

How do you see the case?

DOCTOR

As an atrocious crime.

JULIAN

I am asking for a medical opinion.

DOCTOR

The outcome will show whether, amongst other things, the doctor has not been called too late.

JULIAN

I hope not. Give us proof of your celebrated skill, sir. No expense will be spared.

[198]

The Tower

DOCTOR

Only a quack would attempt to cure the body by the body alone. This monstrous crime is one against all humanity.

JULIAN

Indeed!

DOCTOR *firmly*

This outrage has been committed against Adam, the first-born son of the supreme King.

JULIAN

May I ask for a factual diagnosis?

DOCTOR

Drugs and powders can achieve nothing here. What medicine cannot cure, says Hippocrates, iron will cure. What iron cannot cure, fire will cure.

JULIAN

How do I construe those words?

DOCTOR

Like this: that I am hinting at that keen iron by which men are mowed down like sheaves, and at that fire by which a kingdom is consumed like a barn.

JULIAN

These are strange digressions, sir. We are speaking of a single, private person who has been placed in my charge.

DOCTOR

Not so. Unless God intervenes, majesty itself is being murdered here. At the point where this life is being wrenched away from its roots there will be a vortex that will sweep us all away.

JULIAN *looking at him*

You are taking great liberties.—You are a famous person. The faculty opposes you, but that has made you all the more prominent. You are very much aware of your own importance.

DOCTOR

It is beyond the capacity of Your Excellency to conceive how little I think of myself. Much of my fame is a misunderstanding. To those who walk in the ground mist, every torch seems as tall as the portals of a church. If my body were mightier, so would my works be. How body and soul are for ever struggling for mastery, one over the other, that is my unending study. If any man could divine what power it is that effects these transitions, that man would be truly great. But he who could not only divine, but use this power, would be a mage.

JULIAN

Like anyone who has a strong will.

DOCTOR

Or a strong faith: the two are one.

JULIAN

Do you consider them equal?

DOCTOR

My knowledge proves them so.

[200]

The Tower

JULIAN

So you're a sectarian? A Schwenkfeldian?

DOCTOR

I am a Catholic Christian, like Your Lordship.

JULIAN

walks up and down, then suddenly stops in front of the Doctor

Frankly, then; who do you think the prisoner is? Speak your mind without fear. I ask you as a private person.

DOCTOR

Ask in whatever capacity you like. I have only one thing to say: here the most noble blood is being kept in the most wretched degradation.

JULIAN

In that case, sir, you are falling prey to fantasies.

DOCTOR

Only your most noble person, who has consented to be the guardian and jailer of one unknown—

JULIAN

We shall leave me out of it.—I see that you have come here with a curious preconception.

DOCTOR

No, not that. The person I have seen is of princely quality and predestined for the highest distinction. Never have I stood in an illustrious presence with a reverence more assured. It was difficult to restrain my knees from bending of their own accord.

JULIAN

You are sure of yourself, and loath to be disabused of a fantastic error.

DOCTOR

It is not the rumour that convinces me, only my own impression. That creature I confronted down there, up to his ankles in filth, is a *quinta essentia* of the highest earthly powers. One day this soul will be laid to your charge, and your shoulders are not strong enough to bear a diamond burden.

JULIAN

You are pleased to speak fantastically, without knowledge of the circumstances. I confine myself to reality, in so far as official secrets do not commit me to silence. The young male in question was the victim of a certain coincidence. I did what I could to ease his lot. But for me he would scarcely be alive.

DOCTOR

He would be alive without you as without me, and when his hour strikes he will come forth and be our master. That is the meaning of the coincidence.

A knock at the door.

JULIAN

You have retained a remarkable capacity for enthusiasm. Now I understand the power you exert over men. I wish to talk with you further: above all, about what is to be done.

The Tower

The prisoner, I admit, has been neglected. You will propose drastic improvements to me. (*Doctor bows. Anton has entered with goblets on a silver tray*) For the moment I am otherwise engaged.—Some small refreshment has been prepared for you in the adjoining room; a bite of meat for the road. Two of my men have orders to ride with you and conduct you out of the mountains to the king's highway before nightfall. (*Anton approaches at a sign with the goblets. Julian takes a goblet*) A stirrup-cup, if you please. My thanks again for sacrificing your precious time. I drink to your health.

DOCTOR *after drinking*

But only with the skin of your lips.

JULIAN

Lately it has begun to give me sleepless nights. This noble drink must contain poison as well as a—

He turns to Anton. They confer inaudibly.

DOCTOR

Al-cohol: the noblest. Appearing within our muscles at the very moment—twenty-four hours after death—when the first breath of decay sets in. Out of the unwholesome the means of healing. *Encheiresin naturae,* it is called.

ANTON

reports in an undertone

Simon, the baptized Jew, has come with a letter for Your Excellency.

JULIAN

Show him in.

ANTON

He's here already.

Admits Simon through the large door; Doctor, with a bow, has gone out through the smaller one. Simon hands Julian a letter.

JULIAN

How did you come by it?

SIMON

While returning from my business, in the agreed manner, through the agreed person. I was told to hurry, because it is important for Your Highness. I entrusted my brother-in-law with those affairs that were of importance only to me, mounted my horse, and stayed on the saddle all night so as to be of prompt service to Your Excellency the Burgrave.

Julian quickly breaks the seal, beckons to Simon to with-draw. Exit Simon.

JULIAN

reading the letter

The King's nephew killed while hunting! Fallen into a wolf-pit with his horse!—That's tremendous! That twenty-year-old prince, strong as an ox. God's providence is evident in this! (*Walks up and down, then goes on reading*) The King alone, for the first time in thirty years abandoned by his all-powerful counsellor. (*Reads*) "The Grand Almoner, your mighty enemy, has entered a monastery without so much as taking leave of the King—he has withdrawn his hand from all affairs of state for good—" (*Speaks*) I'm dreaming! It isn't possible that a little scrap of paper should contain so much! (*Goes up to the window, reads in the light*)—fallen into a wolf-pit! The Grand Almoner in a monastery—resigned all his offices—under the name of Brother Ignatius—(*He rings a handbell. Enter Simon*) This is astonishing news you've brought me. Great events have occurred. What's going on in the world? What are people talking about?

SIMON

The world, Your gracious Excellency the Burgrave, the world is one great misery. As soon as money will buy nothing—well, does money buy anything these days? What's money? Money is confidence in the true measure. Where will you find a thaler of the true weight? If any man has seen a thaler of the true weight he must have gone on a long journey.

JULIAN *to Anton*

The key!

ANTON

It is in Your Excellency's hand.

JULIAN

The other!

ANTON

It's lying there in front of you.

SIMON

When the war broke out, the soldier, the tradesman, was paid in silver thalers. When the war entered its second year, the thaler was an alloy; in the third year the silver was plated copper. But people accepted it. The King discovered that you can mint money if you engrave your face and coat of arms on pewter, on tin, on muck. The great nobles discovered it, the townspeople, the little nobles. If the King could mint money, the earls could also mint money. Who didn't mint money? Till everyone rolled in money. (*Julian's attention has turned to the letter again*) But the man who has paid out heavy coins, should he accept light ones? How can he help it? Since His Majesty (*removing cap*) the King's glorious image is engraved on it. But for tithes and taxes the new currency has been forbidden. And will the soldiers and miners accept the light coin? What happens? The miners cease to go down the mines, the bakers cease to bake; the doctor runs away from the sickbed, the student from school, the soldier from his flag. Confidence in the King is gone. Then nothing's right in the whole world. (*At a glance from Julian*) What are people talking about? They're talking about a great rope as long as from here to Cracow, and this rope, they say, is already being greased every night, and this rope will be used to hang the great nobles and the little nobles, and the rich and our own people, all mixed up together, God help us.—Great things must have happened at court, but what need to tell Your Excellency about that? When one of the greatest noblemen of the court will have come riding here tonight. He will discuss these affairs of state and policy with Your Excellency—

JULIAN *startled*

Who will have come riding here? What are you talking about?

The Tower

SIMON

His Grace the Grand Voivode of Lublin, with an entourage of at least fifty men, court pages and men-at-arms among them, the same on whom I gained some two or three hours because I risked my life and rode at full speed on my little Ruthenian horse, through the marshy tracks, to bring you the letter and announcement, because I could work out for myself that it would be important to have the news before His Lordship arrives in person, and worthless later, when he's already standing here in this room in front of Your Excellency's nose.—If I may say so to Your Lordship, Your Excellency is looking at me as though some surprising news had issued from my mouth, although Your Lordship holds in his hands the letter in which it must be set down in black and white.

JULIAN

That will do. Show him out. (*Exit Simon. Anton returns*) Did you hear that, Anton? Not a word about the visit in the letter. Can it be true, Anton?

ANTON

Simon is not usually a liar. Nor would it be a lie with much of a future. I don't think there's anything to be done. It must be so.

JULIAN

You think so? In that case—Anton! The proudest and greatest Voivode at the whole court! Sent to me! Sent by the Master himself—to me! Can you grasp what has happened there, what is about to happen? Anton! They are animating the corpse! The incredible is coming true! Me—me—do you hear me? Why do you make such a face?

[207]

ANTON

Do you think I can't imagine what is going on inside you? Why, this means no more and no less than that they're recalling you to court, thrusting upon you new guerdons—or rather burdens—offices, honours, positions—or rather impositions—sinecures, secret missions—troubles and prohibitions, everything, in short, from which you recoil as a child from bitter medicine!

JULIAN

It probably isn't true.—My God, if it were true!

ANTON

O Lord in Heaven! Now we must make our escape! How shall we get away? That's more easily said than done. What if Your Excellency pretended to be sick? I'll make your bed!

JULIAN

What nonsense is that you're talking?

ANTON

Don't I know what awaits you? And don't I know how you feel about it? To be a great personage again at court! How you get goose pimples at the mere thought of it? You can see through it all, the deceit and flattery, the baseness and the boot-licking and the backbiting, the bowing and scraping to your face, whispered slanders and insinuations, intrigues, cabals, camarillas, and what do you call them when your back is turned!—Dirty world, dirty news—pooh, pooh, pooh! What if Your Excellency were to ride out into the woods and lose his way?

JULIAN

Stop that gibberish without sense or reason, or I'll shut
your mouth. The panelled room will be prepared for His
Grace the Voivode. Put my own bed in there.

ANTON

Anything—and at once—to get rid of him again all the
sooner!

JULIAN

Take out the ermine lining of my best riding cloak and
make a foot-muff of it.

ANTON

What, the green velvet one?

JULIAN

Make a rug out of it to put in front of His Grace's bed.

ANTON

God grant that before long he will set his feet elsewhere
again!

JULIAN

That fine piece of Venetian lace, my mother's—where is it?

ANTON

Why, in the chapel, right on the altar.

JULIAN

Take it off. On His Grace the Voivode's bedside table, so
that you can stand the goblet with his posset on it.

Hugo von Hofmannsthal

ANTON

Very well. Anything you like so that we'll soon be drinking the farewell cup! So that we'll be rid of him as soon as possible! To think of accommodating that puffed-up, creeping nonentity who's coming here, in Your Excellency's own room, though its effect on Your Excellency's nature is like that of stinking-wood or tartar emetic! (*Julian struggles for composure. Anton continues, with a sidelong glance at him*) Must be a glorious feeling to know: I am sure of myself. Approach, Satan, and spread them out before me, all your splendours, like a carpet—and now pack them up again quickly, or I'll spit on them, for I've put all that behind me.

JULIAN

Hold your tongue and keep your Lent sermons till they're more seasonable!—And now send our Ruthenian Hostiniuk up to the outworks.

ANTON

You mean the trumpeter?

JULIAN

To the outworks, where you can see the whole length of the bridle path. As soon as he catches sight of horsemen, one blast! Only one, make that clear to him, as long as they are common horsemen. But if it's a princely cavalcade —if the outriders carry the yellow and red pennants of the Prince Palatine of Lublin—or even the silver lion on the amaranth field—

He has to clutch the table to steady himself in his excitement.

[210]

ANTON

Well?

JULIAN

In that case, three consecutive blasts as for the King!—Why are you gaping at me so inanely! Shall I—

ANTON

I'm reduced to silence. But there's a knock at the door. (*Goes to the door*) The Doctor has finished his meal and begs to pay his respects.—Shall he?

JULIAN

Call him in. And then get on with your business.

Enter Doctor, carrying a note. Exit Anton.

DOCTOR

stopping in front of Julian, who stands lost in thought

I find Your Excellency transformed.

JULIAN

You're an acute physiognomist.—What do you see in my face?

DOCTOR

A powerful, hopeful excitement. Far-flung projects! Momentous projects, embracing a whole realm. *Flectere si nequeo superos, Acheronta movebo!* I have never understood this line so well as in your presence. Your Excellency is of heroic mettle. (*Julian suppresses an involuntary smile*) But —I must say it in the same breath: the source itself is troubled. The deepest root has been gnawed at. Like serpents locked in mortal combat, good and evil struggle desperately in these commanding features.

JULIAN

Make my pulse more steady, that is all I need. Prescribe something that will slow down the beating of my heart. Great perturbations await me.—I need more rest at night.

DOCTOR

From somewhere powerlessness and shame rise up, towards morning, horrible from an inexhaustible chasm.—The hour between night and day it is when the Godhead, horribly separating appearance and reality, approaches us. (*Julian closes his eyes, quickly opens them again. Looking at him, the Doctor goes on*) Your pulse is unsteady, and yet—I give you my word for it—the muscle of your heart is strong. But you deny your heart. Heart and head should be one. But you have accepted the satanic separation, suppressed your noble bowels. Hence those bitterly curled lips, these hands that do not permit themselves to touch woman or child.

JULIAN *nods*

Yes, my life has been one of terrible loneliness.

DOCTOR

Terrible, but self-chosen. What you seek is more poignant gratification: dominance, unlimited power to command. (*Julian looks at him*) Your gait shows me heroic ambition, held back in the hips by an impotent, titanically divided will. This chest is of noble proportions, and yet your breathing is not free. The eyes commanding, and yet a glance that flees in ghastly confusion. The ultimate courage is lack-

ing, that triumphant yet humble self-love, that glorious virtue from which eternal youth flows into every fibre. Your
nights are spent in frantic craving, impotent scheming.
Your days in tedium, self-destruction, despair of what is
highest—the wings of your soul constricted with chains, and
strangers hold the chain and are powerful in you, over you.
Beware! Clear a space in your heart free from striving, and
there will be space enough for you in the world!

JULIAN

Your probing goes deep—too deep!

DOCTOR

To indicate the sickness where I see it is my function. The
offence against that youth, the vast crime against him, the
complicity, the connivance—all these can be read in your
face.

JULIAN

Enough of this fellow whom you persist in placing at the
centre of history!

DOCTOR

You have walled him up in the foundations, turned him
into the slave who works your treadmill for you in the dark:
and he is your master by blood!

JULIAN

Enough, sir. You speak without knowledge of the facts.
(*Goes up to the wall, opens a panel, takes out a document
with a hanging seal attached*) I have saved his life, more
than once. The greatest harshness was enjoined on me, and

no mercy. He was to disappear, to be blotted out. They mistrusted me. I had placed him with kind-hearted peasants. It was imputed to me that I had based ambitious plans on the prisoner's survival.

DOCTOR

I understand.

JULIAN

A commission was despatched to examine the case. I had lavish banquets served to these gentlemen. Then I took them to the kennel and showed them the poor wretch.

DOCTOR

Your Excellency acted like Pontius Pilate.

JULIAN

I transferred him to a dungeon fit for human habitation, with windows.—The very first night a bullet was fired through the window and grazed his neck, a second towards dawn, and it passed between his arm and his chest.—But for me, he would have been murdered.—I am anxious that you should not misjudge me. (*He holds out the document*) See for yourself, sir: the seal of the supreme authority. The personal signature of the sovereign.—I am making great concessions to you.

DOCTOR *reading*

"found guilty of plotting the assassination of His sacred Majesty—" below, the testimony of His Eminence the Keeper of the Seal.—That boy!—The document is nine years old. At that time he was a child!

The Tower

JULIAN

A demon has no age.

DOCTOR

A demon indeed! The lamb with bound feet!

JULIAN

Before he was born stars pointed at him as with bloodstained fingers. What they predicted occurred, item by item, as a horrible confirmation that he was one beyond the pale of society. He was found guilty before his lips could form a single word.

DOCTOR

raising his arms to heaven

Found guilty!

JULIAN

Of attempted regicide.—What can I do!

Locks up the document.

DOCTOR

taking a chit of paper from his belt

While eating I noted down the most indispensable improvements I would recommend. A prison fit for a man, facing the sun, clean food, the attendance of a priest.

JULIAN

Let me have it.

DOCTOR

No, it's not enough, I shall tear it up. (*Does so*) Nothing less than rebirth can heal one so nearly destroyed. Let him

[215]

be taken to his father's house, not in a year's time, not in a month's, but tomorrow night!

JULIAN

You don't know what you are saying.

DOCTOR

I can, I have the power, I am—that is the medicine you must give him; then heap the world on his shoulders, and he will bear it!

JULIAN

I need to spend a day in conversation with you, and my lips are sealed just as my hands are bound. I have already confided more to you than to anyone.

DOCTOR

Your salvation will proceed through his, or you will sink in this whirlpool: one chain controls both your fates.

JULIAN

You know the world as a philosopher, not as a man of action.

DOCTOR

Infamy—that is the one word inscribed above their actions.

JULIAN

Call it that, if you please; in that case infamy is supreme.

DOCTOR

The right of cloddish earth over the living body that has sprung from it.

[216]

JULIAN

You are right.

DOCTOR

But the decision rests with strength and free will.

JULIAN

How should it!

DOCTOR

It is the body alone that subjects you to the infernal web. But this (*he points behind him and down*) is your handiwork which will bear witness against you.

JULIAN

I am an instrument, no more.

DOCTOR

So speaks the body; but the spirit knows its guilt. (*Julian raises his arms to heaven*) This is your handiwork. Anything else to which you may have applied your hands is nothing. This alone counts.

JULIAN

I wish that you knew me better.

DOCTOR

It is written: by their works ye shall know them. For works are the fruit we bear.

JULIAN

You are making insinuations against me.

[217]

DOCTOR

Thus, and not otherwise, does your conscience speak to you between day and night. The yellow spots in the white of your eyes tell me that. (*Julian walks up and down*) You have abused your power over God's creature. You have transgressed against God Himself.

JULIAN

And what if this creature is a demon and a devil, arrogant man? A rebel against God and the world?

DOCTOR

"Nemo contra Deum, nisi Deus ipse."

JULIAN

stopping in front of him

You are exceeding the bounds of your authority, sir. What is your warrant for attributing such incommensurable worth to the creature of whom we are speaking?

DOCTOR

The question has already been answered within your heart, and was only put with your mouth for the sake of appearances. But I shall answer it from my heart and not for the sake of appearances.

JULIAN

I am eager to hear you.

DOCTOR

The first is the voice of a man. He speaks a word, and it is as though he offered his soul to us, so that we may eat it like

bread and drink it like wine. The second is the gaze of a
man. This gaze of a creature lying in chains pierces the
soul more sharply than a bugle's blare. This is neither man
nor woman, but superior to both. His heart is as patient as it
is powerful. His nature is simple. There are no foreign elements in it. He is holy and intact. He has been chosen as a
vessel whose use no man can know.

Trumpets in the distance.

JULIAN

growing pale and closing his eyes

You are accustomed to auscultation, sir, and your ear is keen.
May I ask whether I heard correctly?

DOCTOR

Three trumpet blasts at a great distance. (*Julian opens his
eyes again and draws a deep breath*) Now you've suddenly
hatched a bold and terrible idea.—Your face is flickering.
Do not betray him! Don't let this trumpeter be like the cock
that crowed thrice. Do not deliver up for the heathen's sake
him who has been placed in your charge.

JULIAN

As though by a sudden illumination I see the possibility of a
test.

DOCTOR

By which the victim might be saved?

JULIAN

I consider it possible that much authority will be conferred
on me. You are capable, sir, of concocting a powerful sleeping-draught, of reliable and—?

[219]

DOCTOR

I possess a kind of theriac which will plunge the faculties of the soul into thousandfold sleep.

JULIAN

And could send it to me by a trustworthy person?

DOCTOR

May I ask—

JULIAN

I should send a mounted messenger for it.

DOCTOR

I divine your purpose. You wish to transport the unconscious man to a different environment. To confront him with certain persons?

JULIAN

Let us say no more than is needed. At this juncture my life is at stake if I go too far.

DOCTOR

And if he fails the test?—Your eyes pronounce a ghastly verdict and the curl of your lip, which bares the canine tooth, sets the seal to it. And I am to connive in that?

JULIAN

Great fates are decided by great trials.

DOCTOR

If he fails to please—if the encounter—I shudder at the thought. What will become of him?

[220]

JULIAN

In that case—perhaps—it will be possible to prolong the same form of existence he has led hitherto.

DOCTOR

What? What are you saying?

JULIAN

Imprisonment for life, in the tower which you know, sir— at best.

DOCTOR

I will have no part in this.

JULIAN

In that case assuredly it will be you, sir, who is leaving the creature to his fate. The sleeping-draught, which before and after the test will wholly obliterate consciousness so that the journey taken can be presented to the half-demented victim as something that never occurred, as a mere figment of his brain—this is the indispensable condition.

DOCTOR *retreating a pace*

This would be to drive one of God's creatures out of his mind.

JULIAN

There is no other way. I give you half a minute to decide. Think about it.

DOCTOR *after a few seconds*

The messenger may call for the sleeping-draught tomorrow night.—The dose is strictly measured. Your Excellency must swear to me that the prisoner will receive the sleeping-draught from no other—

JULIAN

I will administer it in person. That is, if I can obtain permission for the test. That is for superiors to decide.

DOCTOR

The sleeping-draught works in a disquieting way.—The first effect on the patient is a great anxiety and restlessness. The elemental faculties of life sense that they are to be bound, and revolt with all their strength against this violation. Next—

JULIAN

has gone to the window, listens, then turns

Next?

DOCTOR

Your Excellency will see a sight such as meets the priest at the death-bed of a righteous man. Like a sky suffused with fire the spirit of this man elect will reveal itself to Your Excellency. The true glory of the human soul will be manifest, for a period not to be computed: minutes, half-minutes by the clock. This continues until the body can no longer endure the subjecting power, relieves its anguish in a scream and plunges inert into a deathlike sleep. (*Trumpets. Julian trembles, rings the handbell*) I am dismissed?

JULIAN

With the request to accept this modest fee (*hands him a purse*) and also this ring as a token.

The Tower

Draws the ring from his finger, hands it to the Doctor with a violently trembling hand.

DOCTOR

Your Excellency pays princely fees.

Bows and withdraws.

Enter Anton by the other door, a fine overcoat over his arm and shoes in his hand. He helps Julian to remove his house-gown and put on the coat.

JULIAN

How near are they?

ANTON

The Cossack outriders are trotting over the second bridge.

JULIAN

I saw a single horseman cantering up.

ANTON

Oh, yes.

Laces up the coat.

JULIAN

An outrider, a courier? What?

ANTON

I'm giving nothing away. It would only annoy you. A puffed-up fellow!

JULIAN

It's for me, then? What do they want of me?

ANTON

Only to be carrying a royal writ, that goes to the head of a stinking stable-washer like him. Why shouldn't the King write a letter or two when he wants to? What's he got hands for?

JULIAN

Addressed to me? To my person?

ANTON

putting the shoes on him

Didn't I say it would only upset you? But I didn't think it would disturb you so cruelly. (*Julian keeps silent*) How shall we wriggle out of it now? Especially as they've brought a horse for you as well! What excuse could we make?

JULIAN

A horse?

ANTON

A Russian chestnut, with a silver bridle and saddle-cloth. So that you can mount at the crack of dawn and ride to court. His Lordship the Voivode is to act as your escort and retinue, as it were, all to increase the pomp and distinction of the occasion.

JULIAN *panting*

Are my men at their posts?

ANTON

Lining the approaches.

Laces the shoes.

[224]

The Tower

JULIAN

Go on to the gate with the candelabra.

ANTON

But there are torches on the staircase. Why should we wear ourselves out for those people who are only bringing trouble into the house?

JULIAN

Light them! You will kneel down on the bottom landing. When His Highness the Voivode has passed you, run ahead of him, light his way up the stairs. I shall go to meet him, three steps from the top landing, not a pace further.

ANTON

Very well. It will be made clear to him that we haven't been waiting for him—these nineteen years.

Curtain

Act Two

Cloisters in the monastery. In the background, the porch.

On the right, the entrance to the interior.

Porter unlocks gate. Enter King Basilius and Courtiers.

Behind them a Beggar.

KING

Is this the place where Brother Ignatius receives those who come to him with petitions?

PORTER

Stand here, all of you, and wait.

YOUNG CHAMBERLAIN

Go to him, man, and deliver the message which I shall tell you.

PORTER

I am not allowed to deliver messages. That is not my business. My business is to lock and unlock.

YOUNG CHAMBERLAIN

Do you know in whose presence you are?

PORTER

Don't know. Not allowed to know. It's not my business. (*Pointing to the Beggar, going up to him*) But I know this one. Stand here, so that he'll see you. He'll be pleased that you've come again.

Beggar silently takes up his place to one side.

YOUNG CHAMBERLAIN

Here stands His Majesty of Poland, King and Sovereign of us all! Did you hear me, porter?

KING

Let him be.—This is a hard errand. I shall raise up all those cousins who have accompanied me higher than all our voivodes, palatines, and ordinants.

Courtiers bow. Young Monk enters, right; handsome, quiet, with a fixed smile. Chamberlain goes up to him, talks softly with him.

YOUNG MONK

looks at the King, then approaches him and the Courtiers, with a slight bow

It is not fitting for me to know names. I have to report to him: there is a man here in great distress—or: there is a woman with her sons, from such and such a place—or: a sick man has come to ask for your blessing.

Bows, steps to the other side.

COURTIERS

talking among themselves in low voices

That is preposterous! The arrogant, satanic Pharisee! Unheard-of insolence!

YOUNG MONK *smiling*

Not so loud!

Hugo von Hofmannsthal

KING

Is he asleep at this early hour and must not be disturbed?

YOUNG MONK

Towards morning, when the stars grow pale, only then he goes to sleep, in a wooden coffin; and when the birds begin to stir he is awake again. (*Walks up to the Beggar, who prays, his face buried in his hands*) What is it you want?

Beggar does not stir.

PORTER

He's the one without a name, who wanders from one holy place to another and in winter and summer alike spends the nights on the stone steps of the churches. He has already spoken to him once. He said to him: Are you, then, St. Hilary reincarnate, or the blessed Abbot Makarion returned to this world?

BEGGAR

uncovering his face; one of his eyes has been put out

Not worthy!

PORTER

He has just come from Our Lady on the White Mountain. Runaway soldiers, such as you see everywhere these days, were about to break into the church and steal the black statue that glitters with jewels more brightly than a lamp. He was lying on the step, they kicked him, so he cried out and the monks had time to barricade the church and keep them out. For that they beat him till they thought he was dead. And they knocked out one of his eyes. But he has forgiven them and is praying for them.

[228]

The Tower

BEGGAR

Not worthy!

Takes up his place behind the Courtiers.

PORTER

The halberd has been taken from the hand of the watchman and placed in the hand of the brigand. What will become of us now?

YOUNG MONK *smiling*

Our protecting garment has been removed, so now we are naked, as is fitting for chastisement.

KING

Tell him, tell him that a man has come, Basilius, in great distress, and that his petition is urgent.

YOUNG MONK *bowing*

He will soon be here. Be patient, sir.

Exit right.

VOICES

Singing in the distance, barely audible

"Tu reliquisti me—et extendam manum meam et interficiam te!"

KING

takes a step forward, raises his eyes

It is St. Egidius' Day: when the stag begins to rut.—A fine, clear evening, the magpies fly from their nests in pairs without fear for their young, and the fisherman is glad: soon the fish will be spawning, but they are greedy still and leap in the mist of early moonlight, before it is night. For a long time still it is half-light between river and forest, then, tall and princely, the stag steps out of the wood, parting his lips as if in laughter and bellows mightily, so that the beasts in the undergrowth huddle together with quivering flanks, in terror and desire.—We were like that stag and enjoyed majestic days before the weather turned, and the knees of lovely women loosened at the sound of our approach, and where we were pleased to enter, the silver candelabrum or the rosy taper illumined the union of Jupiter and the nymph. (*He supports himself on the Young Chamberlain*) And it seemed that no end had been set to this, for our stamina was regal.—But now, for many a year, hell has been let loose against us, and a conspiracy against our happiness crouches under our feet and above our hair, which stands on end, and we cannot lay our hands on the ringleaders. We go now here, now there, to reassert our power, and it is as though the soil had turned soft and our marble thighs sank into the void. The walls are shaken at their foundations and our path has strayed into impassable wastes.

ONE OF THE COURTIERS

an old man, goes to his side

There is a thing that buys all other things, and so it is sovereign over things: that is why your face has been imprinted upon it and your royal arms and the people love it and call it "good money": but where has the good money gone? How did it come about that it fled the country and, together with it, obedience? For where there are no wages there is no respect; and where there is no respect there is no obedience.

The Tower

ANOTHER COURTIER

That's the fault of the fat tradesmen in the towns, the pepper-bags and wool-scrapers and glue-boilers who have done well out of the war, not at ten percent but at a hundred for ten, and above all the Jews, those stinking vampires; they have sucked the marrow out of our country's bones. They have extracted the silver from our coins, and left us the red, evil-smelling copper resembling that which they wear on their heads, the Judases!

A THIRD

joining them from behind

They lie upon royal bonds as upon eiderdowns, their reeking foxholes are papered with vouchers from counts and knights —and if you will seize some ten thousand of them, having first put iron gloves on your hands, and press them till they are squeezed out, then blood and sweat will flow upon the earth and the fields will be fertile again, and gold and silver will fall from the ears of corn upon our Polish earth.

THE SECOND

Let Your Royal Majesty command us to ride with our loyal and noble vassals against the Jews and the helpmeets of Jews, who sit behind pales, against rebels, renegade monks, runaway schoolmasters, and work upon them with as many swords, pikes, and bludgeons as still remain in our possession—before it is too late.

KING

I cannot get to grips with that rabble. I ride out, and they are beggars. They come crawling to meet me out of roofless hovels and extend skinny arms towards me. The woods in which I hunt are full of beggars: they eat the bark off the trees and stuff their bellies with clods of earth. (*He gazes in front of him; his head sinks pensively to his breast*) This too was in the prophecy: it contained things that no one would have thought possible, and they are beginning to seem so! It contained horrors of which anyone would have said that their meaning could only be symbolic, and they are beginning to come literally true. Hunger is in the prophecy; epidemics are in it; darkness, lit up by blazing villages—the soldier who tears down the banner and thrusts the horse's halter into his officer's mouth; the peasant who runs away from the plough and converts his scythe into a bloody pike; the comets, the splitting earth, the packs of stray dogs, the ravens that hover all day and night over the open fields —all these are in the prophecy. (*Softly, to himself*) I burnt the parchment with my own hands behind locked doors, but just as I saw each line curl up in the embers, so now they flare up again in the pit of my heart, whether I lie or walk or stand. (*He heaves a deep sigh, oblivious of the others*) Now we come to the chief items: that the sun will go out in broad daylight over a great city, but no, before that the rebellion will receive its standard: that is, a bundle of clanking, broken chains on a bloody pole, and he before whom it is borne is my own son, my only son, begotten in lawful wedlock—and his face is like a devil's face reborn in the flames of Hell, and he will not rest until he has found me and set his foot upon my neck. I hear the sound of my head striking the earth! And he treads on my face and presses it down until I eat earth and the earth eats me—so it will come about in broad daylight and the sun will go out with horror. Thus it is prophesied, word for word, set down there item by item exactly as I have said. (*He groans, comes to his senses and looks at his retinue*) I am very sick, my loyal friends. I hope you have accompanied me to a physician who can help me.

THE OLD COURTIER

close to his ear

Sire, remember the keenness of that glance which unravelled the most intricate knots in the Council of State—

KING

I do not wish to think of his glance. Like the gryphon's, his eyes pierce to the very depths, and one's entrails cannot resist it. (*He pulls himself up, his voice changes*) We are still the King of Poland! We shall assert our will; if our wish is not granted forthwith, we shall turn our back on this den of monks and ride wherever it pleases our eagle's eye to disport itself!

The Grand Almoner is led in from the right, supported by two monks. The Young Monk already seen walks beside them, an open book in his hand; a lay brother follows carrying a folding chair. The folding chair is set down and the Grand Almoner is lowered upon it. He is an old man of ninety; his hands and face are a yellowish white, like ivory. His eyes are usually closed, but when he opens them his glance can still arouse fear and awe. He wears the habit of a simple monk. All fall silent as he enters. The singing becomes clearly audible.

A SINGLE MENACING VOICE

"Ecce ego suscitabo super Babylonem quasi ventum pestilentem. Et mittam in Babyloniam ventilatores et ventilabunt eam et demolientur terram eius."

[233]

Hugo von Hofmannsthal

GRAND ALMONER

his eyes half open

What they call daylight reigns here. A dun-coloured darkness. Read to me from Guevara. This is a flower-garden—a jelly, many-coloured and stinking.

He closes his eyes.

CHOIR

"Et demolientur terram eius! Et cadent interfecti in terra Chaldaeorum."

YOUNG MONK

reading from the book

"Depart, World, for thou art not to be trusted; in thy house the past lingers on as a mere phantom, the present crumbles under our hands like a rotten and venomous fungus, the future knocks at our door incessantly like a thief's fist at midnight, and in a hundred years thou grantest us scarcely one hour of true life."

GRAND ALMONER

Not one hour of true life. (*Opens his eyes, sees the Beggar, beckons to him with animation*) Ah, what a guest has crossed our threshold!

King, thinking he is meant, makes to step forward. Grand Almoner, without looking at him, contemptuously waves him aside, as if brushing away a fly.

COURTIERS *angered*

Ha!

King motions to them to control themselves.

[234]

The Tower

GRAND ALMONER

to the Beggar, with intense sympathy

How is it with you, my dear friend? And whence have you
come to us? And will you stay with us now, at least for a
day and a night?

BEGGAR

Take no thought for the day which you call the morrow,
for in the Lord's eyes there is none, but all lies before him
as a moment, indivisible.

GRAND ALMONER *to the monks*

Treasure his words! (*Beggar is silent*) Lead me to him, if he
will not come to me, that I may kiss him and receive his
blessing.

Tries to rise, supported by monks.

BEGGAR

Unworthy!

Runs away.

CHOIR

"Et demolientur terram eius! Et cadent interfecti in terra
Chaldaeorum."

GRAND ALMONER

Read to me from Guevara as long as it is light. In the dark
I see visions: truth.

YOUNG MONK

raising the book to read

"Depart, World, in thy palaces men serve without wages—"

[235]

Hugo von Hofmannsthal

KING

going up to the Grand Almoner

My Lord Cardinal, the King of Poland wishes you a good evening.

GRAND ALMONER

I hear an importunate voice that interrupts from some corner. Read on in Guevara.

YOUNG MONK *reading*

"Depart, World—in thy palaces men serve without wages, men caress to kill, redeem to cast down, honour to defile, borrow not to repay, punish without forgiving. In thy hall of state a stage has been erected; on it thou playest some four or five barbarous scenes that are tedious to look upon; there they bargain for power and grovel for grace; there the wise are overthrown, the unworthy lifted up, the traitor regarded with favour, the honest man pushed to the wall—"

King approaches once more.

GRAND ALMONER

with eyes closed

Who are you that thrust your way forward unbidden?

KING

It is I!

GRAND ALMONER

I hear the word I. I hear the abominable word of pride. (*Very loudly*) Read on, boy.

Young Monk raises the book to read.

The Tower

KING

imperiously striking the book

I, the King, approach my former counsellor and most grievously lament my country's distress. The widows and orphans wring their hands, the fire has gone out in the baking-ovens, but hamlets and towns are ablaze; no one can use the roads for bandits, murderers, and incendiaries, and the graveyards have already swallowed the villages.

Grand Almoner sweeps the air with his hand, as though warding off a fly.

COURTIERS

mutter, and turn as though to leave

Preposterous, disgraceful spectacle!

KING *approaching them*

Stay, my loyal subjects! Do not leave me now!

A COURTIER

enraged, but with lowered voice

Someone should lift him from his chair and press his ugly mouth to the ground!

KING

I will deprive the cities of their liberties! I will withdraw my protection from the Jews, and all shall be placed in your hands, as it was at the time of our predecessors! (*Courtiers make a genuflection, kiss his hands and the hem of his robe. Smiling, he continues*) Oh, my loyal subjects! So these hands have not wholly lost their fertilizing warmth!

GRAND ALMONER

Read on in Guevara. It wearies me to think that it is daylight still.

YOUNG MONK *reading*

"—there the honest man is pushed to the wall and the innocent man condemned. There credit is given to him who covets power, and to the righteous man no credit is given.—"

GRAND ALMONER

Insipid stuff! Like tepid water! There is—and there is—and there is! (*In a powerful voice, rising and throwing up his arms in the air*) There is nothing! There is nothing! Nothing but the inexorable judgment and the separation of the chaff from the grain.

Silence. The singing has ceased.

Grand Almoner, exhausted by the exertion, collapses into his chair, his eyes closed.

KING *to the Courtiers*

Withdraw, all of you! Look the other way. It must be. (*Approaches, kneels down before the Grand Almoner*) You must hear me!

GRAND ALMONER

after a long piercing look

I do not know you, sir!

Laughs silently.

KING

Cardinal Grand Almoner! Lord Chancellor of the Realm! Lord Keeper of the Royal Seal! The great kingdom of Poland lies at your feet.

The Tower

GRAND ALMONER

laughing still more, but silently

Oh, say it again! Ah, yes, but what is this thing—the great kingdom of Poland?

KING

Did you not wield our seal? Did you not wield our sword of justice? Now we need you.

GRAND ALMONER

Do not raise your voice in vanity. The word vanity has two meanings: First it means to brag to oneself, to be one's own spectator, to practise spiritual whoredom upon oneself.— Second, it means nothingness, to be as nothing, for nothing, lost in the womb.—Vanity is what you have done, what you have thought, what you have engendered—reduced to vanity by yourself in the womb.

KING

Father, punish me, but do not forsake me!

GRAND ALMONER

Father? That is a dreadful word. Do you really utter that word? Does not your tongue perish when it tastes the unending implications of its flavour?

KING

half rising, softly

I cast off my only son—to a place where the sun does not shine on him! This deed and all deeds I performed under your power. It was you who showed me—a sacred order established by God. This you told me to maintain, and in its service we were united.

[239]

Hugo von Hofmannsthal

GRAND ALMONER

Where was your humanity that could have united with mine? For a man begins at that point where a bestially concupiscent body is mastered and made subservient to essence. That was not for you. The seat of your will is below the navel and the seat of your impotence in the pit of your heart; under your hair there was malice, and the stench of arrogance passed through your nostrils. Thus you were a body, and with your body practised usury, and it is by your body that you will be seized. You bit into the flesh of fruit that was fragrant and soft; but now you are biting wood, for the hour has come.

KING

forcefully, though with lowered voice

Has the evil hour come? And is that why you forsook me with an embrace and delivered me up with one evasive leap, you Judas? Then may my royal blood be upon your head, and all the blood that will flow and in which they will wade up to their knees!

GRAND ALMONER *smiling*

It is written: the corrupt man loveth not the hand that chasteneth him.

KING *with a keen look*

You basilisk! If only I could tear the truth out of your entrails! For always you kept the last thing hidden from me, as the wicked stepmother from the poor orphan.

GRAND ALMONER

That truth which lies behind all appearances dwells in God.

The Tower

KING

Is it God or Satan, then, who speaks through the stars? Answer me! (*Grand Almoner looks at him*) Or do the stars lie?

GRAND ALMONER

Who are we that they should lie to us?

KING

But it was prophesied: that he would set his foot upon my neck, in broad daylight and in the sight of my people.

GRAND ALMONER

But you will wag your rump at him like a dog at its master, and will beg to kiss the butcher's knife with which he will do away with you.

KING

Do you mock me? Do you not believe in the prophecy? Answer me! How could they have seen what is not? Where is the mirror that catches what has never been anywhere?

GRAND ALMONER

Quite right! Put your trust in that which your eyes can see, and take your pleasure with adulteresses and hunting packs! —But I tell you: there is an eye in whose sight today is like yesterday, and tomorrow like today. That is why the future can be explored, and the Sibyl stands beside Solomon and the astrologer beside the prophet.

KING *to himself*

I was sterile, for all the virgins and women I had known, and it was said: at the harvest moon he shall conceive a child by his queen, and my queen became pregnant at the harvest moon. It was said: he will come like one who batters down doors, for he shall be a violent man from the beginning, and the child was born and rent his mother's body, resisting the midwife and the physician.—His will was to be there, naked from out the naked, bloody from out the bloody, deadly from out the deadly, and to fulfil the prophecy from his first cry.—

GRAND ALMONER

But he is your child, engendered in holy wedlock.

KING

Flesh of my flesh, as you say!

GRAND ALMONER

In wedlock, which is comparable to the mystery of the Church in relation to her Lord and Master.

KING

And I have never set eyes upon him, and must hide from him behind bolts and chains and pikes and staves!

GRAND ALMONER *inscrutably*

No man escapes the great ceremony, but the king and the father have been placed in the midst.

KING

again kneeling before him

Give us back our child! We cry with our hands interlocked: give us back our child!

[242]

The Tower

GRAND ALMONER

In Rome I have seen play-acting, in a great hall, but it was poor stuff. What was beyond their power to convey they mimed with distorted bodies, and dragged puffed-out trains behind them like serpents' tails. Now I see a great actor.

KING

rises, then bends towards the old man, threateningly

Advise me! Intercede for me with God! Give me back the child—or take his blood upon your head.—I must have peace in my conscience—or peace in my kingdom for the remainder of my days. One of the two! One of the two!

GRAND ALMONER

Out of two ends the tongs have been marvellously fashioned, and one works against the other!

KING *more softly*

I have given orders to fetch the man who guards him. I cannot bear the thought of the life led by that child. But my hands shall remain innocent of his blood.—I can bear it no longer! Act as my advocate before God! I pace up and down like a caged animal. I writhe in agony!

GRAND ALMONER *over his head*

Even the flaccid fruit yields a drop of oil in the tongs.

KING

Is God two-faced? Answer me! Does God tell lies?—If I have rendered the creature harmless in a tower with walls ten feet thick, so that rebellion would have no head, why,

[243]

then, did rebellion arise? Are these mere dissimulations? Is
God like the Duke of Lithuania who has taken to cheating
and gambles for whole countries with loaded dice? Prevail
upon God to speak without ambiguity, and I will act according to His will as a Christian monarch!

GRAND ALMONER

God, God! Do you defile that word with your slobbering
lips? I will teach you what God is! You come to me for help
and encouragement, and find what you do not like. Instead
of the familiar being, into which you project yourself as into
a mirror, or into the faces of those who fawn on you, you
find a countenance intact from which you recoil in horror. A
something speaks with my mouth, but as though out of yourself, as though aimed at yourself; it neither grips you nor lets
you go; instead of your going from one thing to another, to
seduce them, one thing after another comes to you; nothing
new, nothing old, done with, yet not done with, dreary,
lame, yet whirling. But you have to stand in the midst as
though tied to a stake.—You would like to slip out of your
skin, offer this and that, even murder if need be, but all in
vain. Very quietly that Hell has grown into you which is
called being forsaken by God.—Nothing remains but your
body, which no living creature now has the power to attract.
You can no longer do anything, or produce anything,
covered as you are with enfeebling sweat, perishing, yet like
stone; in naked need, yet not free. But there is something
else as well: it opens before you as though to swallow you—
you are suspended over its maw—it scorns you and leaves
you there. You cry out: it is behind your cry and compels
you and bids you listen to your cry, feel your body, measure
your body's weight, take in your body's writhings, like that
of snakes with ends that strike, to breathe in your decay, to

smell your stench: an ear behind your ear, a nose behind your nose. It despairs behind your despair, horrifies you behind your horror, and yet will not leave you to yourself, for it knows you and wishes to punish you: that is God!

He sinks back on his chair, his eyes closed.

KING

Your advice is what I want! Your advice! (*Grand Almoner opens one eye, laughs silently*) You there, my vassals. Will no one come to my aid against this Satan and traitor! (*Courtiers turn, take a few steps towards Grand Almoner, who pulls himself up and stares at them*) Forward, my faithful subjects, lay hold of him! My Lord Minister owes us counsel and treacherously seeks to withhold it now. You have heard for yourselves that he still has breath enough and to spare! If he cannot walk, carry him into our castle. He is to preside over the Council of State. I will get out of him what there is to be got, for we lack men and need resourceful minds. Up, then, and at him!

Courtiers leap forward. Monks raise their hands to ward them off. Grand Almoner lies still as a corpse.

CHANT

"Ecce ego suscitabo super Babylonem quasi ventum pestilentem."

ONE OF THE COURTIERS

nearest to Grand Almoner

It would be an exquisite pleasure to tickle his flank with this dagger until he is ready to do Your Majesty's will, but I see that he's half way to being a corpse, and that makes my flesh creep.

Hugo von Hofmannsthal

KING *turning away*

Take him away.

*Monks lift the Grand Almoner and carry him into the build-
ing. A knock outside.*

*Porter opens the gate, admits the Voivode of Lublin and
Julian, followed by Anton.*

YOUNG CHAMBERLAIN

approaching King, with a genuflection

The Voivode of Lublin.

VOIVODE

stepping forward, after a genuflection

Forgive the delay, Your Royal Highness. The roads are
barred by rebels. Zamosk is ablaze. A third of my men were
pulled off their horses. We had to creep here through the
woods. I have brought you the gentleman in command of
the lonely tower.

Julian steps forward, kneels before the King.

KING

This one? His warder? (*Steps back suspiciously. Julian remains on his knees*) We graciously recall an earlier meeting.
(*Holds out his hand to be kissed, motions to Julian to rise*)
We are ready to hear your complaints. It is a raving Samson
that we entrusted to your charge. We shall reward you ac-
cordingly.—But we are afraid of seeing in your eyes the
reflection of an unnaturally raging demon.

JULIAN

rising, but with one knee bent

He is a gentle, handsome, and well-made youth.

[246]

The Tower

KING

Full of hatred within? Saturated with venom like a sponge?

JULIAN

Ingenuous. A blank sheet of paper.

KING

Human? A man? Ah!

JULIAN

Oh, that it might please Your Majesty's inscrutable will . . .
(*King frowns, draws back*) . . . to submit the youth to
a test . . . (*King takes another step backwards*) If he were
to fail it, he would be made to vanish once more into the
eternal night of a dungeon. For the unhappy youth it would
be like a short dream in the midst of leaden sleep.

KING

The dream of one night? This is bold—too bold.

JULIAN *quickly*

Not too bold—it is through action that the world becomes
world to us. He has never acted; he knows only shadows
and images, only dreams.

KING

Too bold! Who would assume the responsibility . . .

JULIAN

I, Your Majesty, for everything! Let my life be the pledge!

KING *smiling*

A generous, manly gentleman! And a counsellor! What a
counsellor!—It may be our Ariadne's thread in the darkness

[247]

of the labyrinth, this you are holding out to us. As yet we do not know whether circumstances will permit us to grasp it. We shall consider it. You have roused our mind from its stupor. A very great boon. (*He beckons him to come quite close*)—For how many years have you held this burdensome office?

JULIAN

Twenty-two years less one month. His age.

KING

Unparalleled! Learn from him, my grandees, learn what devotion is. For twenty-two years this good gentleman has been serving us far from our sight in a remote and deserted place, with every drop of his blood. I am touched. (*He wipes his eyes with a handkerchief*) My heart is simple and susceptible to every manner of goodness, like a child's.— Twenty-two years. We were thirty-four, and our queen a princess of twenty, more lovely and regal than words can convey. Twenty-two years!

JULIAN

bends over the proffered hand, also with tears in his eyes

This moment blots them out.

Anton approaches surreptitiously from behind, pricks up his ears.

KING

This meeting has moved us deeply. It is your arms that protect our relative. (*He draws Julian to him as though to embrace him*) How could we bear the sight of his own. . . . (*His expression alters, but only for a moment*) It is our will to visit a dear grave near by. (*To Julian*) Our queen of blessed memory lies here.—The porter will accompany us, no one else. After a fervent prayer we shall return to you. (*Courtiers bow. As the King leaves, he returns to Julian once more*) The proximity of a loyal friend, what a treasure! Counsellor! Comforter! You have restored my life. (*With a friendly gesture to Julian*) You will follow us to court. We have much confidential business to discuss.

Julian bows low. King beckons to the porter and disappears back left. Courtiers go up to Julian. Anton tries to get nearer and nearer to his master unnoticed.

ONE OF THE COURTIERS

with a slight bow

We are close relations. Your Lordship's grandmother was my late grandfather's sister. I hope and trust, Your Lordship, that you have not grown unmindful of it in all those years when you were not seen at court.

Anton pricks up his ears.

JULIAN

bowing very slightly

How could I have grown unmindful of such exalted kinship? I had all the time in the world to reflect upon my family tree.

Anton smiles.

A SECOND *likewise*

May it please Your Lordship to accompany me to my house, where everyone will be at your service.

[249]

TWO OTHERS *likewise*

May it please Your Lordship to grant us your protection. We remain Your Lordship's most humble and obedient servants even unto death.

YOUNG CHAMBERLAIN

approaching Julian with a low bow

Bacio le ginocchia di Vostra Eccellenza!

King returns, stands at the back. Courtiers form a rank, motion to Julian to take up a privileged position in their midst. As he does so, Julian casts a significant glance over his shoulder at Anton, who crosses himself, as though in mortal fear.

Exeunt all.

SCENE II

In the tower. Pentagonal room with barred window. In a corner, at the back, a small iron door. A large crucifix on the wall. A wooden bench, a bucket, a wash-basin.

Sigismund sits in the background on a pile of half-burnt straw. He wears a clean suit of twill and is barefoot but un-fettered.

A sound of the door being unlocked.

ANTON *entering*

Cheer up, Sigismund, your Tony is back. And where has Tony been? There's no time to tell you now: there's work to be done. (*Takes a broom that leans by the door, sprinkles water on the floor from the bucket, and begins to sweep up.*

Sigismund watches him in silence. As he sweeps, Anton continues) There's a visitor coming to you, or several even. *(Sniffs the air)* What's this? Have you been playing with fire in the straw? Are you two years old, then, or twice ten plus two? You hiding your hands? So that's it! Incendiary! Do you want me to lock your hands up in a wooden vice? Burnt a great pile of straw, twigs, and all! God help you if a guard saw you do it!—What have you been up to, and why? *(No answer. He goes on more gently)* Did you think you were a charcoal burner? The charcoal burner's art is to keep fires down, not to fan them! Answer me! *(Sigismund shakes his head. Anton has begun to sweep again)* Did you think you were a blacksmith? Treading the bellows, striking the iron? As ambitious as that? *(Sigismund shakes his head again. Anton stops sweeping)* If you don't answer soon, Tony will get cross. Do you take pleasure in evil things? Are you a devil? A little nitwit is what you are! A young harum-scarum! Bat's claws will grow on your fingers! *(Sigismund raises his hands, mutely imploring)* Well, out with it, I want you to speak to me. To speak is to be human. If beasts could speak, wolves and bears would be our masters, and rulers of the world. By his speech you know a man.—Did you want to sleep, put out the light?—You forgot how it's done, stuck the spill into the straw, thinking that's how you put it out? Then you pulled out a wisp of your hair, it burnt like blazes and stank like the devil's cloven foot? Is that it?

SIGISMUND

My fire was great!

ANTON

O you little comedian! When you'd burnt your hair you took off your gown, threw it into the fire, cried out: Fire, put on your breeches, so that no one will see you burn!

Hugo von Hofmannsthal

SIGISMUND *quickly*

My father was in the fire.

ANTON

What did he look like, then? A fiery face, a smoky cloak, a blue, blazing belly, and glowing shoes?

SIGISMUND *looking away*

My father has no face!

ANTON

Why, you fire-happy fool, what you did was to dip your spill in the straw, and the blaze singed your hair: you dreamed all the rest!

SIGISMUND

I did not dream. The fire was there, and I was there, so I saw the fire and the fire saw me.

ANTON

You bat! (*Sprinkles holy water on him from a small leaden stoup attached to the wall under the crucifix*) Now let me clean up. Are you human? A human being would be horrified to see his room look like the devil's bedstead.

SIGISMUND *anxiously*

Anton, what is that, a human being—as I am a human being?

ANTON

pouring water into his basin

There, wash your face; it will make you think of other things. (*The door is unlocked*) There's a towel for you.

(*Throws him a coloured cotton cloth; Sigismund dries himself*) And now, look, there are visitors for you! It's a merry prison now. Soon it will be like a dovecote!

The iron door has been opened from outside. A Peasant Woman, Sigismund's foster-mother, has entered, stops near the door. Sigismund turns his face to the wall.

PEASANT WOMAN

approaching, to Anton

Is the creature sick? Has he no knowledge of himself? (*Sigismund hides his head and hands in the straw*) I haven't seen him these seven years. Is it true that he's grown claws? Glowing eyes, like an evil bird of night?

ANTON

A lie! Show your hands, Sigismund.—There he is, look at him!

SIGISMUND *composing himself*

Mother, have you come to me?

PEASANT WOMAN

going up to him

Your hair is all tangled. Where do you keep your comb? Give it to me, and let me comb it. (*Anton hands her a lead comb from a niche in the wall, and she combs Sigismund's hair*) Image of God, respect yourself. Don't you remember how the peasant girls used to peep through the fence because of your white cheeks, your raven hair? Milk and honey set before the door, I had to hide you, keep the shutters down! The order was strict.

[253]

Hugo von Hofmannsthal

SIGISMUND

Where's your husband?

PEASANT WOMAN

Your foster-father has been dead for four years. Pray with
me for his soul: Hail Mary, full of grace. You've understood
me. Pray with me. You'll never see him again.

SIGISMUND

I see him quite often. Only last night. He lies behind the
stove in a dark room. Is that Hell where they lie, on beds of
fire, where their tongues are pulled out of their mouths
with fish-hooks?—Or is this Hell already, here and now?

PEASANT WOMAN

taking her rosary

Pray with me. Pray for light.

SIGISMUND

I am willing enough, but it won't let me.—I can't keep
them separate, myself and the other thing. It grows as I
grow. Toads and wood lice, walls and towers. It's all the
same, now large, now small, so that I feel giddy. A straw
like a beam descends on my soul and crushes it. But a
tower, a mountain—why, I blow them out of my way like
dust, like this—is my soul so powerful?

PEASANT WOMAN

Your soul is a texture woven out of pure, inextinguishable
light, like the sheet that was knotted at its four ends, and
in it were all the creeping things and beasts of the earth.
Unknot it, and the beasts drop out, but the white sheet

remains pure and rises shining again to Heaven, whence it was lowered.

SIGISMUND

But where is my soul?

PEASANT WOMAN

How do you mean? What question is that?

SIGISMUND

A proper question.—Do you remember the pig that father slaughtered, and it cried so loud and I cried with it? And how after that I could eat no meat, not even if you had opened my jaws by force. When it hung on a rafter in the passage, by my bedroom door, its inside so dark, I lost myself in it.—Was that its soul which had fled from it in the last terrible scream? And did my soul enter into the dead animal in its place?

PEASANT WOMAN

You do not speak as you should. Pray with me: Our Father which art in Heaven—

SIGISMUND

Mother, take me into your charge. Your face is like an apple and yet it is earthy, your eyes are clear as water, like things eternal. Take me to where you dwell: for where are you and where am I?

PEASANT WOMAN

We are together in a physical place; and if you pray with me, we shall be in one place in spirit also.

[255]

Hugo von Hofmannsthal

SIGISMUND

You are not my mother according to the flesh; that is why you do not hear my voice calling to you!

PEASANT WOMAN

I do hear your voice.

SIGISMUND

Not the true one, which cannot be heard with these ears, but is heard from mother to child with ears that are beneath the heart. Where is my mother according to the flesh? Why does she not help me? Where is my bodily father, if he leaves me in the lurch—though it was he that made me! I stretch out my hands and cry out for him: Father!

PEASANT WOMAN

pointing at the crucifix

That is your Father and your Redeemer! Fix your eyes on him—imprint his image upon your heart; the heart is soft, the image is hard, imprint it like a seal and a brand!

SIGISMUND

gazes intently at the crucifix, imitates the posture, his arms outspread; then lowers his arms

I cannot keep them separate, me and him, and then again me and the animal that was hung from a cross-beam and drawn, full of bloody darkness inside. Mother, where is my end and where is the animal's end?

PEASANT WOMAN

Love your sufferings! Tear them out of yourself and offer them up to him under his bleeding feet!

[256]

SIGISMUND

I cannot tear my sufferings out of myself! They're all one with me! There would be nothing left inside me!

PEASANT WOMAN

You must be able to! Look at the love in his dying eyes—

SIGISMUND

shuts his eyes

Can't see it. There's red fire and darkness inside me. Let him help me!

PEASANT WOMAN

Open your eyes! Look at him! Forsaken by his Father in Heaven! Crowned with thorns, beaten with rods, spat upon by the soldiers. Make yourself see that!

SIGISMUND

The other way round! He could walk about freely, travel on a boat, take part in the marriage feast, enter the city on an ass with palm leaves, and everyone cheering around him!

PEASANT WOMAN

Look again, you pig-headed boy! That's where the boat took him! That's where the she-ass carried him! Nails through his hands! His ankles pierced! His body pricked with spears! Open your eyes! Fix them on him! Think of him day and night, or you'll go astray!

Sigismund covers his eyes with his hands. The Peasant Woman comes close to him.

SIGISMUND *cries out*

Mother, don't anger me. Ah! (*Peasant Woman steps*

[257]

Hugo von Hofmannsthal

back) No body against my body! Knife and chains, if you must, bludgeon and strap, but no body!

PEASANT WOMAN
folds her hands praying

All you fourteen holy helpers, mighty warriors and servants of God, marvellous in strength, firm in constancy of faith, ranged before the throne of God, crowned and magnified with golden crowns, O descend to succour this creature, deliver him from bared fangs, clenched fists, rather let his hands drop off, his feet go lame, his eyes go blind, his ears go deaf, and preserve his soul from violence and evil. Amen.

SIGISMUND *calm as before*

Mother, you are not my mother, but I was entrusted to you and you fed me in place of my mother—do you turn away from me and leave me? Do you know what they are going to do to me? (*The door at the back has been opened again to admit Julian. Another figure is visible in the doorway, waiting there. Peasant Woman bows, kisses Julian's cloak. Julian stops there. Sigismund flees to his lair in the straw)* Anton, look, over there. My murderer has just crossed the threshold!

JULIAN

So that's what you call calming him? Couldn't the woman do better than that? And you—

ANTON
aside to Sigismund

You mustn't abuse my master. That would be no way to behave. You should never even think such thoughts, let alone shout them out loud.

[258]

The Tower

JULIAN *coming close*

Sigismund, I have come to you. (*Beckons; Anton gives him a low stool, on which he sits down*) I have come to bring you joy, Sigismund. Listen carefully to what I am saying now: You have withstood a long and difficult trial. Do you understand my words? (*Sigismund trembles, says nothing*) You have endured much. Your life was hard and lonely. At times fear and grief deranged your mind. But the trial, so I am told, has not made you feeble-minded, but wise. (*Sigismund hides his hands in his sleeves*) Are you listening to me?

SIGISMUND

You are the supreme power over me; I tremble before you. I know that I cannot escape you. (*He hides his hands involuntarily*) I look at your hands and your mouth, so that I shall understand well what you want.

JULIAN

Power is bestowed from above. By one more exalted than I. Mark my words. But I was your rescuer. In secret I poured oil into your lamp of life; because of me alone there is light in you still. Remember that. Do I seem so strange to you, Sigismund? Did I not let you sit beside me at a wooden table a whole winter long, the great book open before you, and did I not show you the things of this world in it, picture after picture, and call them by name for you, and so set you apart from those of your kind? (*Sigismund is silent*) Did I not tell you of Moses and the tables of the law, and Noah with his ark and Gideon with his sword and David with his harp, of Rome, the great and mighty city, and of her Emperors, and of how our illustrious kings are descended from them? Did I not impart to you the notions of master

[259]

and servant, of near and far, of the heavenly and the earthly? Answer me! (*Sigismund stares at the ground*) Did I not bring you up, that is, draw you upwards, draw you out of that animal nature which keeps its eyes fixed upon the ground, because it is moulded out of clay and ashes, and wrench your face upwards to the vault of Heaven, behind which God has his dwelling?—Look up, answer me at once! Or deny it if you can! (*Sigismund nods his head*) And so I did you invaluable favours: entered into your darkness, like the moon, that silver, crescent-shaped lamp to which the heathens pray. So by rights you should pray to me, go down on your knees before me, and clasp the hem of my cloak!

SIGISMUND

Unlike the animal I have knowledge of my ignorance. I know what I do not see, know what is far from me. This makes me suffer anguish like no other creature.

JULIAN

A wonderful privilege! Thank me for it! Praise me with your last breath! I have made you the spectator of stars, the companion of angels! Made you a mighty mage, like Adam and Moses; for I have laid the miracle of speech into your mouth. (*Sigismund, softly moaning, hides in the straw*) Yes, Sigismund, such is my love for you; for that is how the mouths of men grow mighty, by infusing their spirit into the letter, invoking and commanding!—Why do you moan?

SIGISMUND

But there is one dreadful word, more powerful than all others.

The Tower

JULIAN

What word is that? What is it called? I am eager to know that magic formula.

SIGISMUND

Sigismund! (*He passes his fingers over his cheeks and down his body*) Who is that: I? Where is its end? Who first called me by that name? Father? Mother? Show them to me!

JULIAN

Your parents removed you from their presence. You were guilty in their sight.

SIGISMUND

The animal is a gruesome creature. It eats its own young, still moist from their mother's womb. My eyes have seen it. And yet it is innocent.

JULIAN

Do not pry till the curtain is rent. Rely on yourself, alone! For that I have equipped you. Creeping and mauling beasts, to which your childish mind clings, are wrought out of the earth, trees and fishes out of water, birds out of air, stars out of fire, you out of fire still more pure. Luminous spirit, before whom angels kneel! Son of fire, highest of all! First-born!

SIGISMUND

Why do you speak such great words to me? What is that you are moving to and fro in your hand, that sparkles and glows?

JULIAN

That which stag and eagle and serpent crave; that they may renew their lives by plants and stones, by potions and baths:

[261]

for the elect is twice-born. Fiery air is what I hold, elixir of the new life, sweet-scented freedom. (*Sigismund recoils from the vial in Julian's hand. Julian says softly to Anton*) Encourage him! Speak to him of a journey!

ANTON

Hurray, Sigismund, we're going to do some travelling! The world is wide, the world is beautiful! Get up from that straw!

SIGISMUND

Oh, must I go back into the dark, utterly and for ever!

JULIAN

To the light! So close to the light that all but a young eagle would be blinded. Drink this.

SIGISMUND

You taught me how they do away with prisoners by giving them a potion. Tell me first who I am; and I'll follow you like a lamb.

Julian has gone to the door and beckoned. A masked servant has entered with a goblet. Julian takes it, fills it from the vial, puts the vial away in his belt. Exit servant.

JULIAN

holding out the drink to Sigismund

You are you. What you lack is the faintest notion of what it means to live. Listen to me: it is action that shapes the world. Have you any idea of what action is? Drink and see.

SIGISMUND

falling on his knees

Tell me, who am I?

The Tower

ANTON

They'll tell you, never fear, as soon as you arrive some-where! But don't ask a lot of questions in advance, it riles people. Down the hatch, quick as lightning—you know how!

SIGISMUND *retreating*

I'm afraid. I can see by his face that I'm to die, Anton!

JULIAN

Enough of this chatter. It's time we set out on our journey.

SIGISMUND

Help me, Anton.

ANTON

kneels down beside Sigismund

Only let him live, Your Lordship! Don't kill him, whatever you do. He's so young. You could put a muzzle over his face, so that he can never speak to anyone again, but let him live, Your Lordship!

JULIAN

Must my men take hold of you and thrust your salvation upon you?

SIGISMUND

So that is how you speak to me! (*He gets up and remains deep in thought for a moment, then—*) I'll drink it. (*Takes the goblet and drains it, looking fixedly at Julian all the time; then returns the goblet to him*) And I shall drag you after me, to God's judgment seat. (*His eyes are still fixed on Julian, his expression changes*) Yes, you! I shall drag you after me.

[263]

After this cry he reels and shuts his eyes. Takes a few steps backwards and sits down on the ground.

JULIAN

looking at Sigismund

Drag me after you to the throne!

Anton blows his nose. Julian beckons to him, gives him the goblet. Sigismund sits on the ground; his head droops against the wall.

ANTON

drops the goblet, wants to run to Sigismund

I must hold his head. His dying head must not rest on hard stone.

JULIAN

holds him back

Quiet, fool. Who said anything about dying? He's only just beginning to live.

ANTON

Look at him, Your Lordship, how gentle he looks! (*Kneels beside Sigismund, strokes his feet*) Don't you see, Your Lordship, there's an aureole around his face! O the holy, transfigured martyr!

JULIAN

I see nothing except the proper effect of the elixir. The potion is worth the fee.

Sigismund opens his eyes.

ANTON

kneeling beside him

Just look at him. Now the aureole has been drawn inside

him, like fat into a doughnut!—That must be good stuff, that elixir. I wouldn't mind licking up what's left myself.

JULIAN

putting his foot on it

You dare!

SIGISMUND

standing up and moving forward

What an assembly of thoughts within me. Mighty they stand, like crowned kings.

ANTON

Listen to him! So martial all of a sudden!

SIGISMUND

with a smiling expression

Men think that what they do to one another is evil or good: but who can touch the core? That cannot be touched. —I complained that my father is concealed from me. (*He laughs softly*) But my father is with me. Men find it hard to recognize what is near to them; they can see the walls, but they cannot see who is in the room with them. In here (*folding his arms over his breast*) are the four corners of the world; more swiftly than the eagle I fly from one to the other, and yet I am all of a piece and dense as ebony: that is the mystery.

ANTON

Now the boy's talking so lovely, just like out of a book!

Hugo von Hofmannsthal

JULIAN

Silence! And call my men.

ANTON

walking towards the iron door, which is ajar

They're here!

Sigismund goes up to the two in a friendly way, but without seeming to recognize them. Two masked men have entered silently, wait near the door.

SIGISMUND

to Julian and Anton, but as though to strangers

Do not be afraid in our assembly, you who have not died. And do you see angels standing behind me? Angels and devils are one: they share the same secret thought. (*Takes another step forward*) Do you gaze at my mouth, so that I may tell you what it is? A man's mouth is like a flower, but a flower that does not wilt. From it there rises praise. Man is an endless glory, and his afflictions are not too many, but too few. That is what I have to say to you. (*His voice changes*) It is lifting me up. All fear is gone. Only my feet have turned so cold. Warm them for me, Anton.

ANTON *beside him*

So you recognize me?

SIGISMUND

Lift them into the fiery furnace in which the youths, my brothers, walk singing: Lord God, we praise thee! Face to face! Elect! (*Throws up his hands*) Father, into thy hands—

He collapses. The two masked servants step forward.

JULIAN

Have the princely robes been prepared? The shoes, the girdle, everything? Then dress him, with reverence. (*The servants lift up Sigismund. Julian, who has covered Sigismund with his cloak, speaks to Anton*) Have the carriage prepared, the escort ready to mount, the guard at attention. Give the sign from the window.

Anton pulls out his handkerchief, runs out. The servants carry Sigismund away. Julian follows. Bugle call outside.

Curtain

Act Three

The Queen's death-chamber in the Royal Palace. A tall window in the background. In wall, right, an alcove with the bed, which can be curtained off. In the foreground, left, an oratory, from which one looks down into the chapel. In the middle of the left wall, opposite the entrance door, a fireplace. From the oratory a secret door leads to a narrow passage, the beginning of which can be glimpsed in the left wing. One can stand there unobserved and look through one of the oratory windows into the main room. The room is hung with crimson, also the alcove and oratory. The shutters are closed. A sanctuary light burns in the alcove. The Steward unlocks the door from outside and enters with two servants, who open only one wing of the main entrance. The servants open the shutters of the tall window in the background: it is broad daylight outside.

STEWARD

rattling the great bunch of keys

The death-chamber of our Queen of blessed memory! Which no one has entered by this main door these twenty-one years! The reverend sisters of the Visitation, two of whom watch here in prayer from midnight till dawn, enter by this little door, which leads down to the vestry by a winding stair concealed in the column.

The Tower

From below, the sound of an organ and the singing of the nuns. The Steward goes to the alcove, sprinkles holy water on the bed from a silver basin at the entrance to the alcove, then reverently draws the curtain. Sound of approaching people outside. Then three knocks of a halberd on the stone floor. At a sign from the Steward, the servants hurry to open the entrance wide. The Court enters; attendants, mace-bearers, pages with candles. Then the bearer of the royal banner with the silver eagle, then a page carrying the King's missal and gloves on a crimson cushion. The King, girded with his scimitar, holds his Polish cap. Close behind him his Confessor. Courtiers enter by twos, preceded by Julian alone; behind the Courtiers, four Chamberlains. Last of all the Doctor with his Assistant—a young man with spectacles—and behind the latter, Anton, who carries a covered silver basin.—The King stops in the middle of the room, holds out his cap. A page leaps forward, takes the cap with a genuflection. The King takes his gloves from the cushion proffered by the kneeling page, puts on the left one, tucks the other under his belt. The attendants and mace-bearers have walked round the room and out again by the main door, also the Steward and the servants. The double door is closed. Two of the mace-bearers post themselves in front of it. The noblemen on the left, Julian at the extreme right, in front of the oratory. The Doctor and his Assistant nearest to the door. The King approaches the alcove. A Chamberlain hurries to draw back the curtain. Another hands the King the aspergillum. The King sprinkles holy water on the bed, then kneels down, remains in prayer for a moment. The Confessor kneels beside him. The King rises, goes to the centre, the Confessor a little to the side and rear of him. The singing and organ music have ceased.

Hugo von Hofmannsthal

KING *to Confessor*

I have prayed at the deathbed of my late consort for me and for him. This brief prayer has wonderfully refreshed my soul. (*Hails the Doctor*) You are resolved to retire?

DOCTOR

Your Majesty granted me this one condition: that I should be excused from appearing in person before the Prince, should it prove necessary to renew the narcotic; my assistant has been fully instructed—that is, as regards any operation that may be called for—not as regards the facts of the case. (*Lowering his voice*) To him the Prince is a patient of unsound mind, in whom Your Majesty takes an interest for remote kinship's sake. May it all—I have dipped a sponge into essences of infallible potency. Unconsciousness sets in as soon as their vapour has been inhaled, whether voluntarily or under compulsion. That servant is carrying it in a covered dish. He was well known to the prisoner and can help us if necessary.—May these preparations prove superfluous! For that I pray to God.

KING

Such has been our incessant prayer for nine days and nights.—You have grown very close to us during these last days. We regard your illustrious person henceforth as that of our private physician. (*Holds out his right hand to be kissed; the Doctor bends down to it, then goes to the door, which is opened by mace-bearer. Exit Doctor, after bowing again at the door*) Lend me the constant support of your counsel, reverend Father.—I have yielded to the persuasion of my counsellors.—I have subjected my pliant human nature to higher wisdom.

[270]

The Tower

CONFESSOR

Even holy writ—

KING

I know. And the heathen too. Even the heathen. They
were the most highly placed officials in Rome, comparable
to kings. They did not hesitate to sacrifice their own sons—

CONFESSOR

The consul had the heads of two of his sons laid at their
feet.

KING

Two of them! On one day! What arguments did he adduce?
Ready arguments are everything in such cases.

CONFESSOR

Why, that the law transgressed must be satisfied.

KING

What? The law, you say? The law? Of course—

CONFESSOR

The law and the sovereign are one.

KING

The father's power—the father is the creator—his power
directly derived—

CONFESSOR

From the power of God the Creator, the source of all life.

KING

moves one pace away from the Courtiers, drawing the Confessor with him

And what of absolution, if I should be compelled to have him taken back there—my bodily son—back to that place where the sun does not shine on him?

CONFESSOR

You are in doubt about it? When it will serve to prevent evils without end?

A noise of scraping feet behind the door.

CHAMBERLAIN

has gone to the half-open door, talks to someone outside. Then goes up to the King with a genuflection

The equerry who escorted the unknown Prince at the outset of his journey is at the door. He has ridden on ahead by a shorter route.—The Prince will ride into the palace courtyard at any moment now.

King beckons. Mace-bearer opens the door, admits the Equerry, who approaches hurriedly and kneels down. King motions him to speak.

EQUERRY

May it please Your Majesty, this unknown Prince is a poor talker, for he hardly opens his mouth, but I can swear to it, he's a born horseman.

KING

Indeed!

The Tower

EQUERRY

He went up to the horse that had been led out for him—
and at first behaved as though he had never yet put his foot
in a stirrup. I had to lay the reins in his hand—then he
made to mount and raised his right foot—the grooms burst
out laughing—the roan grew restive—then the Prince gave
us a look that was like cold iron—and then he vaulted on
without using the stirrups, and sat the roan despite its
prancing and rearing like the most princely of horsemen
under the sun.

King glances at Julian.

JULIAN

He had never mounted a horse in his life. I was always
mindful of the strict prohibition.

KING

A self-mastery unparalleled! Must I not fear the immense
power of dissimulation?

JULIAN

May I ask Your gracious Majesty to explain—

KING

He hardly deigns to cast a glance upon those whom we appointed his escort.—What kind of language are we to expect
of him when he enters our presence?

JULIAN

The most respectful; though not, to be sure, the kind that is
spoken at court.

[273]

KING

But what?

JULIAN

But such as the angels may use. His language is the gushing forth of that which wells from within—as with a tree that has been gashed and through its very wound exudes a liquid balm.

The Equerry withdraws, bending his knee.

KING

motions one of the older Courtiers to approach

Has the young nobleman whom we appointed personal attendant to the Prince—

COURTIER

Count Adam of the White Mountain—

KING

Has it been impressed upon him that, by cunning questions and every kind of agreeableness customary among young men—he is to induce the Prince to reveal his nature, to give his true feelings away?

COURTIER

The Count knows that Your Majesty will deign to listen from a concealed place to the ostensibly private conversation that he will have with the young Prince.

KING *to Julian, softly*

Has the supreme principle of authority been inculcated in this youth? The principle of unquestioning obedience?

He scrutinizes Julian sharply.

The Tower

JULIAN

meeting this scrutiny

Consider, my liege, that this youth does not know this world, any more than his place in it. The authority that he knows is one most exalted: he lifts his eyes to the stars and his soul to God.

KING

Let us hope that this will suffice. (*Very audibly*) For the world is topsy-turvy, and we are resolved to quench the raging fire—if need be, with streams of blood.

The Courtiers who are furthest to the rear, nearest to the window, peer down. The pages crowd together near the window and try to look down, with some bustling. The King notices it, looks at them.

CHAMBERLAIN

The Prince is dismounting. Count Adam has tried to hold the stirrup for him, but the Prince has anticipated him. He has turned towards the porch and is entering the palace!

KING

to Julian, controlling himself with difficulty

I do not wish to see him yet. (*Leads Julian away from the Courtiers, to the foreground*) A great moment, a terrible and decisive moment.

JULIAN

going down on his knees

At times his speech seems violent and abrupt.—May Your Majesty consider, in your wisdom and forbearance: this creature has never possessed a friend.

KING

I too have never had a friend at my side.

JULIAN *on his knees*

His young foot has never taken one step without heavy chains, worse than a dog's.

KING

Nor have I, Count Julian, ever taken one step unimpeded.

JULIAN *on his knees*

Be patient, great Prince, with one so sorely tried!

KING *looking at him*

You be his counsellor for ever, my wise Julian, and more indulgent towards him than mine towards me! (*He takes a golden chain with a jewelled image of the White Eagle from his neck and places it on Julian's, saying:*) "Sic nobis placuit."

Holds out his hand for Julian to kiss, helps him to rise. The organ music is heard again, but without the singing. Hearing a sound at the door, a Chamberlain has gone there and talked to the person outside. Then he waits, with his eyes on the King. The King motions him to approach.

CHAMBERLAIN

The Prince desires to rest in an inner room.

KING

What does he say?

[276]

The Tower

CHAMBERLAIN

Scarcely one word, and asks no questions. He uttered nothing but what I reported.

King nods his head.

CONFESSOR

He desires to enter into his father's house. *Ducunt fata volentem.*

The organ music rises to a crescendo, without growing very loud.

KING

growing aware of it

What is this? From the church? Order it to cease.

JULIAN

May it please Your Majesty to let it continue.—His soul is susceptible to sounds and—be so gracious as to remember—he has never heard any other music than the rough drum and the blaring bugle.

KING

motioning one of the Courtiers to come to him

Assemble the Court—outside. (*Mace-bearers open the door, pages run out, mace-bearers leave. Exeunt the two young Chamberlains and some of the Courtiers.—The King addresses those who remain. The Steward has entered with the keys and hands them to the oldest Courtier with a bow, then leaves again*) You that are closest to me, pledged to me by sacred vows—wait here within.—The antechamber, where the Queen's own ladies-in-waiting used to assemble before Mass—attend there. My business with the Prince is such as to brook no witness. But if I should step on the balcony with my young guest and place my arm on his shoulder paternally, in token of concord, let the trumpets sound: for then a great hour will have struck for this realm.

The Courtiers bow and leave. They are seen to pass through the secret door of the oratory into the narrow passage, left, and go off to the left, all except the Father Confessor, followed by the Doctor's Assistant, then Anton.

ANTON

as he passes, to Julian

I dreamed of dirty water and teeth that fell out—it will come to a bad end.

KING

motions to Confessor to wait, then calls Julian by flicking an eyelid

I am reminded of those words spoken by my great-uncle of blessèd memory, the Emperor Charles the Fifth, when he made over his crown and lands to his only son, Don Philip. Had it been my death, he said, that had given you possession of these lands, so precious a heritage alone would have entitled me to sufficient gratitude on your part. But now that I yield them to you of my own free will, that I hasten to die so that you may enjoy them the sooner, I require you to pay to these peoples the debt that you feel you owe to me.—

His eyes have filled with tears.

The Tower

JULIAN

kneels down and kisses his hand

May his soul be revealed to you. Does not the crystal attain
its shape under terrible pressure? Such is he, if your eye be-
holds him aright.

KING

Perhaps I too shall retire to a monastery for the remainder
of my days—may a worthy son repay to my subjects the
gratitude that he feels towards me. (*His expression changes
as he beckons to the Confessor. Julian withdraws. The King
addresses the Confessor*) But where is that narrow boundary
whose transgression would justify the most extreme severity
in the eyes of God and the world? Where, my Father?—You
do not speak. If he were to raise his hand against me?

CONFESSOR

God forbid!

KING

Some would say even then that this victim of policy was
not in command of his grievously troubled senses.

CONFESSOR

Wise judges, my liege, have come to this conclusion: that a
five-year-old child becomes punishable and can be condemned to execution by the sword, provided that it can distinguish between an apple held out before it and a copper
penny.

KING *smiling*

A five-year-old child! Most wisely thought out! A marvellous
paradigm! A prince who sits his horse like a born king and

[279]

whose pride forbids him to waste one word on a retinue of princely distinction is certainly not a five-year-old child.

CHAMBERLAIN

hurrying in the door, right, reports on his knees

They are coming.

KING

Who is with him?

CHAMBERLAIN

With an imperious gesture the Prince commanded those in attendance to remain behind. Count Adam alone has followed, as his duty obliged him to do, and is leading him up the stairs to this room.

KING

Withdraw! In there! Where the others are. You too, reverend Father. (*Exeunt Confessor and Chamberlain. To Julian*) You will stay!

The Confessor, followed by the Chamberlain, is seen to leave by the passage. Then the King and Julian go into the passage and can be seen standing there, peering into the room through the window.

The room remains empty for a moment, then the young Chamberlain, Count Adam, becomes visible at the door, which opens: he opens it from outside. Allows Sigismund to enter, enters after him, closes the door. Sigismund is dressed like a prince, but carries no weapon on his belt. He enters and looks around. Then goes to the window, looks out; then back to the middle of the room.

The Tower

COUNT ADAM

It was your wish to rest, my Lord.—This room has been assigned to you by the royal master of this palace, whose guest you are.

He draws back the curtain of the alcove and points to the bed with a respectful gesture. Sigismund goes to it, looks at the bed, the alcove, the sanctuary light; he shudders, steps back.

COUNT ADAM *with feigned composure*

True, this is not the bed on which you awoke this morning. You arrived at an unexpectedly early hour. You had fallen into a deep sleep in the coach—you were carried into the nearest room. Meanwhile this room, more worthy of you, was made ready for you.

Sigismund looks at everything; sees himself in the mirror above the fireplace; is somewhat startled, hides his hands in his sleeves. His face betrays suspicion and a tense vigilance. —Suddenly his head droops. The Chamberlain leaps to his assistance, draws up a chair that stood beside the fireplace. Sigismund thanks him with a faint smile and a small gesture, drops on to the chair.

KING

visible, together with Julian, outside the room as an onlooker

Most noble! Every gesture is princely!

He leans on Julian.

[281]

SIGISMUND

softly to himself

I'm hungry.

COUNT ADAM

I shall have some light refreshment served here, and shall offer you bread and a cup of wine on my knees—but no more than that, merely to assuage the first sharp pangs of hunger—(*Claps his hands towards the door*) Hey there, servants!—for as for the meal itself, the joy of this festive day, my august lord must have the pleasure of sharing it with you; he desires to see you sit at his right hand and, surrounding you, the great noblemen who are his servants.— He wishes to be the first to catch the look (*he kneels down*) by which you reveal that your soul is equal to a great reversal of fortune.

Sigismund looks him up and down as though to ask: who are you to be so familiar with me?

KING

My wife—the very image of her! Armed against every familiarity with a mute, impregnable *noli me tangere!* (*To Julian*) Go in now! And prepare him completely! Tell him all.

JULIAN *softly*

All? Even the ultimate secret?

KING *overcome by tears*

Even the ultimate secret. Tell him that his father is here, waiting to embrace him. And then open the door for me and leave me alone with him. Quickly now!

The Tower

*Julian enters the oratory by the secret door, thence into the
room. The organ is heard more loudly for a moment, after
that it is heard very faintly now and again. The Chamberlain notices him first, retreats bowing. At a sign from Julian
he goes to the door, and leaves after another deep bow to
Sigismund. Sigismund turns his head, sees Julian, leaps to
his feet, turns his back on Julian. He trembles violently.*

JULIAN

*going down on one knee behind Sigismund, three paces
away. He too can hardly control his excitement. Softly*

Prince Sigismund! (*Sigismund raises his hands as though in
supplication and self-defence, but without turning his face
towards Julian, with a soft, scarcely audible sound of fear*)
Yes, it is I.

Silence

This was the journey I promised you. This house is its
destination. (*Sigismund hurriedly looks around, then quickly
turns his back on Julian once more*) Have I ever lied to
you? (*Sigismund shakes his head, still without turning his
way*) Everything is here. You cannot easily gauge the meaning of that word—but as you hear it, much dawns upon
you.—You are wise: you do not want the world to be different from what it is. You take every moment as it comes,
do not want to change anything—because you have learnt
—to know. (*Sigismund gradually turns his face towards
him. Julian rises and speaks from the same distance away*)
You do not want to leave, since you have been taken here.
You ask for nothing; what you are given you take—for you
know that this is your father's house. (*Sigismund starts*)
You have told yourself that it's your father who has exerted

[283]

such power over you, and that, now that you are here, he is near you too: that is what you have told yourself, Sigismund, for your mind is clear and goes to the heart of things. You grasp that your father's ways must be inscrutable to you, as your way over beasts is inscrutable to beasts. You would not wish to live if there were nothing higher above you; that is your disposition.—You do not ask: What has happened to me? (*Sigismund shakes his head*) Nor: Why has it happened to me? (*Sigismund shakes his head*) For your heart is without vanity. You respect the power that is above you. You divine what is nobler than you, because you yourself are noble. And now, you are ready?

SIGISMUND

Where are you taking me?

JULIAN

Stay. Do not hide your hands. Show them without fear. And remember this one thing: I am your father's servant. A true man is aware of higher things with every breath he takes. (*Sigismund stands there in a state of unspeakable tension. Julian says, after looking in every direction*) Sigismund, Crown Prince of Poland, Duke of Gotland, I am commanded to announce to you the visit of your royal father.

The organ music grows louder, swelling to a great crescendo, the vox humana becomes especially prominent.

Sigismund stands there rapt. Then he searches with his eyes for the source of the music, looks up, trembles violently. Tears close his eyes.

[284]

The Tower

JULIAN

You do well to let the organ thunder the name "Father" into your soul. Father, Creator of Heaven and Earth! Face to face! On your knees!

KING

outside, but visible, kneels down and prays

Work a miracle, Lord in Heaven, and reconcile him to his fate, whose innocent tool I was. Amen.

As he rises, his face is drenched in tears. Sigismund goes down on his knees, covers his face with his hands. Julian hurries to the door, opens it, admits the King. The organ music grows softer again. The King stands in the room. Sigismund is still on his knees, his face covered, when his father stands before him. Julian goes out to the passage, disappears to the left.

KING *after a pause*

Speak, my son. Let me hear your voice. (*Sigismund on his knees, his head to the ground*) My son, we have pardoned you. You have come home to us. Our arms are open. Let us see your face! (*Sigismund trembles, shivers, turns his face to the wall; kneels there, his back turned. Presses his face against the wall*) No, it is for us to crave forgiveness. We humble ourselves before him who has suffered. We bow down. (*He bows his head a little. Sigismund trembles more violently, hides his head behind a chair*) Like St. Martin when he found the beggar, the naked one shivering with cold—we will cut off a part of our mantle. (*He grips his sword*) Look up! Shall we share our royal mantle with you? Or (*he puts the sword back in its scabbard*) will

[285]

you come to our heart in its undivided warmth? (*He opens his arms. Sigismund looks up*) Rise, my son, and approach your father unafraid. (*Sigismund rises*) Let us hear the sound of your voice, young Prince. We long for it. We have long been deprived of that sound. (*Sigismund speaks, but no sound passes his lips*) What is it you whisper to yourself? May it be a good spirit who whispers from within you! (*Sigismund cannot speak*) Utter aloud the word of fervent recognition. You cannot know the nature of your offence against us. (*Sigismund struggles in silent anguish. The King comes a step nearer*) We have need of a wise son. We desire to see a young prince capable of great things. We desire to recognize ourself in the vigour and glory of our youth. We are waiting. (*Sigismund retreats*) Do not recoil from our presence, even out of reverence. Your eye is our own! Understand this, once and for all, Crown Prince of Poland: we can do no wrong as King to our subjects, as father to son. And though we had laid your head upon the block without trial, divine authority was bestowed upon us, and there is no one who could plead against us. For we were before you were—and so you were placed in our hands by God Himself.

Sigismund indicates by signs that he is afraid of power, afraid of the King's hands.

KING

understands him

These hands? Afraid of these royal hands? They are merciful, bountiful, they heal the sick man upon whom I place them. But reverence is due to them: you are right, my clever son. A king's hand is more eloquent than the sage's tongue. Their motion is a command, and that command comprehends the whole world: for it anticipates obedience. In commanding, the King resembles his Creator.—As God commanded: let there be light, so I command you: let there be light in your head and obedience in your heart. And this will be easy for you: for move about, go here and there, and all that meets your eye comes from me! (*Sigismund anxiously touches his own body*) Everything! even your body, to which you point. We engendered you here in this very room—on that royal couch. (*Sigismund groans. The King goes up to him again*) Has your heart been overwhelmed? Does it long to cast you at our feet? Is it reverence that makes you quake?—Yes, you are receiving much in a single hour.

SIGISMUND

Whence does it come—so much power?

KING *smiling*

Only the fullness of power avails: that in which we sit here, as the only one, solitary. Such is the power of kings. All other power is lent by him, and mere semblance.

SIGISMUND *very loudly*

Whence does it come?

KING

Direct from God. From the Father, whom you know.—On the day it pleased God we entered into our right as an heir. A herald's cry bore it to every corner of the earth. The crown touched this anointed head. This mantle was laid on our shoulders. Thus there was a king again in Poland. For Basilius or Sigismund dies, but the King does not die. Do you begin to see who it is that confronts you?

SIGISMUND

Oh, yield up your secret now! Let your face arise to me
now! Reveal yourself to me! I have never kissed a human
being. Give me the kiss of peace, my father! But first raise
me up above yourself to you! Give yourself to me even as
you have taken me. Let your face arise! Show me how you
too were bound, you too were beaten when I was! Let your
wounds open! Mother, father, take me to you!

KING

Enough. I do not like this travesty. Come to your senses,
Prince of Poland. Remember from what depths it was that
I, your king, called you here and to what heights I have
raised you up. (*Sigismund stands bewildered*) Sit down here
at my feet, my son. (*He sits down on the high chair, Sigismund at his feet on the low one. The King scans his face
attentively*) You are ambitious, and long for power; I can
read that in your face.—You have been taught how to win
over hearts with fulsome words.—May such gifts profit you
after my death. (*He takes Sigismund's hand*) Put your trust
in me, and no one else. One thing is needful for kings:
that they learn to be wary of evil counsellors. These are
the vipers at our bosoms. Are you listening to me, my son?
Answer me.

SIGISMUND

I am listening, my father.

KING

You are uncommunicative, my son. You are cunning and
subtle. I see that you are equal to every kind of charge. I
will confer the foremost and greatest upon you. (*He rises,
Sigismund also*) Rid me of this scheming servant. Liberate
us from the serpent Julian, who has wound his coils around
us both.

SIGISMUND *looking at him*

What, my father?

KING

What, my father? What? Put you in chains? The heir to three kingdoms under his lash? And told me tales of your savagery, poisoned my days, undermined my nights with the horrible fiction of a raging boy with murderous eyes! With the phantom of a born rebel!—Do you see through these stratagems of a diabolic wickedness? Do you understand how these twenty years with incessant blows he has driven in the wedge between father and son?—What is this general rebellion with the threat of which he is once again assaulting my guileless heart? In whose hands but his own do the threads converge?—And to what end does he implicate your name in these stratagems? Can you guess, my son, to what end? To bind you to him by making you an accomplice in the crime committed against me—to make himself indispensable to you for ever—to debase you to the status of being your creature's creature—to make a second Basilius of you—a second Ignatius of himself!

SIGISMUND

That is the greatness of a king! Which I seemed to divine when I brandished a horse's bone over vermin!

He covers his face with his hands.

KING

I am not questioning you! Who has been inciting my subjects to rebel this past year? I am not interrogating you. I do not demand of you that you deliver up your teacher. I deliver him up to you. His fate shall be in your hands. I speak as a king to the king that was born to me. Who can oppose two kings who are at one?—Take this ring. Put it on your finger. Whosoever wears it is master. My guards obey him. My ministers are the executors of his commands. I took it from the finger of a powerful devil. You shall wear it, my son. (*He puts the ring on Sigismund's finger*) Now act for us both. Be prudent, be strong, be bold. Issue forth from this embrace of mine and be like lightning. Arrest this Julian and see whether their rebellion that has been so cunningly fanned does not collapse like a bundle of dry twigs. Let every step you take be terrible, swift, and decisive. Overpower the evil-minded before their pale-faced terror has turned to subversive defiance. Embroil one order with another, one province with another, the well-housed with the homeless, the peasant with the nobleman. The weakness and folly of men are your allies, gigantic, inexhaustible.— But let your first deed be sudden, startling, dumbfounding —though it be the execution of this Julian! The prerogatives bestowed upon you by this ring on your finger are boundless. They suspend the course of justice. They place the handle of the executioner's axe into the very hand of the henchman who accompanies you on a nocturnal outing. They make you my equal, my son, so that you may act for us both. Henceforth there is one king in Poland: but he assumes two guises. Woe to our enemies!

He opens his arms.

SIGISMUND

recoils

Who are you, Satan, who rob me of mother and father? Show your credentials!

He strikes the King in the face.

[290]

The Tower

KING

My body-guards! Here! On your knees, maniac!

SIGISMUND *seizing him*

Why do you snarl at me? Why is your face so vile?—Already once I've had to strangle an old fox with my bare hands! He smelled like you!

Thrusts him away.

KING

Down on your knees, rebellious beast! Does no one hear me? We shall chastise you! We shall not hesitate to drag you to the block in full view of the people.

SIGISMUND

Now I am here! All else is fluffy refuse such as the crows spew out!—I am here!—I will!—There is nothing woman-ish about me! My hair is short and stands on end. I show my talons. This hour has brought me forth, to your dismay.

KING

Inviolable! Majesty! To my aid!

Makes to escape to the left, Sigismund bars his way.

VOICE OF A PAGE

from the left

The King is calling.

SIGISMUND

harasses the King, tears his sword from the scabbard, brand-ishes it

I command! Over there with you! Down on the ground! I will tread on you.—Since I came here I have been King!

[291]

Why else did you call me? (*King groans under his grip*)
Go on, then, roar! Make a noise! Scream till you're dead!
Give me that mantle!

King tries to escape. Julian appears in the passage, left, rushes in and out again by the door, right. Sigismund chases the King with the brandished sword. King collapses. Sigismund tears off his mantle and puts it on his own shoulders.

PAGES

in the passage, left, cry out

Help!

Several Courtiers rush in, enter by the oratory. The passage fills up with Noblemen, Chamberlains, Pages.

ALL

crying out in confusion

Who is calling? What's happened? In there! It's forbidden. The King is dead!

Those who have entered stay on the left.

SIGISMUND

fixing them with a firm gaze

Silence! Not one look at that old carcass. Down on your knees, all of you! Kiss the ground before your new master's feet and throw that old carrion into the ditch—step forward now! The first two! (*He points at two of them with the point of the sword*) Away with that giver of heirlooms! Seize him!—That way, I will not endure the sight of that thing!

The Courtiers do not stir. Several more have made their way in behind them. The door on the right opens. Julian's head appears. He looks in all directions, then runs in.

The Tower

JULIAN

has clasped the imperial banner, throws himself on his knees before Sigismund, passing him the banner and calling out

Long live the King!

SIGISMUND

seizing the banner with his left hand

Come in, all of you! Here is your master! Prepare yourselves! I shall deal with you like a hawk in the poultry-yard. My doings shall satisfy my will. Understand me! My power shall reach as far as my will. Down on your knees with you! (*He throws the bare sword at their feet*) There! I have no need of that thing! I am master!

Some of those at the front kneel down.

COUNT ADAM

amidst the Courtiers, cries out

The King is alive! To His Majesty's aid! (*He tears the banner out of Sigismund's hands and clasps it*) There is one king only in Poland! *Vivat Basilius!*

Two Chamberlains edge along the left wall and attack Sigismund from behind. One of them puts his arms around him from behind and pulls him down. Several others now throw themselves on top of him. He is half dragged, half carried to the alcove. The older Courtiers and the Pages hurry towards the King, help him to rise. Pages bring his mantle from back, put it on the King. The Confessor supports him. Simultaneously:

A VOICE FROM THE ALCOVE

He's down!

[293]

ANOTHER VOICE

Fetch the doctor!

The Doctor's Assistant and Anton with the covered dish beside him are the last to enter by the oratory. The Assistant goes to the alcove, where signs are made to him. He looks round for Anton, who presses the covered dish to his body. Several others run to him, tear the dish away from him, carry it quickly to the alcove. The King has managed to rise.

COUNT ADAM

runs breathlessly from the alcove, throws himself on his knees before the King, hands him the ring

I have hamstrung him from behind like a stag. He is down.

ANOTHER YOUNG COURTIER *likewise*

I have pulled him down on the bed.

A THIRD *likewise*

We have held the sponge to his nostrils and now he is powerless.

Julian comes forward. He is deathly pale and as though in a trance. He walks mechanically to the wall, left, and stands where he stood before. A group of older Courtiers take up their positions to one side behind him, fix him with threatening looks and keep their daggers drawn. The King seems not to notice Julian. Julian suddenly grows aware of the situation, falls on his knees facing the King, without going closer. The King turns a little, so that he no longer faces Julian. Some of the Courtiers, touched, kiss the hem of the King's robe, others follow their example. Confessor whispers urgently to the King.

The Tower

KING

It has come to pass as it was prophesied. He set his foot upon me in the people's presence. Now he must die.

CONFESSOR *close to him*

Your thought was lofty, I know, at the decisive moment. Your body lay in the dust, at the raving maniac's mercy, but your soul arose in a trice, and you stood in the presence of God, not brought low, but magnified.

KING

As it was prophesied! But we have retained possession of our crown and can pass judgment on him. Oh! Who would have dared to hope for that!

CONFESSOR

As you lay beneath the sword of the demented slave, like one lost, in truth there was a host of angels between the descending blade and your neck, and your soul lay like a dewdrop within the chalice of a lily that sways in the morning breeze, and its thoughts, I know well, were lofty and calm. What were your feelings, my sacred monarch, at the moment when the blood curdled in our veins? What image filled your spirit with noble radiancy, as the divinely inspired artist's brush renders it on the panel, to adorn the High Altar?

KING

As I was hurled to the ground, a heavy and terrible burden thundered in my ears. As of iron bars and chains. What was that?

CONFESSOR

Most happy King! It was the chains he shall wear in the night of his dungeon. Transmitted to you by God's grace,

[295]

what thundered through you was the emblem of bloodless expiation. Lift up your white hands to God, merciful King. He has made known to you His will, to keep your hands pure of the taint of blood. Let us give thanks to our Lord God.

The door, right, opens, servants bring a drink, Chamber- lains hand it to the King on their knees.

A COURTIER

The King is drinking!

ALL

To His Majesty's health!

King hands back the empty goblet. Then he makes to go, motions the Court to follow him and leaves with firm steps by the door, right, which flies open for him. All follow hur- riedly. Those nearest to Julian spit at him. Julian remains in his place and groans softly.

ANTON

That's right—you relieve your feelings, so that the gall won't stay inside and pour into your heart—(*Julian groans*) O dear! Do you feel so bad?

JULIAN

Not me—it isn't me that you must bleed—but the horned beast, till it's bled dry and falls to the ground: the old he- goat with a crown on his head! All dominion is founded on the absurdity of submissiveness; a fool is ruled with a straw, an elephant obeys a dwarf whom he could easily crush like a gnat.

The Tower

ANTON

Your speech is obscure, but then it's come out of a face that's bluish-black. Talk on, as much as you like, only don't gape at me like a cow at a new gate!

JULIAN *lost*

What was that?

ANTON *frightened*

Of course, of course. Just as you say!

The door, right, opens and one of the Courtiers enters with firm strides, followed by Pages.

COURTIER

stopping in front of Julian

With angelic composure my Sovereign has accepted the recent events—to wit, that, as an ordeal beyond the comprehension of men, a devil, rebellion incarnate, assumed the guise of His own Majesty's flesh and blood, to the infernal mockery of our glorious dynasty. As one nameless, never to be named, he shall remain prisoned in everlasting darkness —the space in which he moves his limbs no greater than a chain permits, thirty pounds in weight, and by this his satanic body shall be welded to the central column of the vault. As for you—

ANTON

May it please Your Grace to consider that my master is not quite well and rather give me leave to run for the doctor—

COURTIER

raises his stick against Anton, then to Julian

As for you, expect an immediate sentence for high treason and satanic conspiracy: only its execution is suspended, the

[297]

sword of justice hangs by one hair over your head each day and each night. In spite of it all, your deeds, and whatever may have driven you to them in the depth of your dark mind, shall be covered with a merciful veil by the indulgence of our exalted monarch. You remain his keeper as before. (*Points at Sigismund*) To watch over his life by day and by night. In your arrogance you recklessly uttered this word in His Majesty's presence: if, you said, your ward did not pass the test, these hours spent here were to be regarded as a brief dream in the midst of heavy sleep. Now live up to those words, and drag out your life in this duty, which has been conferred upon you for an indefinite time. The place where you will end your days is that tower, isolated high up in those mountains. Whoever meets you even a musket-shot away from its walls, whether he be a freeman or serf, shall deal with you as with one twice outlawed and condemned—shall give your blood and your bones to the earth, your eyes to the birds, your tongue to the dogs. Now remove from your belt the royal seal, obtained by stealth and deception, from your neck the glorious chain that does not befit you. . . . Pages, do your work!

Pages fall upon Julian and tear off the chain and seal. Exit Courtier, preceded by the Pages carrying the insignia. Julian groans.

ANTON

Relax! Lie down on this easy chair!

Makes to fetch the chair; Julian refuses to sit down. Enter Doctor with Assistant and servants. He goes to the alcove.

JULIAN

To stand up, to leave this room unbowed—

The Tower

Bandage his feet, this light silk cloth over his face.—Creature fashioned out of a single jewel, you shall suffer no outrage.

He stands lost in thought for a moment.

ANTON

running up to the Doctor

Come this way, sir, our gracious master is the graver case.

Doctor goes there, looks at Julian, who takes one step towards him, falters.

DOCTOR

handing him a vial from his bag

Drink from this, my Lord, and it will give you the strength to walk as far as my room, supported on my arm, and there I shall bleed you. Never before has the noble youth, your ward, been in greater need of all your faculties.

Under the Assistant's supervision, the servants lift Sigismund from the bed and slowly carry him out.

JULIAN

What do you want of me? What hope remains? Are you ignorant of the judgment that has been passed on us?

DOCTOR

Every hope. For he lives and shall live. I give you my word for it. Thus, and not otherwise, since time began have saints been laid down for their awakening.

JULIAN

Walls a fathom deep all around us! The warder's fist over our heads!

The Steward and servants lock up the alcove, and have come closer.

DOCTOR

lowering his voice

Mighty is the age that seeks renewal through one elect. It will break chains like straw, blow away towers like dust.

JULIAN

What is it that binds your soul to this youth with such powerful faith? You have scarcely spoken with him.

DOCTOR *softly*

Acheronta movebo. I shall unlock the gates of hell and turn the lowest into my tools—these words have been inscribed from birth on the tablets of your soul.

JULIAN

Support me! I am seized by the fear that I shall die and leave nothing behind me.

Enter two servants, left, one of them with a torch.

DOCTOR

They are coming—we must leave this room.

ONE OF THE SERVANTS

Is the Doctor here? His Lordship the Count of the White Mountain is looking for him.

The Tower

DOCTOR *stepping forward*

Here I am.

Julian turns aside into the dark, turns his face to the wall.

COUNT ADAM

stopping in the doorway

Your most learnèd person is commanded herewith not to set
out before nightfall with the patient. Unforeseen complications have arisen.

DOCTOR

Of what kind?

COUNT ADAM

Insurmountable for the time being. Raging madness has
seized the common people. Rabble-rousers have disseminated
monstrous rumours among them. They are lying about by
their thousands in front of the churches, praying for a beggar king, a nameless boy who is to be their leader and in
chains will usher in a new kingdom, a new age. We shall
have the roads barricaded by the dragoons and musketeers.
Your convoy will be quite safe.

He nods to the Doctor and leaves, followed by the servants.

DOCTOR *aloud*

I have no fear for the outcome.

Turns to Julian.

JULIAN

Powerful man, how the pupils of your eyes shine! Stay with
me. I shall revere you as one reveres angels.

Hugo von Hofmannsthal

DOCTOR

I doubt that you will see me again. To liberate powers is
our business; as for their end, it is governed by one who is
higher than us.

They go in.

Curtain

Act Four

Subterranean vault, on the left a winding stair hewn out of the rock. Sigismund sits on his bed. Julian comes down the stairs, Anton lighting his way with a lamp; under his left arm he carries a bundle of clothes wrapped up in a cloth.

JULIAN

Wake him up, Anton.

ANTON

Sigismund! Are you asleep? His eyes are open.

SIGISMUND

looking at Julian

My guardian, it's a long time since you last came.

JULIAN

I had to go on a journey, in secret: for your sake. To come to you, one helpless creature to another, had grown insufferable. But now I return transformed. Shake off your sleep, utterly and for ever.—From now on I shall stay with you, as your servant, by day and by night.

SIGISMUND *looking at him*

You are always with me as a whispering breath, familiar to me as this dungeon itself, as its exhalation: that there is no world other than my dreams, this is what you taught me; and that there will be no awakening from my dream.

[303]

Hugo von Hofmannsthal

JULIAN

Anton, go and see whether my messenger is coming; we
have no time to waste, and must be far from here before
daybreak.

ANTON

Did you hear that, Sigismundy, dear boy? Open your ears
wide! There's unexpected news for you!

SIGISMUND

looks around, where the light falls, then at Julian

Again and again you enter into my darkness, like the magi-
cian of whom my foster-mother used to tell me when I was
a child. I dreaded him, but I am not afraid of you. Whenever you came and this rosy light flowed from your lamp on
to the walls of my tomb, I was back in the world. I lie
here, yet at the same time I soar up and away, the night
breeze wafts against my face, and beneath me I see village
and wood in the moonlight, that light in which all things
are cleansed of disgrace, and in the river, beneath the silvery
shimmer, the fishes rest and rejoice in the warm flow of the
depth, and I play in their midst, but then I return to this
place and look at your face and see it transmuted as I look
—I cannot say how—and golden and blue light flows about
your temples and your cheeks—and pregnant with messages
your eyes turn to me, but then your lips part and, oh!—ever
again from them to me there comes only that word which is
hard to take in, oh my teacher—the truth!

JULIAN

Yes. But now listen to me, my son. For you have come from
me, who moulded you, not from him who provided the lump
of clay for it nor from her who gave birth to you amidst

howls before passing on—: I fashioned you for this hour, so do not fail me now.

ANTON

A shot rang out, Your Excellency: and now another, quite close to us. What could it be?

JULIAN

Listen for someone who will knock above, and for nothing else. (*To Sigismund*) My doings, hidden from you, were a fulfilment; one plan, of immense scope, governed them all. Understand me now. Rebellion, open rebellion, claps its jaws tonight like the bear that has climbed to the stable roof. Fires are breaking out all over the forests and mountains. Cells, like this one, burst open and the dungeons yield up their living entrails, and fury hurls itself upon fury. But the ten thousand, who have horses and the swords of knights, are riding across the fields with bloodstained spurs, and their battle cry is your name. (*Sigismund raises his hands, rejecting these words*) But there is more to come. Prepare to hear still more. My projects reached out to the very end, I have tickled awake the very earth and that which dwells within the earth, that to which she gave birth, the peasant, the clod of clay, the terrifyingly strong— I have breathed life into him—have stirred up the fanged and taloned beast, from pig's snout and fox's jaws it belches out your name and with earthy hands it strangles Jack Ketch and his troop of torturers. That is what I have achieved! For where there is intelligence, there is violence—and that man is right who said that the underworld must be roused to action.—Now get up and come with me to where you will see legions of your followers, as the moon will see legions of the resurrected on the Day of Judgment, and her eye will not be great enough to contain their multitude—have yourself dressed and come out with me to see this.—You have stared long enough into blackness.

SIGISMUND

Knowing that these are dreams!—for so you taught me to recognize and to name whatever moves before my eyes. Dreams! That was what you taught me to call it.

JULIAN

Dreams! Quite so. The word was wisdom and a safeguard against yourself. Had I said that this that happened to you was reality, the world would have crashed down on top of you and buried you in the rubble. That is why I said, you are dreaming, and again, you are dreaming.

SIGISMUND

Until it struck home—then it took hold of me, and no hand shall tear that bait out of me except with my entrails.

JULIAN

Your soul had to suffer in order to raise itself up—and all else was vanity.

SIGISMUND

You taught me to grasp it. All is vanity, save only the converse between spirit and spirit.

JULIAN

But now dominion lies spread out before you, supreme power palpable—golden reality! Men on their knees, ten thousand noblemen draw their swords from their scabbards;

whoever listens to the tempest outside hears your name thundered from their lips.

SIGISMUND

But my mind soars higher, and their outcry leaves me unmoved.

JULIAN

It was I who nurtured your mind; for it was I who begot it in you. Fashioned you out of yourself, infusing the essence of myself into you.

SIGISMUND

But now I, whom you begot, am above the begetter. When I lie here in solitude my mind goes where yours cannot penetrate.

JULIAN

Is that so? Are you filled with presentiments? Vast presentiments of yourself? A glorious future?

SIGISMUND

Future and present at once. Understand wholly what you yourself implanted in me, when you carried me up on your breast under the stars that rise above the tower—for so you raised me up to preserve my soul from the rigidity of despair. Because I, powerful in my humanity, am one with the stars, so you taught me, they wait in full awareness for what I shall do. Out of my breast I give birth for them to that world for which they tremble with expectation. To them all is the present, giving birth to itself; of that anguish which befalls base men in their wavering and faltering, and of that fear of being crushed by something more powerful than they are which approaches crushingly, of these they are free.

But of their kind—so you said, my teacher—equal to them in election is the glorious heart of a dreaming man, that creates the world out of itself, enjoying its own innermost essence. Whoever lies in the dark knowing this, what more does he need? So you said to me: this earth can add nothing to that.

JULIAN

Lauded one, whom no royal mantle can raise higher! I led you out once from this tower, arrayed in princely fashion, but what was that beside the departure I have prepared for you now!

SIGISMUND

True! For now there is no danger that the delusion will prove no more than delusion.

JULIAN

You are right, my son, for this time you are secure.

SIGISMUND

That I am. Lord and King for ever in this sure tower!

He strikes his breast.

JULIAN

What is in question now is no sharing-out of an inheritance.

SIGISMUND

No, the whole of it remains with me for ever and ever, and no one shall wrest it from me.

JULIAN

Now we are both the prophets and the executors of prophecy!

SIGISMUND

That we are, indeed. How fortunate that we have learnt by experience!

JULIAN

To do deeds—that is our prerogative now. Only the commander acts—as for the others, he only uses them according to his whims, like tools.

SIGISMUND

Ah, yes, we experienced that when they threw us on the cart, like a calf with bound feet.

JULIAN

My dominion! My realm! Clasp these two words to your heart! Put on your robes! (*He takes a scarlet tunic out of the bundle*) These brave noblemen will take you into their midst; fifty thousand peasants have risen up and turned their scythes into pikes.

ANTON

goes up to Julian

The uproar and shouting are coming closer. Now they are ringing the alarm in our chapel and there's a smell of burning. What could it be?

JULIAN

The living proof of my actions. The nobles have entered. They are ringing the bells. They are lighting immense bonfires. They are firing salvoes to victory! Quickly now. The tunic, the belt!

Hugo von Hofmannsthal

ANTON

runs to the stairs again, listens

I hear something—a kind of burbling. Someone is groaning.
Someone is coming down the stairs.

Goes up the stairs.

JULIAN

unpacks all the clothes and hands them to Sigismund

Quick! Quick! It was in your name I called the nobility to
arms! And dragged the naked out of their burrows into the
light. Take them! Put them on! We are riding out.

SIGISMUND

I understand your will, but it is not my will. I shall stand
fast, and you will not move me from this place. Your
schemes are no business of mine.

ANTON

from the stairs, softly, to Julian

Come at once. The mounted messenger has returned. He is
saying something, but I can't understand.

JULIAN

to Sigismund

Do not fail me now, for our hour has come.

SIGISMUND

What do you know of me? Do you have access to me? When
I am inaccessible, as though guarded by a thousand men.

JULIAN

Put on this tunic. Gird on the belt!

[310]

The Tower

SIGISMUND

I will not.

JULIAN

You will not?

SIGISMUND

resists him, retreats

You laid me into the straw like an apple, and I ripened, and now I know my place. But it is not where you would have me go.

JULIAN

Come to me! I shall tear you out of your tomb!

SIGISMUND

Once, but never again! Now, now I vanish from you, as the treasure does from its seeker when the cock crows!

JULIAN

I shall carry you out of this dungeon on my shoulders!

SIGISMUND

No, that will never be. I belong to myself, and nothing can touch me.

ANTON

drags the Messenger down the steps, followed by a Boy, both black with mud as though they have been rescued from a bog

Well, the messenger has arrived. But our people shot at him. That's what has robbed him of speech.

[311]

JULIAN

What's your message? What do the noble gentlemen report?

MESSENGER

folds his hands, and mumbles

Quibus, quabus, Sanctus Hacabus! Now and at the hour of our death, amen.

ANTON

The boy says that it was by mumbling such tags that they made their way through the rebellious peasantry.

MESSENGER

Sanctus Hacabus! surgite mortis!

ANTON

They're dripping with slime, had to hide three days and three nights in the bogs. That's what drove him out of his mind.

MESSENGER

Pater nisters! gratibus plenis! As we forgive them that trespass against us, and deliver us from evil, amen.

JULIAN

Out with the message! They must have sewn it into his clothes. Look for it!

SIGISMUND

Ignore these men! And listen to my refusal; again and again: I refuse.

Messenger, trembling, cannot utter one word.

[312]

The Tower

BOY

The peasants have come out of their burrows. They carry flails, pitchforks, scythes—

JULIAN

Called up by me! What are you trembling for, fool? Your message from the nobles! Where have the squadrons halted? Answer me!

He shakes the Messenger.

BOY

The nobles are all in the forest, and they won't come out. Their feet are up in the air—so high! (*Laughs confusedly*) The peasants attacked them and hanged them on the trees.

JULIAN

Our horses, quick! Take hold of that one. Out of here! Through the ford to the forest.

BOY *stepping forward*

All the roads are barred. Olivier, that rebel soldier, who had ridden out—

JULIAN

Ridden out by my order. A rebel in my pay. With despatches and letters from me.

BOY *laughs*

To turn back is to travel too. Twenty of them turned back at midnight of their own free will. He and his men are killing off our lot with pikes. You can hear their screams right down to this cellar. Now they're ringing the alarm to col-

[313]

lect more men—brigands, vagabonds, thieves, and murderers!

JULIAN

Where are the horses? (*Shaking him*) Where are our horses?

BOY

Don't know, don't know. All's topsy-turvy. Everyone against everyone.

Messenger slinks away up the stairs.

JULIAN

I raised Hell, and now Hell is at large. So I must face it squarely. Anton, wait here. If I call, you'll bring him up after me, or else (*he draws a pistol*) it's the end of you.

Makes to go up.

BOY *clinging to him*

Don't go up there! They're shooting anyone connected with the nobles, even boys, horses, cats and dogs.

Julian shakes him off, goes up; the Boy creeps after him.

ANTON

prancing with fear

I'm feeling all queer, very queer indeed. Get up, Sigismundy, boy; we need to have our wits about us now.

SIGISMUND *quite calm*

What's the matter with you, Anton? Anton, bring me some fresh water, I'm thirsty.

The Tower

ANTON

trying to put on Sigismund's riding-boots for him

Put them on, that's a good boy, just put them on! We're going for a ride. Clippity-clop, over hills and dales. We must be off. (*Sigismund reflects briefly, then sits down on his bed*) Quickly now, come out of your dream! Do you know me? Sigismund! Prince! Prince!

SIGISMUND

What do you want, Anton? Of course I know you.

ANTON

It's a matter of life and death, my Lord Prince. We must get out of here and away!

SIGISMUND

I'm quite happy here. I have water and bread. It's neither too warm nor too cold. Thank you, Anton. Leave, if you wish. Take the lantern. I need no light.

ANTON

This is no day like any other. Something is going on. Something is up.

BOY *from the stairs*

Your master calls out for you. They're shooting at your master.

ANTON

Who?

BOY

The whole lot of them, the rebels. He wants to make a speech. But they won't let him. They're jabbing at him with their pikes.

Disappears again.

ANTON

Shall I run away without him? Holy Mother of God! Sigismund, listen to me! Trumpets of Heaven! Out of here! Hide! It's our lives they're after!

SIGISMUND

You're wrong to speak like that, Anton. Something new is about to happen to me. I sense it like a foretaste, but not in my mouth—lower down, in my breast.

ANTON

God's wrath! We've done you out of your wits! You really were in the palace a year ago! Your father exists! It was not a dream, but the truth. The high palace stands there as real and solid as this tower. Now you're to go there again, to be King inside it!

SIGISMUND

Oh, I know well that that's your scheme. But I will not do it. I shall stay here. Till it's my will to leave.

ANTON

Now I'm sweating blood!—Now there's only one way out. (*He draws a knife, goes for Sigismund, pretending to threaten him*) Now do what I tell you, pig-headed boy, or else—

[316]

SIGISMUND

looks at him calmly

I will not, for I have nothing to do with those who have swords and knives in their hands. But when I say: I will! you'll see in what glory I shall leave this tower.

ANTON

seeing the glow of fire above

Jesus, Mary, and Joseph!

SIGISMUND *laughing*

Why is my Anton biting his fist?

ANTON

Poor boy, don't you see that red glow? Murder and fire, that means. (*Uproar outside*) Hide in the corner! Now it's coming—the hand at our throats, the knee on our chests! And this has to happen to me, of all people, a gentleman's servant from Vienna, with a spotless record! What on earth ever made me come to these accursed parts? I can't remember a thing.

He runs to the back.

SIGISMUND

glancing round, smiling

Beauty has come to this place; the sun is rising out of the dark, the spiders on the walls are glad as when spring comes overnight and the pike breaks the hard ice with his tail. Listen! People are coming, many of them, like the rushing of a stream!

[317]

VOICES

Sigismund! Sigismund! Sigismund!

ANTON

Now all the devils of Hell are roaring out your name. Hide in that corner!

SIGISMUND

Come here, point at me and cry out: there he stands!

The torchlight grows brighter.

OLIVIER

with rebels, entering from right. Still in the background

Halt! The first to catch sight of the creature will report to me. Call him again by his name.

MANY VOICES

Sigismund!

ANTON *in a low voice*

Careful! That one has hay on his horns; he butts.

Sigismund goes to them.

OLIVIER *recoiling*

Level pikes! Axes at the ready! Is this the creature?

ANTON *aloud*

Let him be! Spare him! He isn't all there; he isn't right in the head.

OLIVIER

Take him into the light. (*Two men with torches go to Sigis-*

mund) Does he open his jaws like a wolf? Where's my charm against wounds? (*Feels for it under his doublet*) Make him understand that he is to regard himself as our ally. We will take two paces towards him, so that he will recognize us and honour us as his rescuers.

He drinks from a pewter brandy-jug which one of his men passes to him. Anton salutes him.

JERONIM *coming forward*

Look at him, naked brethren, first-born sons of Adam. This is the one of whom I spoke to you. Look: the royal Prince who dwells underground, forged with chains to the dripping vault!

More and more armed peasants enter at the back.

ANTON

As you say, sir. He has gone out of his mind with brooding over what his father did to him. It came over him as the staggers does over a horse, if you know what I'm talking about, sir. Not even his food gives him pleasure.

OLIVIER

Keep your mouth shut, lackey. (*To Sigismund*) Come forward, creature. Are you in command of your senses and willing to drink your father's blood out of a silver tankard? (*Sigismund does not answer*) Have they castrated your skull of its brains? Are you capable of recognizing an object held out to you? Draw a weapon against him!

They do so.

[319]

SIGISMUND

A sweet fragrance rises from the steel, as of bean-blossom in the air; that comes from the blood into which you have plunged them.

OLIVIER

So you recognize objects set before your eyes?

SIGISMUND

The tools of the field have been estranged from their function and must now purify the world. That I recognize. And I recognize, too, that you are the right man for a bloody task, just as you are. For you have a bull neck and the teeth of a dog.

OLIVIER

Ah, so my face appeals to you? Good! For I need you and lay my hand upon you. Do you catch my meaning?

SIGISMUND *retreating*

All things enter into me and pass out of me again, and I remain in my own service. I am my own father and son, and live in concord with myself.

The glow grows more intense.

OLIVIER

What are you gaping at? *Bougre, larron, écoute.*

SIGISMUND *raising his hand*

Listen! Now the jackdaws are fluttering round the tower and cawing over their nests, where their young are burning

—but the traveller on the high pass a ten-hour climb from here sees only a tiny, glimmering spark. Such is the humility of all things.

OLIVIER

Open your ears wide! Do you know whose flesh and blood you are?

SIGISMUND *looking at him*

The knowledge was forced upon me.

OLIVIER

Then you know enough. Open your mouth as wide as it will go and cry: Death, death, death! Murder! Justice, justice! Death and damnation upon my murderer!

SIGISMUND

Once I cried out like one oppressed by a nightmare, but my crying brought me no help.—You smell of burnt things, butchered things and of earth! Your sharp odour makes me thirsty!

Anton passes him the jug; he takes a long draught.

OLIVIER

Now fetch that Judas, that maleficent boot-licking courtier, and though he were bleeding from ninety-seven wounds, fetch His Excellency here, alive or dead. For it was for that we rose up, to raise the wheel of justice at all times from the morass that clogs it.

Julian is brought in; his wounds have been roughly bandaged and he keeps his eyes closed; the men set him down on the bed.

[321]

Hugo von Hofmannsthal

JERONIM *with a bow*

Royal Prince Sigismund, do you recognize this man to be
your belialical Judas, your prison warder, who kept you, our
King, chained up more cruelly than a dog?

SIGISMUND

Cruel or not cruel—who can tell?

OLIVIER

What, you goose peering into a new barrel! Raise the
alarm, cry blue murder, bear witness against him!—And as
for you. You give us the answers we need—do you hear?
—I want a trial! Now it's I who dispense summary justice.
Do you get me? (*Julian is silent. Olivier to him*) Did you
draw up the ten prohibitions, or did you not? Did you wash
your hands in a silver basin, or did you not? Eh? So you
won't open your big mouth? Deny it if you can. Fetch me
the wash-basin, so that I can try its metal on his skull! Be
quick about it!

Julian opens his eyes.

ANTON

At once—at your service!

Makes to go, someone trips him up, others hold him back.

SIGISMUND

He did not keep me as he was commanded, but he kept
me as he had planned that he should: for the fulfilment of
his spiritual task. For he was master over it all. And as
long as he lived he did not regard his work as wasted, and
rightly so.

[322]

The Tower

OLIVIER *after drinking*

Silence now till the wash-basin's here. Attention now, I am inspired to issue an order! Regimental clerk, take this down: to the entire army. We set down, order, and command as follows: the peasants everywhere are to be called away from their ploughs, since a new age and a new order are about to begin; henceforth the soil will not be broken up, but the flesh and bones of men will be broken up. All men between the ages of fifteen and seventy are commanded to rally to the flag of blood; those who refuse to leave their ploughs will have their hands chopped off. Nobles and merchants to be harnessed to the ploughs; salt to be sown in the furrows. Under the new order we shall feed on the fat of the land and remain on the move incessantly, so no fields are needed any more. Next: all victuals to be brought here, at the army's service; such as honeycombs and cheeses, gingerbread and brandy, the calves and the pigs, the lambs, the goats, fowls and geese, salt and lard, sturgeon and pike—delivered this day under the flag of blood. (*Signs the order*) Now on with the trial! Squeeze out of him whatever is required according to the letter of the law, so that we can strap him to the wheel.

SIGISMUND

I testify that this man taught me the truth, the sole truth by virtue of which my soul has life, for my soul needs truth like the flame that goes out when deprived of air.

OLIVIER

And what sort of truth might that be, you arch-creature, epileptic boy?

[323]

Hugo von Hofmannsthal

SIGISMUND

There is nothing of which we know the nature, and there is nothing of which we could say that its nature is other than that of our dreams. But don't misunderstand me. What I fear is the error that this should make me different from you or him or one of those men. I am as you are. But I know, and you are without knowledge.

JERONIM

Listen to him! He runs about in broad daylight and thinks he's dreaming! Like a man whose head has been put in a sack, and the sack tied fast round his neck. He testifies that they've driven him out of his wits. That's why they will have to die at your hands.

Some sigh deeply.

SIGISMUND

I tell you there is no thing whose nature is other than that of our dreams—the water that flows from this earthenware source—(*he points at his jug*) what could be more real? But even to this the other has been admixed—and the stars swim like fishes in the kindred substance. That is what they taught me.

JERONIM

Listen, all of you, people! Oh! Oh!

SIGISMUND

They led me blindfold by night into my father's palace, and led me back here again, and said: You have been nowhere but where you are. This and the other are one and the same place.

[324]

The Tower

JERONIM

Hear him, you honest country folk: with such words from their accursed and satanic tongues these drove your poor king out of his senses—that hangman there and his lackey. For that they shall hang seven feet higher and the ravens shall hack the tongues out of their wicked mouths.

ANTON

close to Sigismund

Now it's getting hot for me. Now show them you weren't born yesterday.

SIGISMUND

Be quiet.—They said to me, you were dreaming, and again and again, you were dreaming. And that way, as when someone puts an iron finger under the hinge of a door, they lifted a door from before my eyes and I stepped behind a wall from where I can hear everything you say, but you cannot reach me, and I am safe from your hands.

OLIVIER

Translate that gibberish for them! Cry it out, our clever friend, so that they'll all understand what a damnable and maleficent outrage they committed against this creature.

JERONIM

in a shrill voice

He says that they left him to freeze and starve and, when they were full of drink, they beat him as one beats a stubborn ass.

Groans from the people.

[325]

OLIVIER

We shall hang them, my honourable friends, but before that I must have a confession and hear that one there whine for his life at our feet.

ANTON

This is doomsday for me! Tell them that I'm a foreigner here, a gentleman's servant from Vienna, and that I've nothing to do with all this.

OLIVIER

Speak, prosecutor! Proceed! Conjure forth ingenuities from your belly! Make him speak. Make him neigh with terror! He must plead guilty before we hang him. (*Young gipsy girl enters timidly with the silver basin and a fine towel. They show her the way. Olivier continues to Julian*) I give you as much time to justify yourself as I need to wash my hands. Then I shall give them the suds and they will use them to grease the rope for you.

JULIAN *looking round*

You rat-face! You pig-brow with evil, upward-squinting eyes! You snout of a greedy cur! . . . Clods that you are, walk-ing clods! By the light of this torch that shows me your abominable faces . . . I shall laugh at you without being tickled by you. (*He rises*) Put away your pikes! Ah, you hydra-headed nothing, you shrink back from the dead man I am as a flock of sheep from the dog, and yet, you pile of earth, you crush him who with unspeakable effort stirred you up to pour you by night over his enemy's roof. For I have made a Something out of a Nothing—but my will to do so was the only choice I could rightly make. You cannot undo one jot of that rightness, vile scullion.—Even

[326]

now you serve me, for my sadness at the sight of you grows too great for horror to assail me. Stand fast under my gaze, you nothing, you garbage that I swept up. As long as I tame you with my eyes I shall not lose confidence in myself.

OLIVIER

Can these arrogant jaws spew out nothing but stinking abuse? In that case I shall pour this swill from your own basin over your head, as true as summary justice is now mine to dispense!

JULIAN

looking at him fixedly

You will not dare!

SIGISMUND

My teacher, why do you speak to him? To say those things that would be worth saying our tongues are too thick.

JULIAN *turning to him*

Are you here too, my creature?—What you see of him from top to toe is my handiwork, and piteous.—Who is it that forced this task on me, a task too great for my strength?

SIGISMUND

Your eyes are walled up with that which is not, else you would see that your task was successful and has not been undone.

JULIAN

Turn away from me, you lump of clay in whose mouth I placed the wrong word. I cannot bear to look at you.

[327]

Hugo von Hofmannsthal

SIGISMUND

It was the right word that you placed in my mouth, my teacher, the word of comfort in the desolation of this life, and I give it back to you at this hour.

JULIAN

sitting down again on his bed

I cannot bear to look at you. (*Averts his eyes from him*) I have seen many die in their beds and, in their craven fear, struggle to clutch and hold every possession. But now I thrust everything away and remain alone.

He closes his eyes.

SIGISMUND

I smile on you in your solitude.—Your prayer is not without power, though you clench your fists instead of folding your hands.

JULIAN

opening his eyes and shutting them again

I raised the lowest up to the top, but it was in vain.

SIGISMUND

You torment yourself so that a vein will open within you from which you may drink. But in me it flows unceasingly, and that is your doing.

JULIAN

opens his eyes once more, as though to speak, then closes them and falls back with the one word

Nothing!

[328]

The Tower

OLIVIER *coming closer*

Has he escaped me? For what use is it to me to pour this swill over a dead man's skull? The towel—here—to dry my hands. (*He does so*) . . . and hang that sow of a lackey on one of those window-latches.

He takes a swig of brandy. Men take hold of Anton.

SIGISMUND

going to Julian's bed

Very soon you will feel as I do. There is something better than oblivion: a marvellous illumination in solitude.—He's dead.—And you (*to Anton*) stay with me and have no fear. Even a dog wants to be stroked at times, how much more a man. So let him be.

OLIVIER

Why, you maleficent carrion bird with devil's wings. Did I get hold of you so that you would offer me insubordination under my own eyes?

SIGISMUND

looking at him calmly

You did not get hold of me. For I belong to myself. You cannot even see me, for you do not know how to see.

OLIVIER

Are you opening your big mouth against my illustrious person?—Then I'll have you carted to the midden, sewn up in a dog's skin.—But first I have to issue other more pressing instructions as to you. Attention! (*Roll of drums*) For I need that fantastical mug of his for the womenfolk, so

[329]

that they won't cool off but go for the cuirassiers' horses with knives.

SIGISMUND

There's no need for women, for you will sweep all before you like the east wind, gather up prisoners like hay, and all towers and fortifications will be child's play to you.

OLIVIER

Odsbodikins! Are you the prophet Daniel? In that case you shall always ride in an oxcart in front of the middle ranks, crying: Blood upon those who sold me! Keep the blood-flag flying!

SIGISMUND

Make no mistake. For with me no one thing is in safer keeping than any other.

OLIVIER

In return for that I shall keep him supplied with fodder, and he will have so much to eat on his cart that his belly bursts.—Yet should he wag his tongue like a fool against our cause, drums and trumpets will interrupt his speech, so that he won't be able to hear his own words issuing forth from his trap, . . . that will be your charge, Aron the Tartar, and to this end you shall be the staff-bearer and governor of our baggage-train.

JERONIM

Why, you made me that, Olivier, and swore to it over the brandy-cup.

The Tower

OLIVIER

You are to address me as Honourable Generalissimo and to keep your big mouth shut when I am giving orders. Attention! Who is in command here? (*A roll of drums*) Nevertheless I shall condescend to draw up a permanent list of ranks forthwith, while we partake of a banquet, and this shall be observed by all and in every particular; and on you, my lieutenant-generals, I shall bestow the names of devils, as an old witch once whispered them to me—and under these names you shall command roving bands of incendiaries. Where these appear, the nobles and townspeople shall wet themselves with terror, knowing that their last hour has struck.—Why do you gape at me like that, creature? Don't you believe me? I say that those who live in castles, palaces, and cities shall throw litters out of fear! Their bellies shall be evacuated of their last contents when they stand on their parapets and see us riding in!

JERONIM

And what, honourable Commandant, when one by one we have occupied every house in the streets and opened the doors with one of these whetted keys (*he points to an axe*) what, then, shall be done with the masters of those houses?

OLIVIER

Masters! Masters! May the devil take you and stifle that word in your throat! Those masters shall travel head first into the privies.

JERONIM

And the lords of manors?

OLIVIER

They shall be buried in that soil from which they drew rents.

ANOTHER

And the lords of rivers and ponds? Who demanded a toll and refused fishing-rights to the poor?

OLIVIER

Drowned in the waters they owned!

JERONIM

And the lords of game reserves?

OLIVIER

Sewn up in wolfskins and their bloodhounds set at them!

A THIRD

And the priests and monks, schoolteachers, clerks, tax collectors, lackeys?

OLIVIER

They shall be blotted out like flies! This breed shall perish utterly. After us the vultures and wolves shall come, and they shall not say that we left our work unfinished.—But now I have been sufficiently incommoded and importuned, and everyone of you knows his instructions, and my throat is dry. Now call the staff butchers and the cook, and I shall detail to them that joint of meat which I will have them roast on the spit, and you there, I want to see none but you, gipsy, pour out the brandy—and when I propose some martial toast, I want to have it proclaimed from the balcony with trumpets, and in the courtyard with cannon fire, and this is to proceed until broad daylight.

The Tower

SIGISMUND

Excellent. But one day, too, you will have to drink up the dregs, and this my drink (*pointing at the earthenware water jug*) remains pleasant at all times.

OLIVIER

Keep an eye on this masilisk, and put a muzzle on him if he lets his tongue wag too much.—I make you two men responsible for seeing that this creature is useful to us, not harmful. He is not to move an inch without my permission. . . . The general march-off, to mark my departure! Beat that drum-skin till the sticks fly off together with your fingers! (*Drummer beats the general march-off*) Every man jack shall know that my illustrious person is now proceeding to dinner. Torches at the head! And you there form up behind my gracious magnificence.

Goes up the stairs with his retinue amidst drum-beats and preceded by torches.

ONE OF THE PEOPLE

to Sigismund, with reverence

We are with you. Speak to us!

THE MAN WITH A WOODEN LEG

This is the poor people's King, and they will bear the sword and scales before him.

ANOTHER

Speak to us.

A THIRD

Call him by his name!

ANOTHER

That name must not be uttered.

A FIFTH

Those who named him were struck dumb.

AN OLD MAN *pushing forward*

Look upon him, our King, how he stands there! As though laved in the water of the river of life, he shines from head to foot.

ONE OF THEM

He is afraid of us.

SEVERAL

Are you afraid, Sire?

ONE OF THEM

Speak to us.

ANOTHER

If he were to cry out, our souls would all split like sacks. Do not awaken him. He is not dead, but sleeps.

AN OLD WOMAN

I can see him!

THE MAN WITH A WOODEN LEG

A chasm opens, and the kingdom of this world will fall into it.

SIGISMUND

Mother, come to me.

The Tower

*Several bring him gold-embroidered robes, a dalmatic,
golden shoes—a golden crown.*

ONE OF THEM

They want to put golden robes on him!

ONE OF THEM *holding the robe*

Will our King permit us to robe him?

AN OLD MAN

Let us robe you. We have taken it from the altar and wish
to place it upon you with reverence.

They robe him.

THE MAN WITH A WOODEN LEG

A chasm opens, and the kingdom of this world will fall
into it.

ANOTHER

Stay with us! Endure with us!

ANOTHER

A flaming seraph will descend from Heaven and lop off
the ploughmen's right hands! But their left hands will
brandish swords!

SIGISMUND

to himself, in a low voice

But I shall go forth with you.

ONE OF THEM

He speaks to us!

[335]

ANOTHER

Stay with us!

ANOTHER

So that we shall not die, O our Lord!

ONE OF THOSE AT THE BACK

Let the women see him! Lift him up, our King. But carefully, as though he were a statue made of wax.

INDRIK THE SMITH

Make a lane, so that all those at the sides can see him. Open up, so that all can see him!

They do so.

SIGISMUND

Make way.—I sense a wide, open landscape. It smells of earth and salt. That is where I shall go.

VOICES

Stay with us!

ONE OF THEM

Do you want to ride there?

ANOTHER

We shall prepare a carriage and yoke twelve pairs of oxen to it. On this you shall ride, and a bell shall ring on the carriage, as though you were a church on wheels.

VOICES

Stay with us! Endure with us!

ANOTHER

So that we shall not die, O our Lord!

The Tower

ONE OF THEM

The women want to come in, to kiss his feet.

ANOTHER

Chase them away, those mares. They are not worthy to look upon his face.

The women outside scream.

ONE OF THEM

Are you not hungry? The women scream that we leave you hungry.

ANOTHER

Fetch everything! Take everything down from the army carts that is fit for a prince to eat, and spread it out at his feet.

VOICES

Stay with us! Endure with us!

OTHERS

Fetch everything! Heap up a mountain before him. Bring him meat, bread, and milk. Bring him honey and cream. Bring him smoked food and baked food as though for ten hungry men who have been threshing.

MANY OF THEM

Bring it, bring it, bring it.

SEVERAL

Stay with us, O our Lord!

They bring food in baskets, on leaves, on wooden plates, piling it up.

[337]

Hugo von Hofmannsthal

SIGISMUND

Not what the bird-catcher's snare nor what the angler's hook has brought forth, nor the knife at the pig's throat— but that one made of white flour is a wholesome food. (*He takes some of it, sharing it with Anton*) But this, too, must stay with me (*takes his drinking jug, clasps it to his breast*) for I shall suffer great thirst in your world.

ANTON

gobbling up a sausage

Proverbs are always right. There's nothing like fear to make a man hungry. Now I understand the adage.

ONE OF THEM

who offers food to Sigismund from a multicoloured cloth

Do you still think you are dreaming? When you have tasted all these will you still think that it's all a dream?

ANTON

Oh, he won't think at all! Now he'll soon wake up.

VOICES

Awaken with us!

OTHERS

Do not leave us!

SIGISMUND

pressing the jug to his breast

Like the cock in the farmyard I smell the grey of daybreak and the hour when the stars leave their sentry posts. Let us go away together.

He takes a few steps.

[338]

The Tower

ARON

staggers down the winding stair, a precious coverlet on his shoulders

Where's the creature? Where have you put it?

INDRIK THE SMITH

raising his hammer

Here is our King. What do you want of him?

Sigismund turns to him.

ARON

Up there with you! Come here, you! You're coming with me. Our generalissimo is in great spirits and wants you to drink a swig of priest's wine with him from a special chalice, kneeling at his feet. So up with you at the gallop! That's his order. Do you get me?

He staggers.

INDRIK

trips Aron up with his foot and throws him down

Lie there, you swinish fellow, and die when they throw their torches into the gunpowder store.

SIGISMUND

Let him lie. Where we are going, obedience is done before the command is given, and the mowing done with no hope of supper. But you are a sturdy fellow, and shall give my mowers the lead.

Indrik kneels down and kisses the hem of Sigismund's garment.

Hugo von Hofmannsthal

MANY OF THEM

Protect us, our Lord. Endure with us.

Exit Sigismund, followed by the people.

Curtain

Act Five

The interior of a tent. Main entrance, centre. Two side entrances on the right, two on the left. A broken chair and a tall drum as seats. Near them an iron regimental pay-box.—Foreground, right, a pile of loot—carpets, costly garments, saddlery, linen, all pell-mell in a heap. It is dark, shortly before dawn. Signals from time to time, as though from the surrounding camp. Frequent shots from the distance.

A Tartar leads in the Gipsy Girl, bound, by a rope, preceded by Cavalry Boy.—Simon looks round; he is busy making an inventory of the looted things. Indrik rises from the stool on which he has been sitting. He is armed, and a cudgel hangs from his belt.—The Doctor enters from the darkness at one side, Count Adam from the other side.

CAVALRY BOY

That's the gipsy and the horseman who brought her in. Her feet are bleeding; he made her walk behind his horse.

The Doctor goes to her. Exit Tartar, then Cavalry Boy, after reporting something in a low voice to Count Adam.

DOCTOR

It could have been the death of her. She's pregnant.

INDRIK

Pregnant by Olivier? Then she'll be delivered of Satan himself.

[341]

COUNT ADAM

How could you tell so quickly? I should never have known it.

DOCTOR

It shows, unmistakably. In their posture, their eyes. I can hardly explain it.

INDRIK *to Simon*

Is that really Olivier's chief whore? Look at her, Simon.

ADAM

Not so loud; the King is asleep.

ANTON

coming in quietly from the left

No, he's up, and reading a book.

SIMON

goes towards her, but not close

What's the right one called? Twelve and twenty women he drags behind him by day and by night, but this one has been his great favourite at all times. I wish I'd never seen her enter a town, with my own eyes. What is left behind is a shambles full of twitching carcasses.

Cavalry Boy enters again, looks at Adam.

ADAM

Show them in. (*Exit Boy*) The bannerets are about to pass through here. Remove that thing.

[342]

The Tower

INDRIK

to the Gipsy

Crouch down.

He throws a rug over her. Cavalry Boy draws aside curtain at the main entrance. Enter two Tartars with lances. Then a small group of Noblemen from the Court, unarmed, followed by two more Tartars.

ADAM

Be so gracious as to wait here a moment, gentlemen. (*Pointing at the small entrance, right*) His Majesty will receive you very soon.

ONE OF THE NOBLEMEN

in a low voice

We were assured that our personal liberty would not be restricted. We are unarmed. Why this escort of Tartars?

ADAM

A guard of honour, sir, nothing more.

He leads them over to the right.

ANOTHER NOBLEMAN

in a low voice, as he walks

You, Cousin Adam, were quick to sense which way the wind was blowing. I pay respects to your foresight.

ADAM

opening the curtain, right

Be so kind as to enter here, Your Excellencies.

[343]

He ushers them in and follows.

Two Tartars remain posted at the door, right, two at the main entrance.

INDRIK

pulling away the rug and dragging the Gipsy up into the light

Where's your fellow, your mate? What villages is he burning down? Whose children's heads is he cutting off now? We are without news of his drunken magnificence! Answer me, or we shall find other ways of questioning you!

Gipsy clenches her teeth. Anton listens towards the left, then goes to the left entrance, respectfully raises the curtain.

ADAM

The King!

Bows. Simon steps back.—Indrik pulls Gipsy to the back.

SIGISMUND

entering in a long gown, unarmed, and going to the table

Where have these maps come from?

He sits down.

INDRIK *coming forward*

From the monastery that was on fire on our right, as we passed it on yesterday's march.

SIGISMUND

at the table, without looking up

Let the Tartars beware. Next time I see a red sky I shall

have a dozen of them hanged. (*Feeling the Doctor's gaze fixed on him*) Does it astonish you that I have been so quick to learn the language of the world?—Dear friend, my place is a dreadful place, and even in broad daylight I live under the stars, and nothing is there or not there: all things, because they are, have been there before. (*He beckons to Adam, shows him the map*) A fine representation. There lies the whole country right up to the high mountains. Beautifully it lies there, as in a basket. Here you see the marshes to the south.

ADAM

Into which, with God's help, we shall throw Olivier.

SIGISMUND

Or he us, with Satan's help.

ADAM

A rumour persists among our Tartars that there has been a happy encounter between their men and him.

SIGISMUND

We need more certainty than that, for we are dealing with a powerful devil. Has no news been brought?—Your scouts, Simon?

SIMON *approaching*

None has returned. But that one there is worth more than a report.

He points to the Gipsy, who stands with her back to the table.

[345]

SIGISMUND

Is that one of his women?

SIMON

lowering his voice

More than that. A great accessory to everything he does.

SIGISMUND *to Indrik*

See that you make her talk. Without using force. You go with them, Simon. Take some of this stuff and use it to arouse her greed. (*The Gipsy laughs silently. Exeunt Indrik and Simon, left rear, with Gipsy. Sigismund addresses the Doctor*) I have been reading Plutarch—that life at which you opened the book for me. It contains much that is relevant to us and to our situation, despite the difference between the two periods. I should like to discuss these matters with you. Perhaps there will be time in the evening. (*The Doctor bows. While Sigismund speaks, Anton goes to him and busies himself with one of Sigismund's shoes*) You must eat more, Anton, and take more rest. Tell them to give you double rations. I want to see your old face again, well padded as it used to be. (*Anton kisses his proffered hand. Sitting down at the table again, Sigismund speaks to Adam*) I heard a great deal of shooting among the sentries shortly before midnight. What was going on?

ADAM *going to him*

May I inform Your Majesty that the Palatines and bannerets, as many as remain alive, have passed through the outposts with an escort, and are waiting outside.—The shooting was close to the river; an exchange between our vanguard and men of the Green faction. They have encamped themselves firmly on the other bank. But they declared themselves neutral, and the shooting ceased.

SIGISMUND

The Green faction are marauders, stragglers from the King's army, runaway murderers and incendiaries from Olivier's band. Since when has such a rabble of knaves presumed to establish camps and issue declarations of neutrality?

ADAM

These form a large, well-disciplined corps. It consists of children from all the three realms, and they are ruled by a Children's King.

SIGISMUND

looking up from the map

What do you mean by that, Adam?

ADAM

They are adolescents, who have formed themselves—

DOCTOR

The forests have been full of the like of them ever since the four years' war under Basilius made a wilderness of the border provinces. They are all the orphans from the villages with no houses left in them, and they flock together. Here and there an old man, who leans on the branch of a beech-tree, leads them up to some remote piece of pastureland, until there's a hard winter and they all freeze to death. For years now they have been seen by anyone riding over the mountains.

Enter Simon again, rear, followed by Indrik and the Gipsy.

ADAM

There are nearly ten thousand of them. They have peculiar laws and customs, and are ruled by an elected king,
who is said to be a strong and handsome youth with the
bearing and gaze of a lion. They plough and live again as
men did of old. They practice crafts and sing as they work.

SIGISMUND

I shall not leave an enemy ten thousand strong, with a
fortified camp, at my flank. That would mean leaving three
regiments and artillery behind to safeguard my reinforce-
ments against them; I cannot spare so much cover. They
have a King, you say?

ADAM

Of whom strange tales are told.—He is said to be King
Basilius' son by a beautiful, savage woman who was a
servant at his hunting lodge—but no sooner born than
carried away by his mother to the woods in ignorance—
he of his birth, the King of his paternity.

SIGISMUND

I must see that boy—I offer him safe conduct. Send a
spokesman with a white flag, observing all the formalities.
We must not offend His Green Majesty. (*Turning his head
to Simon*) What did the interrogation reveal?

*Adam gives an order to the Tartars at the door. The Cav-
alry Boy goes to the door.*

SIMON

going to Sigismund

She says: she will not open her mouth to such base ruffians
as ourselves. If she could be alone with Your Majesty.

(*Lowering his voice*) It would not be the first time that
she entered Your Majesty's presence.

SIGISMUND *rising*

I know. I fear there is no other way. Or (*to the Doctor*) can
you suggest another method?

ANTON

Quite alone with you? (*Softly*) What if the bitch has a
dagger on her? Doctor, prevent it, I beg you, sir.

ADAM *in a low voice*

She has been searched down to her skin. She has neither
anything in writing nor any weapon on her.

SIGISMUND

Have a breakfast served to the Counts, meanwhile—if we
have anything to offer them. (*To the Doctor*) Despatch a
horseman to obtain the book of which you spoke to me.
The Emperor Marcus—

DOCTOR

Marcus Aurelius.

*Count Adam has left by the right, after a bow, and after
dismissing the Tartars with a gesture.*

SIGISMUND

His meditations, or whatever you called them. A great
monarch, full of noble thoughts and ambitious plans to
direct the future of Europe along certain paths for centuries to come. But he too was the victim of circumstances,
and died in his tent, in the midst of his projects.—I envy

you your great knowledge. No, I love you for it. For it does not inhabit you like a tenant, but lives in you as in its own palace.—Do not leave me, unless our way of life should become too strenuous for your body. (*Indrik takes the Gipsy nearer to Sigismund, who casts one look at her then turns his back on her again. The following is said half to himself, then again to the Doctor*) In two ways the Oliviers of this world exercise their infernal power— through bodies and through things. (*He grazes the piled-up loot with his foot*)—Take off her ropes. (*To the Doctor, so that the Gipsy does not hear him*) I shall be alone with her by the light of a lamp, like Olivier, but for very different business, God knows.—She is young, and beautiful rather than ugly, yet she makes me shudder. But we have nothing else that could be our mother but this sex, and this is the substance of which the world is made.

ANTON

softly, to Indrik

Leave her hands bound.

SIGISMUND

who has heard him

Free her hands. (*Exit Anton, reluctantly, followed by Indrik. Sigismund is sitting down at the table and studying the map*) It has been reported to me that the band of rebels under the command of your man has been driven up against the mountains and annihilated by my Tartar troops. What have you to say about that, Clairvoyante?

GIPSY

What? The general? (*Laughs coarsely*) Who could destroy him?—You could destroy an unborn child, perhaps— that would be like you!

The Tower

SIGISMUND *looking up*

So you carry an unborn child in your womb?

GIPSY

silently traces circles in the dark with her fingers

You will see what it is I am pregnant with!

SIGISMUND

What is that you mumble?

GIPSY

walking round in a circle with great speed

Svahah! angah!—Ellio! mellio!—Selo, elvo, delvo, helvo!

SIGISMUND

without looking at her

You can go, if you don't want to speak. Run back to your master and say to him: I was an incompetent emissary.

GIPSY

going to him in a strange, dancing gait; her hair crackles

Bleeding feet—bad emissaries! Come from far away—are there others besides? (*Throws herself down, puts her ear to the ground*) Many of them! An army!

She strikes the ground lightly with her palms; immediately the air is full of the sound of many tripping and shuffling feet.

SIGISMUND

looks up, goes to her

Has the time come for that?

Hugo von Hofmannsthal

GIPSY

throwing back her head

The time has come. From out the earth from vault and lair!—From the privy! From the air!

A whistling and scuttling of rats and other vermin: flitting shadows everywhere.

SIGISMUND

Where has this swarm of wood lice come from? And what do they want, these mice and rats as big as cats?

He laughs.

GIPSY

Forward, forward—we are many—he is one! Great shall be small, and small be great! All these one womb can procreate!

SIGISMUND

There is nothing you can shake out of your womb, black angel, that is not familiar to me as my own hands and feet. (*From the darkness there rises something like a woman with a horse's skull in place of her head*) Your sisters with the horse's teeth make no impression on me. I used to share the straw that was my bedding with some of their kind; they don't keep a man very warm. (*The creature comes closer to him from one side. He chases it away*) Leave me, succubus.—And as for you, my little dove of peace, listen to me. I am eager for a message from your noble consort. It's burning your tongue; for you had yourself captured on purpose. As the goat to the milkmaid, so you came running to me.—Open your mouth, therefore, before I lay you into my Tartars' arms.

The Tower

GIPSY

Your Tartars? But no one obeys you! You have no army! All those are phantoms. They all bear the names of devils, your Tartars. Why, you create them out of vapour; out of yellow, venomous night mists you fashion them!—How else could they fall upon one so silently while one is marching? How could they strangle sentries without so much as a cry?—And yet with such conjurer's tricks you have driven our Lord God Himself into the marshes, damned Judas that you are!

SIGISMUND

Is the red Satan dead, then? Hey, ho! I—but you're lying? You're trying to ensnare me?—I want to see his corpse.

GIPSY

Peck out his eyes, gobble them up, you wraiths!—Earth, empty your belly!

Glow of a blaze, a gale that shakes the tent pegs. Great bones come rattling up out of the earth.

SIGISMUND

There he is! As true as I—He stinks of fires and blood like a stag in rut! By my greater power! As true as I pulled you here by the deepest rope that I hold in my hands!

GIPSY *cowering, whimpering*

Help me, vermin. Gnaw away the rope! He is pulling me!

SIGISMUND

Bring it to me at once, the corpse.

The glow deepens.

[353]

Hugo von Hofmannsthal

GIPSY

*on the ground, twists round and points to the back, where
a second figure, exactly like her, is seen standing*

Look at her! Look at her! How her lover lights her way
with blazing villages! She has come from far away! (*Beckons to the figure*) Come here!

SIGISMUND

Hey, ho!—Are you twofold, witch? I also am more than
one—there, let me beat time for you! (*He seizes a large
bone, brandishes it, utters a spell, and takes long, clumsy
paces in time with it like a bear tied to a post*) Thus cry
the seven seals: the fishes shall roar, the angels shall weep,
throwing stones at one another, the grasses shall teethe,
and all the tall pine-trees!

*He drums in the air loudly. The Standing Gipsy approaches
with heavy strides, one at each drum-beat, Sigismund beating time to it with his bone.*

THE STANDING GIPSY

her eyes wide open, but unseeing, as she walks

Walk on, walk on incessantly! Bleeding feet, never, never
give up! You will get there, get there in the end! Rejoice,
my child, my child in the womb! Your father's burning
down the world! That will light you on your way!

Comes close to Sigismund.

SIGISMUND *raising his hands*

Halt! Stay there! There's somebody standing here!

The Cowering Gipsy laughs.

[354]

THE STANDING GIPSY

suddenly quite close to Sigismund's face, changing her expression all at once as though she recognized him

Shame on you, camp thief! Have him whipped with a bridle! —There, bind him! (*Tries to seize him; he brandishes his bone; she retreats*) The parasite! You stole the fiery breezes out of your generalissimo's belly. What you stole is inside there! (*She strikes her abdomen*) You mandrake! Seed that has dripped from the gallows!

THE COWERING GIPSY

passing her hand through the pile of bones. A fox barks hoarsely and digs its way out of the bones with glowing eyes

Have no fear, my old lover! He is chained up.—What, does he bare his teeth at you? Your bodily son, risen up from the burial pit? Bite him, fox, at him! I'll throw you on top of him.

She takes the fox in her arms; suddenly she is holding King Basilius instead, half of whose body rises from the earth.

SIGISMUND

Away! That's past and gone. That lies in the belly of the earth.

Basilius laughs, puts out his tongue at Sigismund and collapses as a crooked fox with its tongue hanging out.

THE STANDING GIPSY

Whatever was prostrate rises up against you. Now everything's up and about!

Hugo von Hofmannsthal

A man with a terrible and unknown face rolls in under the flap of the tent.

SIGISMUND

I am proof against your power. Earth upon you!

THE COWERING GIPSY

Earth does not obey you. Cast out by Earth. Spewed out by air. Mandrake!

SIGISMUND

Who are you, then, old sleepwalker? I always had such as you sitting about in my sty.

THE MAN ON THE GROUND

tears off his strange face and appears as the dead Julian. He sits on the ground and beckons to Sigismund with his green hand

Hear what I have to say. I have little time, Sigismund.—I never taught you the right language. I could tear my hair with remorse. The language I taught you is adequate only for the early stages. But everything moves on all the time. Where I have my dwelling now I am only beginning to divine the new language: this renders the higher and the lower things in one breath.

SIGISMUND

It's coming to me in a flash. But I have no time for it. I am a general in his tent and have to fight on two fronts.

JULIAN

I must lend you my head, so that you will see the world from below.

The Tower

His head alone, with a horribly tense and knowing expression, approaches Sigismund.

SIGISMUND

beating the air with his bone

I learnt that lesson long ago in the tower. Let me be!

The head vanishes. The dead fox, too, has vanished. The gale rises again. A crash, as of a door split open.

THE STANDING GIPSY *into the gale*

Approach, you strong one! Approach, you great one! Fetch him away!

The lamp goes out, the glow in the middle of the tent deepens. Olivier's figure is seen standing in it, but vague as though made of glass. The Cowering Gipsy has now vanished.

SIGISMUND

Answer me! Reveal your presence to me! It is my will. I command you.

Olivier's figure grows more distinct.

GIPSY

Do you stretch out your hand imperiously at your master? You toad! You adder's spawn! We shall paralyse your hand!

Olivier stands and stares. His head is cut and battered

Roar at him so that his guts fall out of his belly.—Ah, how he glares! How he bares his poor teeth. How his hair rises, congealed with blood! Master, master, master!

[357]

Hugo von Hofmannsthal

SIGISMUND

You could never endure my gaze, even when you were in the flesh. Away with you, therefore. But not as you would have it yourself, but as I would have it. You shall vanish from my eyes such as you were at the moment of your death.

Olivier tries to attack Sigismund. He raises the stump of a sword and tries to strike him. But his steps are unsure, as though he were on marshy ground.—Jeronim and Aron, dripping with mud, pull themselves up towards him from the right and left, and cling to him. He roars, and sinks with them.

THE GIPSY *before he has gone*

What? Who? What weapon for you?—Don't punish me, I am here. Your slave is here. Your creature is here.

After Olivier's disappearance, instantly almost complete darkness. At that moment the Gipsy is very close to Sigismund.

SIGISMUND *imperiously*

Lights here, and remove the woman! (*A ray of light from left.—The Gipsy clutches at the air and collapses.—Adam enters hurriedly from the right with a light, the Doctor and Anton likewise from the left, as well as several servants.— At the same time the first light of dawn penetrates through the sides of the tent. Sigismund goes to meet Adam*) Olivier is dead.—Do you understand me? Olivier is dead.

DOCTOR

Is that possible?

The Tower

ADAM

Reliable news? Palpable evidence?

SIGISMUND *with great animation*

He has just convinced me of it.

DOCTOR

How so?

Enter Indrik from the back.

ADAM

What's become of the woman, Indrik?

INDRIK

She's lying here.

ADAM

Dead?

INDRIK

I don't know.

Gipsy is carried out.

SIGISMUND

Friends, I am master in my own house. Give me a cloth. (*Anton hands it to him. He wipes his brow and continues, with great animation*) It is not the perspiration of fear, but a cold dew that has settled there from exhalations of the nether world. To know a thing for certain is worth a little cold sweat. Yes, Doctor, someone has been here. But not in the same way as you or I. It seems there are many other ways, of which we shall not know till presently.—

[359]

This is where it stood. A wind blew from it that put out the light and made my flesh creep a little.—Not many words were spoken. I shouted at the thing and it vanished. —It seems that we are destined to higher things.

DOCTOR

But you are bleeding, Your Majesty!

Searches for a bandage in the bag he carries by a shoulder-strap.

SIGISMUND

What is it?—(*Turning to Adam*) He lies in a bog with his head slashed to pieces.—Adam, these are bloody times. Where am I bleeding?

DOCTOR

Here—it's your hand. How did Your Majesty come by this wound? It's a sharp cut across your whole palm, passing straight through the line of life.

SIGISMUND

How should I know? Oh yes, I did feel something. The woman came close to me.

DOCTOR

The woman! God forbid!

ANTON

searches the ground, picks up a tiny dagger

There! Could it have been that? A knife no bigger than a hairpin?

The Tower

DOCTOR

Very likely. (*To Anton*) A large beaker of the strongest brandy! At once!

Exit Anton.

SIGISMUND *to the Doctor*

This is where the thing stood. A minute ago I should have been able to clarify it for you—so I imagine—but the moment is insanely jealous and leaves nothing to its successor but an empty chest bearing the inscription: here it used to be! (*He goes to the table and peruses the map*) Now my vanguard can wheel into the attack. The two armies without a leader are lost in any case. Well, why don't you bandage the wound?

DOCTOR

while Sigismund studies the map

Count Adam!

ADAM *close to him*

That's a ghastly look on your face! Poison?

DOCTOR

It is more than likely.

INDRIK

has overheard, rushes over, takes Sigismund's hand, kneeling before him

Let me suck the wound!

ANTON

with the beaker, trembling

Oh, Doctor, what's happened, sir?

[361]

DOCTOR

Quiet! (*To Indrik*) Leave it alone; the cut is too deep for that.

ADAM

How do you feel, Your Majesty?

SIGISMUND

As usual. Why do you stare at me like that? Eh? What's wrong with you all? Have I been poisoned?

DOCTOR

May it please Your Majesty to drain this beaker in any case. The gipsies, I know, make use of the viper's venom. This is the only antidote I have at hand.

SIGISMUND

I am quite well and, as you know, brandy is repulsive to me.

DOCTOR

It will not disgust Your Majesty now. I beg you to drink it. And then a brief rest. Perhaps the heart needs all its strength now to resist the poison.

He bandages Sigismund's hand.

SIGISMUND

draining the beaker

We must attend to our business, and cannot choose the hour at present. (*To Adam*) Ask the Counts to enter. We can now confront these dubious grandees with blood less troubled than only an hour ago.

DOCTOR

May God make those words true!

SIGISMUND *to Adam*

Tell them that the black faction has been dispersed to the four winds. There is no army of Olivier's now to oppose me, and they are no longer what they believed themselves to be, the index of the balance of power. Now go—but keep them in doubt as to the reception I have prepared for them. And—one more thing—have their swords given back to them: they shall not appear before me like cooks or grooms. (*Exit Adam to the right. The Doctor has had the beaker filled by Anton once more and now approaches Sigismund with it*) What! Another one? There's nothing wrong with me.

DOCTOR

I beseech you.

SIGISMUND

I am perfectly well, except for—

He passes his hand over his knee.

DOCTOR

Except for—?

SIGISMUND

A trifle. A great heaviness in my legs. But, then, for three days and three nights we scarcely quit the saddle.

He sits down, picks up the map.

Anton looks at him anxiously, with an expression of despair, and bites his knuckles.

The Doctor goes to Sigismund and makes him drink the brandy.—At a sign from Adam, the curtain of the main entrance is raised. Enter: one officer bearing the royal standard; an armed peasant with the rebels' standard, a black pole bearing a bundle of broken chains; and a Tartar captain with a standard consisting of a gilt crescent moon and a horse's tail. The three standard-bearers line up on the left side of the tent. Enter Indrik, who seizes the standard with the broken chains. The bannerets enter from the left, preceded by Adam. They at once kneel down before Sigismund. At the same time Sigismund's generals enter by the main entrance; they are five or six men of the lower orders, wearing armour, and they line up at the back, left, near the entrance.—Adam, who has re-entered, takes the sword of state in a velvet scabbard, offered to him by a boy, and takes up his position behind, and to the left of, Sigismund.

SIGISMUND

sitting at the table on a drum, scrutinizes each of the kneeling men very attentively, then

Rise, gentlemen. We are in camp, not at court.—But, my vassals, I await your unanimous homage—at last.

THE SENIOR BANNERET *kneeling*

Most illustrious Majesty! Most mighty! Most invincible!— Your supreme Highness! Sovereign Lord and King of us all!

SIGISMUND

But rise, cousins, rise!

[364]

The Tower

THE SENIOR BANNERET

standing up, as all the others do

As the morning ray appears to the shipwrecked after a night of terrible squalls, so does the merciful speech of our gracious King appear to us. Blessed are we to have known such trials: twice blessed after such a night of terror. What human mouth can find words to describe the events of recent times!—The cities swept away from the face of the earth as though with a broom, the castles and monasteries mere gaping cinders, the fields morasses of blood, the survivors in hollow trees or in chasms beneath the earth. But our lawful King speaks to us with indulgence; and, with that manly eye in which glistens no tear but that of awed emotion, we see the most venerable banner of our ancient kingdom raised again in this tent of victory—and look upon this one alone, that now and for ever it may wave over the head of our rightful King.

SIGISMUND

You may look upon all three of them, gentlemen; united they flap and clatter in the wind, wherever we ride. Continue, Palatine.

THE SENIOR BANNERET

Dreadful beyond measure was the threat of the age, but more dreadful still the discord that divided our hearts. Power and law, these two pillars that support the world, horribly pulled apart before our eyes! Son against father, dominion against dominion, power against power like water against fire, yet a third against both, as if on the Day of Judgment the earth were to split asunder and swallow both water and fire. Together with the fools and knaves, the

[365]

blasphemers and heretics, the levellers and the self-helpers, Asia invaded us and sought to be master in our house as in the gruesome times of our ancestors. Awful above this chaos, the banner of the broken chains was brandished by the hand of a mighty one, so that it rang out over our bowed heads like the scourge of God!—How in this hand could we recognize the hand of our anointed King?—Who overthrew the sacred authority of a father, stripped the cities of their protecting walls, laid waste the castles, did not oppose the burning down of churches or the ruins of monasteries! Whom the homeless, trembling on battered highroads, trudged out to meet that they might offer him bread salted with their own tears—but it was he!

SIGISMUND

It was he. It is he. Your Lord and King by power and by necessity, here I am.—The old kings are dead, old customs destroyed, old allegiances dissolved. From the North Sea to the Black Sea in the south, where this nation of horsemen has its dwelling, no power but mine remains unshaken. Out of blacksmiths and cowherds I made my generals, turned ploughshares into swords—and all that had been called impossible proved possible to me.

INDRIK

You showed us power, irresistible, and above this power a higher thing for which we have no name; and so you became our Lord, our one and only Lord, sacred and inviolable.

THE FIRST BANNERET

True. From the burning nest a phoenix rose, and as it soared up, we recognized the mettle of our kings and the mighty wing-beats of your Northern forebears, and now the nightmare is ended, and the desert of our lives grows passable again.—Lord, let us see a great King, who will oppose the constant north of manly power to the seething impotence of our time: just and magnanimous, merciful and mighty!

SIGISMUND *rising*

Such I will be.

THE COUNTS

Long live the King!

SIGISMUND

taking a step towards them

But let there be no misunderstanding between us! I reserve the right to combine both in my lifetime: both to impose order and to transcend the bounds of the old order. And for that I need you: consent is what I ask of you, consent that is more than submission.

THE COUNTS

Impose order, Lord! Give us peace! Let justice reign!

SIGISMUND

What you call peace is your power over the peasantry and the earth. What you call justice is your prerogative, to be wolves rather than dogs. Can you not rid yourselves of this greed? Do you know of nothing better than to sit entrenched in your possessions and to struggle for precedence? —What I bear within me is the spirit of foundation, not the spirit of possession; and the order I seek to establish is based on self-denial, self-dedication. For I do not seek to

[367]

change this or that, but to change the whole, all at once; and then we shall all be citizens of the new age. (*He paces the length of the tent, intently watched by the Doctor, then returns to the Counts*) Cousins, you think that your destiny can still be bounded as a farm is bounded by fence-posts; but that is not so—for the world is ripe for renewal, and when the mountains begin to move, they pay no heed to an old church tower upon their flanks. What has long stood upright now lies prostrate; the Teutonic Order has crumbled away, its power usurped by the merchants' guilds; a strangled child sits on the Muscovite throne, and at the centre of the earth no one holds sway but he, the Grand Turk (*pointing to the Tartars*), my ally, and myself. He has built the great Eastern Empire; in him converges all the strength of Asia under the crescent moon and the flowing horse's tail, and he does not count the peoples that are subject to him, and between him and me he has set that great river in the south, Borysthenes or Oglu, as they call it, and its wide waters mirror the smile of our amity, and perhaps I shall cede Constantinople to him as a pledge; for the time has come when the great must deal greatly, magnanimously, with each other.—But as for your little realms, your houses, which you build in rivalry, and your creeds, which you hold in rivalry, I will not respect them, but confound your frontiers: I will mix all you little peoples anew in a great melting-pot.

THE SENIOR BANNERET

Our lives and lands are yours, our Lord and King; but let your loyal subjects acclaim you. Do not let the horse's tail of the heathen wave beside your holy banner! And have the banner of the broken chains buried in the earth: for why the emblem of rebellion, since you are supreme?—

But let the saving crown touch your head, to render it sacred and invulnerable! Make a covenant with us, who are your vassals, and permit us to crown you with the crown of your fathers!

INDRIK

His brow bears the sign of dominion for all to see, and he has no need of your old crown. No covenant between him and you!

THE COUNTS

Permit the coronation! Permit it, Sire.—Long live our crowned King!

SIGISMUND

Desist! I will not be your lord in the manner habitual and agreeable to you, but in a manner that will astonish you. It is not yet time for you to see my gentle face, though that will come later.—If that which I bring about has not the strength to endure, then throw me on the shambles with Attila and Pyrrhus, the kings who established nothing. But if my work is lasting, then we shall put on crowns and present a smiling face. May the god of Time, that friend of my days in the dungeon, be kind to us!—Why has it grown so dark all of a sudden? (*He reels*) Open the shutters! Let in the light!

He falls back into the arms of Anton, who has run to him. The curtain before the tent entrance is drawn back. Outside the people wait, many of them armed, all bareheaded. From the midst of the camp rises a great mast with a bundle of broken chains.

[369]

Hugo von Hofmannsthal

DOCTOR

Gentlemen, I beg you to retire. The King is unwell.

Anton and Adam, who hands the sword of state to one of the generals, run to Sigismund and lay him on a couch made of the clothes and rugs piled up in the foreground, right.—The Counts step aside.

ONE OF THEM *softly*

What's this? Has he the falling sickness like his father?

ANOTHER

Look how pale his face is. What do you think our lives will be worth, gentlemen, if he never opens his eyes again?

ANTON

kneeling by Sigismund

Give us a sign of life, supreme Majesty! Just give your Anton a little sign! Only move one finger!

DOCTOR

to the generals, who have approached

Step back there, so that the light and air can reach him. The King is very ill. Step back, I beg you.

The crowd outside increases, but in utter silence.

SIGISMUND *opening his eyes*

Who is that lean fellow there? He looks like my old Anton. (*Anton weeps*) And what is that great blaze, growing stronger and stronger? Hang the Tartars for setting fire to the tower again!

The Tower

DOCTOR

It is the rising sun that dazzles Your Majesty. Hold up a shield.

They do so.

SIGISMUND

No! Let me see it!—My teacher in the tower taught me to call things by their right name, but the present moment has moved me to take that flaming tower up there for my dwelling-place.—What I mean is this: a man needs a space no smaller than the whole world, to exist in truth—but for twenty years I lived in a hollow stone, and there was *one* word that I did not know: the word "longing." For wherever I am, I permeate all with my being, am present, and rule.—No need to look overawed, cousins. Did I show you a stern face? A certain stringency was added to our nature, without which one cannot win battles—but our mind has also gained a little: from the marrow of our bones and the marriage of our inwardness with necessity.—I ask you—inasmuch as you are men: is there not something in you that says "yes" to me in spite of all?

He props himself up, looks at them, and sinks back. Some kiss his hands and the hem of his robe.

THE COUNTS

kneeling round his couch

Lord, let your vassals testify to their loyalty!—Permit us to crown you!—Let the sacred unction touch your limbs, and they will be healed!

The Doctor bends over Sigismund.

[371]

Hugo von Hofmannsthal

SIGISMUND

opens his eyes and shuts them again at once; softly but clearly

I am about to die.

ONE OF THE YOUNGER BANNERETS

nearest to Sigismund

You will live, Sire, and be anointed with the sacred oil. Miraculously the emerald vessel escaped all damage in the vault beneath those smouldering ruins.

ANOTHER

Miraculously that ancient man has survived, the centenarian, Ignatius, once the hidden ruler of this realm, and his hands shall set the crown upon your anointed head; fate has spared him for that.

SIGISMUND *sitting up*

Ah, where was I? Back in the tower? In the blackness! Ah, ah, kill that old man! Batter down the tower! Break the chains! I am here! I will not die! Draw the sword. Give it to me! I will hold it! (*He tries*) There is no one here but myself! You do not see the world as it is. Only I, because I have been dead once already. (*He stands up with a great effort*) Come to me, all of you! With this sword we shall break open the door to the new age!—I will sweep you along with me—into the—into the sun—poison and light —and—yet, and yet!

He collapses.

THE PEOPLE *crying out*

Ah!

[372]

The Tower

ADAM

Has our King left us with no farewell?

DOCTOR

holding Sigismund's limp hand

He's alive, he has not died. His pulse-beat is light and quick, like a little bird's.

Sigismund opens his eyes.

DOCTOR

How do you feel, Your Majesty? You give me cause for new hope.

SIGISMUND

Abandon it. I am far too well to hope.

Silence. He lies there with his eyes open.

The Counts whisper together and listen. A little bell is heard, like the acolyte's bell at Mass. It comes nearer.

ONE OF THE COUNTS

You are drawing strength in advance from the anointing oil, which is being brought to you on a cart.

ANOTHER

Hear the fanfares! Hear the little bell! They are carrying in Brother Ignatius, who is to crown you.

The soldiers outside make a lane.

THE CAVALRY BOY

enters with a white flag

They're coming. Not only the young King, whom our Sovereign summoned here with this flag, but many of his followers too have joined him, all unarmed and dressed in white. They've already reached our men, and no one bars their way.

Enter two Boys in white robes, barefoot. One of them holds a little bell, the other a white twig, peeled of its bark.

THE CHILDREN'S KING

who has approached through the lane, a little way behind the two Boys. He wears a white robe and a crested helmet on his head. He stops in the middle of the tent

I shall stay here and these two, who can divine water and ore, will tell me whether this place is safe. (*Sigismund lies motionless. The Doctor never takes his eyes off him*) It does not befit me to look on evil things.

THE FIRST BOY

to those crowding around Sigismund

Step back and let him breathe!

ADAM

Who presumes to give orders here?

THE CHILDREN'S KING

I. For those who will live have appointed me their ruler. (*The Counts make to draw their swords*) Let our unarmed hands fill you with shame, and put back your swords.

DOCTOR

to the Boy nearest to him

Have you no medicinal herbs? Is there no wise shepherd among you? In the name of Christ I beseech you: we need an antidote to strengthen his heart.

THE SECOND BOY

We ourselves are medicinal herbs. We grew up in the mountains.

He turns away from the Doctor. The two Boys take up their position some distance away from Sigismund. All have stepped back to make room for them.

THE FIRST BOY

after inhaling the air with his head raised, singing

The light is mild, and I hear the sickle move in the grass and the sheaves fall over the scythe-blade.

THE SECOND BOY *singing*

Most mighty! The lark is most mighty! And the sun displays his glorious house, and all points to one place.

THE FIRST *singing*

Mighty is the earth, and mightier still is man. There is nothing else but he. He is a measure, and he is measured.

THE SECOND *singing*

Here is the rock from which flows the source, milk and honey.

BOTH *together*

Here all is purified! And no dread is near.

They kneel down, facing Sigismund.

SIGISMUND *opening his eyes*

What rouses me yet again? Who is it that dwells in me still unknown? (*The Children's King takes a step towards him. Sigismund speaks to himself*) Someone.

Hugo von Hofmannsthal

He directs his gaze on the Children's King. They look at each other.

THE CHILDREN'S KING

taking two more paces towards him

I know your name and honour you according to your deeds. My wounded mother told it to me before she bade me go down into the well so that I would live.

SIGISMUND *smiling*

Who are you?

THE CHILDREN'S KING

A King. (*He bows down towards Sigismund*) You know, there is that in me a little measure of which makes men stubborn, but a large measure as tame and meek as dogs. You must give me your sword and judgment scales: for you were only an interim King.—We have built cottages, and we keep fires alight in the forge, and turn swords into ploughshares. We have proclaimed new laws, for it is always from the young that laws should come. And we set lighted candles beside the dead. (*Sigismund looks at him, smiling*) Step back, all of you, and leave me alone with my brother. (*The two Boys rise and stand side by side behind the Children's King, who goes quite close to Sigismund. Sigismund closes his eyes*) There was one man in this world with whom I was destined to enter into blood-brotherhood—and now . . . (*He kneels beside Sigismund*) Don't be startled. I ask you nothing but that which you cannot say.

All kneel down, both those in the tent and those outside. The people outside heave a deep sigh.

[376]

The Tower

SOME OF THE PEOPLE

We cannot see his head. Hear us! We are calling you. Your
people. You, our head. Do not speak with the stranger!

*Sigismund opens his eyes and raises his right hand, for all
to see.—The people weep.*

THE CHILDREN'S KING *softly*

Your face! What divine being is it that crosses the threshold now?

SIGISMUND *looking at him*

That will soon dissolve. Give me your friendship as long
as I am here.—It is terrible how the soul clings to the body.
But, as the clairvoyante told me, there is no place for me
in time.

ANTON

kneeling at Sigismund's feet

And us? Has my King nothing to say to us?

SIGISMUND

looks round, then in a clear voice, looking at the Doctor

Bear witness: I was here. Even though no one knew me.

THE PEOPLE

Do not leave us! Endure with us!

THE TWO BOYS

Let him die!—Rejoicing!

SIGISMUND

in a very clear voice, drawing himself up a little

Here I am, Julian!

Hugo von Hofmannsthal

He falls back, takes a deep breath and dies.

The Children's King rises and raises his right hand.—All rise and do likewise.—The three standard-bearers lower the banners at Sigismund's feet.

THE PEOPLE

Tear our standards to pieces!

THE CHILDREN'S KING

Quiet, you people.—In time you cannot measure this man; but out of time, like a constellation.

THE PEOPLE

Sigismund! Your name remains with us!

BOYS

who have stepped forward from the crowd of soldiers, singing with clear voices

"Mitte spiritum tuum, et creabuntur, et renovabis faciem terrae!"

THE CHILDREN'S KING

clasping the sword of state in its scabbard

Take him up. We need his grave to sanctify our dwelling. (*Boys take up Sigismund's corpse*) Forward, and follow the deceased with me.

Trumpets.

Curtain

[378]

THE CAVALIER OF THE ROSE

A Comedy for Music

Translated by

CHRISTOPHER HOLME

PRINCESS WERDENBERG, *Field Marshal's wife*

BARON OCHS OF LERCHENAU

OCTAVIAN, *nicknamed Quinquin, a young gentleman from a great house*

HERR VON FANINAL, *a rich man recently ennobled*

SOPHIA, *his daughter*

MARIAN LEITMETZERIN, *the duenna*

VALZACCHI, *an Italian*

ANNINA, *his companion*

MAJOR-DOMO OF THE PRINCESS

MAJOR-DOMO OF FANINAL

A SINGER

A FLAUTIST

A NOTARY

HIS CLERK

A HAIRDRESSER

HIS APPRENTICE

A NOBLE WIDOW

HER THREE NOBLE DAUGHTERS

A MODISTE

AN ANIMAL DEALER

A SCHOLAR

A POLICE COMMISSIONER

TWO WATCHMEN

A DOCTOR

AN INNKEEPER

A PORTER

A LITTLE BLACKAMOOR

[381]

Hugo von Hofmannsthal

Footmen, runners, haiduks, waiters, servants in the Faninal household, servants at the inn, musicians, suspicious-looking figures.

The place: Vienna.

The time: The first decade in the reign of Maria Theresa.

Act One

The Princess's bedroom. Left, in the alcove, the great tent-shaped four-poster. Near the bed a three-leaved Chinese folding screen, with clothes lying about behind it. Further away from it, an occasional table and a few chairs. On a chaise-longue left lies a sword in its scabbard. Right, big double doors into the antechamber. Centre, barely visible, is a small door let into the wall. Otherwise no doors. Between the alcove and the small door stand a dressing table and a few chairs against the wall. The bed curtains are drawn back.

Octavian is kneeling on a footstool before the bed, left, with his arm half round the Princess, who is lying in bed. Her face cannot be seen, only her very beautiful hand and her arm with the lace sleeve falling from it.

OCTAVIAN

What you were! What you are!
No one can know, no one can guess!

PRINCESS

sitting up among the cushions

Is that a complaint? Would my Quinquin
prefer that many knew it?

OCTAVIAN

Sweetheart, no, blessed am I
to be the only one that knows what you are.

[383]

No one can guess! No one can know!
You, you—what does the "you" mean, what "you and I"?
Has it a meaning?
Words, just words, isn't that all it is? Tell me!
And yet, and yet—there's something in them,
a swaying, a tugging, a squeezing, a yearning,
as my hand now moves to yours,
the will to be near you, to enfold you,
this is what "I" am and it wants you near,
but the "I" dissolves in the "you,"
I am your boy—but when my senses are reeling,
then where is your boy?

PRINCESS *softly*

You are my boy, you are my treasure!

OCTAVIAN

Why is it day? I don't want the day!
What is day for? Then you belong to everyone.

The Princess laughs softly

OCTAVIAN

Are you laughing at me?

PRINCESS *affectionately*

Am I laughing at you?

OCTAVIAN

Sweetheart.

PRINCESS

Treasure, you, my treasure child.

The Cavalier of the Rose

A soft tinkle of bells

Listen.

OCTAVIAN

I don't want to.

PRINCESS

Quiet, pay attention.

OCTAVIAN

I don't want to hear *any*thing! What could it be?

The tinkling comes nearer

Footmen perhaps, with letters and cards
from Saurau, or Hartig, or the Portuguese envoy.
But I'll let nobody in here. Here I am master.

*The small door in the centre opens and a tiny Blackamoor
in yellow, hung with silver bells, carrying a tray with the
chocolate, trips over the threshold.*

PRINCESS

Quick, there—hide there. It's the breakfast.

*Octavian slips behind the nearer leaf of the screen. The
door is shut behind the Blackamoor by invisible hands.*

PRINCESS

For heaven's sake, throw your sword behind the bed!

*Octavian dashes for his sword and hides it. The Princess
lies back after pulling the bed curtains to. The little Blackamoor puts the tray on the small table, pushes this forward,
moves the left-hand sofa nearer it, bows deeply to the bed,*

[385]

his little arms crossed over his breast. Then he dances daintily backwards, his face turned always towards the bed. At the door he bows once more and vanishes.

The Princess comes out between the bed curtains. She has put on a light, fur-bordered wrap.

Octavian comes out from between the wall and the screen.

PRINCESS

Madcap, careless boy!
Leaves his sword lying about in a lady's bedroom?
Don't you know any better manners?

OCTAVIAN

If my behaviour is beginning to offend you,
if it irks you to find me so unpractised in such matters,
then I really don't know what you see in me at all.

PRINCESS

affectionately, on the sofa

Let my lord and treasure stop philosophizing and come
  here.
There's a time for everything, and now it's breakfast.

OCTAVIAN

sits down next to her. They breakfast very affectionately. Octavian lays his face on her knee. She strokes his hair. He looks up into her face. Softly

Marie Thérèse.

PRINCESS

Octavian.

OCTAVIAN

Bichette.

PRINCESS

Quinquin.

OCTAVIAN

Treasure!

PRINCESS

Darling boy!

They continue breakfast.

OCTAVIAN *gaily*

The Field Marshal's stuck in the Croatian forest hunting
   bear and lynx.
And I, a mere youngster, I stick here, and what do I hunt?
Oh, I can't believe my luck, my luck!

PRINCESS

as a shadow crosses her face

Leave the Field Marshal in peace.
I dreamt of him last night.

OCTAVIAN

Last night you dreamt of him? Last night?

PRINCESS

I'm not responsible for my dreams.

OCTAVIAN

Last night you dreamt about your husband?

Hugo von Hofmannsthal

PRINCESS

Don't make such big eyes at me, I can't help it. All at once
there he was, at home again.

OCTAVIAN

The Field Marshal?

PRINCESS

There was a clatter down in the yard, horses and people,
and there he was.
Suddenly I woke up in a fright—why, just look at me,
look how silly I am—I can still hear the bustle in the yard,
I can't get it out of my ears. Don't you hear something too?

OCTAVIAN

Yes, of course I hear something, but why must it be your
husband?
Think where he now is—in the Raitzenland, beyond Esseg.

PRINCESS

That's really a long way, is it?
Good, then it must be something else. All is well.

OCTAVIAN

You're looking so worried, Thérèse.

PRINCESS

Well, you know, Quinquin—even if it is a long way—
the Field Marshal's so quick. Once—

OCTAVIAN *jealously*

What happened once?

The Princess listens distractedly.

[388]

OCTAVIAN *jealously*

What happened once? Bichette?
Bichette! What happened once?

PRINCESS

Oh, be a dear boy now, you don't have to know everything.

OCTAVIAN

throws himself on to the sofa

Look how she treats me! Oh I'm a miserable creature!

PRINCESS *listening*

Don't be difficult now. Now it's serious—it *is* the Field
   Marshal.
If it were a stranger, the noise would be over there, in my
   antechamber.
It must be my husband, trying to come in through the
   dressing-room
and arguing with the footmen.
Quinquin, it's my husband!

   Octavian makes a dash for his sword and runs right.

PRINCESS

Not there, that's the antechamber.
That's where the tradespeople are waiting and half a dozen
   footmen.
There, that way!

   Octavian runs across to the small door.

PRINCESS

Too late. They're in the dressing-room already.
There's only one thing for it. Hide! There!

Hugo von Hofmannsthal

OCTAVIAN

I'll bar his way! I'm staying with you!

PRINCESS

There behind the bed! There among the curtains! And don't stir!

OCTAVIAN *hesitating*

If he catches me there, what'll become of you, Thérèse?

PRINCESS *pleading*

Hide, hide, treasure.

OCTAVIAN *by the screen*

Thérèse!

PRINCESS *stamping impatiently*

Quiet, I said!

With flashing eyes

          I should like to see them try!
Let anyone just try to get through with me standing here.
I'm not a Neapolitan general—where I stand, I stand.

Goes resolutely up to the small door and listens

Splendid fellows, my footmen, won't let him in,
telling him I'm asleep. Splendid fellows!
That voice?
Why, that isn't the Field Marshal's voice!
They're calling him "Your Lordship." It's a stranger.
Quinquin, it's a caller.

She laughs

[390]

The Cavalier of the Rose

Quick get into your clothes,
but keep hidden,
don't let the footmen see you.
That loud, stupid voice—I ought to know that.
Who can it be? Oh heavens, it's Ochs.
It's my cousin, Lerchenau, Ochs of Lerchenau.
What can he want? Oh my goodness!

She cannot help laughing

Quinquin, do you hear, Quinquin, don't you remember?

She goes a few steps over to the left

Five or six days ago—the letter—
we were sitting in the carriage
and they brought me a letter to the carriage door.
That was the letter from Ochs.
And I have no notion what was in it.

Laughs

You know who's to blame for that, Quinquin.

VOICE OF MAJOR-DOMO *outside*

May it please Your Lordship to wait in the gallery!

VOICE OF THE BARON *outside*

Where did the fellow learn his manners?
Baron Lerchenau don't kick his heels in an anteroom.

PRINCESS

Quinquin, what are you up to? Where've you got to?

OCTAVIAN

in a woman's skirt and bodice, his hair done up in a hand-kerchief and ribbon like a mob-cap, comes forward and curt-seys, speaking like a country girl

[391]

Please Your Highness, not been long in Your Highness's service.

PRINCESS

You darling boy.
And I can't give you more than just a peck.

Kisses him quickly

He's breaking my door down, my lord cousin.
But you, go on, be off with you!
Slip boldly out through the footmen.
You're a clever rascal. And mind you come back, treasure,
but in man's clothes and through the front door, if you
please.

Sits down, her back to the little door, and begins to sip her chocolate. Octavian goes quickly towards the little door and tries to get out. At the same moment the door is wrenched open and Baron Ochs forces his way past the footmen who are trying to hold him back. Octavian, as he is trying to make his escape with lowered head, collides with him. Octavian presses himself back coyly against the wall to the left of the door. Three footmen who have been swept in with the Baron stand uncertain what to do.

BARON

with hauteur to the footmen

No question that Her Highness'll receive me.

He comes forward, while the footmen on his left try to bar his way. To Octavian, with interest

Your pardon, my pretty child!

Octavian turns coyly against the wall.

The Cavalier of the Rose

BARON

with graciousness and condescension

I said, "Your pardon, my pretty child!"
*The Princess looks over her shoulder, then stands up, and
comes to meet the Baron.*

BARON

with gallantry to Octavian

Haven't really hurt you, my dear, have I?

THE FOOTMEN *pulling at his clothing*

Her Serene Highness!
The Baron makes a French bow with two repeats.

PRINCESS

How well Your Lordship looks.

BARON

bows again, then to the footmen

Now d'you see how charmed Her Highness is to see me?
*Advances towards the Princess with cavalier nonchalance,
offers her his hand, and leads her forward*

And why shouldn't Your Highness be charmed?
What's an early call among people of rank?
Why, I remember Princess Brioche now,
called on her day after day to pay my compliments
while she was in her bath,
with nothin' but a little screen between her and me.
I must say I'm astonished

[393]

Hugo von Hofmannsthal

Looking round angrily

that Your Highness's fellows—

PRINCESS

Forgive us,
they did but do as they were told,
I had a bad headache this morning.

*At the Princess's nod the footmen have brought forward a
small sofa and an armchair, and gone off.*

The Baron keeps looking over his shoulder.

*Octavian, having sidled along the wall towards the alcove,
tries to busy himself as inconspicuously as possible about
the bed.*

*The Princess sits down on the sofa, after offering the Baron
the armchair.*

BARON

*tries to sit down, his attention wholly taken up with the
pretty chambermaid. To himself*

A pretty child! A precious little morsel!

PRINCESS

*standing up and once more, with ceremony, offering him a
seat*

I pray Your Lordship.

*The Baron sits down reluctantly and tries not to turn his
back completely on the pretty maid.*

PRINCESS

I'm still not quite recovered.
So my cousin will perhaps have the indulgence to—

BARON

Of course.

He turns round to look at Octavian.

PRINCESS

My chambermaid, a young thing from the country,
I'm afraid Your Lordship finds her a nuisance.

BARON

Quite delightful! What? Oh, not the least little bit. Me? On
the contrary!

*He beckons to Octavian with his hand, then turns to the
Princess*

Your Highness will be surprised perhaps
that a betrothed man

Looking around

should none the less—in the meantime—

PRINCESS

A betrothed man?

BARON

As to which Your Highness, of course, will be sufficiently
informed from my letter—
Delicious little creature! Can't be fifteen!

PRINCESS

The letter, of course, yes, the letter, now who is it then,
who's the lucky girl?
I have the name on the tip of my tongue.

[395]

BARON

What?

Over his shoulder

Fresh as a kitten! Washed and bloomin'! Delightful!

PRINCESS

Who is she, just remind me, your lady bride?

BARON

The young Miss Faninal. I made no secret of the name to
Your Highness.

PRINCESS

Of course. Where's my memory? Only, the family—not local
people, are they?

*Octavian busies himself with the tray, thus getting still
more behind the Baron's back.*

BARON

Yes, local people indeed, Your Highness.
One ennobled by Her Majesty's gracious favour.
He has the contract for supplyin' the army in the Nether-
lands.

*The Princess impatiently signals with her eyes to Octavian
to remove himself.*

BARON

completely misunderstanding her look

I see Your Highness knittin' her lovely brows at the misal-
liance.
But let me say, the girl's as pretty as an angel.

[396]

Fresh from the convent. She's an only child.
The father owns twelve houses in the Wieden,
as well as his town house on the Platz am Hof,
and his health is said to be not all that good.

PRINCESS

My dear cousin, I understand very well what quarter the
  wind is in.

Nods to Octavian to remove himself.

BARON

And if Your Highness will graciously permit the expression,
of good noble blood I have enough, I think, for two in my
  veins.
A man is what he's born, *corpo di Bacco!*
My lady wife shall have the precedence where her rank
  entitles her,
we'll see to that, and as for the children,
if there's any reluctance to allow them
the golden key—*va bene!*
They'll content themselves with the twelve iron keys
to the twelve houses in the Wieden.

PRINCESS

Indeed, yes, my cousin's children, I feel sure,
will not go tilting at windmills.

Octavian tries to back across towards the door with the tray.

BARON

Why such a hurry with the chocolate?
There now, easy does it!

Octavian stands uncertainly, turning away his face.

[397]

Hugo von Hofmannsthal

PRINCESS

Go on, be off with you!

BARON

If I confess to Your Highness
that I've hardly tasted a morsel of breakfast.

PRINCESS *resigned*

Here then, Mariandel. Serve his lordship.

Octavian comes and offers the tray.

BARON

taking a cup and helping himself to chocolate

Hardly a morsel, Your Highness. Sittin' up in the coach
since five o'clock this mornin'.

Softly

Really delicious creature. Stay here, my love. I've got somethin' to tell you.
My whole domestic staff, grooms, attendants, the whole
lot—

He eats noisily

all down in the courtyard here, complete with my almoner—

PRINCESS *to Octavian*

Go now.

BARON

Just another biscuit? Stay a moment!

Softly

You're a sweet little creature, you're a precious thing!

[398]

The Cavalier of the Rose

To the Princess

—are on the way to the "White Horse," that's where
we're puttin' up, till the day after tomorrow, that is.

Half aloud

I'd give a lot just for a little tête-à-tête—

To the Princess, very loud

—the day after tomorrow—

Quickly to Octavian

—somewhere with you, just the two of us.

*Princess cannot help laughing at Octavian's impudent im-
personation*

BARON

Then we move to Faninal's.
Of course I must first send my best man—

Angrily over his shoulder

can't you just wait?—
to announce me to the lady bride
and present her with the silver rose
as is customary among the high nobility.

PRINCESS

And which of our relations has Your Lordship chosen
to perform this office?

BARON

The desire to seek Your Highness's advice
has emboldened me to present myself thus attired at Your
Highness's levee.

[399]

Hugo von Hofmannsthal

PRINCESS

My advice?

BARON

As solicited, with all respect, in my humble missive.
I have surely not had the infelicity with my poor
    supplication
to arouse Your Highness's displeasure?

Leaning back

You could turn me round your little finger,
and well you know it!

PRINCESS

Why, of course, a best man
for Your Lordship's first visit to the bride,
one of our relations—now whom could we—I'll—
Cousin Jörger? Or let me see—Cousin Lamberg?

BARON

I leave it in Your Highness's most lovely hands.

PRINCESS

Very well. Will you dine with me, cousin?
Tomorrow, shall we say? By then I shall have a name to
    suggest.

BARON

Your Highness is condescension itself.

PRINCESS *trying to get up*

Meanwhile—

[400]

BARON *half aloud, to Octavian*

Mind you come back to me! I shan't go until you do.

PRINCESS *to herself*

Oho!

Aloud, to Octavian

Stay a moment!

To the Baron

Can I now be of any further service
to my cousin?

BARON

I am almost ashamed to trouble Your Highness—
a recommendation to Your Highness's notary—
it's a matter of the marriage contract.

PRINCESS

My notary often comes in the mornings. Go and see,
    Mariandel,
if he's not waiting in the antechamber.

BARON

Why send the girl?
Your Highness deprives herself of service
for my sake.

Holds Octavian back.

PRINCESS

Let her be, cousin, she can perfectly well go.

Hugo von Hofmannsthal

BARON

That I cannot allow. Stay here at Her Highness's nod.
There'll soon be one of the footmen comin' in—
'pon my word, I'll not let this little pearl
be cast among the swinish herd of flunkeys.

Strokes her.

PRINCESS

Your Lordship shows too much concern.

The Major-Domo enters.

BARON

There, didn't I say so?
He's come to report to Your Highness.

PRINCESS *to the Major-Domo*

Struhan, is my notary waiting in the antechamber?

MAJOR-DOMO

Your Highness's notary awaits Your Highness,
the steward too, then Your Highness's chef,
then too, sent by His Excellency Count Silva,
a singer with a flautist.
Otherwise the usual riff-raff.

BARON

*has pushed his chair behind the Major-Domo's broad back
and is tenderly pressing the supposed maid's hand*

Ever had dinner alone
with a man of the world
in a private room?

[402]

Octavian pretends to be very embarrassed.

BARON

No? You'd be surprised! Like to try?

OCTAVIAN *softly, shamefacedly*

Oh I'm sure I don't know if I ought.

The Princess, inattentively listening to the Major-Domo, notices the two and cannot help laughing softly.

The Major-Domo bows and steps back, giving the Princess an unobstructed view of the tableau.

PRINCESS *to the Major-Domo*

Ask them to wait.

The Major-Domo goes off.

The Baron sits back in his seat as unconcernedly as he can manage and assumes a ponderous expression.

PRINCESS *laughing*

I see my cousin doesn't waste his chances.

BARON *relieved*

With Your Highness I see one can be quite open.
No shifts and evasions, no false proprieties,
no standing on ceremony.

He kisses the Princess's hand.

PRINCESS *amused*

But, as an engaged man?

[403]

Hugo von Hofmannsthal

BARON

half standing up, coming close to her

Does that make a lame duck out of me?
Should I not rather be like a good hound on a trail,
double keen to sniff out every bit of game?

PRINCESS

I see Your Lordship makes a profession of it.

BARON *standing up*

I should think I do.
Like to see anythin' which'd suit me better.
Must say I'm sorry for Your Highness
that Your Highness—how shall I say?—
has experience only in defence.
Parole d'honneur! There's nothin' like the attackin' side.

PRINCESS *laughing*

I can well believe it has many attractions.

BARON

There's not a season of the year, not an hour of the day—

PRINCESS

Not one?

BARON

Which isn't—

PRINCESS

Which isn't?

[404]

The Cavalier of the Rose

BARON

Right for coaxing some small favour
out of the boy Cupid.
A man's not a stag or a capercailzie
held at the mercy of the seasons
but a lord of creation free of the calendar.
May, for instance, is a good month for the love game
as every child knows,
but I say:
June, July, August are better still.
Those are the nights!
Up in our country then there's an influx
of young girls over from Bohemia—
they come for the harvest and are otherwise good and
    biddable.
I often keep two or three of them for myself
in the house till November.
Then, and not before, I send them home.
And what a mixture they make,
the round young Bohemian maids,
sweet and heavy on the palate,
with those of our own sort, the German strain,
dry and sharp-tastin' as a mountain wine.
And what a mixture they make all together!
And everywhere there's watchin' and lyin' in wait
and slippin' through the palin's,
creepin' to one another and lyin' around together,
and everywhere there's singin'
and swayin' of hips
and milkin'
and mowin'
and dabblin' and splashin' in brook and horsepond.

Hugo von Hofmannsthal

PRINCESS

And my cousin lets nothing escape him?

BARON

Could I but be as blessed Jupiter
in a thousand shapes,
I'd have a use for every one.

PRINCESS

What, even the bull? Would you be as rough as that?

BARON

All accordin'! Accordin' to the case.
There are as many ways to a woman's favour
as there are women.
I know how to take them each one as she wants.
There's the little waif
stands there as if she couldn't count up to five
and yet when it comes to the point, upon my word
she's all there, I can tell you.
And then there's the one that loses her head
with giggles and sobs—she's a particular favourite.
Or at the other extreme the one
in whose eye sits a cold, hard devil,
but even for her there comes the moment when that eye
    melts.
And when that same devil inside her lets it be known
that the hour of reckonin' has struck,
like a fish gaffed and landed,
if I may so put it, that's a game worth the candle—
can't have too much of that.

PRINCESS

A devil, my word, that's yourself!

[406]

The Cavalier of the Rose

BARON

And is there some poor Cinderella, savin' your presence,
for whom no one has a glance,
sloppin' about in a dirty smock, savin' your presence,
squattin' in the ashes behind the kitchen range,
even she, even she taken at the right moment,
even she has everythin' that's needed.
That look of astonishment! Can't understand what's
    happenin'!
And terror! And last of all such overpowerin' bliss
that the master himself
should graciously stoop to her lowliness.

PRINCESS

My cousin knows his business, that I can see.

BARON

Then there are those who want you to creep up on them
soft as the wind caressin' the fresh-mown hay.
Others again you have to stalk from behind
like a lynx,
catch hold of the milkin' stool and tip them over
headlong—first makin' sure there's some hay nearby.

PRINCESS

No! You're altogether too expert.
Be my good cousin and leave this child alone.

BARON *back on his dignity*

Let Your Highness but give me the little creature
to wait upon my future wife.

[407]

Hugo von Hofmannsthal

PRINCESS

What, my little girl here? What should she do?
The lady bride must be well provided already
and not dependent on Your Lordship's selection.

BARON

That's a fine piece of goods, God damn it!
There's a drop of the best blood there all right.

PRINCESS

Your Lordship has a keen eye.

BARON

It's only fittin'.

Confidentially

See nothin' wrong in people of quality being thus waited
    on by noble blood,
I've a child of my own pleasure here with me.

PRINCESS

What? Not a girl? I sincerely hope not!

BARON

No, a son: has the lineaments of a Lerchenau in his face.
Keep him as a valet.
When Your Highness shall please to order me
to place the silver rose in your hands,
he it will be who brings it.

PRINCESS

It will be a pleasure. But wait a moment. Mariandel!

[408]

BARON

Let Your Highness give me the maid. I won't let go.

PRINCESS

Oh dear. Mariandel, go and get that miniature.

OCTAVIAN *softly*

Thérèse, Thérèse, take care.

PRINCESS *softly*

Go on, bring it. I know what I'm doing.

BARON

gazing after Octavian

Could be a young princess.
It's my intention to present my bride
with a true copy of my family tree
together with a lock of the first Lerchenau's hair—
he was a great founder of monasteries
and chief steward of the imperial domains in Carinthia
and the Wendish March.

Octavian brings the miniature.

PRINCESS

Will Your Lordship have the young gentleman there as
best man?

BARON

At Your Highness's recommendation, unseen—no need to
look.

PRINCESS

My young cousin, Count Octavian.

[409]

BARON

Octavian—

PRINCESS

Rofrano, second brother of the Marquess.

BARON

Could wish for no one of better quality.
Should be exceedingly obliged to his young Lordship.

PRINCESS

Look at him.

Holds out the miniature to him.

BARON

looking alternately at the miniature and the maid

The likeness!

PRINCESS

Is it not?

BARON

Feature for feature.

PRINCESS

I have often had my thoughts about it.

BARON

Rofrano! One is somebody, comin' from such a house,
even if only by the servants' entrance.

PRINCESS

That's why I keep her as something extra special.

BARON

It's only fittin'.

PRINCESS

Always about my person.

BARON

Quite right.

PRINCESS

But now go, Mariandel, be off with you.

BARON

How so? She'll be comin' back?

PRINCESS *ignoring his remark*

And let the people in from the antechamber.

Octavian goes towards the double doors, right.

BARON *after him*

My lovely child!

OCTAVIAN *at the door, right*

You may go in.

Runs to the other door.

BARON *after him*

Your humble servant! Grant me a moment's audience.

OCTAVIAN

shutting the small door in his face

Be back soon.

[411]

At the same instant an elderly chambermaid comes in through the same door. The Baron retires disappointed. Two Footmen come in from the right and bring a screen out from the alcove. The Princess goes behind the screen, accompanied by the chambermaid. The dressing table is pushed forward into the centre. Footmen open the double doors right. There enter: the Notary, the Chef, followed by a scullion carrying the menu book; then the Modiste, a Scholar with a folio, and the Animal Dealer with several minute dogs and a little monkey. Valzacchi and Annina, gliding swiftly behind these, take up the front place left. The Noble Mother with her Three Daughters, all in mourning, take up their position on the right. The Major-Domo leads the Tenor and the Flautist to the front. The Baron, towards the back, beckons a Footman to him and gives him an order, signalling: "Here through the back door."

THE THREE NOBLE DAUGHTERS

kneeling down

Three poor but noble orphans
implore Your Highness' aid.

MODISTE

Le chapeau Paméla. La poudre à la reine de Golconde.

ANIMAL DEALER

Monkeys, Your Highness, all mischief and slyness!
Birds of Africa too, in every hue.

THE THREE ORPHANS

Our father on the field of honour
gave his young life, his daughters three
have but one wish, to do the same.

The Cavalier of the Rose

MODISTE

Le chapeau Paméla! C'est la merveille du monde!

ANIMAL DEALER

Parrots gay in every hue
from Africa and India too.
Lap-dogs so small,
house-trained one and all.

*The Princess steps forward and everyone bows or curtseys
deeply.*

The Baron has come forward left.

PRINCESS

May I present the Notary to Your Lordship?

*With a bow to the dressing table, where the Princess has
seated herself, the Notary approaches the Baron, left. The
Princess beckons the youngest of the Three Orphans to
herself, takes a purse handed her by the Major-Domo, and
gives it to the girl with a kiss on the forehead. The Scholar
is about to step forward and present his folio when Valzacchi bounds forward and pushes him to one side.*

VALZACCHI

producing a black-bordered newspaper

The Black Gazette, Serene Highness!
All secret news printed here!
Only for high-placed personage!
Corpse found in back room
of noble count's town house.
Citizen's wife and her lover
poison the husband—
last night at three A.M.

[413]

Hugo von Hofmannsthal

PRINCESS

Don't bother me with this tattle!

VALZACCHI

Your pardon!
Tutte quante confidences
from high society!

PRINCESS

I won't hear a word of it!

Valzacchi with a regretful bow jumps back.

*The Three Orphans, with their Mother bringing up the
rear, have kissed the Princess's hand.*

THE THREE ORPHANS

in marching order for departure

May Providence upon Your Highness all its wealth and
blessings show'r!
In our hearts Your Highness' bounty be remember'd every
hour.

They go off with their Mother.

*The Hairdresser moves up hastily, his Apprentice dashing
after him with flying coat-tails. The Hairdresser scrutinizes
the Princess, then puts on a gloomy expression as he takes
a step backwards to study her appearance on this particular
day. The Apprentice meanwhile unpacks, laying the things
out on the dressing table. The Hairdresser pushes some of
the people back to give himself room for manoeuvre. After
brief consideration his plan is formed, he throws himself
with determination upon the Princess, and begins to dress
her hair. A Footman in pink, black, and silver approaches,*

[414]

*bringing a note. The Major-Domo is quickly on the spot
with a silver salver on which he presents the note to the
Princess. The Hairdresser breaks off, to let her read it. The
Apprentice hands him a fresh curling-iron. The Hairdresser
brandishes it. It is too hot. The Apprentice, after a questioning look at the Princess, who nods, hands him the note,
which he smilingly uses to cool his iron. At the same time
the Singer has taken up his position, holding a sheet of
music before him. The Flautist reads his accompaniment
over his shoulder.*

*Three Footmen have taken up position right front, while
others stand in the background.*

SINGER

Di rigori armato il seno
Contro amor mi ribellai,
Ma fui vinto in un baleno
In mirar due vaghi rai.
Ahi! che resiste puoco
Cor di gelo a stral di fuoco.

*The Hairdresser hands the iron to his Apprentice and ap-
plauds the Singer. Then he continues his arrangement of
the curls.*

*A servant has meanwhile admitted through the small door
the Baron's valet, almoner, and body servant. They are
three dubious-looking figures. The valet is a tall young lout,
both stupid and impudent. He carries under his arm a red
morocco casket. The almoner is a village curate run wild,
a four-foot-high but strong and insolent-looking gnome. The
body servant, before he was stuck into ill-fitting livery, no
doubt carted dung. The almoner and the valet seem to be*

[415]

*quarrelling about the precedence and treading on one an-
other's toes. They make a course along the left-hand side
of the stage towards their master and take their stand near
him.*

BARON

*seated, to the Notary, who stands before him taking his
instructions*

As bride-gift—entirely separate, however,
and before the dowry—you take my meanin', Mr. Notary?—
the house and estate of Gaunersdorf returns to me,
free of encumbrances and with undiminished privileges
as they were by my late father possessed.

NOTARY *short of breath*

If Your Right Honourable Lordship will permit me most
     humbly to advise,
a bride-gift is only to be demanded or stipulated
as given by the husband to the wife,
not by the wife to the husband.

BARON

That may be so.

NOTARY

It is so—

BARON

But in a special case—

NOTARY

The forms and provisions know no special case.

[416]

The Cavalier of the Rose

BARON *shouting*

Damn the forms and provisions!

NOTARY *terrified*

Craving your pardon!

BARON

softly again, but insistently and in a tone of lofty self-respect

Where the lusty scion of a great and noble house
condescends to grace with his presence,
before God and the world, and, so to speak,
in view of Her Imperial Majesty,
the marriage bed—you take my meanin'?—
of a young Miss Faninal who's as good as a commoner,
corpo di Bacco then if that isn't a case
where a bride-gift as a fittin' token of grateful devotion
in return for the conferment of such noble blood
can very well pass from wife to husband.

The Singer makes as if to start singing again but waits until the Baron is quiet.

NOTARY *softly to the Baron*

Perhaps if the affair is separately—

BARON *softly*

You miserable pedant, as bride-gift I want the place!

NOTARY *softly*

—treated as a part of the dowry well hedged round with
stipulations—

[417]

Hugo von Hofmannsthal

BARON *half aloud*

As bride-gift! Can't you get it into your thick head?

NOTARY *the same*

—as a presentation *inter vivos* or—

BARON *shouting*

As bride-gift!

SINGER

during the conversation between the two

Ma sì caro è'l mio tormento
Dolce è si la piaga mia
Ch' il penare è mio contento
E 'l sanarmi è tirannia.
Ahi! che resiste puoco—

Here the Baron raises his voice so loudly that the Singer breaks off abruptly, and the Flautist with him.

The terrified Notary retires into the corner.

The Princess nods to the Singer to approach her and reaches out her hand for him to kiss. Singer and Flautist withdraw with deep bows.

The Baron acts as though nothing had occurred, nods affably to the Singer, then joins his servants, pushes back the forelock which has been combed in peasant fashion on to his valet's forehead. Then he goes to the small door as if he were looking for somebody, opens it, peeps outside, is angry that the maid does not return, in his anger sniffs around the bed, shakes his head, comes forward again.

[418]

The Cavalier of the Rose

PRINCESS

looking at herself in the hand-glass, half aloud

My dear Hippolyte,
today you have made an old woman of me.

The Hairdresser, much distressed, goes feverishly to work again on the Princess's coiffure and alters it once more. The Princess's face remains sad.

PRINCESS

over her shoulder to the Major-Domo

Everybody out!

Four Footmen form a chain and push the waiting people out through the doors, which they then fasten shut.

Valzacchi, with Annina behind him, has crept right round the stage behind everybody's backs to where the Baron is standing and they introduce themselves to him with exaggerated servility. The Baron steps back.

VALZACCHI

Your Lordship looks for something, I can see.
Your Lordship in need of something.
I can find it. I can provide it.

BARON

Who are you, what do you know about me?

VALZACCHI

Your Lordship's face speaks without tongues.
Like antique. *Come statua di Giove.*

[419]

BARON

Quite an intelligent fellow, this.

VALZACCHI

Attach us to Your noble Lordship's suite!

Falls to his knees, and Annina likewise.

BARON

You?

VALZACCHI

Uncle and niece.
Two work better than one, at everything.
Per esempio: Your Lordship has young wife—

BARON

How do you know that, you devil you?

VALZACCHI *zealously*

Your Lordship has cause for jealousy: *dico per dire!*
Could happen today or tomorrow. *Affare nostro!*
Every step the lady she take,
every carriage the lady she ride,
every letter the lady get—
we're on the spot.
There we are.
At the corner, in the chimney, under the bed—
there we are.

ANNINA

Your Lordship will not regret.

*They hold their hands out to him, soliciting money; he acts
as if he did not notice.*

[420]

BARON *half aloud*

Hm! The things you can find in Vienna!
Just as a test. D'ye know the girl Mariandel?

ANNINA *half aloud*

Mariandel?

BARON *the same*

The little maid in the house here with Her Highness.

VALZACCHI *softly to Annina*

Sai tu, cosa vuole?

ANNINA *the same*

Niente!

VALZACCHI *to the Baron*

Sure, sure! My niece will provide.
Be sure of it, Your Grace.

*Holding out his hand once more, which the Baron again
affects not to see.*

*The Princess has got up. The Hairdresser makes a deep bow
and hurries off, the Apprentice after him.*

BARON

leaves the two Italians standing and approaches the Princess

May I present the counterpart to Your Highness's dainty
   chambermaid?
The likeness, I am told, is unmistakable.

The Princess nods.

[421]

Hugo von Hofmannsthal

BARON

Leopold, the casket.

The young valet awkwardly presents the casket.

PRINCESS *laughing a little*

My warmest congratulations to Your Lordship.

BARON

*takes the casket out of the youth's hands and nods to him
to withdraw*

And now let me show you the silver rose.

Is about to open it.

PRINCESS

Pray do not bother to open it.
Be so good as to put it down there.

BARON

Perhaps the maid might take charge of it?
Shall she be called?

PRINCESS

No, let it be. She's too busy now.
But let Your Lordship rest assured: I shall bid Count
    Octavian wait on you
and the Count will do it for my sake
and as Your Lordship's cavalier will call
to present Your Lordship's rose to his lady bride.
Meanwhile just put it there.
And now I must bid my cousin adieu.

The Cavalier of the Rose

It is time now for the company
to withdraw, and I must to church.

Footmen open the double doors.

BARON

By your inexhaustible favour to me
Your Highness this day has put me to shame.

Bows formally and makes a ceremonial departure.

*The Notary follows him at his nod. After him the Baron's
three servants, in shambling procession. The two Italians in
lithe and obsequious silence attach themselves to it. The
Footmen close the doors and the Major-Domo withdraws.*

PRINCESS *alone*

There he goes, the puffed-up evil wretch,
and gets the young and pretty thing
with a pocketful of money thrown in
as if it were a law of nature.
And prides himself moreover on its being himself
who is giving something away.
Why should I worry myself about it then? It's the way of
   the world.
I, too, can remember a girl who once
was drafted fresh from the convent into the holy estate of
   matrimony.

Takes the hand-mirror

Where is she now? Might as well look for the snows of yester-
   year!
It's easily said, but can it really be true
that I was that little Resi
and that it's I who will one day be the old woman?

The old woman, the old princess.
"Look, there she goes, the old Princess Resi!"
How can such a thing happen?
Why does the good God arrange it so?
When I am still the same person.
And if He must arrange it so,
why then does He let me look on at myself
with such a clear understanding? Why doesn't He hide it
    from me?
It's all a mystery, so much is mysterious.
And we are here to endure it.
And in the How, there lies the whole difference—

*Octavian enters from right, in morning dress with riding-
boots.*

PRINCESS *half smiling*

Ah, there you are again.

OCTAVIAN

And you are sad.

PRINCESS

It's all over. You know how I am.
Half the time gay, half the time sad.
I cannot choose my thoughts.

OCTAVIAN

I know why you are sad, my treasure.
Because you're upset and have had a fright.
Aren't I right? Confess!
You had a fright,
my darling, my love,
because of me, because of me.

PRINCESS

A little bit perhaps.
But I took hold of myself and told myself:
Nothing will come of it.
And would much have come of it?

OCTAVIAN

And it wasn't the Field Marshal after all.
Only a comic cousin, and you belong to me.
You belong to me.

PRINCESS

Careful, Tavie, not to hug me too often.
Who hugs most, they say, holds least.

OCTAVIAN

Say you belong to me, say you belong to me.

PRINCESS

Oh be gentle now, be gentle and clever and good
No, please do not be as all men are.

OCTAVIAN

As all men?

PRINCESS

As the Field Marshal and Cousin Ochs.
Let my boy not be as all men are.

OCTAVIAN *angrily*

I don't know how all men are.

Hugo von Hofmannsthal

Gently

I know only that I love you,
Bichette, they've changed my Bichette for another.
Where's my Bichette?

PRINCESS *calmly*

She's here, let my lord and treasure be reassured.

OCTAVIAN

She's here, is she? Then I will hold her
and press her to me so that she doesn't escape me again.

PRINCESS

disentangling herself from his embrace

Oh let my Quinquin be good. I have a feeling
as if the frailty of all temporal things
had seeped into my very heart—
for we can hold nothing,
for we can grasp nothing,
for everything runs through our fingers,
everything, as we reach for it, dissolves,
everything melts away like dream and mist.

OCTAVIAN

When my Bichette has me here,
my finger hooked in hers,
my eyes seeking hers,
is that the moment for such feelings?

PRINCESS *very seriously*

Quinquin, today or tomorrow you will go off
and give me up for the sake of another,

[426]

The Cavalier of the Rose

Octavian tries to stop her mouth

one younger and more lovely than I.

OCTAVIAN

Are you trying to thrust me from you with words,
because your hands will not do it for you?

PRINCESS

The day will come quite of its own accord. For who are
    you?
A young lord, a younger son.
Your brother the head of your house.
Is he not bound to seek you a bride?
As if everything in the world
hadn't its proper time and its laws.
Today or tomorrow the day will come, Octavian.

OCTAVIAN

Not today, not tomorrow. I love you.
Not today, not tomorrow.

PRINCESS

Today or tomorrow or the day after.
I don't want to torment you, my love.
I'm saying what is true, saying it to myself as much as to
    you.
Easy for you and me I want to make it.
Easy is what we must be,
with heart and hands at ease,
holding and taking, holding and letting go. . . .
Those who are not so,
are punished by life and get no pity of God.

[427]

Hugo von Hofmannsthal

OCTAVIAN

My God, how she says it—only to show me
she doesn't care for me any more.

He weeps.

PRINCESS

Be a good boy, Quinquin.

He weeps more violently

Be a good boy.
Now it's I who must console the child
for the prospect that he will sooner or later leave me.

She strokes him.

OCTAVIAN

Sooner or later!
Who's putting the words into your mouth today, Bichette?

He stops his ears.

PRINCESS

Sooner or later.
Do those words offend you so?
Yet time, when you get down to it, Quinquin,
time doesn't alter circumstances.
Time is a strange thing.
While one just lives for the moment, it is nothing.
But then all at once
we feel nothing else but it,
it's all around us, it's right inside us,
it trickles away in our faces, it trickles in the mirror,
in my temples it flows away.
And between me and you there it is flowing too.

[428]

The Cavalier of the Rose

Soundless, as an hour-glass.
Ah Quinquin!
Often I hear it flowing incessantly.
Often I get up in the middle of the night
and stop all the clocks.

OCTAVIAN

My lovely darling, are you determined to *make* yourself
   miserable?

PRINCESS

Only we must not be afraid of it.
Time too is a creature of the Father
who has created us all.

OCTAVIAN

Today you talk like a parson.

An awkward silence

Does that mean that I shall never again
be allowed to kiss you
till you gasp for air?

PRINCESS *gently*

Quinquin, you must go now, you must leave me.
I am going to church now.
And later I shall drive to see my uncle Greifenklau,
who is old and paralysed,
and lunch with him—that will cheer the old man.
And this afternoon I will send you a footman,
Quinquin, and let you know
whether I am driving in the Prater.
And if I drive

[429]

and you would like,
you shall come to the Prater too
and ride beside my carriage.
Be good now and do as I say.

OCTAVIAN

As you command, Bichette.

He goes. A pause.

PRINCESS *alone*

I didn't even kiss him.

She rings agitatedly. Footmen come in from right

Run after His Lordship the Count
and ask him back for a word with me.

A pause

I let him go and never even kissed him.

The Footmen come back out of breath.

FIRST FOOTMAN

His Lordship's off and away.

SECOND FOOTMAN

Right at the gate His Lordship mounted.

THIRD FOOTMAN

The groom was waiting.

FOURTH FOOTMAN

Right at the gate they mounted and off like the wind.

The Cavalier of the Rose

FIRST FOOTMAN

Off round the corner, gone like the wind.

SECOND FOOTMAN

Ran after them, we did.

THIRD FOOTMAN

Shouted we did.

FOURTH FOOTMAN

All to no purpose.

FIRST FOOTMAN

Off round the corner, gone like the wind.

PRINCESS

Very good, you may go now.

The Footmen withdraw.

PRINCESS *calling after them*

Send Mohammed.

The little Blackamoor enters with a tinkling of bells and bows.

PRINCESS

There take this casket—

The Blackamoor zealously takes the morocco casket.

PRINCESS

But you don't know where. To Count Octavian.
Hand it over and say:

[431]

Hugo von Hofmannsthal

The silver rose is inside.
His Lordship knows all about it.

The Blackamoor runs off.

The Princess rests her head on her hand.

Curtain

Act Two

State room in Herr von Faninal's house. Centre door leads to the antechamber. Doors left and right. Right, a big window. On either side of the centre doorway chairs against the wall. In the corner on either side a great fireplace.

HERR VON FANINAL

about to take his leave of Sophia

A great day, a solemn day!
A glorious day, a holy day!

Sophia kisses his hand.

MARIAN LEITMETZERIN *the duenna*

Joseph's just driving up with the new carriage,
it's got sky-blue curtains,
drawn by four dapple-greys.

MAJOR-DOMO

with a touch of familiarity

High time that the Master was leaving.
The noble father of the bride,
so etiquette decrees,
must have left the house
before the silver Cavalier of the Rose arrives.

[433]

Hugo von Hofmannsthal

Would not be fitting
that they should meet at the door.

Footmen open the door.

FANINAL

God be with you. When I return,
it will be to lead your future husband by the hand.

MARIAN

The stern and noble Lord of Lerchenau,
Chamberlain of Her Imperial Majesty,
Assessor of Common Law for Lower Austria.

Faninal goes.

Sophia comes forward alone while Marian stays at the window.

MARIAN *at the window*

Now he's getting in. Xavier and Anthony are jumping up
behind.
The groom hands Joseph his whip.
All the windows are full of people.

SOPHIA *in front, alone*

In this solemn hour of trial,
when Thou, my Creator, art minded to raise me above my
deserts
and lead me into the holy estate of matrimony,

It costs her a great effort to control herself

to Thee in humbleness, in humbleness I offer up my heart.
To awaken humbleness in me
I must humble myself.

[434]

The Cavalier of the Rose

MARIAN *very excited*

Half the town's afoot.
The right reverends are looking down from the Seminary.
There's an old man sitting on top of the street-lamp.

SOPHIA

collecting herself with an effort

Humble myself and well consider—sin, guilt, meanness,
temptation, my forlorn state!
My mother is dead and I am all alone.
I for myself must answer.
But marriage is a holy estate.

MARIAN *as before*

He's coming, he's coming in two carriages.
The first has four horses, and it's empty.
The second has six and in it sits
himself, the Cavalier of the Rose himself.

SOPHIA *as before*

May I never presume upon my new rank—

*The voices of the Footmen in threes ahead of Octavian's
carriage in the street below: "Rofrano! Rofrano!"*

—never presume—

She can no longer contain herself

What are they calling?

MARIAN

The name of the Cavalier of the Rose and all the names
of your new princely and lordly relations they're calling
out.

[435]

Now the servants are forming up.
The footmen jump off the back.

*The voices of the Runners in threes come nearer: "Ro-
frano! Rofrano!"*

SOPHIA

Will they call out my bridegroom's name like that
when he comes driving up?

*The voices of the Runners close under the window: "Ro-
frano! Rofrano! Rofrano!"*

MARIAN

They're flinging open the carriage door! He's getting out!
All decked out in silver, he is, from head to foot.
He looks like a holy archangel.

She hastily shuts the window.

SOPHIA

Oh God in Heaven, yes,
I know that pride is a heavy sin,
but now I cannot humble myself, not now.
It just isn't possible.
It's all so beautiful, so beautiful!

*Footmen have quickly opened the centre doors. Octavian
enters, clothed entirely in white and silver, bareheaded, the
silver rose in his hand, behind him his suite of servants in
his own colours: white with pale green. The Footmen, the
Haiduks with curved Hungarian sabres at their side, the
Runners in white chamois with green ostrich feathers. Close
behind Octavian a Blackamoor carrying Octavian's hat and
another servant carrying in both hands the morocco casket
for the silver rose. Behind, the Faninal servants in livery.*

The Cavalier of the Rose

Octavian, the rose in his right hand, advances towards her with an aristocratic demeanour but his boyish face tense and blushing from shyness. Sophia is pale as death with excitement at his appearance and over the whole ceremony. They confront one another.

OCTAVIAN

after a slight hesitation, during which they increase one another's confusion by their beauty and embarrassment

To me has fallen the honour
to be permitted to present,
in the name of my cousin Lord of Lerchenau,
to the high-born maiden his bride
the token of his love, this rose.

SOPHIA *taking the rose*

I am much obliged to Your Lordship.
I am eternally obliged to Your Lordship.

A pause of confusion. She smells the rose

Smells very strong. Like roses, live ones.

OCTAVIAN

Yes, there's a drop of Persian attar of roses been put in it.

SOPHIA

Like heavenly, not earthly ones, like roses
of the blessed paradise. Don't you think so?

Octavian bends over the rose which she holds out to him; then straightens himself as if stunned and looks at her mouth

[437]

Hugo von Hofmannsthal

SOPHIA

It's like a greeting from Heaven. It's even too strong.
It draws one after, as with cords about one's heart.
Where have I been once before
and felt so blissful?

OCTAVIAN

*saying the words after her as if unconsciously and more
softly*

Where have I been once before
and felt so blissful?

SOPHIA

I must go back there, though it be the death of me.
Where must I go
to feel so blissful?
There must I go, though I die upon the way.

OCTAVIAN

*saying the first words while she is still speaking, then speak-
ing alone*

I was a child,
was it yesterday or an eternity ago?
A time when I did not yet know *her*.
Did not know *her*?
Who then is *she*?
How does she come to me?
Who then am I? How do I come to her?
Were I not a man, my senses well might leave me.
But I'll hold on to them, I'll hold on to them.
It is a blissful, blissful moment
never to be forgotten till the day of my death.

The Cavalier of the Rose

Meanwhile Octavian's suite has arranged itself in the rear, left, the Faninal servants with the Major-Domo right. Octavian's manservant presents the casket to Marian. Sophia shakes off her absorption and hands the rose to Marian, who shuts it in the casket. The Blackamoor steps up to Octavian from the back and hands him the hat. Octavian's suite withdraws, at the same time as Faninal's servants bring three chairs to the centre, two for Octavian and Sophia, one a little to the back and side for the Duenna. Simultaneously the Faninal Major-Domo bears the casket with the rose off through the centre doors. Sophia and Octavian stand opposite one another, having more or less returned to the everyday world, but with constraint. At a gesture of Sophia's they both sit down, as does the Duenna.

SOPHIA

I already know you quite well.

OCTAVIAN

You know me, *ma cousine?*

SOPHIA

Yes, from the book with the family trees in it, *mon cousin.*
The Mirror of the Austrian Peerage.
I take it to bed with me every night
and look up all my future relations there.

OCTAVIAN

Do you really do that, *ma cousine?*

SOPHIA

I know how old Your Lordship is—
Seventeen years and two months.

[439]

I know all your Christian names—Octavian Maria
　　Ehrenreich
Bonaventura Ferdinand Hyacinth.

OCTAVIAN

Better than I know them myself.

SOPHIA

Something else I know.

Blushes.

OCTAVIAN

What do you know? Tell me, *ma cousine.*

SOPHIA *without looking at him*

Quinquin.

OCTAVIAN *laughing*

That name you know too?

SOPHIA

So you are called only by your best friends
and fine ladies, if I am not mistaken,
with whom you are on good terms.

Short pause

Naïvely

I so look forward to being married. Do you look forward to
　　it too?
Or haven't you yet thought about it, *mon cousin?*
Think how different it is from the single state.

The Cavalier of the Rose

OCTAVIAN

softly, while she is speaking

How beautiful she is.

SOPHIA

Of course, you are a man, you are what you will be.
But I need a man before I can be anything.
I shall be much indebted to my husband for that.

OCTAVIAN *as before*

Heavens, how beautiful and good she is.
She makes me quite confused.

SOPHIA

And shall take care that I do not disgrace him.
And should one that thinks herself better than I
dispute my rank and precedence
at a christening or a funeral,
then will I, upon my soul,
show her who is the better
and put up with anything
rather than insult or unseemliness.

OCTAVIAN *warmly*

How can you even suppose
that you will be met by unseemliness,
when you'll be the most beautiful everywhere you go,
admitting no comparison?

SOPHIA

Are you laughing at me, *mon cousin?*

[441]

OCTAVIAN

What, could you think that of me?

SOPHIA

You may laugh at me, if you will.
I'll gladly submit to anything from you,
because it's the first time a young cavalier . . .
But now here comes my future lord.

*The doors open at the back. All three stand up and move
to the right. Faninal ceremoniously leads the Baron over the
threshold and towards Sophia, giving him the precedence.
The Lerchenau suite follows close behind—first the almoner with the valet-son. Then follows the body servant
with a similar lout, wearing a plaster over his broken nose,
and two others of the same sort, taken from the fields and
stuck into livery. Like their master, all wear myrtle. The
Faninal servants remain in the background.*

FANINAL

I present to Your Lordship his future wife.

BARON

makes a formal bow, then to Faninal

Delicious! I congratulate you.

He kisses Sophia's hand, slowly, scrutinizing it as he does so

A fine wrist. Attach a lot of importance to a wrist.
Mark of distinction not often found among commoners.

OCTAVIAN *half aloud*

I'm going hot and cold.

The Cavalier of the Rose

FANINAL

Permit me now to introduce a faithful friend of the family
Marian Leitmetzerin—

Introducing Marian, who curtseys three times.

BARON *waving her aside*

Don't bother with that.
Let's go and pay our compliments to my Cavalier of the
    Rose.

*With Faninal he approaches Octavian, with a bow, which
Octavian returns. The Lerchenau suite at last comes to a
stop, after it has almost knocked Sophia over, and draws
back a few paces.*

SOPHIA

standing right with Marian, half aloud

What kind of manners are these? Does he think he's a
    horse-coper?
Does he imagine he's bought me?

MARIAN *the same*

A gentleman's behaviour
is unconstrained, you see, and affable.
Remind yourself who he is
and what he is making you
and you'll soon clear your head of such humours.

BARON

to Faninal as he leads him forward

It's astonishin', the young Count's likeness to someone I
    know.

Hugo von Hofmannsthal

He's got a little sister, between you and me, a bastard, a
  pretty one, too.

Awkwardly confidential

It's no secret among people of quality.
Have it from the Princess's own mouth,
and as Faninal here is now so to speak a relation.
Doesn't distress you, does it, Cousin Rofrano,
that your father did a bit of philanderin' in his day?
He's in good company there, the late Right Honourable
  Marquess.
I myself make no exception of my own case.
Let Your Worship look at that long fellow there,
the blond one, behind.
Don't want to point my finger at him,
but he stands out from the rest
by a nobility of feature.
He is, too, a quite exceptional fellow,
though I say it as shouldn't, bein' his father,
but he's got his head well screwed on.

SOPHIA *meanwhile*

And now he leaves me standing, the coarse creature.
And that's my future husband.
And pock-marked all over his face, into the bargain,
  Heaven help me!

MARIAN

Now, now, if you don't like the front view, Miss Arrogance,
have a look at him from behind,
there you'll see something to put you in a good humour.

The Cavalier of the Rose

SOPHIA

I'd like to know what that could be.

MARIAN

copying her scornfully

She'd like to know what that could be.
That it's an Imperial Chamberlain
which your guardian angel has bestowed upon you
as your lord and husband.
You can see that at a glance.

*The Major-Domo politely approaches the Lerchenau servants
and leads them away. The Faninal servants also withdraw,
except for two who remain to hand wine and confectionery.*

FANINAL *to the Baron*

Will it please Your Lordship to partake? An old Tokay.

Octavian and the Baron help themselves.

BARON

Well done, Faninal, you know what's what.
Serve an old Tokay with a young maid.
I'm very pleased with you.

To Octavian

Must always show these upstart nobility
they're not to think themselves the likes of us,
must always be a touch of condescension there.

OCTAVIAN

I am full of admiration for Your Lordship,
you conduct yourself like a real man of the world,
could play the part of an ambassador any day.

[445]

Hugo von Hofmannsthal

BARON

I'll fetch the girl over.
She shall show us her conversational paces,
we'll see what the filly can do.

Goes over and takes Sophia by the hand, leading her across

Eh bien, now talk to us a little, me and Cousin Tavie.
Tell us what you most look forward to in marriage.

Sits down and tries to pull her on to his lap.

SOPHIA *resisting him*

What are you thinking of?

BARON *comfortably*

I'll show you what I'm thinking of! Come snuggle up to me
and let me tell you what I'm thinking of!

As before, Sophia resisting him more strenuously.

BARON *comfortably*

Would it be more to your taste if I should act
the master of ceremonies with you?
With *"mille pardons"* and "humble servant"
and "Spare me, Sir" and "Pray restrain yourself"?

SOPHIA

Really and truly it would be more to my taste!

BARON *laughing*

Not to mine either! There you see! Absolutely not to mine
either!
I, I'm all for a bit of decent, open-hearted flirtation.

He makes a move to kiss her but she resists energetically.

[446]

The Cavalier of the Rose

FANINAL

*after offering Octavian a seat in the second chair, which he
declines*

I can't get over it, there sits a Lerchenau
fondling, in honourable intimacy, my little Sophia
as if they were married already.
And there stands a Rofrano, as if it were
the most ordinary thing in the world.
I can't get over it. A Count Rofrano, no less,
brother of the Marquess the Lord High Steward.

OCTAVIAN *angrily*

There's a fellow I'd like to meet with my sword
somewhere with no watchman to hear him cry out.
Let me meet him, that's all I ask.

SOPHIA *to the Baron*

Stop it now, we're not yet on such terms.

BARON *to Sophia*

Does it embarrass you in front of Cousin Tavie?
There's no good reason. Let me tell you somethin'.
In Paris, which is the high school of good manners,
there's nothin', so I am told,
of what goes on between young married couples
to which they wouldn't send out invitations
to come and look on, even to the king himself.

*He gets more and more affectionate, she hardly knows what
to do.*

FANINAL

Were all the walls here of glass
so that all the envious citizens of Vienna

[447]

might see us so sitting *en famille!*
I'd give my corner house in Lerchenfeld for that, upon my
soul!

OCTAVIAN *enraged*

I'm doing penance for all my sins!
Oh to be out and away from here!

BARON *to Sophia*

Enough of these humours! Now you belong to me.
Everythin's all right. Be a good girl. All in apple-pie order.

Half to himself, coaxing her

Made to measure! Shoulders like a barnyard hen!
Thin as a rake still, no harm in that.
White too, with a bloom on her, just as I like it!
The luck of the Lerchenaus is with me yet!

Sophia tears herself free and stamps her foot.

BARON *delighted*

Temper! Is it a spirited little thing then?

Up and after her, Sophia having drawn back a few paces

Does the blood rush into its cheeks, then,
and will it burn a man's hand to touch them?

SOPHIA *flushed and then pale with anger*

Take your hands off me!

*Octavian in silent rage crushes the glass in his hand and
throws the pieces on the floor.*

The Cavalier of the Rose

DUENNA

runs daintily over to Octavian, picks up the pieces, and whispers delightedly to him

How delightfully informal, His Lordship!
The things he thinks of, it's an entertainment just to be
    with him!

BARON *close to Sophia*

Nothin' I like better!
'Pon my soul, you couldn't make me half so happy
with meltin' looks and lovin' ways.

SOPHIA *sharply, to his face*

I haven't a thought of making you happy!

BARON *genially*

You'll do it, though, whether you think to or not.

OCTAVIAN *aside, pale with anger*

Out, out, and no goodbyes,
or I'll not answer for myself,
I'll be doing some violence!

Meanwhile the Notary has entered with his Clerk, led in by Faninal's Major-Domo, who now announces him softly to Herr von Faninal. Faninal goes up to the Notary at the back, speaks with him, and looks through a sheaf of documents handed him by the Clerk.

SOPHIA *between her teeth*

No man has ever spoken to me in such a way!
What do you think we are to one another, I should like to
    know?
What are you to me?

[449]

Hugo von Hofmannsthal

BARON *genially*

The night'll come
when you'll learn, quite gently,
what I am to you.
Just as it goes in the song—d'ye know the song?
"Lalalalala—when I'll be your all!
With me, ah! with me, no garret's too small,
When I am away, daylight's terrors are strong,
But with me, ah! with me no night is too long."

*Sophia, as he presses her more closely to him, tears herself
loose and pushes him violently back.*

DUENNA *hurrying to her*

How delightfully informal, His Lordship!
The things he thinks of, it's an entertainment just to be
with him!

OCTAVIAN

without looking, but seeing what is going on none the less

I'm treading on coals of fire!
I'll be beside myself!
In this one hour I'm doing penance
for all my sins.

BARON

to himself, delightedly

Really and truly the luck of the Lerchenaus is with me.
There's nothin' in the world which so inflames me
and so effectively renews my youth
as a regular little termagant.

[450]

The Cavalier of the Rose

*Faninal and the Notary, the Clerk behind them, have come
forward left.*

BARON

*as soon as he sees the Notary, eagerly to Sophia, without
guessing what is going on in her*

There's business to be done now, I must excuse myself,
I'm needed over there. Meanwhile
Cousin Tavie will keep you company.

FANINAL

Now, if my noble son-in-law pleases—

BARON *eagerly*

Of course I please.

*As he passes, to Octavian, confidentially putting his arm
round his shoulders*

I've no objection
if you want to flirt with her a little, cousin,
now or in future.
She's still a regular touch-me-not.
She'll be all the better
for havin' some of the stiffness taken out of her.
Like a young filly that's not yet broken in.
It all accrues in the end
to the benefit of the rightful owner
if he knows how to make the best, that is,
of his marital privileges.

*He goes off left. The servant who admitted the Notary
has meanwhile opened the door left. Faninal and the Notary are about to pass through it. The Baron measures*

Faninal with a look and indicates that he is to keep three paces distance. Faninal obediently draws back. The Baron takes the precedence, assures himself that Faninal is three paces behind, and goes portentously off through the door, left. Behind him Faninal, then the Notary, then the Clerk. The servant shuts the door left and goes off, leaving open, however, the double doors to the antechamber. The servant handing wine has gone off earlier.

Sophia, right, stands confused and shamed. The Duenna, beside her, curtseys towards the door until it shuts.

OCTAVIAN

with a glance behind him to make sure that the others have gone off, walks quickly over to Sophia; quivering with emotion

Are you going to marry that man there, *ma cousine?*

SOPHIA

taking a step towards him, softly

Not for the world!

With a glance at the Duenna

Oh heavens, were I but alone with you,
so that I might beg of you, so that I might beg of you!

OCTAVIAN *half aloud, quickly*

What is it you would beg of me? Tell me quickly.

SOPHIA

taking another step nearer him

Oh heavens, that you would help me! But you'll never want to help me, because it's your cousin!

The Cavalier of the Rose

OCTAVIAN *violently*

I call him cousin from politeness,
the relationship doesn't go far, God be praised and thanked!
I never saw him in my life before yesterday.

*Some of the Faninal maids here flee right across the stage,
the Lerchenau servants at their heels. The valet and the
one with plaster on his nose chase a pretty young girl and
corner her right on the threshold of the salon.*

THE FANINAL MAJOR-DOMO

comes running anxiously in, to get the Duenna's help

The Lerchenau lot are drunk with brandy
rampaging among the servants, twenty times worse
than Turks or Croats!

DUENNA

Fetch some of our people, where are they?

*She runs off with the Major-Domo, they snatch their prey
from the two intruders and take the girl away. Everyone
disappears and the antechamber is left empty.*

SOPHIA

*now she knows there is no one in charge of her, in a
normal voice*

And now you will go away from me,
and I—what will become of me?

OCTAVIAN

I mustn't stay—
how I should like to stay with you.

[453]

Hugo von Hofmannsthal

SOPHIA *sighing*

You mustn't stay—

OCTAVIAN

Now you must, all on your own, stand up for us both.

SOPHIA

What? For us both? I don't understand.

OCTAVIAN

Yes, for us both! You *will* understand, I'm sure.

SOPHIA

Yes, for us both! Say that again.
Never in my life have I heard anything so beautiful.
Oh, say it once again.

OCTAVIAN

For your sake and my sake that's what you must do,
defend yourself, save yourself,
and stay as you are.

SOPHIA

Stay with me, then I can do all you could wish—

OCTAVIAN

My heart and mind—

SOPHIA

Stay with me!

OCTAVIAN

—will stay with you wherever you go or are.

[454]

SOPHIA

Stay with me, oh stay with me!

From the secret doors in the two corners at the back Valzacchi, left, and Annina, right, have slipped out soundlessly, spying on the couple. Soundlessly, slowly, they creep on tiptoe nearer and nearer.

Octavian draws Sophia to him and kisses her on the mouth. At this moment the Italians are close behind them, crouched behind the armchairs. Now they leap out, Annina seizing Sophia, Valzacchi catching hold of Octavian.

VALZACCHI AND ANNINA

shouting together

My Lord Baron of Lerchenau!—My Lord Baron of Lerchenau!

Octavian jumps sideways to the right.

VALZACCHI

who has trouble in holding him, breathlessly to Annina

Run and bring His Lordship!
Quick, only quick. I must hold this gentleman.

ANNINA

If I let the young lady go, she run away from me.

BOTH TOGETHER

My Lord Baron of Lerchenau!
My Lord Baron of Lerchenau!
Come to see the lady bride!
With a young Cavalier!
Come quickly, come here!

[455]

Hugo von Hofmannsthal

The Baron comes out of the door left. The Italians let go of their victims, jump to one side, and bow obsequiously to the Baron with meaningful gestures.

Sophia presses herself close to Octavian.

BARON

arms crossed over his breast, considers the group. Ominous pause. At last

Eh bien, mam'selle, what have you got to say to me?

Sophia is silent.

BARON

who is not at all put out

Now then, make up your mind!

SOPHIA

Oh heavens, what should I say?
You will not understand me.

BARON *genially*

That we shall see.

OCTAVIAN

taking a step towards the Baron

I have to advise Your Lordship that a change has occurred in one important particular of his affair.

BARON *genially*

A change? Hm, none that I know of.

[456]

OCTAVIAN

That is why you must now be informed.
The lady—

BARON

You move fast! You don't waste your opportunities
for all your seventeen years! I must congratulate you!

OCTAVIAN

The young lady—

BARON *half to himself*

A lad after my own heart, just as I was at his age.
Can't help laughin' at the young cub.

OCTAVIAN

The young lady—

BARON

Why, lookee, she's struck dumb and has engaged him
as her advocate.

OCTAVIAN

The young lady—

He breaks off again, as if to let Sophia speak.

SOPHIA *fearfully*

No, no, I can't open my mouth. You speak for me.

OCTAVIAN

The young lady—

[457]

Hugo von Hofmannsthal

BARON

stammering after him

The young lady, the young lady! The young lady! The
    young lady!
What kind of Punch and Judy show is this?
Be off with you now, or I shall lose my patience.

OCTAVIAN

with great decision

The young lady in a word,
the young lady does not like you.

BARON *genially*

Don't fret yourself about that. She'll learn to like me well
    enough.

Moving towards Sophia

Now you come in there with me. It'll soon be your turn
to give your signature.

SOPHIA *drawing back*

For nothing in the world will I give you my hand!
How can a gentleman be so lacking in delicacy?

OCTAVIAN

*who is now standing between the two of them and the
    door, left, very sharply*

Do you not understand plain language? The lady has made
    her mind up.
She desires Your Lordship to give up all thought of marry-
    ing her
now and for evermore.

The Cavalier of the Rose

BARON

with the look of a man in haste

Fiddlesticks! Maid's prattle'll get us nowhere!
By your leave now!

Takes her by the hand.

OCTAVIAN

taking up position in front of the door

If you've a spark
of gentlemanly feeling
what you've just heard from me
will be sufficient.

BARON

acting as if he had not heard him, to Sophia

Only congratulate yourself that I can wink an eye.
That will show you how a gentleman behaves.

He makes as if to pass Octavian, taking her with him.

OCTAVIAN

striking the hilt of his sword

There is one language at any rate
will be understood by the likes of you.

BARON

not letting go of Sophia and pushing her towards the door

I'd like to know what it is!

OCTAVIAN

I'll make no further effort therefore
in front of all these people—

[459]

BARON *as before*

I've got no time to lose.

OCTAVIAN

—to treat you with consideration.

BARON

Another time you can hold forth to me,
here or elsewhere.

OCTAVIAN *breaking out*

I'm talking to you here and now,
you're not a gentleman!
I don't even regard you as a man.

BARON

Truly, did I not know
that you had respect for my rank,
and were you not related to me
I should now find it hard
to avoid an appointment with you!

*He makes as if to lead Sophia, with affected unconcern, to
the centre doors, after the Italians have made lively signals
to him to take this route.*

BARON

Come, we'll go to your father that way.
It's nearer.

OCTAVIAN

after him, close to her

I hope Your Lordship will rather come with me behind the
  house.
There's a convenient garden there.

[460]

The Cavalier of the Rose

BARON

continues on his way, trying with pretended unconcern to lead Sophia by the hand in that direction, back over his shoulder

Shouldn't dream of it. I don't find it convenient now.
Don't want to keep the Notary waitin' at any price.
Would be an insult to the young bride.

OCTAVIAN

seizing him by the arm

The devil! You've got a thick skin!
I shan't let you pass that door either.
I'll shout it to your face,
I consider you a scoundrel,
a fortune-hunter,
a designing ruffian and filthy peasant,
a rogue without honour or decency.
And if you insist I'll give you your lesson here and now.

Sophia has torn herself loose from the Baron and jumped behind Octavian. They stand left, somewhat in front of the doorway.

BARON

*puts two fingers in his mouth and makes a piercing whistle.
Then*

What an impudent vocabulary
a lad of seventeen here in Vienna
already has at his command!

He looks round towards the centre doorway

However, thank God, the man who stands before him
is not unknown in this city

[461]

even to Her Imperial Majesty herself.
A man is what he is and doesn't need to prove it.
So take note of that and allow me to pass.

The full complement of Lerchenau servants has gathered within the centre doors; he assures himself of this by a glance to the rear. He now advances upon the two of them, determined to get possession of Sophia and a free passage

Should be really sorry if my people back there had to—

OCTAVIAN *enraged*

Do you dare involve your servants in our quarrel?
Now draw, or God have mercy on you!

Octavian draws.

The Lerchenau servants, who had already advanced a few paces, are rendered somewhat uncertain by this sight and check their advance. The Baron takes a step forward to get hold of Sophia.

OCTAVIAN *shouting at him*

Draw, damn you, or I'll run you through!

SOPHIA

Oh heavens, what will happen now?

BARON *withdrawing somewhat*

In front of a lady! Shame! Be sensible.

Octavian rushes at him in a rage.

The Baron draws, but manages it clumsily, and already has the point of Octavian's sword in his right upper arm. The Lerchenauers bound forward.

BARON

letting his sword fall

Murder! Murder! My blood! Help! Murderers! Murderers!
Murderers!

The servants all fall upon Octavian together. He leaps across to the left and holds them off his body by rapidly whirling his sword about him. The almoner, Valzacchi, and Annina hurry over to the Baron, whom they prop up and set down on a chair in the centre.

BARON

surrounded by them and hidden from the audience

I've a hot blood! A doctor, a bandage!
Bind it here! I'll bleed to death in an instant.
Stop him! Send for the police! Police!

THE LERCHENAUERS

closing in on Octavian with more ostentation than determination

Cut him down there! Slice him through!
Bring the pistols! Tinder too!
Get his sword, here catch a hold!
Knock him senseless, knock him cold!

The entire Faninal domestic staff, including the female house servants, kitchen staff and grooms, have streamed in through the centre doors.

ANNINA *in their direction*

The young Cavalier
and the lady bride, you see,

[463]

had a secret understanding
on the side, you see.

*Valzacchi and the Almoner pull off the groaning Baron's
coat.*

THE FANINAL DOMESTIC STAFF

Somebody ran him through?
That one? The stranger? Who?
The bridegroom, did you say?
Don't let the swordsman get away!
What swordsman? There in the light!
That one dressed all in white!
What, the Cavalier of the Rose?
On account of what? Who knows?
Knock him down! Get him outside!
On her account! The bride!
Why did he do it?
Love drove him to it.
Hate more like, and wickedness.
See how pale the mistress is!

DUENNA

*cleaves a way through to the Baron; they surround the
Baron in a close group, out of which over all the other
voices that of the Duenna rings out in lamentation*

Such a fine gentleman! Such humanity!
What a disaster, what a calamity!

OCTAVIAN

holding his assailants at arm's length

If you value a whole skin
keep away from my sword!

I'm quite ready to answer
for what has occurred.

SOPHIA *left front*

All is confusion,
excitement and thrill!
How like a god he was
imposing his will!
I feel him embracing me,
the touch of his hand,
and then it's as if
at the wave of a wand,
nothing could trouble me,
pain and terror depart,
and I feel his look piercing me
through to the heart.

THE LERCHENAUERS

*turn away from Octavian and make purposefully for the
maids nearest them*

Linen from Your Ladyships!
Tear your blouses into strips!
Don't be shy, you'll take no harm!
To bandage up His Lordship's arm!

*They make as if to seize for this purpose the blouses of the
younger and prettier maids. At this moment the Duenna,
who had dashed out, returns breathlessly, loaded with
linen; behind her two maids with sponge and basin full of
water. They surround the Baron with zealous attention.*

*Faninal dashes in at the door, left, behind him the Notary
and Clerk, who remain standing anxiously in the doorway.*

[465]

Hugo von Hofmannsthal

BARON

his voice is heard, but not much of him is seen

I can endure the sight of any amount of bloodshed,
only not my own! Oh! Oh!
So please use all your skill, do something to save my life!
Oh! Oh!
Sophia, as soon as she sees her father, has run forward,

right, and stands beside Octavian, who now sheathes his
sword.

ANNINA

curtseying officiously to Faninal, forward, left

The young Cavalier
and the lady bride, Your Worship,
had a secret understanding
on the side, Your Worship!
We in His Lordship's service
full of zeal, Your Worship,
kept after the pair
close at heel, Your Worship!

DUENNA

busy about the Baron

Such a fine gentleman! What a calamity!
What a disaster, what inhumanity!

FANINAL

clapping his hands over his head

My Lord son-in-law! What do I see? My Lord and saviour!
That such a thing should happen to you in my house!
Run for the doctor! Fly like the wind!

Ride them to death, my ten costly horses!
What, did none of my servants spring to your defence?
Is it for that that I feed a host of flunkeys tall as trees
that such outrage should befall me in my own brand-new
   town house?

Moving towards Octavian

I had really expected a different behaviour from Your
   Lordship!

BARON

Oh! Oh!

FANINAL

moving back to the Baron

Oh, the rich baronial blood running to the ground!

Now back to Octavian

Shame on you, a vulgar brawl!

BARON

I've got such young hot blood, it's a real tribulation to me,
nothing will stanch it. Oh!

FANINAL

breaking out at Octavian

I had really hoped to be taking another kind of pleasure
in Your Lordship's right honourable company here.

OCTAVIAN *politely*

Your Worship must excuse me.
I am beyond measure exceedingly distressed at the incident.
It was, however, not my fault. At a more convenient time

[467]

Your Worship will no doubt learn the course of events
from your daughter's own lips.

FANINAL

controlling himself with an effort

I must earnestly request it.

SOPHIA *determined*

As you command, father, I shall tell you everything.
That nobleman there has not behaved himself as he should.

FANINAL *angrily*

Eh, who are you speaking of? Of His Lordship your
  intended?
I certainly hope not! Those are not the manners I like.

SOPHIA *calmly*

It isn't so. I don't consider him as such.

The Doctor enters and is immediately led to the Baron.

FANINAL *more and more angry*

You don't consider him as such?

SOPHIA

No longer. I most respectfully beg your forgiveness for that.

FANINAL

*at first dully muttering the words, then bursting out into
furious rage*

Does not consider him as such. No longer. Begs my forgiveness.

The Cavalier of the Rose

Lies there spitted. Stands beside her. The youngster.
Disgraced. My marriage all to pieces.
All the envious citizens of Vienna
in the seventh heaven! Now the doctor. May have his death
    on my hands.

Moving towards Sophia, in blazing anger

You'll marry him!

*Towards Octavian, his coarseness damped down by respect
for the Count Rofrano to a fuming civility*

I humbly beg that Your Lordship may be pleased
with all haste to retire from hence
and never be seen here again!

To Sophia

Listen to me!
You'll marry him! And if he bleeds to death
you'll marry him dead!

*The Doctor indicates by a reassuring gesture that the
wounded man is not in any danger.*

*Octavian looks for his hat, which had fallen among the
servants' feet.*

A maid hands him the hat.

*Faninal makes Octavian a bow, exaggeratedly polite, but
unambiguous. Octavian, it is clear, must go, but he would
like to say one more word to Sophia. First of all he returns
Faninal's bow with an equally ceremonious one.*

SOPHIA

*hastens to say the following while Octavian can still hear
it, with a curtsey*

Neither living nor dead will I marry that nobleman!
I'll rather shut myself in my room!

FANINAL

*in rage and after making another furious bow to Octavian,
which Octavian promptly returns*

So! you'll shut yourself in your room.
There are servants enough in the house
to carry you into the carriage.

SOPHIA *with another curtsey*

I'll jump out of the carriage which takes me to church!

FANINAL

*going through the same performance between her and Oc-
tavian, who keeps making a further step towards the exit,
 but cannot tear himself away from Sophia at this moment*

So! you'll jump out of the carriage! Well, I'll sit next to you!
I'll hold you right enough!

SOPHIA *with a new curtsey*

I'll give the priest at the altar
No instead of Yes for an answer.

*The Major-Domo meanwhile gets the people out of the
room. The stage begins to empty. Only the Lerchenauers
stay behind with their master.*

FANINAL *as before*

So! you'll answer No instead of Yes!
In a trice I'll shut you in a convent!
Quick march! Out of my sight! This very day!
For life!

SOPHIA *struck with terror*

I pray your forgiveness! I've been a good daughter to you!
Pardon me just this once.

FANINAL

stopping his ears in his rage

For life! For life!

OCTAVIAN *quickly, half aloud*

Keep calm, my dearest, at all costs.
You'll be hearing from me.

The Duenna pushes Octavian towards the exit.

FANINAL

For life!

DUENNA

dragging Sophia with her towards the right

Come, get out of your father's sight!

Drags her to the door, right, pushes her out, and shuts it.

Octavian has departed through the centre doorway.

The Baron, surrounded by his domestics, the Duenna, two maids, the Italians, and the Doctor, is now fully visible reclining on a couch improvised from two or three chairs.

FANINAL

shouting once more after Sophia through the door, right

For life!

Then hastens to the Baron

[471]

Hugo von Hofmannsthal

I'm overjoyed! I must embrace Your Lordship!

BARON

whose arm has been hurt by the embrace

Oh! Oh!

FANINAL

O goodness gracious!

Then, raging inwardly, in the right-hand direction

Villainy! A convent.

In the direction of the centre doorway

A prison!
For life!

BARON

All right, all right. A mouthful of somethin' to drink.

FANINAL

A glass of wine? Or beer? A ginger cordial?

The Doctor makes an anxiously deprecating gesture.

FANINAL

To reduce a gentleman to such a state
in my town house! She'll marry you all the sooner!
I'm man enough to see to that.

BARON

All right, all right.

FANINAL

in an access of rage at the door, right

I'm man enough, I say!

[472]

Turning back to the Baron

I kiss His Lordship's hand in appreciation of his kindness
    and indulgence.
Everything in the house is his to command. I'll run, I'll
    bring him—

Towards the right

A convent's too good for her. Let Your Lordship not be
    anxious.
I know what satisfaction I owe you.

*Dashes off. The Duenna and maids also go off. The two
Italians have already slipped out during the foregoing.*

BARON *half sitting up*

There I lie! The things that can happen to a gentleman
    in this city of Vienna!
Wouldn't suit me—one is altogether too much the sport of
    fate—
rather be at home.

*A servant has appeared with a decanter of wine and glasses
on a tray.*

BARON

makes a movement which renews the pain in his arm

Oh! Oh! The young fiend! Oh! Oh! Devil take the lad!
Scarcely out of the nursery and can't keep his sword in its
    scabbard!
Young puppy, confounded dago, wait till I get hold of you!
I'll shut you in the kennels, upon my soul,
in the hen-house, in the pig-sty!
I'll tan your hide! Ye'll sing to another tune when I've done
    with ye!

Hugo von Hofmannsthal

The Doctor pours out a glass of wine and offers it to him.

BARON *after he has drunk*

And yet I can't help laughin' how a lad like that
at seventeen pictures the world to himself;
thinks perhaps, heaven knows, he's crossed me properly.
Hoho! quite the contrary—I wouldn't for the world
have missed the girl's rebellious outburst.
There's nothin' in the world which so inflames
and so effectively renews my youth
as a regular little termagant.

Turning to the Doctor

I've a mind now to go back to my room and rest a little.
So, learned sir, pray go ahead of me.
Make me a bed entirely of feather-bolsters.
I shall come after. But first I must drink a little. You go
   ahead.

The Doctor goes off with the valet.

*Annina has come in through the antechamber and glides
   furtively up to him, a letter in her hand.*

BARON

to himself, emptying the second glass

A feather-bed. Two hours to dinner. All that time to kill.
"When I am away, daylight's terrors are strong,
But with me, ah! with me no night is too long."

*Annina so places herself that the Baron must see her, and
   signals to him mysteriously with the letter.*

BARON

For me?

[474]

ANNINA

comes closer

From one you know.

BARON

Who do you mean by that?

ANNINA *quite close*

To be given into your own hands alone, in secret.

BARON

Give me air there!

The servants step back and without more ado take the decanter from the Faninal servants and drink it empty

BARON

Show me the scrawl.

Tears open the note with his left hand. Tries to read by holding it away from his eyes.

BARON

Look in my pocket, will ye, for my spectacles.

Mistrustfully, as she is about to do so

No, better not! Can you read handwritin'?
Here.

ANNINA

takes it and reads

"My cavalier, could be free Saturday evening.
I liked you well, but was ashamed

in front of Her Serene Highness
because I'm so young still. The Mariandel you know,
your loving chambermaid.
If my cavalier hasn't forgotten my name already.
Waiting for a reply."

BARON

She's waitin' for a reply.
Everythin's fallin' neatly into place
just as at home, but with a different twist.
The luck of the Lerchenaus is really with me.
Come to me after dinner, I'll give you the answer in writin'.

ANNINA

Entirely at your orders, my lord cavalier.
You won't forget the messenger?

BARON *to himself*

"When I am away, daylight's terrors are strong."

ANNINA *more insistent*

Your Lordship won't forget the messenger?

BARON

Don't worry.
"But with me, ah! with me no night is too long."
Later. All in one payment. At the end.
Wait for my reply. Leave me meanwhile.
Have writin' materials sent to my room. Over the way
    there,
so that I can dictate my reply.

Annina goes off.

[476]

The Cavalier of the Rose

BARON

*one last mouthful, then as he leaves, accompanied by his
servants*

"But with me, ah! with me no night is too long."

Curtain

Act Three

A private room in a tavern. In the background, left, an alcove, in which is a bed. The alcove can be shut off by a curtain which can be opened and closed. Forward left, a door to the neighbouring room. Right, stands a table laid for two, and on it a large, many-branched candlestick. In the centre at the rear a door on to the passage. Beside it, left, a sideboard. On the right at the back a blind window, in front, left, a window on the street. Chandeliers with candles in them on the side tables as well as on the walls. The only candles alight are one in each of the chandeliers on the side tables. The room is half in darkness.

Annina is standing there, dressed as a lady in mourning. Valzacchi arranges Annina's veil, plucks here and there at her dress, steps back and surveys her, takes a crayon out of his pocket, and draws shadows under her eyes. The door right is carefully opened, a head appears, disappears again, then a decently clothed but still somewhat dubious-looking old woman slips in through the rear door, opens it soundlessly and respectfully admits Octavian, in woman's clothes, with a mob-cap such as the daughters of the citizenry wear.

Octavian, the old woman behind him, goes up to the two others. They are at once noticed by Valzacchi, who stops what he is doing and bows to Octavian. Annina does not at once penetrate his disguise, she is quite at a loss from astonishment, then curtseys deeply. Octavian puts his hand in his pocket (not as a lady would but as a gentleman, and it can be seen that under his hoop-skirt he has men's clothes and

*riding boots, but without spurs) and throws Valzacchi a
purse.*

*Valzacchi and Annina kiss his hands, Annina makes some
last adjustment to Octavian's fichu. Meanwhile five suspicious-looking gentlemen have entered cautiously from the
right. Valzacchi signs to them to wait. They stand right,
near the door. Valzacchi pulls out his watch and gestures to
Octavian that it is high time. Octavian goes hurriedly off
through the centre door, followed by the old woman, who
plays the part of his companion. Annina goes to the
looking-glass (all with great care, avoiding noise), makes
further adjustments to her costume, then pulls out a scrap
of paper, from which she appears to be learning her part.
Valzacchi leads the suspicious-looking characters to the
front, impressing on them with every gesture the necessity
for the utmost caution. The five follow him on tiptoe to
the centre. He signs to one of them to follow him, quietly,
with scarcely a sound; leads him to the wall right, opens,
soundlessly, a trap door not far from the laid table, makes
the man climb down into it, and shuts the trap door after
him. Then he beckons two more to him, creeps in front of
them as far as the main door, sticks his head out, assures
himself that the coast is clear, beckons them to him, and
lets them out. Then he shuts the door, leads the last two
softly to the door into the next room and pushes them out
through it. Then he beckons Annina to him, and goes off
with her softly left, shutting the door after him soundlessly.
After a moment he comes in again and claps his hands.
One of those hidden raises himself head and shoulders
out of the floor, while up above the bed and from other
places heads appear and immediately disappear again, shutting secret sliding doors without a sound. Valzacchi looks at*

his watch again, goes to the back, opens the main door, then pulls out a fire-lighter and begins busily lighting the candles on the table. A waiter and a boy come running through the centre door with two long candle-lighters and some steps. They light the chandeliers on the side tables, then the numerous wall chandeliers. They have left the door open behind them, and in another room dance music is heard playing. Valzacchi hurries to the centre door, of which he obsequiously opens the second leaf, and jumps aside with a bow.

Baron Ochs appears, his arm in a sling, leading Octavian with his left hand, the valet behind him. The Baron scrutinizes the room. Octavian looks round, takes the looking-glass, and adjusts his hair. The Baron notices the waiter and boy, who want to light more candles, and signs to them not to. In their zeal they do not notice.

The Baron impatiently pulls the boy off the steps and extinguishes with his hand some of the candles burning nearest him. Valzacchi discreetly shows the Baron the alcove and through a gap in the curtains the bed. The Tavern-keeper hurries in with several more Waiters, to greet the distinguished guest.

INNKEEPER

Has Your Lordship any further commands?

WAITERS

More lights? A larger room? More silver on the table?

BARON

zealously occupied in putting out all the candles he can reach with a napkin he has taken from the table and unfolded

Make yourselves scarce! D'you want to get the girl all
    flustered?
What's the music for? I didn't order it.

INNKEEPER

Shall I arrange for it to come closer perhaps?
In the antechamber there, as music at table?

BARON

Leave the music where it is.

*Notices the window at the back, right, behind the laid
table*

What window is that?

Tries whether it lets in a draught.

INNKEEPER

Just a blind window.

Bows

May dinner be served?

All five waiters are about to hurry off.

BARON

Stop, what do these maybugs want?

WAITERS *at the door*

To serve Your Lordship!

BARON

waves them away

Don't need anyone. My valet there will serve
and I'll pour out myself. Understand?

Valzacchi indicates that they are to follow His Lordship's wishes without a word. Pushes them out of the door.

BARON

to Valzacchi, while he again puts out a number of candles, among them, with some trouble, those burning high up on the wall

You're a good fellow. If you'll help me knock a bit off
    the bill,
there'll be a little something for yourself. Sure to cost a
    fortune here.

Valzacchi goes off with a bow.

Octavian is now ready.

The Baron leads him to table, and they sit down.

The valet at the sideboard looks on, with unashamed curiosity, at the development of the tête-à-tête, and places carafes of wine from the sideboard on the dining-table.

The Baron pours out the wine. Octavian sips. The Baron kisses Octavian's hand. Octavian pulls his hand away. The Baron nods to the valet to withdraw, but has to repeat it several times before the valet at last goes.

OCTAVIAN

pushing back his glass

No, no, no, no! Wine fuddles so!

BARON

Come, come, love, what's the matter? Stop your fussin'!

OCTAVIAN

No, no, I'll not stay here.

The Cavalier of the Rose

Jumps up, makes as if to run out.

BARON

seizing him with his left hand

You'll drive me frantic.

OCTAVIAN

Oh I know what you think! Oh you're a wicked man!

BARON *in a very loud voice*

Damnation take me! Swear by my guardian angel!

OCTAVIAN

*acts as if terrified, runs as if in confusion not to the door
but to the alcove, pulls open the curtains and sees the bed.
Pretends to be exceedingly astonished, and comes back on
tiptoe, quite upset*

Dear Jesus, there's a bed in there, a mortal big one.
Oh my stars, I wonder who sleeps there?

BARON

leads him back to the table

You'll soon see. Now come, and sit down.
Somebody'll be comin' with the dinner in a minute.
Aren't you hungry?

Puts his left arm round his waist.

OCTAVIAN

Oh lord, and you a bridegroom and all.

Pushes him away.

[483]

Hugo von Hofmannsthal

BARON

Oh let's not hear that tedious word!
You're sittin' here with a man of the world,
Not a candlestick-maker.
A man of the world leaves everythin'
that doesn't suit him
outside the door. There's no bridegroom sittin' here
and no chambermaid neither.
Here sits a lover with his lovely mistress.

Draws him to him.

Octavian leans back coquettishly in the armchair, with half-closed eyes.

BARON

raises himself; the moment for the first kiss, he thinks, has come. As his face comes quite close to that of his companion, he is sharply struck by the likeness with Octavian. He starts back and his free hand goes involuntarily to his wounded arm

That face! that cursèd lad!
Follows me around wakin' and dreamin'.

Octavian opens his eyes, looks him boldly and coquettishly in the face. The Baron, now reassured that it is the maid, forces himself to smile. But the fright has not quite left his limbs. He must get air, and the kiss is postponed. The man under the trap door opens it too soon and shows himself. Octavian, who is sitting opposite him, nods emphatically to him to disappear. The man at once does so. The Baron, who, in order to shake off the unpleasant impression, has taken a few steps and is about to embrace her and kiss her from behind, just catches a glimpse of the man. He gives a violent start and points towards the spot.

[484]

OCTAVIAN

as if he did not understand

What ails you?

BARON

pointing to the spot from which the apparition has vanished

What was that? Didn't you see it?

OCTAVIAN

There's naught!

BARON

There's naught?

Once more anxiously scrutinizing her face

No?
And isn't there aught either?

He passes his hand over her face.

OCTAVIAN

That's my face.

BARON

breathing heavily, and pouring himself out a glass of wine

That's her face—and there's naught—seems
I've got an attack of giddiness.

*He sits down heavily, thoroughly upset. The valet comes
and serves food. The music off plays louder.*

OCTAVIAN

Oh the lovely music!

[485]

Hugo von Hofmannsthal

BARON *again very loud*

My favourite song, d'ye know that?

Nods to the valet to withdraw. The valet goes.

OCTAVIAN

listening to the music

Oh it makes you want to cry.

BARON

What?

OCTAVIAN

'Cause it's so beautiful.

BARON

What, cry? What a notion!
Merry as a cricket you ought to be,
the music goes into your blood.
D'ye feel it now,
now at last, d'ye feel it there,
feel you can do with me
anythin' you want?

OCTAVIAN

*leaning back, speaking as if to himself, with immoderate
sadness*

Faith, it's all one, faith, it's all one,
what the heart craves, be it ever so strong.

As the Baron takes her hand

What's the use of it all, give over your game,
I tell you it's not worth the candle.

[486]

The Cavalier of the Rose

BARON

What ails the lass? It's worth it every time.

OCTAVIAN

in the same melancholy mood

As the hour do go, as the wind do blow,
we two will soon be gone.
We're but human after all, that's a thing beyond our call,
there's none will mourn us after, not you and not me.

BARON

Does the wine always make you like this?
No doubt but it's your bodice
pressin' on your heart.

Octavian, with his eyes closed, makes no reply.

BARON

gets up and seeks to unlace her

Now I'm feelin' it a bit hot too.

With a quick decision he takes off his wig and looks for somewhere to put it down. As he does so he sees a face which shows itself over the alcove and stares at him. The face vanishes again almost immediately. He says to himself, "A giddy fit!" and shakes off his fright, but has to mop his brow none the less. Once more he sees the maid sitting there, her body relaxed and as if deprived of all will to resist. This overcomes every other consideration and he approaches her affectionately. Then he seems to recognize Octavian's face quite close to his own and starts back again. Mariandel hardly stirs. Once more the Baron shakes off his fright, forces a look of gaiety on to his face, when his eye

[487]

once again lights on a strange head staring out of the wall. This makes him exceedingly frightened, he utters a muffled roar, seizes the hand-bell from the table, and starts ringing it in a fury.

There, there, there, there!

Suddenly the supposedly blind window springs open, and Annina appears, in black mourning costume, and points with outstretched arms to the Baron.

BARON

distraught with terror

There, there, there, there!

Cowers away, at the same time covering himself against an attack from the rear.

ANNINA

It's he! It's my husband! It's he!

She disappears.

BARON *fearfully*

What is this?

OCTAVIAN

The room's bewitched.

Crosses himself.

ANNINA

rushes in through the centre door followed by Valzacchi in disguise, pretending to hold her back, then by the Innkeeper and three Waiters; she speaks with an educated but foreign accent

It's my husband, I claim this man as husband!
God is my witness, you are all my witnesses.
I'll take him to court! To the Privy Council!
The Empress herself shall give him back to me!

BARON *to the Innkeeper*

What does this hussy want with me, proprietor?
What does *he* want, and he, and he?

Points in all directions

The devil haunt your God-damned private room!

ANNINA

He dares to disown me, oh!
He acts as if he did not know me.

BARON

*has laid a cold compress on his head and holds it fast with
his left hand while he goes close up to the Waiters, the
Innkeeper, and last Annina, to assure himself of their reality. Facing Annina*

This one's alive too!

Throws the compress away. Very emphatically

As God is my witness I've never seen the baggage.

ANNINA *plaintively*

Oooh!

BARON *to the Innkeeper*

Send them packing and get on with the dinner.
It's the last time I set foot here in your tavern.

Hugo von Hofmannsthal

ANNINA

as if she had only just discovered Octavian's presence

Oooh! It's true, what they told me,
he's planning to make a second marriage, the scoundrel,
with a second innocent girl such as I was.

INNKEEPER, WAITERS

Oh Your Lordship!

BARON

Am I in a mad-house? God in Heaven!

*Violently shakes Valzacchi, who is standing nearest to him,
with his left hand*

Am I the Baron Lerchenau or am I not?

Pushes his finger through a candle-flame

Is that a candle, is that a napkin?

Beats the air with a napkin

Am I in my right senses?

ANNINA

Yes, yes, husband, that you are,
and as sure as you're in your right senses,
so sure am I in mine, and well you know me,
Leopold Anthony von Lerchenau,
consider well, above us stands a higher power,
which sees through your wickedness and will judge you.

BARON

stares at her, completely at a loss. To himself

She does remind me of someone.

[490]

The Cavalier of the Rose

Looks again at Octavian

They're one and all double-faced.

Looks fearfully towards the places in the wall and in the floor

Something up with me, something terrible.

Goes, like one lost, right forward to the footlights.

WAITERS *in hushed voices*

Oh the poor lady, oh the poor Baroness!

ANNINA

Children! here, come in!
And lift up your hands to him.

Four children between the ages of four and ten tumble into the room and at Annina's nod make for the Baron.

CHILDREN *piercingly*

Papa! Papa! Papa!

ANNINA

Don't you hear your own blood speaking to you?

BARON

hits out at them furiously with a napkin which he snatches up from the table

Send them packing, clear them out of my sight!
All of them, him, and him, and him, and him!

Pointing in all directions.

[491]

Hugo von Hofmannsthal

INNKEEPER

at the Baron's shoulder, softly

Saving your presence, don't go too far!
Could have very unpleasant consequences
for Your Lordship, the affair.

BARON

What? Me? Consequences? From that baggage there?
Never touched her in my life, not with the fire-tongs!

ANNINA *wailing aloud*

Aaah!

INNKEEPER *as before*

Bigamy's no joke—it's—begging Your Lordship's pardon—
it's a capital offence!

VALZACCHI

similarly slinking up to the Baron

Your Lordship take my advice, be careful!
The vice police don't brook no trifling.

BARON *in a rage*

Bigamy? No triflin'? Papa, Papa, Papa?

Clasps his head

Throw her out, that undertaker's mare there!
Who? What? You won't?
What? Police! The ruffians won't?
Are the whole crew of you in league against me?
Are we in France? Are we among the wild men?
Or in the Imperial City? Police!

[492]

The Cavalier of the Rose

Tears open the window on to the street

Up here, there, police! Up and restore order,
there's a person of rank here needs your help.

INNKEEPER

Oh my house and its reputation!
Oh what a black day for my house!

CHILDREN

Papa! Papa! Papa!

Valzacchi meanwhile says something in a low voice to Octavian.

OCTAVIAN *softly*

Has someone gone to fetch Faninal?

VALZACCHI

Right at the beginning. Be here any moment.

VOICES FROM OUTSIDE *smothered*

The police, the police!

*A Commissioner and two Watchmen enter. Everyone takes
up position so as to make room for them.*

VALZACCHI

softly to Octavian

Oh my goodness, what shall we do?

OCTAVIAN

Rely on me and let the affair take its course.

[493]

VALZACCHI

As Your Excellency commands.

COMMISSIONER *sharply*

Halt! No one must move. What's going on?
Who shouted for help? Who made an uproar?

BARON

goes up to him with the assurance of a great lord

Everythin's all right now. I'm very pleased with you.
Just as I had hoped—that in Vienna here
everythin' would be in apple-pie order.
Get this crew off my back, will you?
I want to have supper in peace and quiet.

COMMISSIONER

Who are you, Sir? What is your authority?
Are you the proprietor?

The Baron's jaw drops.

COMMISSIONER *sharply*

Then kindly be quiet
and wait till you are questioned.

The Baron falls back somewhat perplexed and begins looking for his wig, which has vanished in the disturbance and cannot be found.

Commissioner seats himself, and the two Watchmen post themselves behind him

Where's the proprietor?

[494]

The Cavalier of the Rose

INNKEEPER *obsequiously*

Tender my humblest respects to the Commissioner-General.

COMMISSIONER

The goings-on here seem anything but respectable.
Now make your report.

INNKEEPER

Your Worship.

COMMISSIONER

I trust you're not going to start off with denials.

INNKEEPER

Your Worship.

COMMISSIONER

From the beginning!

INNKEEPER

This one here, the Lord Baron—

COMMISSIONER

The big fat man there? What's he done with his wig?

BARON

who has been searching for it the whole time

I'm askin' you that.

INNKEEPER

That's the Lord Baron of Lerchenau.

[495]

COMMISSIONER

Not enough.

BARON

What?

COMMISSIONER

Have you any person with you?
Who can vouch for you?

BARON

Right here. My secretary here, an Italian.

VALZACCHI

exchanging a look of understanding with Octavian

I excuse myself. I know nothing. The gentleman
may be Baron, may be not. I know nothing.

BARON *beside himself*

How dare you, you filthy dago, you lyin' cheat!

Goes for him with his left hand raised to strike.

COMMISSIONER

sharply to the Baron

First of all control yourself.

A Watchman springs forward and holds the Baron back.

OCTAVIAN

*who has stood quietly on the right hitherto, now behaves
as if he were wandering desperately to and fro looking for
the way out and had mistaken the window for the door*

[496]

The Cavalier of the Rose

Oh goodness gracious, I could sink into the earth!
Holy Mary Mother of God!

COMMISSIONER

Who is the young person there?

BARON

She? Nobody. She's in my charge.

COMMISSIONER

You'll soon be given in charge yourself, I'm thinking.
Who is the young creature? What's she doing here?

Looks around him

I much hope you're not one of these damned seducers
and debauchers of the young. It'll go badly with you if so.
What are you doing with the girl? I want an answer.

OCTAVIAN

Oh I could drown myself!

*Runs to the alcove, as if to escape, tears open the curtains
and reveals the bed, peacefully illuminated.*

COMMISSIONER *getting up*

Proprietor, what do I see here?
What kind of business are you carrying on here?

INNKEEPER *embarrassed*

When I have persons of rank here to dinner or supper—

COMMISSIONER

Hold your tongue, I'll hear you later.

Hugo von Hofmannsthal

To the Baron

Now I shall count three, then I want to know,
what are you doing here with this young commoner?
I trust that you will not demean yourself to make a false
    statement.

*The Innkeeper and Valzacchi indicate to the Baron by ges-
tures the danger of the situation and the importance of his
statement.*

BARON

*nods to them with great assurance to rely on him, for he is
no greenhorn*

I presume you will have no objection, Commissioner,
to a person of rank takin' supper
at nine of an evenin' with his affianced bride.

Looks around to watch for the effect of his cunning reply.

COMMISSIONER

So this is your fiancée? Declare her father's name
and place of residence. If your declaration is confirmed
you may leave here with the young lady.

BARON

I am really not accustomed to be talked to in this—

COMMISSIONER *sharply*

Make your statement or I shall change my tune once more.

BARON

I shall not fail you. She's young Miss Faninal,
Anna Barbara Sophia, legitimate daughter

[498]

of the noble Master Faninal,
resident in his own house on the Platz am Hof.

At the door the inn staff, other guests, and also some of the
musicians from the other room have collected, curious to
see what is happening.

Von Faninal pushes through them, in haste, excited, in hat
and overcoat.

FANINAL

Here I am. What is required of me?

Moving up to the Baron

What a sight you look!
I could hardly have reckoned with a summons
at such an hour to a common tavern!

BARON

thoroughly astonished and upset

Who summoned you here? In the devil's name?

FANINAL

half aloud to the Baron

What's the idea of asking such a stupid question, son-in-
law?
When you've almost had my door beaten in with messengers
urging me to come here quickly and help you
out of an unpleasant situation, in which you found yourself
through no fault of your own.

The Baron clasps his head.

COMMISSIONER

Who is this gentleman? What is his business with you?

BARON

Nothin' of importance. Just an acquaintance
who happens to be stayin' here in the inn.

COMMISSIONER

Will the gentleman please give me his name?

FANINAL

I am the noble Master Faninal.

COMMISSIONER

So this is the father—

BARON

*putting himself between Octavian and Faninal, so as to
conceal him from him, zealously*

Oh dear me no, not he! He's a relation,
a brother, a nephew. The real one's twice as fat.

FANINAL

What's going on here? What a sight you look!
Of course I'm the father.

BARON

trying to get rid of him

It'll all be explained, only withdraw.

FANINAL

I must really beg—

BARON

Drive off home, in the devil's name!

[500]

FANINAL

Really, son-in-law, to compromise my name and honour
in such an affair!

BARON

trying to hold Faninal's mouth, to the Commissioner

It's an *idée fixe*.
Calls me so only for fun.

COMMISSIONER

That's quite enough, thank you.

To Faninal

So you recognize
in this gentleman here your son-in-law?

FANINAL

Perfectly! How so should I not recognize him?
Perhaps because he's got no hair?

COMMISSIONER *to the Baron*

And you now, I presume, recognize in this gentleman too,
for good or ill, your father-in-law?

BARON

*takes the candlestick from the table and shines it on Fani-
nal, inspecting him*

So, so, well, well—Yes, yes, it must be the same after all.
Haven't been quite myself all this evenin'.
Can't believe my own eyes today. I must tell you,
there's somethin' in the air here causes giddy fits.

[501]

Hugo von Hofmannsthal

COMMISSIONER *to Faninal*

On the other hand you repudiate the paternity
of this daughter here stated and alleged to be yours?

FANINAL

noticing Octavian for the first time

My daughter? This baggage here
gives herself out my daughter?

BARON *with a forced smile*

A bit of fun! A pure misunderstandin'! The innkeeper here
told the commissioner some story
of my engagement in the family Faninal.

INNKEEPER *excited*

Not a word! Not a word did I say to His Worship!
According to your own statement—

FANINAL *beside himself*

Arrest the hussy! To the pillory!
Have her whipped! Shut her in a convent!
I—I—

BARON

Drive off home—tomorrow mornin' first thing
I'll explain everythin'. You know what a debt you owe me.

FANINAL

beside himself with rage

According to his own statement! My daughter shall come up!
She's sitting in the sedan-chair below. Up at the gallop!

[502]

Some of those at the back go.

You'll pay for this! I'll bring you to court!

BARON

Harkee, you're makin' a regular hullabaloo
out of nothin', nothin' I say! A gentleman needs
the patience of an ox to be your son-in-law.

Shakes the Innkeeper

My wig! Find me my wig!

*As he thrashes around wildly looking for his wig, he catches
hold of a child or two and pushes them aside.*

CHILDREN *automatically*

Papa! Papa! Papa!

FANINAL

starts back

What's this now?

BARON

*succeeds in finding his hat at least, and strikes at the chil-
dren with it*

Nothin' at all, a swindle. I don't know the hussy!
Says she was married to me.
And me, I'm as innocent as the day.

*Sophia arrives in a cloak, and the people make way for her.
At the door the Faninal servants are seen holding the left-
hand carrying-poles of the sedan-chair.*

*The Baron seeks to screen his bald pate from Sophia, more
or less, with his hat.*

[503]

Hugo von Hofmannsthal

MANY VOICES

as Sophia goes over to her father

There's the bride! Oh, what a scandal!

FANINAL *to Sophia*

There, look round you. There stands your bridegroom.
There's the family of the noble Lord.
Wife and children all complete. And that wench there
Belongs to the family on a morganatic footing—
Oh, no, that wench is you, according to his own statement.
D'you feel like sinking in the earth? So do I!

SOPHIA

I'm heartily glad of it, I don't consider him as such.

FANINAL

Doesn't consider him such! Doesn't consider him such!
Oh, my good name! The whole city of Vienna! The Black Ga-
zette!
Tongues'll be wagging all the way up
to the Imperial antechamber.
I'll never dare set foot again on the Graben.
There's not a dog'll take a bone from me after this.

He is near to tears.

THE HEADS

popping out of the wall and floor, in muffled tones

The scandal! The shame!
On Faninal's good name.

[504]

They disappear again, but muffled voices are heard, coming out of the floor and walls

The scandal! The shame!

FANINAL

There! Out of the cellar! Out of the air!
The whole city of Vienna!

Advancing on the Baron with clenched fist

Oh you scoundrel! I'm not feeling well. A chair!

Servants spring forward to catch him.

Sophia anxiously occupies herself with him. The Innkeeper also joins her. They take him up and carry him into the neighbouring room. Several Waiters go ahead, showing the way and opening the door.

The Baron at this moment spots his wig, which has suddenly appeared again as if by magic; rushes upon it, snatches it up, puts it on and adjusts it correctly. With it he more or less recovers his bearing but contents himself with turning his back on Annina and the children, whose presence still makes him uneasy. The door has closed, right, behind Faninal and his attendants.

The Innkeeper and the Waiters soon after come softly out, fetch medicines, jugs of water, and so on, which are carried to the door and taken from them by Sophia at the opening.

BARON

now advancing on the Commissioner with his old self-assurance

I assume that everythin' is now clear. I'll pay and go.

Hugo von Hofmannsthal

To Octavian

I'll take you home now.

COMMISSIONER

There you're mistaken. You're to be examined further.

At the Commissioner's nod the two Watchmen remove all other persons from the room, only Annina with the children remains standing by the left-hand wall.

BARON

Let matters rest there. It was a joke.
I'll tell you later who the girl is.
Give you my word, I'll probably marry her one of these
    days.
See, the clothes-horse back there is mum already.
You'll soon see who I am and who I'm not.

Makes as if to lead Octavian away.

OCTAVIAN

frees himself

I'll not go with the gentleman!

BARON *half aloud*

I'll marry ye, just stay with me.
You'll be the Lady Baroness yet, I like ye very much!

OCTAVIAN

Mister Commissioner, I want to make a statement!
But His Lordship mustn't be there listening.

At the Commissioner's nod the two Watchmen push the Baron towards the front, right.

[506]

*Octavian seems to be giving the Commissioner some infor-
mation which greatly surprises him.*

BARON

*to the Watchmen, familiarly, indicating Annina in a half
whisper*

Don't know the hussy there, 'pon my honour.
Was just eatin'. No idea what she wants.
Otherwise I'd never've shouted for the police myself.

*The Commissioner accompanies Octavian to the alcove.
Octavian disappears behind the curtain. The Commissioner
seems to be amused and stands close to the parting of the
curtain without embarrassment.*

BARON

very excited over this inexplicable occurrence

What's happening there? No, it can't be! The rascal!
So that's what they call vice police?

He can hardly be held back

An unmarried girl!
Under my protection. I complain!
It's my turn to speak now!

*Tears himself loose and makes for the bed, but they catch
and hold him again. From the alcove there appear, piece
by piece, the clothes of Mariandel. The Commissioner
makes a bundle of them.*

BARON

*continues excitedly struggling to free himself from the two
Watchmen*

[507]

Must go to her now at any price!

*They have trouble in holding him, while Octavian's head
looks out from a gap in the curtains.*

INNKEEPER *entering*

Her Serene Highness the Princess Werdenberg!

*Waiters come in and throw open the doors. At first some
people in the Princess's livery become visible and take up
positions. The Princess enters, with the little Blackamoor
carrying her train.*

BARON

*having torn himself loose from the Watchmen, wipes the
sweat from his forehead, and hastens over to the Princess*

I'm happy beyond measure, have scarcely deserved the favour,
esteem Your Highness's presence here as an unexampled act
of friendship.

OCTAVIAN

sticks his head out of the curtains

Marie Thérèse, how did you get here?

*The Princess stands motionless, does not answer, looks
questioningly around her.*

COMMISSIONER

approaching the Princess

Suburban Assistant Commissioner—
obediently reporting to Your Highness.

[508]

The Cavalier of the Rose

BARON *simultaneously*

You see, Commissioner, Her Serene Highness has personally exerted herself.

Now you know with whom you have to deal.

PRINCESS

to the Commissioner, without paying any attention to the Baron

You know me? Don't I know you too? I almost think so.

COMMISSIONER

Very well.

PRINCESS

Once orderly to His Excellency the Field Marshal, wasn't that it?

COMMISSIONER

At Your Highness's command!

Octavian once more sticks his head out of the curtains.

BARON

nods vigorously to him to disappear, anxiously concerned that the Princess should notice nothing. In a half whisper

Stay behind there, for God's sake!

Then he hears footsteps approaching the door, forward right; throws himself towards it, puts his back against the door at the same time as he tries by courteous gestures in the Princess's direction, to give his behaviour an appearance of complete unconcern.

Hugo von Hofmannsthal

*The Princess crosses over to the right, looking at the Baron
expectantly.*

*The door, right, is forced open, obliging the Baron to step
back angrily.*

OCTAVIAN

*half dressed as a man, comes out between the curtains as
soon as the Baron has turned his back on him; in a half
whisper*

This isn't what we agreed. Marie Thérèse, what's come
over you?

*The Princess behaves as if she had not heard him, her look
of courteous expectancy still fixed on the Baron, who in the
utmost embarrassment divides his attention between the
door and the Princess.*

*The two Faninal servants have forced open the door with
some violence, and now Sophia is able to come in.*

The Baron steps back in an agony of embarrassment.

SOPHIA

*without seeing the Princess, who is concealed from her by
the Baron*

I've a message from my father for you.

BARON

breaking in, in a half whisper

Another time, God damn it!
Couldn't you have waited till called?
Do you think I want to present you here in a tavern?

Tries to push her out.

OCTAVIAN

*simultaneously stepping softly out, in a half whisper to the
Princess*

That's the young lady—who—because of whom—

PRINCESS

over her shoulder to Octavian, half aloud

You're a little too much in a hurry, Rofrano.
I don't need telling who she is. A charming girl, I find.

Octavian slips back through the curtains.

SOPHIA

*her back to the door, so sharply that the Baron takes an
involuntary step back*

You will present me nowhere and to nobody,
for I will have nothing more to do with you.
And my father sends you this message:
If you should ever have the impudence
even to show your nose
within a hundred paces of our town house,
you'll have only yourself to thank for the consequences.
That is my father's message.

BARON

beside himself, tries to go past her through the door

Hey, Faninal, I must—

SOPHIA

Don't you dare!

*The two Faninal servants come forward, stop him, and
push him back.*

Sophia goes in through the door, which shuts after her.

BARON *to the door, roaring*

I'm willin' to let everythin' that's occurred
be forgiven and forgotten!

PRINCESS

approaching the Baron from behind, taps him on the shoulder

Be a good fellow, now, and make yourself scarce.

BARON

turns round and stares at her

How so?

PRINCESS

cheerfully, mistress of the situation

Consider your dignity and drive off home.

BARON *speechless*

I! What?

PRINCESS

Put a *bonne mine à mauvais jeu*
and you may still pass, almost, for a person of rank.

The Baron stares at her, struck dumb.

Sophia has softly come out again. Her eyes seek Octavian.

PRINCESS

to the Commissioner, who is standing behind, right, with his watchmen

You see, Commissioner,
the whole thing was just a practical joke and nothing more.

COMMISSIONER

I'm satisfied. Tender my humble obedience and withdraw.

Goes off, followed by his two watchmen.

SOPHIA

to herself, horror-struck

The whole thing was a practical joke and nothing more.

The glances of the two women meet. Sophia makes the Princess an embarrassed curtsey.

BARON

standing between Sophia and the Princess

I for one am not so minded!

PRINCESS

impatiently stamping her foot, to Octavian

You tell him then, *mon cousin!*

Turns her back on the Baron.

OCTAVIAN

goes up to the Baron from behind, very manly

Must earnestly beg you.

BARON

turns round

Who? What?

[513]

Hugo von Hofmannsthal

PRINCESS

from the left, where she is now standing

The Right Honourable Count Rofrano, who else?

BARON

after closely scrutinizing Octavian's face, to himself with resignation

So it is. Had enough of that face.
So my eyes didn't deceive me. It's a young man all right.

Octavian stands there, haughty and impudent.

PRINCESS *taking a step closer*

It was a Vienna masquerade and nothing more.

BARON *very much put out*

Aha!

To himself

They're all in league against me.

PRINCESS *haughtily*

It would have gone ill with you
had you ventured in reality
to seduce a Mariandel of mine.

BARON

as before, brooding to himself

Aha!

PRINCESS

as above and without looking at Octavian

Just now I'm out of humour with all men—
I mean the sex in general.

[514]

The Cavalier of the Rose

BARON

gradually realizing the situation

Confound it! Can't get over my astonishment!

*with an eloquent look which wanders from the Princess to
    Octavian and from Octavian back again to the Princess*

Really don't know what to make
of the whole farrago.

PRINCESS

with a long look, then with great assurance

You are, are you not, a man of the world?
A man of the world as you are—or am I mistaken?—
you'll make nothing of it at all.
That's what I should expect of you.

Pause

BARON

with a bow, carrying it off like a man of the world

Charmed, I am sure, by so much refinement, I can't tell you
    how much.
No Lerchenau was ever yet a spoilsport.

Moving a step closer to her

A most entertainin' farrago of nonsense.
But now in return I need Your Highness's support—
I'm willin' to let everythin' that's happened
be forgiven and forgotten.

Pause

Eh bien, may I go to Faninal and—

He makes as if to go over to the door, right.

[515]

Hugo von Hofmannsthal

PRINCESS *impatiently*

You may—you may, in all tranquillity, make your departure!

The Baron is brought down to earth with a crash.

PRINCESS

Do you not understand when something is at an end?
The whole transaction, your engagement and everything else
that goes with it, is now a thing of the past.

SOPHIA

very distressed, to herself

Everything that goes with it, a thing of the past!

BARON

to himself, indignant, in a half whisper

All a thing of the past! All a thing of the past!

PRINCESS

*seems to be looking round for a chair, Octavian jumps to
give her one. The Princess seats herself, left. Meaningfully,
to herself*

All past and gone.

SOPHIA

right, to herself, pale

All past and gone!

*The Baron is quite unable to accept this turn of events,
rolling his eyes with rage and embarrassment.*

At this moment the man from the trap door emerges.

[516]

Valzacchi enters from the right, the doubtful characters following modestly behind him. Annina takes off her widow's cap and veil, wipes off her make-up, and shows her customary face. All this to the Baron's steadily increasing astonishment. The Innkeeper, a long bill in his hand, enters by the centre door, followed by waiters, musicians, porters, coachmen.

BARON

on seeing them all, gives his game up for lost. Quickly making his mind up, he calls out

Leopold, we're going!

Makes a deep but angry bow to the Princess. The valet snatches a candlestick from the table and is about to go ahead of his master. Annina impudently puts herself in the Baron's way. The children get under his feet. He hits about them with his hat.

CHILDREN

Papa! Papa! Papa!

The valet has cleared a way to the door. The Baron is about to pass.

WAITERS

Beggin' Your Lordship's pardon.
The candles is our affair.

MUSICIANS

Two hours' music at table.

COACHMEN

There's yer journey to pay—
our nags has wore their feet away.

Hugo von Hofmannsthal

PORTER

So, for openin' the doors to ye, milord Baron.

WAITERS

Candles, one gross—the candles is our affair.

BARON *in the throng*

Back there, make way, damnation take ye!

CHILDREN

Papa, Papa, Papa!

The Baron forces his way through the street door, as they all cluster tightly around him.

PORTER

Carriage and porterage! Out of town!

All together in the doorway, where the candlestick is torn from the valet's hand.

WAITERS

Candles is our affair!

They storm after him, the noise gradually dies away. The two Faninal servants meanwhile have gone off, left.

SOPHIA *standing right, pale*

Oh God, nothing more than a practical joke.
Oh God, oh God.
How he stands beside her, and I might as well not be here.

OCTAVIAN

behind the Princess's chair, embarrassed

This isn't what we agreed, Marie Thérèse, I'm surprised at you.

[518]

In acute embarrassment

Is it your command that I—should I not—the young lady—
the father—

PRINCESS

Go to her, quickly, and do what your heart bids you.

OCTAVIAN

Thérèse, I don't know.

PRINCESS

laughs angrily

Just like a man. Go to her.

OCTAVIAN

As you command.

Goes across.

Sophia is speechless.

OCTAVIAN *beside her*

Eh bien, haven't you a kind word for me?
Not a look, not a kindly greeting?

SOPHIA

I'll bury myself in a convent this very day, young as I am.
Let me go.

OCTAVIAN

I shall not let you.

Seizes her hand.

[519]

SOPHIA

That's easily said.

OCTAVIAN

I love you exceedingly.

SOPHIA

You don't love me as much as you pretend.
Forget me.

OCTAVIAN

It's for you I care and only for you.

SOPHIA

Forget me.

OCTAVIAN

I see your face always before me.

SOPHIA

weakly fending him off

Forget me.

OCTAVIAN

I too dearly love your dear self.

Clasps both her hands in his.

PRINCESS

to herself, together with Octavian and Sophia

Today or tomorrow or the next day after that.
Didn't I tell myself it would happen?

It's a thing that happens to every woman.
Didn't I know it then?
Didn't I make a vow
that I would bear it
with a calm and collected heart . . .
Today or tomorrow or the next day after that.
So God has created the world
and could not have done it any other way.

She wipes her eyes, and stands up.

SOPHIA *softly*

The Princess there, she's calling you, go to her.

Octavian has taken a few steps towards the Princess, and now stands embarrassed between the two.

Pause

Sophia at the door, uncertain whether to go or stay. Octavian, in centre, turns his head from one to the other. The Princess sees his embarrassment, and a sad smile passes over her face.

SOPHIA *at the door*

I must go in and ask how my father is.

OCTAVIAN

I must now speak, and the words fail me.

PRINCESS

The boy, how embarrassed he stands there in the middle.

OCTAVIAN *to Sophia*

Stay here whatever you do.

[521]

Hugo von Hofmannsthal

To the Princess

What, did you say something?

SOPHIA

together with the Princess, to herself

It's not for nothing she must've come here.
She's a good friend of his, no doubt of it.
Oh, I wish I'd stayed in my convent
and still knew nothing of the great world.

PRINCESS

together with Sophia, to herself

I vowed to myself to love him in the proper way
so as to love even his love for another . . .
Though truly I never thought
I should be so soon put to the test.

She goes across to Sophia.

Octavian takes a step backwards.

The Princess stands in front of Sophia, and looks at her quizzically but kindly. Sophia is embarrassed and curtseys.

PRINCESS

So quickly you love him, and so much?

SOPHIA

I don't know what Your Highness means by that question.

PRINCESS

Your pale face already gives the right answer.

[522]

The Cavalier of the Rose

SOPHIA

No wonder if I am pale, Your Highness.
I had a great fright over my father.
To say nothing of my justifiable indignation
against the outrageous Lord Baron.

PRINCESS

Don't talk too much, my dear, you're pretty enough.
As for your respected father's illness, I think I know a
remedy.
And for your paleness perhaps my cousin there knows the
remedy.

OCTAVIAN

Marie Thérèse, how good you are!
Marie Thérèse. I really don't know—

PRINCESS

with an indefinable expression

I don't know anything either.
Not a thing.

Nods to him to stay behind.

OCTAVIAN

Marie Thérèse!

*The Princess remains standing in the door. Octavian stands
the nearer of the two to her, Sophia further to the right.*

PRINCESS

*together with Octavian and Sophia, but without looking at
them*

[523]

There's many a matter here on earth
nobody could ever believe
did they but hear the story told.
But the one it happens to, that one believes and knows not
    how. . . .
There stands the boy and here I stand and with that stran-
    ger girl there
he'll be as happy as happiness
is understood by men. In the name of God.

OCTAVIAN

together with the Princess and Sophia, first to himself, then
face to face with Sophia

Something has happened, something has changed.
I'd like to ask her, Can it be? and yet I feel
that just that question is the forbidden one.
I'd like to ask her, Why is there something shaking in me?
Has some great wrong been done? And yet she's the one
of whom I can never ask that question—and then, Sophia,
I look at you, see only you, feel only you, Sophia,
know nothing else but one thing only—it's you I love.

SOPHIA

together with the Princess and Octavian, first to herself,
then face to face with Octavian

I feel as if in church, a holy feeling, and so fearful,
and yet I feel unholy too, I don't know how I feel.
I'd like to kneel down there before the lady and I'd like
to do her some hurt too, for I feel she gives me him
and at the same time takes something of him from me. I
    don't know how I feel.

The Cavalier of the Rose

I'd like to understand everything, I'd like to understand
    nothing,
to ask and not ask. I'm feeling hot and cold,
feel only you and know one thing only—it's you I love.

The Princess goes softly into the inner room, right, un-
noticed by the two. Octavian has come close up to Sophia,
and a moment later she is lying in his arms.

OCTAVIAN

together with Sophia

Feel only you, feel only you alone,
together, you and I as one.
And all else like a dream now flies
before my eyes.

SOPHIA

together with Octavian

Dream and reality are one,
together, you and I alone,
always together, you and I,
to all eternity.

OCTAVIAN *as before*

Was once a house that you were in,
they picked me out, they sent me in,
the highway to eternal bliss—
what a stroke was this!

SOPHIA *as before*

You can laugh! Pity my state,
poor trembling soul at Heaven's gate,
weak thing as I am, enfold me,
I'm sinking, hold me.

She has to lean on him. At this moment the Faninal serv-
ants open the door and come out, each with a candlestick.
Through the door comes Faninal, leading the Princess by
the hand. The two young people stand a moment confused,
then make a deep bow and a deep curtsey, which are re-
turned by Faninal and the Princess.

FANINAL

giving Sophia a good-humoured, fatherly pinch on the
cheek

Young people, they're all the same!

Then he gives the Princess his hand and leads her to the
centre door, which is simultaneously opened by the Prin-
cess's footmen, the little Blackamoor with them. Outside is
light, here inside half darkness, the two servants with the
candlesticks having preceded the Princess.

Octavian and Sophia are left alone in the half-dark room.

OCTAVIAN

Feel only you, feel only you alone,
together, you and I as one.
And all else like a dream now flies
before my eyes.

SOPHIA

Dream and reality are one,
together, you and I alone,
always together, you and I,
to all eternity.

She sinks into his arms, he quickly kisses her. Without her
noticing it, her pocket handkerchief falls out of her hand.

The Cavalier of the Rose

Then they run out hand in hand together. The stage remains empty, then the centre door opens once more. There enters the little Blackamoor with a candle in his hand. He looks for the handkerchief, finds it, picks it up, trips out.

Curtain

ARABELLA

A Lyrical Comedy in Three Acts

Translated by

NORA WYDENBRUCK
and
CHRISTOPHER MIDDLETON

COUNT WALDNER, *captain of Horse (retired)*

ADELAIDE, *his wife*

ARABELLA
ZDENKA } *their daughters*

MANDRYKA

MATTEO, *officer in the Rifles*

COUNT ELEMER
COUNT DOMINIC } *admirers of Arabella*
COUNT LAMORAL

FIACRE-MILLI

A FORTUNE-TELLER

WELKO, *Mandryka's valet*

DJURA
JANKEL } *Mandryka's servants*

A FLOOR-WAITER

ARABELLA'S DUENNA

THREE GAMBLERS

A DOCTOR

GROOM

Coachmen, guests at the ball, hotel guests, waiters.

The place: Vienna.

The time: 1860.

[531]

Act One

Drawing-room in a private suite in a Vienna hotel. Folding doors in centre, window on the right, door further back. Another door on opposite wall. The room is newly and sumptuously furnished in the style of 1860.

Adelaide is sitting with the Fortune-Teller at a table on the left. Zdenka, disguised as a boy, is sorting papers at another smaller table.

FORTUNE-TELLER

The cards are better than the time before.

ADELAIDE

Please God it's true.

A knock at the door

We must not be disturbed!

ZDENKA

runs to centre door; something is handed in to her

My father's not at home, my mother has migraine.
Come later.—It's a bill again, another bill!

ADELAIDE

motions her away

Not now! Put it down there.

[533]

Hugo von Hofmannsthal

ZDENKA

There are so many there already.

ADELAIDE

Quiet now. What's in the cards this time?
This worry and impatience, they're killing me.

FORTUNE-TELLER

bending over the cards

Be calm. The bequest is coming nearer—but slowly.

ADELAIDE

wringing her hands

No, we can't wait any longer!
There's only one hope left us:
that Arabella should get married quickly.
What's in the cards about it now, my friend?

FORTUNE-TELLER

They show me everything as in a mirror;
I see the father—the count, your husband;
O dear, he has his cares, it's dark all round him.
He tries his luck—O dear, and he's losing again,
the highest bid.

ADELAIDE

Holy Mother of God!
So help me now, and through my lovely daughter!
For heaven's sake, is it soon she'll be betrothed?
No one will give us credit any more, my friend.

[534]

Arabella

FORTUNE-TELLER

gazes at the cards a long time

Here is the officer.

ADELAIDE

An officer? O dear!

ZDENKA *to herself*

Matteo!

FORTUNE-TELLER

No! He is not the man in the cards.

ADELAIDE

I should hope not indeed!

FORTUNE-TELLER

He'll come from over there, the stranger, the bridegroom.

ADELAIDE

My emerald brooch will be your very own,
if what you prophesy comes true this week.

FORTUNE-TELLER

slowly, as if deciphering the book of fate

He comes from farther away. A letter called him here.

ADELAIDE

From farther away? It is Count Elemer, that's certain.

FORTUNE-TELLER

I see enormous forests, it's from there he comes.

ADELAIDE

That's him! How well you have described our Elemer.
Splendid! But why does he hesitate?

FORTUNE-TELLER

The hesitation comes from her.

ADELAIDE *delighted*

You see through human beings as through glass.
It's her incredible pride. Please God to soften it!
Her pride is as great as her beauty is.

A knock. Zdenka hurries to the door.

ZDENKA

No, it's impossible at the moment.

She is given another bill which she puts on the table.

ADELAIDE

What can you see? Why do you frown like that?

FORTUNE-TELLER

pondering as she studies the cards

Someone is thrusting himself
between the beautiful daughter and the rich man.

ADELAIDE

Holy Mother of God, don't let that happen!

FORTUNE-TELLER

bending over the cards

What's this? Has your ladyship a second daughter?
Now things are getting very dangerous.

[536]

Arabella

ADELAIDE *softly*

Not so loud! You've touched on a family secret.

Zdenka, on the right, is listening.

FORTUNE-TELLER

How does she come in so suddenly, this other girl?
It is she who brings misfortune to her sister.

ADELAIDE

For heaven's sake, speak quietly!

FORTUNE-TELLER

bending over the cards

Keep the sisters carefully apart.
Or else things will go wrong.

ADELAIDE *close to her*

Tell me, what can you see?

FORTUNE-TELLER

I see a violent quarrel—separation—
The suitor wants to leave!
Terrible things are being said! Strangers listen!

ADELAIDE

Merciful Lord in heaven!

FORTUNE-TELLER

It's all because
of the little fair-haired girl and the officer.

[537]

Hugo von Hofmannsthal

ADELAIDE

kneels beside the table

Angelic hosts of heaven, hear the prayer of a mother
whose heart is torn by fear!

ZDENKA *frightened*

Mamma!

ADELAIDE

Zdenka, be quiet, these things are no concern of yours.

Rises, whispers, pointing to Zdenka

Quietly, that's the girl!

FORTUNE-TELLER

That young man there?

ADELAIDE

She is a girl. But she was such a boyish madcap
that we allowed her to remain a boy.
We can't afford, in this expensive city,
to bring two daughters out, as would suit our standing.
Yet Zdenka is devoted to her elder sister.
How could she ever do her harm?

FORTUNE-TELLER

The cards can never lie.
Here is the officer. And there the fair-haired girl.
I can see drawn swords, and the bridegroom is going away.
The cards are warning you!

[538]

Arabella

ADELAIDE

gets up

You are my guardian angel.
Come to my room here. Try the cards **again**.

FORTUNE-TELLER

The cards take nothing back.

ADELAIDE

Hurry, I implore you.

Leads her into the room on the left.

ZDENKA

takes up the heaped bills, scrutinizes them

They all want money, they threaten with the law.
What's this? This is news to me; they write:
They've heard that we intend to be leaving soon,
O that would be the end.
I'll never see him again.

In her fear, runs to the door on the left and listens

She says some danger is threatening Arabella,
through an officer.
And Mamma is saying that he must not come here again.
He's compromising her.
Never come here again! Heavens, he'll kill himself.
And they'll all know: it is because of her—
and she, at last she'll know how much he loved her.

Leaves the door

O God, do not let it happen that we must leave,
make Papa win! Make the old aunt in Gorizia die!

[539]

Make Bella love Matteo with all her heart.
Let him be happy, and stop us being poor!
I vow to sacrifice myself; as long as I'm alive
I'll wear men's clothes and give up everything, everything!

*A knock, she goes to the centre door; it is carefully pushed
open from outside. Enter Matteo, in uniform, carrying his
hat, without his sword.*

ZDENKA

has gone pale

Matteo!

MATTEO

Zdenko! You here! Are you alone!

ZDENKA

in a low voice, timidly

Mamma's in there.

MATTEO

And Arabella?

ZDENKA

She's gone for a walk on the Ring with the duenna.

MATTEO

comes a step nearer

Nothing for me? No message? Not a letter?

Zdenka shakes her head sadly

Where did she go last night?

[540]

Arabella

ZDENKA

She went to the Opera
with our Mamma.

MATTEO *jealously*

Alone with your Mamma?

ZDENKA *hesitantly*

I think the three young counts were there as well.

MATTEO

And this afternoon?

ZDENKA

hesitantly, timidly

They're going to take her out for a sleigh ride.
I'm to go too. She must be chaperoned.

MATTEO *deeply wounded*

So that is how things stand between her and me;
if it were not for you I would not even know her plans.
She has not a moment for me now, only at times
a half disapproving, half indifferent look.

ZDENKA

And yet she loves you. Believe me, I . . . I know!

MATTEO

with sudden brightness

Zdenko, you're my only friend!
You know? Did she confide in you?

[541]

Hugo von Hofmannsthal

ZDENKA

You know how she is secret as the grave itself.
She doesn't say it in words.
But I just know—besides, didn't she write three days ago
the letter which gave you so much happiness?

MATTEO

Blissful happiness—that letter came from heaven!
But then she treats me coldly again, like a stranger.
Zdenko, what does it mean? And however can I bear it?

ZDENKA

softly, mysteriously

That's how girls are. A girl will gladly give you more and
    more,
but keeps her feelings secret. You see, she's so ashamed.

MATTEO

How much you know, you darling boy!
So you must know—

        Grasps Zdenka's arm; she draws away

            how terrible it is,
and what obsessive thoughts can often master me
when she looks through me, just as if I were not there,
and you fail to bring me a sign
that would make me hope and live again.

ZDENKA *quickly*

I know! I'll bring you another letter like that,
today, or tomorrow!

[542]

Arabella

MATTEO *urgently*

Please, today! You are my only friend.
Give me your word as a gentleman, I count on you!
And if I found I could count on you no longer—
there would be sweeping changes.

ZDENKA *with alarm*

What would be changed, Matteo?

MATTEO *gloomily*

I should apply tomorrow for a transfer to Galicia,
and then, if even there I find myself
unable to forget Arabella,
there's one resort remaining: the revolver.

ZDENKA

O God in heaven!

MATTEO

Think of a way to help me.

He hurries away.

ZDENKA

*almost beside herself with excitement and fear at all the
dangers and difficulties besetting her*

Help *him*—dear God! And me, who shall help *me*?
There are words enough in me to write a hundred letters.
Her writing too—I could copy it in my sleep.
And yet such letters cannot help him, when it's myself
who must invent these tender words of love.
I must find the words that will go to her heart

[543]

and make her recognize the only man who deserves her
love—
that's far more difficult, and if I don't succeed—the game
is up!

*Enter Arabella, wearing a hat, veil, and fur jacket, followed
by the duenna.*

ARABELLA

Thank you, Fräulein. Fetch me at the same time tomorrow.
I do not need you any more today. Adieu.

Exit duenna.

ARABELLA

*takes off her hat and jacket, notices the roses on a small
table*

What lovely roses! Was it a hussar brought these?

She takes the roses.

ZDENKA

What? A hussar?

ARABELLA

The servant of some stranger on a journey.

ZDENKA

No, they are from Matteo.

*Arabella puts the roses quickly down. Zdenka replaces them
in the vase.*

ZDENKA *gently*

That's how you treat Matteo's flowers,
and yet he brings you fresh ones every day.

ARABELLA *tersely*

Perhaps. And the other posy over there?

ZDENKA

From Elemer.
The perfume is from Dominic. The lace from Lamoral.

ARABELLA *sarcastically*

Those three! They throw away money together, love the same girl together,
in the end all three together will get engaged to me!

ZDENKA

They're no good at all—this is the only good one, this!

She holds Matteo's roses towards Arabella.

ARABELLA

Perhaps. Those three are far more fun, and interest me more.

ZDENKA *reproachfully*

How can you say that? Interest you more than Matteo?
Does he not love you with all his heart, with all his soul?

ARABELLA *sarcastically*

–and with all his strength as well!
It's just that he's not very strong.

ZDENKA *passionately*

How dare you speak like that?
You used to be fond of him.

[545]

Hugo von Hofmannsthal

ARABELLA

Perhaps!
I used to be—that's over: you say so yourself.

ZDENKA

Don't let him ever hear you speak that way.
It would be the death of him.

ARABELLA *flippantly*

Men don't die all that easily.

ZDENKA *more passionately*

It would be the death of him! He worships you!

ARABELLA

looks at her

My pet, you've caught that highfalutin tone from Mamma!
You must watch out!

ZDENKA *ardently*

Because it breaks my heart to see him suffer!

ARABELLA

without looking at her

Are you in love with him?

ZDENKA

I am his friend—
his only friend, in all the world!

[546]

Arabella

ARABELLA

looks at her attentively again

My little Zdenka, there's been something dangerous about
   you for some time.
I think it's time that you became a girl
quite openly, and ended this masquerade.

ZDENKA

I'll be a boy until I die. I will not be a woman—
a woman such as you. Flirtatious, cold, and proud as well.

ARABELLA

My dear, it seems to me that it's high time indeed.

ZDENKA *passionately*

It's time you stopped trampling underfoot
the only heart that is worthy of you.

ARABELLA *very seriously*

He's not the man that I could marry!
He's not a manly man. I could never feel afraid of him;
with me, a man like that has played his hand.

ZDENKA

Now you are speaking like a witch!

ARABELLA

has sat down

I'm speaking seriously and telling you the truth.
It's not my fault that I am made this way.
A man may suddenly mean very much to me,
and just as soon I find he does not mean a thing!
It happens in my mind, quicker than I can say.

[547]

Questions begin to come, and I cannot find
the answers to these questions, day or night.
Then quite against my will my heart will turn away,
and turn from him. That's out of my control—
but the right man for me, provided he exists, one day
will suddenly be standing here before me,
and he will look at me and I at him,
and there'll be no more doubting, no more questioning.
It will be bliss, and I'll obey as gladly as a child.

ZDENKA

gazes at her lovingly; after a slight pause

I don't know what you're like, I don't know if you're
    right—
because I'm far too fond of you! All I want is your happi-
    ness
with a man who deserves you—and I'll help you win it.

More warmly, half to herself, together with Arabella

That's just as the prophetess has seen it—
she bathed in light, while I go down in darkness.

To herself

She is so sweet and beautiful—I'll go away,
and even as I go, I'll bless you, my dear sister.

ARABELLA

to herself, together with Zdenka

The right man, if there is one for me at all,
will look at me, and I at him,
and there'll be no more doubting, no more questioning.
It will be bliss, and I'll obey as gladly as a child.

The jingling of sleigh bells is heard.

[548]

Arabella

ZDENKA

That's Elemer's sleigh. I know the sound of his bells.

ARABELLA

lightly and gaily again

And Dominic will be following in his sleigh
and Lamoral behind him. That's how they go on.
And I join in the fun—because it's carnival.

ZDENKA

No. Elemer will come alone today.
For that is the agreement they have made.
Are you glad? No—he cannot be the man for **you.**
No, no, that must not happen.

ARABELLA

How should I know?
He's certainly a man. Or too much a man,
an untamed, violent man. Perhaps I must accept **him.**

She pauses thoughtfully.

ZDENKA

If you do that, Matteo will shoot himself—

As in a trance

I'm knocking at his door, but there's no answer,
I throw myself on him—for the first time I kiss
his ice-cold lips! Then that is the end of it.

ARABELLA

to herself, taking no notice of Zdenka

Perhaps I must. I'm sure I'll be given a sign.
Tonight is the end of carnival. Tonight I must decide.

[549]

Hugo von Hofmannsthal

My little one, why do you look at me so sadly?
I know too well our parents cannot wait
to rid themselves of me. How can I go
unless there's something urges and pushes and throws me at
  that one man?

She goes to the window

Listen, this morning I caught sight of a stranger,
as I walked from the house on to the street,
standing just at the corner there—tall, in a fur-lined coat,
behind him his servant—a gentleman from Hungary
or from Wallachia.
He looked at me with large, grave, steadfast eyes.
Then he turned to say something to his servant.
I could have sworn that he would send me flowers.
Today, flowers from him would mean the world to me.
I'd take them to my room and keep them there,
and in the night, returning from the ball,
I would find them again, and keep them alive,
until he came in person. Never mind,
these are just dreams—
why do you look so scared?

ZDENKA

takes Matteo's roses from the vase and holds them out

Take these! They come from the loyalest man on earth.
Take them to you, hold these close and these alone.
I feel: your fate, and mine, depend on it.

Sleigh bells are heard, louder.

ARABELLA *amazed*

What's the matter? What has come over you?

[550]

Arabella

ZDENKA

Quiet now! Here comes Elemer.

The centre door opens revealing Elemer. He throws off the fur-lined coat he had slung round his shoulders. A groom behind him catches it. Closes door from outside. Zdenka quietly exit right.

ARABELLA

Why this triumphant entrance?

ELEMER

This day is mine. We have drawn lots for it.
And I have had my Russian horses harnessed,
to take you in my sleigh this afternoon,
and at the coachmen's ball, this evening,
I'll be your master.

Arabella frowns

           I mean to say: your foremost servant,
for you remain our undisputed queen.

ARABELLA

You three drew lots for me! You ought to be ashamed!

ELEMER

No—we have made a decision and sworn an oath
that the man you choose must be one of us three.

ARABELLA

Indeed? I'm forced to choose one of you three?
And I? Am I a slave girl that you should wager for me?
In what war have you captured me, if I may ask?

[551]

Hugo von Hofmannsthal

ELEMER

It is she herself who asks to be the prize.
Her looks have summoned us to face the competition.
A look from a girl is strong, and gives and takes,
and promises even more.

ARABELLA *to herself*

What a difference was in the other eyes that looked at me
    today.

Looking steadily at him

Yes, you demand—and you desire—perhaps even love me!

ELEMER

Perhaps? You dare say that word, to *me*, after these weeks?

He grips her wrist angrily.

ARABELLA

frees herself and moves away

I have my pride and there are things I never could forgive.
And I refuse, entirely, to be fettered!

ELEMER

Your pride demands one thing alone, to yield to a man!

ARABELLA

It asks for that? Then I should be angry with you
for having courted me through an entire carnival
and failed, in spite of it, to free my heart
from this my pride, and given me nothing in place of it.
And all the time I am what I have always been,
and savour that bitter-sweet and only joy

[552]

Arabella

which is all a girl retains: in hiding herself,
still undecided, never giving all,
and hesitating still—
perhaps—perhaps a change is coming, Elemer.

With a sweet smile

Who knows? Perhaps quite soon, perhaps this very night!

ELEMER

That change will come the moment—and that moment
I do implore to come from heaven, Bella—
when you will throw off all your cowardly hesitating doubts,
and become what you really are, the most divine of crea-
    tures,
made to bring bliss. And for me, for me alone.
Can you hear my horses? How they stamp their hooves,
and shake their bells. Their ringing says:
You're willing! Come; then away we shall rush with you.
To reflect is death; joy is to follow impulse!

ARABELLA

Are they the Russian horses? Shaking their heads with im-
    patience?
Yes, yes, I'll come. For today is Shrove Tuesday,
and at midnight everything will reach an end.
Drive through the Prater fast, to take my breath away
—but Zdenko must come with us.

ELEMER

angrily, unhappily

Not a word,
am I not allowed to speak a single word to you?

[553]

Hugo von Hofmannsthal

There are words in me, burning ones, for you alone!
Words that none else may hear.

ARABELLA *firmly*

The boy comes too.

ELEMER

How cruel you are.

ARABELLA

In half an hour I'll be downstairs,
with him. Till then your horses stand and wait.

She dismisses him

Au revoir!

ELEMER

You are a creature to be adored,
Impossible to understand! A cruel, enchanting creature!

Exit

ZDENKA

enters from right

Have you sent him away?

ARABELLA

We're going out with him. Quick, get your things.
Out sleighing.

ZDENKA

And you need me for that?

[554]

Arabella

ARABELLA

Yes, I need you for that.

Sounds of stamping and sleigh bells

How fine those black horses are, so fiery and impatient.

Her voice suddenly changes

Zdenka!

ZDENKA

What is it? What makes you start so?

ARABELLA

It's him, it's him! My stranger. Look! Just over there,
with his servant. Surely he wants to find out where I live.
Just watch—now he's scanning the windows to find mine.
You must look at his eyes—you never saw such large and
  serious eyes.

ZDENKA *behind her*

How can I see his eyes? He isn't looking up.

ARABELLA

waits

No, he's not looking up.

Turns back into the room

He's walking on. Somewhere else another woman is waiting for him.
And now I hate her and wish her all the ill in the world.

ZDENKA

And by tonight you'll have forgotten her and him as well.
I know your little fantasies.

[555]

Hugo von Hofmannsthal

Arabella stands unsmiling.

ZDENKA

comes closer, lays her head on her sister's shoulder

It is the men alone who are allowed to choose.
And we, we have to wait till they have chosen us,
or we have no hope left.

ARABELLA

What wisdom!

Raises Zdenka's head

Let me look at you! Your eyes are full of tears.
Zdenka, now tell me what is wrong with you.

Sleigh bells louder.

ZDENKA

frees herself

Nothing. You're going out with Elemer then?

ARABELLA

Yes, yes. Go and get dressed. You're coming with us. I wish it.

ZDENKA

Sh! Here's Mamma.

Adelaide enters from the left, listening. She hears Waldner coming.

Enter Waldner through centre door, well-dressed in fur-lined coat, top hat, gloves, walking stick. He looks elegant but exhausted. Crosses the stage as though unaware of the others, and sits down in an armchair in front on the right.

[556]

Arabella

ADELAIDE

Leave us alone now, children,
Your father has his worries.

Exit Arabella on the left, Zdenka on the right.

WALDNER

*rises, removes his outdoor things behind a screen and puts
his top hat on the table. Sees the envelopes containing
bills, automatically opens one, then another*

Only this rubbish? Has no other letter come?

ADELAIDE

You've been gambling. Have you lost again, Theodor?

Waldner remains silent

Have you written to your old comrades in the regiment?

WALDNER

Not one of them has answered; it is hard.

*throws himself into the armchair; half to himself, half to
Adelaide*

One of them, a certain Mandryka,
was as rich as Croesus and a real eccentric.
One day, to please a girl, he had the streets of Verona
covered with three thousand bushels of salt,
because she wanted to go sleighing in the middle of August!
I appealed to his generosity
and enclosed a portrait of our daughter Bella,
in her steel-blue ball dress trimmed with swansdown.
I thought to myself, perhaps he will come here,
being crazy as he is, and marry the girl.

[557]

ADELAIDE

O God! my pretty child and such an old old man.

WALDNER *passionately*

There's got to be a substantial suitor,
and an end to these everlasting flirtations
which come to nothing.

Gets up and paces round the room

And I know no other way!

ADELAIDE

suddenly ecstatic

Let's go away! To Aunt Jadwiga.
She'll take us on at her château!
You can be bailiff—
I can look after the house!

WALDNER

And the girls?

ADELAIDE

Zdenka will be a groom for ever after—
we are not in a position
to keep a couple of daughters!
And Arabella—it has been foretold
she'll make her fortune through a splendid marriage!

WALDNER *grimly*

Meanwhile our last fifty florins will have gone.

ADELAIDE

Keep calm, Theodor, three numbers came to me in a dream!
Infallible, wonderful numbers!

[558]

Arabella

WALDNER

Pah! Rubbish!
Pawn the emerald brooch and give me the cash.
What? You've no longer got it? Pawned it already?

ADELAIDE

Last week. It was my last.

WALDNER

And it was to be my lucky day.
I feel it in every finger!
You unhappy woman!

He catches sight of the boxes as he paces around

What's all this stuff I see?

Has quickly opened the boxes.

ADELAIDE

Chocolates from Dominic, perfume from Elemer, lace from
    Lamoral.
These young gentlemen are most attentive!

WALDNER *comes nearer*

Did you say lace? Where's the lace?

ADELAIDE

There. Point d'Alençon.

WALDNER

Go out at once and see if you can get a price for it.

ADELAIDE

The lace that belongs to our child?

[559]

Hugo von Hofmannsthal

WALDNER

At once, I've not a florin left in my pocket.

ADELAIDE

O this Vienna!

She takes the little parcel of lace

But I foresaw this in my dreams.
We shall be raised from the very depths,
up to the heavens by the hand of beauty!

Waldner crossly signs to her to go.

ADELAIDE

turns to go, stops in the left-hand doorway, ecstatically

You won't be telling me they never married for love
in the Imperial family?

Exit quickly.

WALDNER

returns to the bills, reads the first

"I am unable to wait any longer."

Takes the second

"Otherwise I shall have to obtain a writ."
My poor wife! My poor daughters!

He reaches behind him and pulls the bell. Enter Floor-waiter

WALDNER *loudly*

Brandy!

[560]

Arabella

WAITER

My instructions are to serve nothing to Number Eight
unless the gentleman pays in cash beforehand.

WALDNER

Be off with you. There's nothing I require.

Exit Waiter.

Waldner walks up and down

Now they'll be sitting down and starting to play again,
and everything else is just a waste of time!

WAITER

enters with a salver

A gentleman to see you.

WALDNER

You are to say that I've gone out.
Put the thing there!

Waiter puts a visiting card on the table, exit.

WALDNER *looks across*

Why, this is not a bill. Since when have tradesmen
taken to sending in their visiting cards?

He walks across, looks at the card, pleased and surprised

Mandryka!

With increasing astonishment

The chap with the money! My best friend in the regiment!

[561]

Hugo von Hofmannsthal

WAITER *at the door*

The gentleman begs to be admitted.

WALDNER

Tell him I'll be delighted.

Goes to meet the visitor with outspread arms

Ciao! Comrade!

Enter Mandryka, tall, very powerfully built, elegant, thirty-five at the most. Something about him suggests the country, but he is extremely well dressed, not at all like a provincial.

Welko follows Mandryka as he enters, but he stays at the door.

Waldner steps back, perplexed.

MANDRYKA

Have I the honour to address Captain Count Waldner?

WALDNER

Waldner is my name, but I am no longer captain.

Mandryka reaches back with his right hand without turning round.

Welko bows and hands him a letter.

MANDRYKA

steps up to Waldner with the letter

Are you, Count Waldner, the man who wrote this letter?

Waldner takes the letter, which is crumpled and blood-stained.

[562]

Arabella

MANDRYKA

very politely, in a gay and casual tone

Some blood got on it and it's not legible any more.
The very day this letter was delivered
I went to hunt an old she-bear; she and I had a scrap,
and she scratched me a little—that's how it happened.

WALDNER

giving him back the letter, having glanced at it

As a matter of fact, I wrote this to someone of the same
    name—
we were friends and served in the same regiment.

MANDRYKA

That was my uncle. He is dead. I am the only Mandryka.
So forgive the liberty I took
in opening the letter. But now the most important thing:
Welko, the picture!

WELKO

handing him a photograph

It is quite right, master,
the beautiful girl with the face lives here.

MANDRYKA

holding the photograph

Count Waldner, in the letter which you wrote
as an old friend to your comrade my uncle,
you enclosed this portrait of a young lady.

Hugo von Hofmannsthal

WALDNER

looking at it casually, lightly

Ah, yes, it's the photograph of my daughter Arabella.

MANDRYKA

obviously excited, but not changing his posture

Is your respected daughter still unmarried?

WALDNER *nodding*

Still unmarried—

MANDRYKA

—and not till now engaged?

WALDNER

No, not as yet.

MANDRYKA

with gravity verging on solemnity

Then may we talk for five minutes?

Welko quickly draws up two easy chairs opposite each other and then withdraws.

Waldner and Mandryka sit down. Short pause, with Mandryka embarrassed and Waldner tense.

MANDRYKA

May I be so immodest as to ask you a question?

WALDNER

You're the nephew—and heir—of my dear old comrade. I'm at your disposal.

Arabella

MANDRYKA

Thank you.

Ponders a moment

When you thought to enclose in your letter
to my lamented uncle the charming portrait
of your honoured daughter,
may I assume—forgive me please—
that an intention was involved?

WALDNER *cautiously*

O well, I just thought to myself
it might please the old fellow to see it.

MANDRYKA

*very attentively, concentrating on the purport of every word
Waldner has uttered*

Please my uncle? Yet if this had had the following result:
that my esteemed uncle, who was a most manly man,
in the best years of his manhood, had fallen in love with
    the portrait,
and had presented himself to you here, most honoured sir,
as one frank-minded nobleman to another,
and had said: whoever has seen this face
and fails to press his suit upon you,
does not deserve to be allowed to live in this beautiful world:
So give me your daughter as my wife and queen.
What would have happened? Assuming he said such things!

WALDNER

We would surely have found ourselves in an unexpected
    situation.

[565]

Hugo von Hofmannsthal

MANDRYKA

stands up, most agitated, but with self-control

My uncle has passed on. Now I am Mandryka, the only one.
Mine are the forests, mine the villages.
Four thousand people on my land pray for my happiness,
and I, with upraised hands, now beg of you,
my lord and father, give me your honoured daughter,
grant me her hand in marriage. For fourteen weeks,
she has been mistress of every thought I've had.

Waldner, amazed, says nothing.

Mandryka continues very gravely

I am a widower—will that alarm your daughter?
My sweet Maria was too good for me!
Only two years she stayed beside me.

Waldner signs to him to sit down again

Does your hesitation condemn me? No!

Waldner shakes his head

May I see her?

Waldner nods

Imagine! This letter comes, and in the very same hour
the old she-bear takes me in her arms
and manages to crush four of my ribs.
For twelve weeks I had to stay in bed—
before my eyes this picture—and one thought that grew and
    grew
until it dragged the soul out of my breast!

Arabella

Naïvely, with no trace of boasting

Here come my bailiffs: what's up with our master?
Here they come from the dairy farms: what's up with our
    master?
Here they come from the studs: doesn't our master like horses
    any more?
Here come my gamekeepers: doesn't our master care to go
    shooting?
I do not answer any of them. Welko, I shout,
Go fetch the Jew. Now what's that Jew in Sissek called,
who wants to buy my forest? There's the oak forest!
Go fetch him quickly, tell him to bring the money,
for tomorrow I must go to the Emperor's City,
and that costs money with every breath you draw,
and there must be no hindrances when I go courting!

He draws out a large but elegant wallet; it contains a thick
bundle of thousand-florin notes

That is the forest!
It was a fine one; hermits used to live there,
and there were gipsies in it and old stags,
and many charcoal piles sending smoke up—
now it's all changed into these few scraps of paper!

Together with Waldner

But there are still forests enough growing on my land,
for children and grandchildren—God keep them safely!
O please forgive me for talking about such things!
I haven't the faintest idea how it started!

Is about to replace the wallet in his pocket.

[567]

WALDNER

restrains him with an involuntary movement

O but I find it tremendously interesting.
To think of it—a forest—hermits lived there,
and there were gipsies in it, and old stags,
and hey presto!—such a fat wallet!
For many, many years I have not seen one like it.

Stares spellbound at the wallet.

MANDRYKA

offers him the wallet, very amiably and casually

Might I perhaps? Do you need . . . perhaps?
Just for the time being? You'll do me a favour.
Please help yourself.

WALDNER

after hesitating a moment, takes a thousand-florin note

My banker has just left town.
You'll have it back this evening at the latest.

MANDRYKA

holds out the wallet again, very cordially

That's all? But take some more! Yes do, go on!
Please help yourself.

*Waldner takes a second note, puts it nonchalantly with the
first in his waistcoat pocket.*

MANDRYKA

replaces the wallet in his breast pocket.

A somewhat embarrassed pause

[568]

And when would it be convenient
to introduce me to your Countess
and to your honoured daughter?

WALDNER

rises

They are both here in the next room.

Mandryka also rises

Do you want to see them? I'll call—
I'll introduce you.

MANDRYKA

Now? Just like this? O no, I beg you, no!

WALDNER

Your uncle was never as shy as this!

MANDRYKA *very seriously*

This is quite a different case.
For me this is something sacred.

WALDNER

Just as you wish.

MANDRYKA *his tone changed*

I shall take rooms here, in this same hotel,
and wait for the commands your Countess sends me,
as to when she can receive me in the afternoon,
or evening—or whenever she may choose.

*Bows. Waldner shakes hands and accompanies him to the
door. Exit Mandryka.*

[569]

Hugo von Hofmannsthal

WALDNER *alone*

Did I dream it all? He was here, on this very spot,
my friend Mandryka's nephew.
Things like that simply do not happen.

*Draws out a crumpled thousand-florin note, then the sec-
ond, smooths them and puts them in his empty wallet*

Did I dream it all? No, it wasn't a dream!

*He extracts one note absent-mindedly, folds it into a small
paper cone which he keeps in his hand. Gaily imitating
Mandryka's tone, rather loudly*

Please help yourself!

WAITER

enters

Did you call?

*Notices the thousand-florin note in Waldner's hand, and
changes his tone at once*

You had an order, sir?

WALDNER

tenderly to himself

Please help yourself!

WAITER

Do you wish me to change the thousand florins?

WALDNER

Later perhaps. Not now.

Exit Waiter.

Arabella

To himself, playfully

Please help yourself!

Tenderly, in melting tones

Please help yourself!

Majestically

Please help yourself!

Takes his coat, hat, and stick.

ZDENKA

enters by the door on the right

Did you call someone, Papa?

WALDNER *with wild joy*

Please help yourself.

ZDENKA

Who are you speaking to, Papa? Is anything wrong?

WALDNER

notices at last that he is not alone

Nothing at all. I'm going out. They're expecting me.

He waves the thousand-florin note at her

Do you want some, perhaps? I'll get some change.
Goodbye.

Exit through centre door.

ZDENKA *alone*

Papa! Now he has gone.
I've never seen him like that.

[571]

Hugo von Hofmannsthal

His worries have driven him out of his mind!
We must leave this town, and tomorrow too.
Today perhaps I'll see Matteo for the last time.
O God! Do not forsake me in my sorrow!

Enter Matteo quickly and surreptitiously through the centre door. Zdenka starts.

MATTEO

He did not see me. I pressed myself against the door.

ZDENKA

points to the door at the back on the left

Sh! She's in there.

Listens

She's calling me.

MATTEO

Can't I see her now?

ZDENKA

Not now! I beg you, not now.

MATTEO

Where's the letter?

ZDENKA

Letter? Yes! No! She won't just now.
She says—she intends—this evening—come to the coach-
   men's ball.
And first be here,

here in the hotel, I can bring it perhaps
to your room—or you shall have it when you're there.

MATTEO

O please don't fail me now! I have your word.

Zdenka points in alarm at the door on the left.

Exit Matteo quickly.

*Enter Arabella from the left, wearing another dress, in coat
and hat.*

Zdenka stands looking confused and embarrassed.

Sleigh bells are heard.

ARABELLA

Aren't you ready? Whatever have you been doing?
O do get dressed. The horses are very impatient.

ZDENKA *furiously*

The horses! And your Elemer!

Runs into room on the right.

ARABELLA *sitting down*

My Elemer! How extraordinary that sounds.
He mine—I his. What can this be?
It is as if I were suddenly afraid
and full of longing. But what am I longing for?
For Matteo?

She gets up

Because he always says
he cannot live without me and keeps gazing at me
with eyes like those of a child?

[573]

Hugo von Hofmannsthal

She reflects

There's nothing in me yearns for poor Matteo.

Hesitates, then breaks out

I long to see my dark-eyed stranger again!
I long to hear, just once, his voice. To hear his voice
would make him seem to me like other men.—
What did Zdenka say? We must wait for a man to choose
or otherwise there's no hope left for us.
It is high time she wore a woman's clothes,
my little sister's eyes look sometimes very strange.
Then, when I'm married, she must live with me.
I—married to that Elemer?

Shudders involuntarily

Why this shivering, as if I walked over a grave?
Is it the dark-eyed stranger, to whom I never spoke one
   word,
drawing me towards him in the darkness?
Dear God! I'm almost sure he is a married man,
and I shall never be allowed to see him again.
And today, today's Shrove Tuesday, and tonight there'll be
   my ball—
And I shall be queen, and after that—

ZDENKA

enters wearing a short fur coat, with top hat in hand

There, I'm ready now.

ARABELLA

Come then!

*Zdenka opens the door for her. Arabella goes out. Zdenka
puts on her top hat and follows her. The sleigh bells jingle.*

Curtain

[574]

Act Two

Foyer to a public ballroom, with sumptuous décor in the style of the 1860's. Boxes with pillars and curtains left and right. In centre, stairs leading to a gallery from which one can look down on the ballroom, which is reached by descending the stairs right and left.

Arabella, followed by Adelaide, and accompanied by several gentlemen, slowly descends the staircase from the gallery. Waldner and Mandryka stand on one side at the foot of the stairs. Both are wearing black tails, knotted black ties.

MANDRYKA

It is an angel coming down from heaven!

WALDNER

At last. She's always half an hour late.

MANDRYKA

O Waldner, Waldner!

WALDNER

If you press my hand so hard,
I'll be unable to hold my cards for three days at least.
Come now, I'll introduce you. Why are you stepping back?

Adelaide and Arabella are now downstairs and moving left.

The gentlemen with them have remained behind.

[575]

Hugo von Hofmannsthal

ADELAIDE

softly to Arabella

There he is. Do you find him elegant?
Did I exaggerate?

ARABELLA

without appearing to look at him

Mamma—now comes the moment of decision!

ADELAIDE

You're very pale. Don't you feel well, my child?
Do you want to sit down? Or leave?

ARABELLA

No, no, Mamma.
Leave me alone a moment.

Adelaide walks across to Waldner and Mandryka.

WALDNER *coming toward her*

What is the matter?

ADELAIDE

Leave her alone a moment.

WALDNER

Whatever for?

ADELAIDE

She suddenly felt faint.
You know what she is like.

WALDNER

This isn't the time for fads like that!
Let me introduce Herr von Mandryka.

Adelaide gives Mandryka her hand, he kisses it.

ARABELLA *joining them*

Here I am, Mamma.

WALDNER

My daughter Arabella.

*Mandryka makes a low bow. Adelaide takes Waldner to
one side. They disappear on the right. Mandryka gazes at
Arabella, unable to speak a word.*

ARABELLA

You don't seem the person to be interested in all this.

Fans herself

Whatever brought you here?

MANDRYKA

To Vienna?

ARABELLA

No, here, to this ball.

MANDRYKA

You ask what brought me here, Countess Arabella?

Enter Dominic from behind to fetch Arabella for a dance.

DOMINIC

May I have the pleasure of a waltz, perhaps?

[577]

Hugo von Hofmannsthal

ARABELLA

Later. I am speaking with this gentleman.

Walks to the left. Exit Dominic to the ballroom.

MANDRYKA

after a short dance with her

Hasn't your father told you anything?

ARABELLA

*sitting down and signing to him with her fan to sit beside
her*

What did you expect him to tell me?

Enter Elemer from behind.

ELEMER

May I have the pleasure of this waltz, perhaps?

ARABELLA

Later. For the moment I'm staying here.

Elemer bows, exit. Arabella looks at Mandryka

Explain. What was my father to have told me?

MANDRYKA

You know nothing about me?

Arabella shakes her head

I had a wife who was lovely and good as an angel.
Only for two years could she remain with me.
Then the Lord God quickly called her back.
I was too young and not good enough for an angel.

He bows his head.

[578]

Arabella

ARABELLA

after a short pause

Was it this my father was supposed to tell me?

MANDRYKA

very seriously and ponderously

You must forgive me. I am half a peasant.
With me, things happen slowly, but they're strong.

With sudden decisiveness

You are beautiful, Arabella—your lovely face—
even on paper it can burn a man's very soul!

ARABELLA *frowning*

What do you mean? How did it happen that a picture of
   me
came to Slavonia?

MANDRYKA

gazes at her

How did it happen that—what does it matter?
You are so beautiful—there's a power in your face
to print its features on a soul as on soft wax.
Over a simple man, who lives among fields and forests,
such a power is very great, and he becomes a dreamer,
he becomes like a man possessed, and his soul decides,
a complete decision—and as he decides, so he must act!

*Arabella is alarmed by his ponderous and passionate man-
ner, she rises to her feet*

Countess, I had forgotten the world is different elsewhere.

He gets up

[579]

Hugo von Hofmannsthal

Here I am far from my fields and forests, and you must forgive me
for my inept remarks, which have kept you from dancing.

Enter Lamoral from behind.

LAMORAL

May I intrude and ask you for a waltz?

ARABELLA

No, later, Lamoral. I would like to speak a little more with
   this gentleman,
if he'll be good enough to sit down again.

Lamoral bows, exit.

ARABELLA

sits down, signs to Mandryka to do likewise

You wish to marry me, my father tells me.
But have you any idea who we really are?
We're not so grand by the usual worldly standards.
We live rather dubious lives on the edge of society.

MANDRYKA

Your pedigree, Arabella,
is written in the features of your face!
And should it be enough for you to rule a man,
who in his turn rules over many others,
then come to my home with me and be its mistress,
you shall have peacocks that strut on silken soil,
and no one shall ever come to think himself above you
unless it be the King and Emperor and his Empress! No one
   else!

Arabella

ARABELLA *to herself*

The right man—so I once said quietly to myself,
the right man—if he exists for me at all,
will be here all of a sudden, so I said then.
I shall look at him and he at me,
and then there will be no tricks and no questions.
No, all open and light, like a clear stream shining in the
    sun!

MANDRYKA

That is the way the clear quiet Danube passes my house,
and has brought you to me! Loveliest of women!

Mysteriously

Even this evening, when it's time to sleep,
if you had chanced to be a girl from my village,
I would tell you to go to the well behind your father's
    house
and draw up a beaker full of cool fresh water
and give it me at the door to prove I'm your betrothed be-
    fore God,
and before every man, my loveliest!

ARABELLA

Never have I met a human being like you!
You carry your own breath of life about with you,
and what does not pertain to you does not concern you.

MANDRYKA

That's why I cannot live without something splendid,
high above my own self, and in this moment
I raise you to the heights, choose you as my wife.

[581]

And where I'm master, you shall be the mistress,
you shall command wherever I'm the master.

ARABELLA

softly in unison with him

And you shall be my master, I your subject.
Your house shall be my house, I want to be buried in your
    grave.
I give myself to you for all eternity.

> *In an entirely changed tone, but seriously*

But now drive home. Please do so for my sake.

MANDRYKA

And you?

ARABELLA

I shall stay here.

Mandryka bows

I'd like to dance once more and take my leave
from all my girlhood years, just for a single hour.
Will you let me do so?

MANDRYKA

But if you stay here,
my place is nowhere else than at your side!

Arabella frowns

But there's no need for you to say a single word to me.

*A crowd of coachmen and guests, among them Fiacre-Milli
and other girls of the kind, also the three counts, come up
on to the stage from the ballroom.*

Arabella

ARABELLA

looks at Mandryka

May I?

MANDRYKA

Of course you may! You may do whatever you wish!

He steps aside and clears the way for the others. Fiacre-Milli, a pretty girl in a very showy ball-dress, carrying a large bouquet, comes out of the crowd and approaches Arabella, who now stands in the centre.

DOMINIC *beside Milli*

It's time now for our ball to have its queen.
Our Milli is the herald of the coachmen,
and we have placed our words of homage on her lips.

MILLI

handing Arabella the bouquet with a curtsey, light-heartedly, almost impertinently

The gentlemen of Vienna know
Just all about astronomy:
Each one of them must be employed
Somehow at the Observatory.
They're very sharp to notice when
A new star swims into their ken,
To be their heaven's queen!
And then with single voice they call:
We crown you Queen of Carnival!

THE COUNTS AND COACHMEN

We crown you Queen of Carnival!

As Fiacre-Milli's song ends she begins at once, without any break, to yodel gaily and exuberantly; her yodelling blends

[583]

into the waltz which now begins. As the waltz is being played, with Milli yodelling to it, Arabella takes flowers from the bouquet and distributes them among the gentlemen and coachmen. Finally she throws among them all that remains of the bouquet, takes Dominic's arm and descends with him into the ballroom, followed by all the others. Mandryka gazes after her, then turns away. At this moment Adelaide appears from the right. Simultaneously Matteo has come from the left. Zdenka humbly follows him, in boy's clothes, but in a kind of black dress-coat. She hides behind a pillar.

ADELAIDE

going toward Mandryka

You are alone? Where is Arabella?

MANDRYKA

Where duty summons her, as queen of the ball.

MATTEO

speaking up into the air

How she forgets me—in the ecstasy of her beauty.

ADELAIDE

Your eyes are shining. How may I interpret this?

ZDENKA

behind Matteo, timidly

She's thinking of you, Matteo, I know it!
Only she's being careful where she looks.

Arabella

MANDRYKA

going toward Adelaide

·O Countess, you yourself so young, so charming—
and you her mother! How can I find on earth
the words with which to express my thanks to you?

He kisses her hand with great warmth.

MATTEO

takes one step forward

Flowers for everyone! For everyone her smile!
Herself for everyone! What's left for me?

ADELAIDE *to Mandryka*

O if you could guess how I am feeling now!
My son! My friend! And my knight-errant!
Too much for my heart. I must, I must share it.
To him, to her! No, you must stay here!
I'll find him myself! And he shall embrace you!

She hurries off right.

ZDENKA

intensely, but tenderly, to Matteo

For you, everything's left; she needs your sorrow,
deep as a well,
to throw all her soul into—
others are shallow!

MATTEO *to himself*

All that is left is: to go to Galicia,
and to forget her—if I still can!

He walks forward, Zdenka remains left, afraid to be seen.

Hugo von Hofmannsthal

ZDENKA

Papa! Mamma! I mustn't be seen.
Where are you going, Matteo?

Matteo walks backstage, gazes mournfully down into the
ballroom; Adelaide and Waldner enter right and walk to
Mandryka. Zdenka vanishes, left.

ADELAIDE

O Theodor! Here he is, Theodor!

WALDNER *jovially*

How good to see you, nephew of my old Mandryka!
Well! Please—embrace me!

MANDRYKA

My good friend, and you see me happy—

A brief embrace

So very happy that I am almost ashamed—
it's not as a man that you see me before you,
but as a boy, waiting for the evening
—in our villages—
when everything's dark, and the fires are out!
But he knows that a girl is waiting in her father's house,
then out she slips to the well and draws for him
a drink of clear water:
that's what she gives him on the darkened doorstep!

ADELAIDE

What delicacy, O what a charming country custom!
I feel the air of my old home round me and my father's
    castle,
down there the village sleeping—

[586]

Arabella

WALDNER *to Mandryka*

I shall be with you at once.

He makes as if to go, Adelaide holds him back

Let me go! I am winning.

Exit right.

Mandryka raises his hand and snaps his fingers. At once, Welko, Djura, and Jankel surround him, all in black evening dress, but with metal buttons.

MANDRYKA

Bring a table. We shall have dinner.

A waiter promptly appears, with a menu, and pageboys.

MANDRYKA *to Adelaide*

Will you order champagne? Whichever you wish!

Waiter presents Adelaide with the wine list.

ADELAIDE

Moët-Chandon, half-dry, half-sweet, we had this at my engagement.

MANDRYKA

Thirty bottles of this one.

Points to the wine list

Six for the table,
and serve the others around in the ballroom.
And another thirty!
And another thirty!
Welko, see to it. Coolers in every corner!

[587]

Hugo von Hofmannsthal

Till no one in the ballroom knows any more
if he is a count, magically changed into a coachman,
or if he's a coachman turned into a count!
Let everyone be happy, when I am happy!

To Adelaide

What else would you order?

ADELAIDE

as lobster, pheasant, ice cream, and so on, are presented

Have we flowers?

MANDRYKA

calls

Listen, Djura!
Take a coach, no, take two coaches;
open up all the flower shops,
wake the pretty flower girls,
tell them to empty out their storerooms!
Fill one whole carriage with roses,
another with red and white camellias!
On flowers she shall dance her waltzes,
she shall say goodbye to her girlhood.
Afterward I'll spread my hands,
then she shall dance no more waltzes,
but dance on the palms of my hands!

ADELAIDE

O this is the dream of my girlhood days again!
You are generous and full of strength,
curt in command, and surely terrible in anger—
what confidence you inspire, O, it's beyond words!

[588]

Arabella

She takes his arm and they walk backstage up the stairs.
From the right a table is pushed in and lavishly laid for a
cold buffet.

ARABELLA

comes on Dominic's arm from backstage out of the ball-
room; they turn left

And now I say adieu to you, dear Dominic.

DOMINIC

Adieu? You're going home already?

ARABELLA

with composure, serenely

That was the last dance we shall dance for all time.
Perhaps one day we two shall meet again,
then we shall just be friends of our past youth.

DOMINIC

takes her arm

Arabella!

ARABELLA

No, Dominic.

She quickly releases herself

You were the first man ever, Dominic—
I'm not talking of boys—who said to me
that he liked me, and it made me very happy.
But the right person for you—I was not that—
and you were not the right person for me.
Don't speak, Dominic. Here comes Elemer, adieu!

She nods to Elemer. Dominic slowly leaves.

[589]

Hugo von Hofmannsthal

ELEMER

coming from the ballroom, approaches Arabella

I've never seen you looking so beautiful!
Something has happened to you!

ARABELLA

Yes, Elemer, something has happened to me,
and because of it, I shake you by the hand,
and say adieu, and thank you, Elemer—
there were many enchanting moments that we had—

ELEMER

There were, Bella, there shall be!

ARABELLA

Do not hold my hand, just quickly feel the pressure of my
    fingers,
and know that we are good friends,
even if we shall not see each other again.

ELEMER *passionately*

It is the stranger, you've fallen in love with him,
this Wallachian, or whatever he is!

ARABELLA *gently*

Please do not spoil this last moment for me,
here, Lamoral is coming, and he's waiting
for his last dance!

*Lamoral appears at the top of the stairs from the ballroom;
the laying of the table continues.*

[590]

Arabella

ELEMER *close to her*

Marry me!
What person in the world can stand in my way?

ARABELLA

No. No. It's just that a different joy was meant for me.

She leaves him and goes to Lamoral; exit Elemer, left.

LAMORAL

O Arabella, can anything at a ball be more beautiful than
you!

ARABELLA

Yes, it is sweet to be in love, sweet this rise and fall:
but there is something a thousand times greater and lovelier.
And one day you will understand it too, perhaps—

LAMORAL

Do not speak of things that are far away—

ARABELLA *gravely*

For you it is still far away, you are right.

LAMORAL

I am afraid. You've changed so much, Arabella.
Someone is taking you away from me!

ARABELLA

Taking me away? Nonsense, little man!
But here is your first kiss, and your last one too.

*She leans over and kisses him quickly and lightly on the
forehead. They stand, left, partly concealed by the curtains.*

LAMORAL *radiant*

Who can it be, gave me this wonderful kiss?

ARABELLA

entirely at ease, walks away from him to the centre of the
stage

It was a girl, a girl who is happy today,
so happy she must be completely alone,
completely alone by herself, up in her room,
and lie there, long unsleeping, for the joy she feels.

Her tone changes

But now let's dance this last waltz to the end,
then I shall leave, never to see you again!

Exit with Lamoral to the ballroom.

Matteo enters, right, past the waiters laying the table.

Zdenka enters, left, afraid to be seen; she stares across at
Matteo.

MATTEO *to himself*

I am a coward. I must go. And end it all!

ZDENKA

O God! The look on his face! How terribly determined!

She signs to him; he crosses over to her.

Mandryka descends the stairs from the gallery, crosses the
stage to the laid table, listens to what Welko has to say to
him.

ZDENKA *frightened*

You are like that again? Has it got you again?

[592]

Arabella

MATTEO

It's driving me mad, consuming me.

ZDENKA

She's thinking of you! Thinking of nothing else!

Matteo laughs bitterly.

ZDENKA

She has given me a letter to give to you.
Here it is.

*She puts her hand in the inside breast pocket of her tail-
coat*

MATTEO

retreats towards the centre of the stage

I won't take it!
It means the end for ever!
I can feel it!

Zdenka follows him as he retreats, the letter in her hand.

Mandryka begins to pay attention to them.

Jankel enters, right, with people carrying a load of flowers.

Zdenka has followed Matteo to the centre of the stage.

MATTEO

Take it back! I feel it says I must go!

ZDENKA

You must take it, everything has changed.
Just feel it!

Hugo von Hofmannsthal

MATTEO

takes the envelope

A key?

ZDENKA

Take it! You've only to take it!

MATTEO

opens the envelope

No letter, only a key?
What sort of a joke is this, Zdenko, I ask you!

ZDENKA

pale, almost swooning

That is her key.

MATTEO

Her key?

ZDENKA

with hardly any tone in her voice

Of her room. Be careful. Hide it.

MATTEO

This is the key? I must be dreaming!
Are we at the ball? And are you Zdenko?
Is she your sister? The girl dancing downstairs?
This is the key?

ZDENKA

To her room!

[594]

Arabella

MATTEO

The key to Arabella's room.

He holds out the key in front of him.

MANDRYKA

winces

I must have misheard!

Jankel approaches him. But Mandryka signs to him to keep away, walks closer to the others.

ZDENKA

panic-stricken, overcoming her shyness

You are to go home—she'll be there in fifteen minutes.
The key fits the door that's next to hers.
She'll come to you without a sound—Matteo, she does not
want you to be unhappy! She'll do anything, anything
that may bring happiness to you, and tonight.

MATTEO

Swear to me that it is true!
The key to Arabella's room!

ZDENKA

You have it there as truly as it fits,
as truly as she who gives it to you
will do today anything to make you happy!
Now I must go. No one must see me here.

Runs out left.

MATTEO *to himself*

Mystery of a girl's heart, O unfathomable!

Exit quickly left.

[595]

Hugo von Hofmannsthal

MANDRYKA
suddenly roused out of fixity

Stop! Someone, or whoever you are!
Welko, Djura! Stop that person there!
Bring him to me! The man there with the key!

*Dominic has entered with Adelaide from the left, front.
Welko and Djura are not sure whom they are expected to
chase.*

WELKO

Which one, master?

DJURA

What sort of a man?

WELKO

This one?

*points to Dominic. Dominic and Adelaide sit down on a
sofa, left.*

MANDRYKA *to himself*

And if there are many here called Arabella—
my damned huntsman's ears
hoax my hard stupid skull—
shall I make a fool of myself before a stranger?
Would she send out the key of her room then,
while she herself is dancing here in the ballroom?

He looks at his watch

And it is not even an hour yet
since I let her go, like that, in freedom—
am I then a fool, an utter ass?

[596]

Arabella

To the three

Let it pass! And carry on there at the table!

He walks rapidly up and down

Marvellous music, not a damned key there,
violins in it, not a murmur of keys,
and in a few moments she will stand there,
in front of me, and I shall scatter flowers
that will kiss her feet in place of me.
Ah! how she dances now and says goodbye
this very hour to all her girlhood days!

DOMINIC

left, beside Adelaide

O enchanting lady! Lovelier than your daughter ever was!
How well you would know how to cure my melancholy—

Kisses her shoulder.

ADELAIDE

pulls her stole up over her shoulder

Dominic! No! But later, I shall always be alone,
without my child—

DOMINIC

And we shall read Lenau together.

ADELAIDE

Or I shall play Chopin to you.

DOMINIC

No. Lenau! Only Lenau! dear melancholy Lenau!

Many couples are coming up from the ballroom.

[597]

Hugo von Hofmannsthal

MANDRYKA

looking towards them fiercely

Why are many coming, but not she among them?
Why do I keep on hearing a damned jingling of keys?

Fiacre-Milli, on Elemer's arm, comes up to Mandryka, other couples gather round.

FIACRE-MILLI

Kind sir, I must come to you again,
and ask you to give back to the ball its queen!

MANDRYKA

angrily to himself

What is the woman saying? That I
should give her back? I never locked her up.
I haven't got the key. It's in the envelope.

He grasps a chair so strongly that its back cracks. Welko comes with champagne.

MANDRYKA

mastering his feelings

I ask you please, to do me the honour—
all of you, as you are, acquaintances or strangers.

ELEMER

But we do not want the Countess Arabella
to absent herself from us at the supreme moment.
Surely you'll know, if anyone, where to find her?

MANDRYKA

puts his hands to his throat, loosens his tie

Find her? Find her? Keys! Djura! And Welko!

[598]

Arabella

The two run up.

Look for the lady, everywhere in the ballroom!
You found her in the great city of Vienna,
you'll find her simply enough at this local hop here.

Djura and Welko hurry out.

MANDRYKA

shouts after them

—and ask her to come, if she would be so kind!

Then, to Milli, who has left her place on Elemer's arm

A sweet little mouth like yours must have a sweet drink
too.

He hands her a glass of champagne.

DOMINIC

beside Adelaide, with a glass of champagne

We are always poised on the edge of an abyss—

ADELAIDE

How clever! And how true, my friend!

With a glass of champagne

The Prussian threatens to the left, the Russian to the
right—
but yet our guardian angel will protect us!

DOMINIC

It's love that will protect us, love alone!

*At the same time Jankel goes up to Mandryka and takes
him a note on a tray.*

[599]

JANKEL

This must be a letter for Your Honour.

MANDRYKA

Feel if there's a key in it.

JANKEL

What? A key?

Mandryka quickly takes the note but hesitates before opening it.

MANDRYKA

Dear God, who gave this face such power over me,
that I should be afraid?—

*Walks aside, opens the envelope, reads. Repeats its contents
fiercely*

"I say good night to you just for today.
I'm going home,
and from tomorrow on I shall be yours."
A little A instead of a signature!
Not even her name! She won't answer for it
to a silly nincompoop she's taken in.

With bitter joviality

Naturally she must say goodbye to her girlhood days,
and for that she needs all the tenderness she has got:
she has no time for a more tender signature!

*He assumes a forced gaiety, walks back to the others, makes
a sign*

Now throw away the flowers! Bring champagne!
Serve up all round, till everyone's under the table,

[600]

the counts and the coachmen and fiacre girls all in a heap!
Today everything, and I mean everything,
is on me.

Waiters disperse, serving everyone quickly with champagne

Now shall I perhaps sing lovely Milli a song?

He pulls her towards him

I feel like it.

*Fiacre-Milli answers softly, using no words, by yodelling.
Mandryka, between self-derision and angry tears*

"Went through the wood, don't know through which one!
Found there a girl, don't know whose daughter!
Trod on her toe, don't know on which one,
She began to scream, I don't know why though,
Look at the rogue, some way to make love, that!

*Milli repeats the refrain yodelling, Mandryka pulls her
down beside him on the sofa. Adelaide releases herself from
Dominic and stands up*

Right thing for him would be the wine jug.
Give him the wine, but not the wine glass,
Let the rogue drink from the heavy jug then,
It's his hard luck, until he learns his lesson!

Milli yodels the refrain

Give him the girl; that would be the right thing,
The girl, that's me, let him do without a bed though.

Fiercely

Let the lad sleep on the ground without blankets,
It's his hard luck, until he learns his lesson."

He leaves Milli, suddenly stands up. Milli repeats the refrain. Mandryka, more and more angrily, to himself

Today she's going home to her master of the keys,
and from tomorrow on, she will be mine.
How about a kiss, Milli?

Kisses her

How much does one pay
for the keys of Countess's rooms here in Vienna?

ADELAIDE

planting herself suddenly in front of him

Herr von Mandryka, where is my daughter?

MANDRYKA

standing, embracing Milli

Don't know! She was not courteous enough
to tell me. Do you want more Moët-Chandon?
It's here. Now pour a glass for the Dowager Countess.

ADELAIDE

hurries excitedly right

Where is my husband? Someone look for him!

Dominic exit right, quickly, to look for Waldner.

ADELAIDE *back to Mandryka*

Now I implore you, where is Arabella?

MANDRYKA *impertinent*

I ask the Dowager Countess that herself!

Arabella

Waldner appears right, with Dominic; behind him the three men with whom he has been gambling.

ADELAIDE

O Theodor!
O now you must protect your wife and daughter!

WALDNER

What's going on? Mandryka, what a way to behave
in the presence of my wife.

MANDRYKA

It is entirely appropriate.
I have sloughed off the stupid lout from the provinces,
and am as suits the style of these Viennese counts.
Sit down and join us, there are girls here, and champagne!
Please help yourself!

WALDNER *close to him*

Where is my daughter?

MANDRYKA

I'm sorry, I can give no information.
Countesses, so it seems, sometimes retire
at moments of excitement.

WALDNER

to Adelaide, furiously

Where is the girl? I want to know where she is!

ADELAIDE

—at home!

[603]

Hugo von Hofmannsthal

WALDNER

You are sure? What does this mean?

ADELAIDE

An impulse! A sudden fit of melancholy!
A caprice! You know her little ways.

WALDNER

You swear she is at home?

ADELAIDE

We are speaking of your daughter and of mine.

WALDNER

Very good, we'll go home too. This very moment.
You'll knock at her door, and tell us afterward
if she's all right: only to calm our minds.

To Mandryka angrily

Then I shall have some words to speak with you;
so you will be so good as to come with us.

MANDRYKA

For me that will be a very special honour.

Bows and gives Adelaide his arm.

WALDNER

to his fellow-gamblers

We'll go on playing at once, in the hotel,
as soon as we've settled this small misunderstanding.

MANDRYKA

stopping by the door, calling back

These ladies and gentlemen remain my guests!

[604]

FIACRE-MILLI

Hurrah! We are your guests!

GUESTS IN CHORUS

Hurrah! We are your guests!

All raise their champagne glasses.

*Mandryka has already left with Adelaide; Welko and Djura,
preceded by Waldner with the gamblers, follow.*

Curtain

Act Three

The hotel. Large foyer, from which stairs lead upward, turning twice. Below, several tables with newspapers, rocking chairs, armchairs. Right, front, the porter's box and exit to street. Night; the foyer is lit with oil lamps.

Matteo, in a uniform blouse, appears on the staircase at the height of the first floor. He peers down.

The doorbell rings, Matteo vanishes. The floor-waiter (of Act One) comes out of the porter's box and opens the door.

Arabella enters, in cloak and hood, coming from the ball. The waiter disappears. Arabella slowly walks to the staircase. Her eyes are half-closed, her face has an expression of happiness. The music of the ball enswathes her, its dance rhythms intertwined with Mandryka's Slav speech rhythms. She smiles, sits as if daydreaming on the rocking chair nearest to the front of the stage, and gently rocks herself, thinking aloud.

ARABELLA

Over his land the coach will travel,
and through his tall and silent forests—
yes, he suits them: tall silent forests—
and then his horsemen come riding towards us.
"This is your mistress," he will be saying,
"whom I have brought," he will be saying,
"from the Emperor's City and never shall she wish to return—
she will wish to stay with me in my forests."

[606]

Arabella

MATTEO

appears again at the top of the stairs and leans over the banisters. He catches sight of Arabella, can hardly believe that it is she, whispers to himself

Arabella! Impossible! It is unthinkable!

Arabella's happy dream is suddenly broken. She does not see Matteo; he is behind her. But she feels that she is no longer alone.

Matteo has quietly come down the stairs and stands in front of her and bows.

ARABELLA

surprised, but not disturbed

You, my dear?

She corrects herself

Are you still here?

She stands up quickly

So late?
So you are still living in the hotel?

MATTEO

with knowing intimacy

You here? I ask you too, Arabella!

Comes one step closer

You are going out again, so late?

ARABELLA

I have come back from the ball and am going to bed. Good night.

She gives him a nod and tries to pass him up the stairs.

MATTEO

infinitely ironic

You have come back from the ball! You are going to your
room?

Half to himself

Mystery of a girl's heart, O unfathomable!

ARABELLA

Yes. And good night. You find it so amusing?

MATTEO

O Arabella!

He gives her an adoring and suggestive smile.

ARABELLA

If you have anything more to say to me,
then, please, tomorrow, but not now, not here.

MATTEO

Anything—more? I—anything—more?
O sweetest Arabella, just to give you thanks
from this day on, to the end of all my days!

ARABELLA

Thank me? For what? It is over now, once and for all.

MATTEO

with the strongest irony

Thank you? For what? Such art is quite beyond me.
Such virtuosity I find terrifying!

[608]

Arabella

ARABELLA

What is the matter?

MATTEO

To act a comedy for the comedy's sake so consummately,
to act a comedy without a public!
That is too much! That's coming near to witchcraft!

ARABELLA

I do not understand a word of what you say,
and so good night.

MATTEO

stands in her way

Very well. But one more look, a single look, to tell me
that in your heart of hearts you are the same!

ARABELLA

The same?

MATTEO *fervently*

As you were a quarter of an hour ago!

ARABELLA *in all innocence*

A quarter of an hour ago I was somewhere else!

MATTEO

as if transfigured with memories

A quarter of an hour ago! Yes! Upstairs!

He gazes fervently at her.

[609]

Hugo von Hofmannsthal

ARABELLA

glancing up the stairs, uncomprehending

I don't know what you mean and have no wish to stay here
  any longer!

MATTEO

This is too much! Such cold mastery of every nerve!
After such moments—a man just cannot bear it!
I appeal to the single drop of blood in you
which is incapable of hypocrisy!

He grasps her arm.

ARABELLA

You are out of your mind!
Matteo! Out of my way, or I'll call someone!

MATTEO

You, you could drive a man stark staring mad,
more quickly than anyone on earth!
Confirm, with only a single, final glance,
what there has been between us, there upstairs,
and I'll have nothing more on earth to ask of you!

*The waiter enters softly from the porter's box and goes to
open the door.*

ARABELLA

There are people coming, now, will you let me go!

MATTEO

I have given my word that you shall be rid of me,
I gave my word into your tears, your whispering kisses—
from tomorrow on! And I shall keep my word!

[610]

Arabella

We were in the dark, I did not see your eyes.
Now with a glance set your seal for the last time on every-
    thing,
and you are free for ever!

*Adelaide, behind her Mandryka, who immediately stops, then
Waldner, finally the three gamblers, who stop in the half-lit
    vestibule; Welko and Djura behind them.*

ADELAIDE

What an animated tête-à-tête at the foot of the stairs!
So after all you did not go to bed?
My child, what does this mean?

ARABELLA

Nothing, Mamma, nothing at all.

MANDRYKA

looking rigidly at Matteo

Yes. It is that accursèd man with the key.

ARABELLA

takes a step towards Mandryka, quite at her ease

I did not expect to see you again today, Herr von Mandryka.

MANDRYKA

sternly, to Adelaide

May I have your permission, Countess, to withdraw?

He steps back

Welko!

WELKO *beside him*

The master has recognized him?

[611]

Hugo von Hofmannsthal

MANDRYKA

Now go and pack. We take the first train home.

ARABELLA

walking up to Mandryka

There is nothing here that is your concern, Mandryka.
I came home, and I met this gentleman.
He is a good friend of ours. I shall tell you
everything later, if you wish me to.

MANDRYKA

I must ask you, please, to let me leave you now.

He is about to go.

Arabella, astonished, shakes her head.

ADELAIDE

O Vienna! City of scandal and intrigue!

Turning to Matteo

Unhappy man!

WALDNER *retaining Mandryka*

But you must stay another moment!
It seems that there are still some misunderstandings.

To Arabella

I ask you now, my child: how did you get here?
Did the lieutenant bring you home from the ball?
With your consent?

ARABELLA

Papa, look me in the eye!
Can a single madman make all other men mad?

[612]

Arabella

WALDNER

You have nothing to tell me?

ARABELLA

No, nothing, really,
except what you know already, dear Papa,
since this evening. Or perhaps you do not know it?

WALDNER

Then I am very much relieved.

> *Kisses Arabella on the forehead. To Mandryka*

So, you see?
Nothing has happened. Nothing has happened at all!
All the excitement for nothing at all, and that's that.

> *To the gamblers*

Would you come in here. Let's play on, and at once.

MANDRYKA

> *goes to Arabella, speaks only to her*

I shall help, as far as money and good will can help,
to cover up this hideous comedy,
since I am not the man to play, Arabella,
the rôle you have allotted to me to play in it.

ADELAIDE

O thrice unhappy meeting!

MANDRYKA

> *turns away, to himself*

No, no, how can it be? No, how can it be possible!

[613]

Hugo von Hofmannsthal

ADELAIDE

O thrice unhappy meeting!

WALDNER

Please, this is not the time for arias!

ARABELLA *to Mandryka only*

Mandryka, listen, as true as there's a God in heaven,
there is nothing here for which you must pardon me!
Much rather it is for me, if I can, to pardon you
for what you have said to me and for the tone you used.

MANDRYKA

staring angrily at Matteo

I should have been blind, but alas have good eyesight,
I should have been deaf, but alas have good hearing,
I should have been weak in the head—then, perhaps,
I would not have known this individual,
and not understood the game that is played here by night.

MATTEO

takes the insult in Mandryka's look and expression

Sir, should there be any rights in this
that are yours, even if only a short time since—
I am at your service.

ARABELLA

standing between the two men

Yes, this gentleman has every right, for I am engaged to him,
and you do not possess the smallest right, not even the shadow
     of a right!
Say so yourself!

[614]

Arabella

MATTEO *hesitant, agonized*

No . . . none . . .

ARABELLA *to Mandryka*

You see!

MANDRYKA

You should have let the gentleman have his say!
He had one small word still on the tip of his tongue.
"No . . . none . . . except" is what he meant to say,
and he quickly stopped himself!
But I! I saw it when it was on his lips.

ARABELLA

Matteo, I never thought that you were mean!
What are you doing to me now!
You want to compromise me in public out of defiance!
You want to ruin my marriage for me!

ADELAIDE

Miserable intriguer! So he means to steal my daughter's
hand!

MANDRYKA

Takes a step closer to Matteo

"Except"—now, out with the truth you are hiding!

MATTEO *firmly*

Not a word! Not a word!

MANDRYKA *to Arabella*

Except the rights, he was about to say,
which this night gave to him.

You try; perhaps for you and you alone
he'll find and speak these little words!

ARABELLA *to Matteo*

              Now have you
anything more to say before this gentleman?

MATTEO

bows his head

No!

MANDRYKA

I congratulate you, lieutenant,
on your luck with beautiful women, and your discretion,
you have equal measures of both.

ARABELLA

Did you hear that, Papa!

WALDNER

Mandryka, you must account for this to me!
Now come to me, my child!

ARABELLA

stays where she is, with an expression of deep sorrow

Whatever happens, it doesn't matter, life is a worthless thing!
What's left in all the world, if this man can be
so weak and has not the strength to believe in me?
And gives me up, simply because of nothing!

Arabella

THE GUESTS

murmuring at the top of the stairs

What did you say? You know them? Who caught whom?
What happened? She was running away? Really? With the
    lieutenant?

ADELAIDE

walking across to Waldner with an expansive gesture

No, Theodor, this young man is not worthy
to stand before your pistol-point. This is
merely the villainous intrigue, nothing more,
of a suitor who has had his suit rejected.

WALDNER

That one does not come into it. Mandryka here,
it's he who owes me satisfaction! And at once.
Where are my pistols? What? They're sold? O heavens
    above!
But never mind, I can get myself some others.

THE THREE GAMBLERS

We protest!
First we must play the return game that you owe us!

MATTEO

It is I alone who am the guilty one. I take back every word,
and every look! It has all been misconstrued,
I never meant a word of what you thought I said.
If anyone here needs punishing, it's me.

[617]

Hugo von Hofmannsthal

WALDNER *acidly*

You plunge in headfirst, then in the same breath clear yourself!
This was not done among officers in my time!

MANDRYKA

to Arabella only

The young man is being as good as he can.
It is time you showed for him
a little sympathy and some concern, sweet child.
Confess the truth to me, to me alone!
He is your lover! I shall do everything—
you can have every confidence in me, Arabella!

ARABELLA

looks at him firmly

I swear, Mandryka, by my very soul,
the truth is on my side.

MANDRYKA

Do not forswear your soul this way, my girl!
My heart grieves for you.

To himself

O God, what disgrace are you bringing me through this
woman!

Again to Arabella, quietly

Considering I even saw the boy
as he handed the key to him, the key
of your room.

[618]

Arabella

ARABELLA

What boy?

MANDRYKA

The boy, your groom, the one you sent to him!

ARABELLA

Zdenko! My God! You mean him?

MANDRYKA

Aha! Confess. I want it. To me alone!

ARABELLA *to herself*

Has hell decided to conspire against me?

MANDRYKA

That man there, that man who has ruined my life,
should I spare him, as he is your lover? Tell me!

ARABELLA

The truth is on my side. Mandryka, only the truth,
for everything else—as I can see—is against me.

MANDRYKA

For the last time! Do you want to marry that man there,
with whom you had your little rendezvous
ten minutes after we had become engaged?

ARABELLA

I have no answer, Herr von Mandryka, to your questions.

She walks away from him.

[619]

Hugo von Hofmannsthal

MANDRYKA *angrily*

Very well then. Welko, go, and take Djura with you.
Go to the gunsmith, make him open his shop,
it does not matter what it costs, I need sabres!
Two heavy sabres, make sure they're sharp!
Bring them at once. And have a doctor wakened,
that's all I need. The conservatory is there.

Half turning to Matteo

We'll make an end of it all, and without witnesses.

*He takes out his cigar case, reflects, offers Matteo one, who
refuses, lights one himself*

Perhaps you people would be good enough
to leave us alone till then.

He smokes.

They wait, gloomily.

ZDENKA

her voice from above

Papa! Mamma!

All look up.

*Zdenka, in a house-coat, with hair loose, undisguisedly a
girl, rushes down the stairs, falls on her knees before her
father*

Papa!

ADELAIDE

covers Zdenka with her stole

Zdenka! What behaviour! You'll disgrace us all!

[620]

Arabella

ARABELLA

What has happened? Zdenka, dear. Tell me. I am here.

ZDENKA

I must say goodbye, and quickly, to you all. I'm going.
I must throw myself in the Danube before dawn comes.

WALDNER

What do you mean?

THE GUESTS *murmuring*

Now who on earth can she be, this pretty girl?

MANDRYKA *to himself*

Surely I've seen that face somewhere before today?

ZDENKA

Only forgive me everything—and let me go.
I'm so ashamed—dying of shame—so let me go!
Before sunrise, I must be lying there, deep down—
then afterward they will all forgive me, even Papa!

ARABELLA

embraces her and draws her close

You stay with me. And whatever has happened to you,
nothing has happened to make us love you the less.

ZDENKA

pointing at Matteo

He is innocent. He did not know anything.
It was only I—

[621]

Hugo von Hofmannsthal

ADELAIDE

Not a word, unhappy child!
Silence to the grave!

WALDNER

Silence yourself, and let the girl speak out!
Now you shall have the reward for your masquerades.

ZDENKA *to Arabella*

I can tell it only to you, to you and you alone!

ARABELLA

I am here, I'll not desert you, I am here!

ZDENKA

nestling against her

He thought that it was you! I did it all,
out of fear for him, Bella, do you understand?
And still he does not know that it was me!

Timidly

Matteo!

MATTEO

What sweet voice calls to me?

ZDENKA *bashfully*

The voice of your deceiver, Matteo!
Your friend, your only friend, your Zdenko stands before
 you!

MATTEO

O my dear friend! Dear girl! O my sweet angel, you!

Arabella

ZDENKA

It is you whom I must ask for pardon, you and her,
both of you—O my God!

She covers her face with her hands.

ARABELLA

If too much love must ask to be forgiven,
then simply ask him to forgive you.

Holds her tight and kisses her.

MATTEO

In the room it was too dark, I did not hear your voice—
and yet I feel as if, from the very start,
I guessed what was happening, O sweet little Zdenko!

*Zdenka looks at him affectionately, but stays in Arabella's
embrace.*

MANDRYKA *to himself*

The girl, she was the groom! Fool, fool that I am!
How should she ever pardon me for this,
unable as I am to pardon myself for it?

*Welko comes from the right, carrying two cavalry sabres.
Behind him Djura with two pistols in a case; behind them,
the doctor.*

*Mandryka sees them, waves them away, they remain stand-
ing, right.*

WALDNER

has seen them too; with the cold decisiveness of the gambler

Very good. Now at last I know whom I am playing against.
This is the concern of no one but her father.

[623]

Hugo von Hofmannsthal

THE THREE GAMBLERS

Oho! Oho!

MANDRYKA

ignoring Waldner, to Arabella only

How can I look you in the face, Arabella?
I know that I shall never in my life deserve a glance from
  you.
Like a ruffian, with my two bare fists
I thought that I could grab the joy of joys,
and am become unworthy—in the twinkling of an eye,
and now am penitent and ashamed, to the end of my days.

ARABELLA

Zdenka dear, you are the better of us two.
You have the kinder heart, and nothing for you exists,
nothing in the world, except what your heart dictates to you.
Thank you so much, you have taught me a great lesson,
that we should not want anything, nor ask for anything,
not calculate and not barter and not covet,
only give and go on loving always!

*As she is speaking she does not give Mandryka the glance
which he so ardently desires and which would solve all
problems.*

ZDENKA

together with Arabella

How gently you speak to me! You are not angry with me!
You are so inexpressibly kind, I know you better than anyone,
and I want to do everything always for your sake—

Arabella

Alone

—and all I wanted was quietly to run away,
and not offend you. But you understand me, you,
and you will not desert me now, whatever happens!

MANDRYKA

to himself, very irresolute

Whatever happens . . .

ADELAIDE

O God! Our terrible disgrace!
O had this evening never, never happened!
The prophetess did not foretell all this!

WALDNER *firmly*

What happens now is clear beyond a doubt.

He takes a resolute step, eyeing the pistols.

ARABELLA *to Zdenka*

Whatever happens, I am here with you!

MANDRYKA

looking at Arabella, in a choking voice

What happens now . . .

ZDENKA *frightened*

Papa!

MATTEO

Angel from heaven, sent down to raise me up in flight,
God forbid that the world should ever sully you!

[625]

Hugo von Hofmannsthal

MANDRYKA

his voice even more choking

What happens now . . .

He turns to go.

ARABELLA

softly, over Zdenka's shoulder

Mandryka!

She raises her hand.

Mandryka fervently grasps and kisses her hand.

MANDRYKA

I do not deserve such forgiveness!

ARABELLA

Quiet, Mandryka!
We'll speak no more now. Now we have forgotten
the things that have just happened to us here!
It was no fault of ours.
Let us all go to meet, with a good will,
what is yet to happen.

MANDRYKA

What is yet to happen?

*He grasps, quickly and resolutely, Matteo's hand and leads
him over to Waldner*

What happens now is the wooing!
I stand before you with this gentleman, most noble sir,
I bow, and on my friend's behalf, request
that you do not deny him the hand of this young lady.

Waldner makes a gesture of demur.

[626]

MANDRYKA

Do not deny him that which great love has given him!
And the lordship of two villages, two of my own,
between the mountains and the quiet Danube,
I make it my privilege to lay at her feet,
with the castle as well;
that she may possess the place where she is mistress,
and need not feel her sister puts her to shame.

ZDENKA *faintly*

Matteo! Papa! What does it mean?
I mustn't go away?

ARABELLA

You must be happy now, as you deserve to be!

WALDNER

is touched, kisses her

Now do not cry, little one. Give me your hand, my son.

He takes Matteo's hand.

ADELAIDE

O Theodor, how everything has changed!

WALDNER

Marvellous!

ADELAIDE *in tears*

O Theodor!

WALDNER

*hurriedly embraces Adelaide, then turns promptly to the
gamblers*

[627]

Now I am at your service, gentlemen!

Exit quickly into the conservatory, the gamblers follow him.

THE GUESTS *murmuring*

We'll go to bed. There's nothing more can happen.

They return to their rooms.

ARABELLA

Take her to bed, Mamma!

Mandryka takes a step towards Arabella

ARABELLA

We'll speak no more now,
till another day has dawned. Don't you agree?

Adelaide and Zdenka go up the stairs to the first-floor level.

ZDENKA *affectionately*

Matteo!

ARABELLA

Go on now, he will come tomorrow morning,
and you shall have him for ever.

Matteo disappears.

Mandryka stands there, worried and tense.

ARABELLA

goes to Mandryka, nonchalantly

Could your servant go to the fountain in the courtyard and
    bring
a glass of very fresh water up for me?

[628]

Arabella

Welko hurries off

After this interlude, I think it would do me good.

She walks up the stairs.

MANDRYKA

gazes after her, until she is at the top. Someone must have
turned out another lamp—it is now noticeably darker

She does not look at me, she does not say good night,
she leaves me here, and goes. Have I deserved any better?
What is deserved in this world? Deserved is nothing.
A thrashing is deserved by a fellow like me—
but I would like to have had a glance from her—
just half a glance!

Welko appears with a glass of water on a tray, looks ques-
tioningly at Mandryka

MANDRYKA

Go up to her then!

Welko goes up the stairs

She thought of nothing but to have a glass of water,
and relief from the sight of me. Or she wanted to mock me.
Perhaps—? Even if she mocks, at least
that is itself a mercy, undeserved, God knows it is!

Arabella appears at the top of the stairs, looks down to see
if he is there, her face brightens. She takes the glass and
comes down the stairs, Welko behind her.

Mandryka turns, sees Arabella slowly and solemnly coming
downstairs with the glass, which she carries on the tray
using both hands; he steps back with a shock of joy.

[629]

Hugo von Hofmannsthal

ARABELLA *on the last step*

It was very good, Mandryka, that you had not left—
it was very good for me and also for you.
I wanted to drink this glass all on my own
to the oblivion of the trouble there has been,
and to go quietly to bed and not think any more of you and
    me,
till another bright day had dawned over us both.
But then, as I felt that you were standing here in the dark,
there came a great power from above,
and touched me to the heart,
so that I do not need a drink to refresh myself;
no, the very feeling of my joy refreshes me,
and this untouched drink I give now to my friend,
on the evening which ends for me my girlhood days.

*She descends the last step and passes him the glass. Welko
takes the empty tray deftly from her and disappears.*

MANDRYKA

*drinks the water quickly in one draught and holds the glass
up high in his right hand*

As sure as none shall drink from this glass after me,
you are mine and I am yours to the end of time!

He smashes the glass on the stone stairs.

ARABELLA

*stands on the last step again and lays her hand on his shoul-
der*

And so we are to be married and are joined
for sorrow and joy and injury and forgiving!

[630]

MANDRYKA

For ever, my angel, and for all that may ever happen!

ARABELLA

And you will believe—?

MANDRYKA

And you will remain as you are?

ARABELLA

I cannot change, so take me, just as I am!

She sinks into his arms, he kisses her, she quickly releases herself and runs up the stairs. He gazes after her.

Curtain

THE DIFFICULT MAN

A Comedy in Three Acts

Translated by

WILLA MUIR

HANS KARL BÜHL, *Count*

CRESCENCE, *his sister, Countess Freudenberg*

STANI, *her son, Count Freudenberg*

HELEN ALTENWYL, *daughter of*

ALTENWYL, *Count*

ANTOINETTE HECHINGEN, *wife of*

HECHINGEN, *Count*

NEUHOFF, *Baron*

EDINE

NANNI } *Antoinette's bosom friends*

HUBERTA

AGATHE, *Antoinette's maid*

NEUGEBAUER, *Count Bühl's secretary*

LUKAS, *Count Bühl's butler*

VINCENT, *a new footman of Bühl's*

A FAMOUS MAN

SERVANTS *of Bühl and Altenwyl*

Act One

A medium large room in a rather old Viennese palace, fitted up as a study.

SCENE I

Lukas comes in with Vincent

LUKAS

This is called the study. Relations and close friends are shown in here, or else, but only on special instructions, into the green drawing-room.

VINCENT

coming farther in

What does he study? Estate business? Or what? Political affairs?

LUKAS

This door in the wall is for the secretary to come in by.

VINCENT

So he has a private secretary, too? Miserable creatures, they are. Slinking good-for-nothings. Does this one count for anything in the house?

LUKAS

This door leads into the dressing-room. We'll go in there now and lay out his dinner jacket and his tails so that he can choose which he likes, since he hasn't given any special instructions.

VINCENT

nosing round all the furniture

So what? Do you think I need to be taught my duties? There's time enough till tomorrow morning, and we'd do better to have a heart-to-heart talk now. It's a good many years since I learned all about gentlemen's service, so just stick to the needful; I mean the special peculiarities. Come on! Put me in the picture.

LUKAS

straightening a picture that is hanging a little askew

He can't bear to see a picture or a looking-glass hanging the least bit awry. When he starts pulling out all the desk drawers or hunting for a mislaid key, he's in a very bad mood.

VINCENT

Oh, trifles like these don't matter. But didn't you tell me that the sister and the nephew who live upstairs in the house have to be announced every time they come to see him?

LUKAS

polishing a looking-glass with his handkerchief

Exactly like any other visitor. He insists on that.

VINCENT

What's he getting at? He must want to keep them at arm's length. Then why does he let them live here? I suppose he has more than one house? But they're his heirs. They must be wishing him dead.

LUKAS

Her ladyship Countess Crescence and Count Stani? God forbid! I don't know what to make of you.

VINCENT

You can cut out the preaching. What's he after, keeping them in the house? That's what interests me. You see, it throws a light on his future intentions. These I must know before I let myself in for this job.

LUKAS

What future intentions?

VINCENT

Don't throw my words in my teeth! This all means a lot to me. If things suit me here, I might settle down for life. When you've retired, I could take everything in hand. From all I hear, this place would probably suit me very well. But I want to know where I am. Now, since he's bringing his relations into the house, it looks as if he means to begin a new kind of life. At his age and after his years at the front that's quite understandable. When a man won't ever see forty again—

LUKAS

His lordship will be forty next year.

VINCENT

Put it in a nutshell, he wants to be done with love-affairs. He's had enough of little bits of fluff.

LUKAS

I don't understand that kind of talk.

VINCENT

But of course you understand me very well, my *dear* sir.—
Anyhow, that bears out what the woman at the lodge told
me. The main point now is: does he mean to get married?
In that case there'll be nothing in it for me, with a lawful
mistress in the house. Or might he settle down to a bachelor life with me? Tell me what you think about it. That's
the main point for me, that is, you see. (*Lukas clears his
throat loudly*) What's the idea, making me jump?

LUKAS

Sometimes he's actually in the room before you hear a
footfall.

VINCENT

What's he getting at? Does he try to trap people? Is he as
spiteful as that?

LUKAS

When that happens, you have to go away quietly.

VINCENT

What a horrible habit to have. I'll soon break him of that.

SCENE II

HANS KARL

has come in noiselessly

Just wait a moment, Lukas. Is that you, Neugebauer?

Vincent is standing to one side in the dark.

LUKAS

Beg to inform your lordship this is the new footman, who
was four years with His Highness, Prince Palm.

HANS KARL

Just carry on what you were doing with him. Let Mr. Neugebauer bring me the papers about Hohenbühl. And I'm not
at home to anyone.

A bell is heard.

LUKAS

That's the bell in the small antechamber.

He goes out.

Vincent stands still.

Hans Karl has moved up to the desk.

SCENE III

LUKAS

comes in and announces

Her ladyship Countess Freudenberg.

Crescence has come in on his heels.

Lukas leaves the room, Vincent likewise.

CRESCENCE

Am I disturbing you, Kari? Do forgive me—

HANS KARL

Not at all, my dear Crescence.

CRESCENCE

I'm on my way up to dress—for the soirée.

HANS KARL

At the Altenwyls'?

CRESCENCE

You're coming too, aren't you? Or not? I should just like to know, my dear.

HANS KARL

If it's all the same to you, I'd rather perhaps make up my mind later, and then perhaps ring up from the Club when I've decided. You know how I dislike being tied down.

CRESCENCE

Oh yes.

HANS KARL

But if you have been counting on me—

CRESCENCE

My dear Kari, I'm old enough to get home by myself—besides, Stani will be there and he'll pick me up. So you're not going?

HANS KARL

I'd rather think it over a while yet.

CRESCENCE

A soirée's none the more attractive for being thought over, my dear. Besides, I fancied that being at the front would have got you out of the way of thinking things over quite so much. (*Sits down beside him as he stands beside the desk*) Let Kari be a good boy now and give up being so horribly erratic and so unable to make up his mind about anything that I have to carry on a war to the knife with his friends, what with one of them calling him a hypochondriac and another saying he's a wet blanket and a third that he can never be depended on.—You've come back in such excellent shape, too, exactly as you used to be when you were twenty-two and I was infatuated with my brother.

HANS KARL

My dear Crescence, are you paying me compliments?

CRESCENCE

Not at all, I'm just telling you the truth: now Stani is an excellent judge of such things, and he thinks you simply the finest gentleman in society; with him it's Uncle Kari this, and Uncle Kari that, and the greatest compliment one can pay him is to say that he resembles you, which of course he does—in his movements he's just you all over again. He has never known anything more elegant than your way of handling people, the grand air, the distance you set between you and everyone else—and yet the complete composure and *bonhomie* you show even to the humblest—but, like me, he can't help noticing your weaknesses; he adores decisiveness, strength, positiveness, and he hates shilly-shallying just as much as I do!

HANS KARL

Let me congratulate you on your son, Crescence. I am sure you will always find great happiness in him.

[643]

CRESCENCE

Still—*pour revenir à nos moutons*—goodness me, when a man's been through what you've been through and yet has carried on as if it were nothing at all—

HANS KARL *embarrassed*

But everyone did that!

CRESCENCE

Allow me to say: by no means everyone. But I should have thought that it would enable a man to get over his fits of nerves!

HANS KARL

People in a drawing-room still make me nervous. An evening party gives me the horrors, I simply can't help it. I can quite well understand people who keep open house, but not those who go there.

CRESCENCE

Then what is it that frightens you? Surely we can talk it over. Are you bored by the old people?

HANS KARL

Oh, I find them charming, they have such good manners.

CRESCENCE

Or is it the young ones who get on your nerves?

HANS KARL

No, I don't mind them at all. It's the occasion itself that is simply a horror, don't you see, the whole thing—the whole thing is such a twisted tangle of misunderstandings. Oh, these chronic misunderstandings!

CRESCENCE

After all you've gone through at the front, I simply don't understand why it hasn't hardened you.

HANS KARL

Crescence, that doesn't make a man less susceptible, but more so. How is it you don't understand that? I find tears starting to my eyes over some little stupidity—or I grow hot with embarrassment about some trifling nuance that nobody else even notices, or it happens that I say out loud what I am thinking—in any such state it's impossible to mix with people. I can't describe it more precisely, but it's too much for me. To be honest with you, two hours ago I gave instructions to make my excuses to the Altenwyls. Perhaps another soirée, sometime soon, but not this one.

CRESCENCE

Not this one. But why not this particular one?

HANS KARL

It's too much for me, just in general.

CRESCENCE

When you say in general you mean something in particular.

HANS KARL

Not at all, Crescence.

CRESCENCE

Of course you do. Aha. Well, on this point I can reassure -you.

HANS KARL

On what point?

CRESCENCE

As far as Helen is concerned.

HANS KARL

What has Helen to do with it?

CRESCENCE

My dear, I'm neither deaf nor blind, and that Helen was head over heels in love with you from the time she was fifteen until not so long ago, let us say until the second year of the war, I have plenty of evidence, in the first, second, and third place.

HANS KARL

But, Crescence, you're just imagining things—

CRESCENCE

Do you know, about three or four years ago, when she was quite a young débutante, I used to fancy that she was the one person in the world who could hold you, who could be your wife. But as sure as I live I'm glad that it hasn't turned out like that. Two such complicated people, that would be no good.

HANS KARL

You do me too much honour. I'm the least complicated person in the world. (*He has pulled out a drawer of the desk*) But I cannot think how you should hit on such an idea—I'm fond of Helen, she's a kind of cousin—after all, I've known her since she was little—she could be my daughter.

Hunts in the drawer for something.

CRESCENCE

More likely mine. But I shouldn't like her to be my daughter. And much less should I want that Baron Neuhoff for a son-in-law.

HANS KARL

Neuhoff? Is that really a serious affair?

CRESCENCE

She's going to marry him.

Hans Karl slams the drawer shut.

CRESCENCE

I regard it as a settled thing, in spite of the fact that he's a wild outsider, blown in from some Baltic province or other where the wolves howl good night in the snow—

HANS KARL

Geography was never your strong point. Crescence, the Neuhoffs are a Holstein family.

CRESCENCE

Well, it's the same thing. Wild outsiders, that's what I said.

HANS KARL

And, besides, one of the first families. As well-connected as anyone could be.

[647]

CRESCENCE

But, really, that's only what it says in the *Gotha*. How could one make sure of that from as far away as here?

HANS KARL

You're very set against the man.

CRESCENCE

Why shouldn't I be? When one of the best of our girls such as Helen gets notions about a wild outsider like him, in spite of the fact that he'll never in his life have any position here—

HANS KARL

You think not?

CRESCENCE

Never in his life!—In spite of the fact that she's not taken in by his high-flown talk, flying, in short, in the face of her-self and the world— (*A short pause.—Hans Karl with some violence jerks out another drawer*) Can I help you to look for something? You're upsetting yourself.

HANS KARL

Oh, thanks very much, I'm not really looking for anything, I put the wrong key in the lock.

SECRETARY

appears at the little door

Oh, I beg your pardon, please excuse me.

HANS KARL

I'll be free in a minute or two, my dear Neugebauer.

The Secretary retreats.

CRESCENCE

rises and comes up to the desk

Kari, if it's to do you even a small favour, I'll put an end to that affair.

HANS KARL

What affair?

CRESCENCE

The one we're speaking of: Helen and Neuhoff. I could put an end to it overnight.

HANS KARL

What?

CRESCENCE

As sure as I live, she's as much in love with you now as she was six years ago, and it would need only a word, the merest shadow of a hint—

HANS KARL

Which I beg you for God's sake not to give her—

CRESCENCE

Oh, sorry. Very well.

HANS KARL

My dear, with all due respect to your energetic temperament, people, thank goodness, are not so simple as all that.

CRESCENCE

My dear, people, thank goodness, are very simple if one takes them simply. Well, this bit of news, I see, is no great blow to you. All the better—you've stopped being interested in Helen, I'll keep that in mind.

HANS KARL *standing up*

But I don't know how you ever got the idea that I needed to stop being interested. Do other people have the same fantastic notion?

CRESCENCE

Very likely.

HANS KARL

You know, that's enough to make me want to go to the soirée.

CRESCENCE

To give Theophilus Neuhoff your blessing? He'd be delighted. He'd crawl on hands and knees to be taken into your confidence.

HANS KARL

Don't you find that, considering all this, I should have shown myself at the Altenwyls' long ago? I'm extremely sorry that I made my excuses today.

CRESCENCE

Well, ring them up again: say it was a mistake made by a new footman and that you're coming.

Lukas comes in.

HANS KARL *to Crescence*

You know, I'd still like to think it over.

LUKAS

There's someone waiting to see your lordship.

CRESCENCE *to Lukas*

I'm just going. Get on the telephone quick to Count Altenwyl, and say that his lordship will be coming to the soirée tonight. It was a mistake.

Lukas looks at Hans Karl.

HANS KARL

not meeting Lukas's eyes

In that case he'd have to ring up the Club first and say that Count Hechingen is not to expect me for dinner, or later on.

CRESCENCE

Of course, he can do that too. But first Count Altenwyl, so that people know where they are. (*Lukas goes out. She rises to her feet*) And now I'll leave you to your business affairs. (*On the way out*) Which Hechingen were you going to see? Nandi?

HANS KARL

No, Adolf.

CRESCENCE *coming back*

Antoinette's husband? Isn't he an utter fool?

HANS KARL

Do you know, Crescence, I'm no judge of that. Long conversations always make me feel that the clever things people say are foolish and that the foolish things, if anything, are clever.

[651]

CRESCENCE

And I'm convinced, anyhow, that there's more to him than to her.

HANS KARL

Well, in the old days I never knew him at all, or, rather— (*He has turned towards the wall and pokes at a picture which is hanging not quite straight*)—only as the husband of his wife—and then out there at the front we became friends. You know, he's a thoroughly decent fellow. We were together in the winter of '15, twenty weeks in our station in the Carpathian forest, I with my gunners and he with his sappers, and we shared our last crusts together. I developed a great respect for him. There were plenty of brave men out there, but I never met one who faced death with such complete equanimity, almost a kind of comfortable ease.

CRESCENCE

If his relations could hear you they'd fling their arms round your neck. You'd better speak to his fool of a wife, then, and bring about a reconciliation between them, you'd make two families happy. This idea that she keeps dangling over them of a divorce or a separation, it's all the same, is getting on everyone's nerves. Besides, it would be to your own advantage to have the situation made regular.

HANS KARL

How so?

CRESCENCE

You may as well know it: there are people spreading the absurd rumour that if she got an annulment you'd marry her. (*Hans Karl is silent*) I don't say that it's people of any standing who are making up such unlikely nonsense. (*Hans Karl is silent*) Have you been to see her at all since you came back from the front?

HANS KARL

No. I ought to go, of course.

CRESCENCE

looking at him sideways

Well, go to see her tomorrow and stir up her conscience.

HANS KARL

bends down as if to pick up something

I don't really know if I'm exactly the right man to do that.

CRESCENCE

It would be an act of simple kindness. It would let her understand that she was on the wrong track when she tried her hardest two years ago to get you involved with her.

HANS KARL

not meeting her eyes

That's only a notion of yours.

CRESCENCE

Exactly as she's trying to do with Stani today.

HANS KARL *in astonishment*

Your Stani?

[653]

CRESCENCE

Ever since springtime. (*She had got as far as the door, but turns round again and comes back to the desk*) There's a great, great favour my Kari could do me—

HANS KARL

But for goodness' sake, you've only to tell me what it is!

He offers her a chair, she remains standing.

CRESCENCE

Let me send Stani downstairs for a moment or two, and Kari can make the situation clear. Tell Stani that Antoinette is—well, the kind of woman who's not worth compromising oneself for. In a word, put Stani off her.

HANS KARL

And how do you think that's to be done? If he's in love with her?

CRESCENCE

But men are never so much in love as all that, and you're an oracle for Stani. If you would just bring the conversation round to that point—will you promise?

HANS KARL

Yes, well—if it can be done naturally—

CRESCENCE

again at the door, speaks from there

You'll find the right approach. You have no idea what an authority you are for him.

[654]

On the point of going out, she turns once more and comes forward to the desk

Tell him that you find her anything but elegant—and that you would never have had anything to do with her. Then he'll drop her overnight. (*She makes for the door again, and again turns round*) You know, don't be too severe about it, but not too casual either. Don't be too subtle about it. And he mustn't have the slightest suspicion that I'm behind it—he has the fixed idea that I'm trying to marry him off—of course I am, but all the same—he mustn't suspect it; he's exactly like you in that: the mere idea that anyone might try to influence him—! (*Once more she makes the same manoeuvre*) Do you know, I'd very much like to get it all settled at once, why waste an evening? And that provides you with a line of action too: you make it clear to Antoinette how much you disapprove her goings-on—you lead her round to the subject of her marriage —you sing Adolf's praises—and that gives you something to do and keeps the whole evening from being aimless.

She goes out.

SCENE IV

VINCENT

has come in from right, looks round first to see if Crescence has gone, then

I don't know if the butler has mentioned it, there's a young woman out there, a lady's maid or something like that.

HANS KARL

What does she want?

VINCENT

From Countess Hechingen, to be precise. Seems to be a kind of confidential messenger. (*Coming still nearer*) Not a poor creature with nothing to say for herself.

HANS KARL

That I shall judge for myself, show her in.

Vincent goes out right.

SCENE V

LUKAS

comes in quickly through the middle doors

Has it been announced to your lordship? Countess Hechingen's maid, Agathe, is here. I told her I absolutely could not say whether your lordship was at home.

HANS KARL

Good. I have sent to say I am at home. Did you ring up Count Altenwyl?

LUKAS

I beg your lordship's pardon. I noticed that your lordship didn't want the call to be made, but didn't want to contradict her ladyship—so for the time being I have not telephoned.

HANS KARL *smiling*

Well done, Lukas. (*Lukas goes as far as the door*) Lukas, what do you think of the new footman?

LUKAS *hesitating*

Perhaps we should wait to see how he turns out.

[656]

The Difficult Man

HANS KARL

An impossible man. Pay him off. Send him packing!

LUKAS

Very good, your lordship. I thought as much.

HANS KARL

But say nothing about it for tonight.

SCENE VI

Vincent shows in Agathe. Both servants go out.

HANS KARL

Good evening, Agathe.

AGATHE

To think of seeing you again, your lordship! I'm all of a flutter.

HANS KARL

Won't you sit down?

AGATHE *standing*

Oh, your lordship, only don't be angry because I've come instead of that Brandstätter.

HANS KARL

But, my dear Agathe, we're old acquaintances. What has brought you to see me?

AGATHE

Oh dear, your lordship knows quite well. I've come about the letters. (*Hans Karl is taken aback*) Oh, my goodness, oh, excuse me, I can't bear to think of how my lady impressed on me not to spoil things by putting my foot in it.

HANS KARL *hesitatingly*

The Countess did write to tell me that certain letters belonging to her which are in my possession would be called for by a Herr Brandstätter on the fifteenth. Today is the twelfth, but of course I can hand over the letters to you instead. Immediately, if that is what the Countess wishes. I know that you are very devoted to the Countess.

AGATHE

Certain letters—what a way to speak, your lordship. I know quite well what letters these are.

HANS KARL *coldly*

I shall have them brought in at once.

AGATHE

If she could only see us together like this, my poor lady. It would be a comfort to her, it would do her a little good. (*Hans Karl begins to hunt about in a desk-drawer*) After these dreadful seven weeks, since ever we knew that our Count had come back from the war and yet we hadn't a single sign of life from him—

HANS KARL *looking up*

You hadn't a sign of life from Count Hechingen?

AGATHE

From him! When I say "our Count" that's what we call *you* between ourselves, your lordship. We don't call Count Hechingen "our Count"!

The Difficult Man

HANS KARL *very embarrassed*

Ah, excuse me, I couldn't be expected to know that.

AGATHE *tentatively*

Until this very afternoon we believed that you were to be at Count Altenwyl's soirée. And then Countess Altenwyl's maid told me on the telephone: he's made his excuses. (*Hans Karl stands up straight*) He's made his excuses, Agathe, cried my poor lady, he's not going because he's heard that I'm to be there! That means it's all over—and she gave me a look that would have melted a stone.

HANS KARL

very politely, but with the intention of putting an end to this

I fear that the letters in question are not here in my desk. I'll send for my secretary at once.

AGATHE

Oh, goodness, does the secretary have these letters? My lady must never find that out!

HANS KARL

The letters, needless to say, are in a sealed package.

AGATHE

A sealed package! Have things gone as far as that?

HANS KARL

speaks into the house telephone

My dear Neugebauer, could you come over here for a moment? Yes, I am free now.—But never mind those papers

[659]

—something else has cropped up. At once? No, just finish adding up your figures. In three minutes' time, that will do.

AGATHE

He'd better not catch sight of me, he'll remember who I am.

HANS KARL

You can slip into the library, I'll put on the light for you.

AGATHE

How could we imagine that all of a sudden everything would be over.

HANS KARL

escorting her to the library door, stops, wrinkles his fore-head

My dear Agathe, since you are so well-informed—I don't understand it, for I wrote to the Countess from the field hospital, a long letter, this last spring.

AGATHE

Yes, that abominable letter.

HANS KARL

I don't understand you. It was a very friendly letter.

AGATHE

It was a treacherous letter. How it made us tremble when we read it, that letter! Upset we were, and humiliated.

HANS KARL

But why on earth, I should like to know!

AGATHE *looking at him*

Why? Because you praised Count Hechingen in it up to the skies—and said that in the end one man is the same as another and any man will do instead of any other.

HANS KARL

I certainly never used such expressions. Thoughts of that kind never entered my head!

AGATHE

But that was what it all amounted to. Oh, we've read the letter often enough. And this, cried my lady, this is the result of nights spent under the stars in solitary meditation, this letter, in which he says plainly: one man is the same as another, our love was only moonshine, forget me and turn to Hechingen again—

HANS KARL

Not one single word of all that was in the letter.

AGATHE

The words don't matter. We understood the sense of it well enough. The humiliation of it, the mortifying conclusions to be drawn. Oh, we know well enough what was meant. This self-deprecation is just a deceitful trick. When a man starts accusing himself in a love-affair, he's accusing the affair itself. And in no time it's us who are standing in the dock. (*Hans Karl is silent. Agathe comes a step nearer*) I put up a good fight for our Count, when my lady said: Agathe, you'll see, he wants to marry the Altenwyl girl, and it's only because of that he's trying to patch up my marriage again.

[661]

HANS KARL

Did the Countess actually think that of me?

AGATHE

In her worst hours, when she'd been brooding over it. Then she would have a flash of hopefulness again. No, she would cry then, no, I'm not afraid of Helen—for she runs after him; and anyone who runs after Kari is done for as far as he's concerned, and she doesn't deserve him, either, for she's quite heartless.

HANS KARL

setting something straight

If I could only convince you—

AGATHE

But then she would suddenly despair again—

HANS KARL

How far I am from—

AGATHE

O God, she would cry, he hasn't been seen anywhere yet! Could that mean—?

HANS KARL

How far I am from—

AGATHE

Suppose he were to get engaged to her before my very eyes—

HANS KARL

How *can* the Countess—

AGATHE

Oh, men do that kind of thing, but not you, surely, your lordship?

HANS KARL

Nothing in the world is farther from my thoughts, my dear Agathe.

AGATHE

Oh, I kiss your hand, your lordship!

Quickly kisses his hand.

HANS KARL

withdrawing the hand

I hear my secretary coming.

AGATHE

For we know, we women, that something so blissful can't last for ever. And yet that it should suddenly stop all at once, that's what we can't get used to!

HANS KARL

You'll see me in a minute. I'll give you the letters myself and— Come in! Just come in, Neugebauer.

Agathe goes off right.

SCENE VII

NEUGEBAUER

comes in by the wall door

Your lordship summoned me.

HANS KARL

If you would be so good as to come to the help of my bad memory. I'm looking for a packet of letters—private letters, sealed up—about two fingers thick.

NEUGEBAUER

Inscribed by your lordship with a date? June 15 to October 22, 1916?

HANS KARL

That's right. Then you know—

NEUGEBAUER

I've had those documents in my hand, but I can't think where, for the moment. In the pressure of work among so many different memoranda that are piling up daily—

HANS KARL

without the slightest reproach

I can't understand how these very private letters should come to be mixed up with business documents—

NEUGEBAUER

If there is occasion to fear that your lordship has the faintest doubt of my discretion—

HANS KARL

But that has never entered my mind—

NEUGEBAUER

Be so good as to let me look for them at once; I'll do my utmost to clear up this very regrettable mishap.

The Difficult Man

HANS KARL

My dear Neugebauer, you're making far too much of a trifling occurrence.

NEUGEBAUER

For some time now I have been aware that something in me has begun to irritate your lordship. It is true that my education has been confined to inward accomplishments, and if it has perhaps failed to equip me with an unimpeachable social manner, this defect might perhaps be balanced in the eyes of a benevolent judge by other qualities, which it would certainly be difficult for a man of my character to remind you of, if I had to do so in person.

HANS KARL

I have no doubt of it, my dear Neugebauer. You give me the impression of being overworked. I wish you would stop work rather earlier of an evening. Why not go for a stroll in the evenings with your fiancée? (*Neugebauer is silent*) If it is private affairs that are worrying you, perhaps I could come to your assistance in some way and lighten your burden.

NEUGEBAUER

Your lordship takes it for granted that it's only financial worries a man of my kind can have.

HANS KARL

That's not at all what I meant. I know you are engaged to be married, and so of course a happy man—

NEUGEBAUER

I don't know if your lordship is referring to the housekeeper of Castle Hohenbühl?

HANS KARL

Yes, haven't you been engaged to her for five years?

NEUGEBAUER

The lady I'm at present engaged to is the daughter of a senior civil servant. She was engaged to my best friend, who lost his life in the war six months ago. Even while he was alive she was fond of me—and I have regarded it as a sacred trust from the deceased to offer this young girl a support for her lifetime.

HANS KARL *hesitatingly*

And your former long-standing engagement?

NEUGEBAUER

I brought it to an end, of course. Naturally, in the most correct and conscientious manner.

HANS KARL

Ah!

NEUGEBAUER

Naturally I shall honour all the commitments I had entered into, and take that extra burden with me into my new marriage. No small burden, I admit. (*Hans Karl is silent*) Perhaps your lordship does not sufficiently appreciate the severe moral seriousness that presses down on life in our lowly circles, so that the only course open to us is to exchange hard duties for others still harder.

HANS KARL

I always supposed that when a man thought of getting married he felt happy about it.

NEUGEBAUER

Personal inclinations cannot take first place in our humble world.

HANS KARL

To be sure, to be sure. Well, you'll find me the letters if you can.

NEUGEBAUER

I'll hunt for them until midnight if necessary.

Goes out.

HANS KARL *to himself*

I wonder what it is about me that makes everyone so much inclined to read me a lesson, and that always makes me wonder ever so faintly whether I don't deserve it?

SCENE VIII

STANI

appears in the middle door, in full evening dress

Excuse me, I only want to say good evening, Uncle Kari, if I'm not disturbing you.

HANS KARL

on his way to the library door right, stops and stands still

Not at all.

Offers him a chair and a cigarette.

Hugo von Hofmannsthal

STANI

taking the cigarette

But of course it puts you out when people come in without being announced. You're very like me in that. I can't stand it either when somebody gate-crashes me. I need time to put my thoughts a bit in order first.

HANS KARL

Please don't apologize, this is your home.

STANI

I beg your pardon, it's yours—

HANS KARL

Go on, sit down.

STANI

No, truly, I shouldn't have had the face to come in if I hadn't heard Neugebauer squawking away—

HANS KARL

He's just this moment gone.

STANI

Or else I should never have— You see, the new footman ran after me in the corridor about five minutes ago and told me—without being asked, mind you—that you were talking to Antoinette Hechingen's maid and shouldn't be disturbed.

HANS KARL *half to himself*

He did, did he?—Delightful fellow!

STANI

So of course I wouldn't have on any account—

HANS KARL

She was only bringing me back some books.

STANI

Does Toinette Hechingen read books?

HANS KARL

Apparently. One or two old French things.

STANI

Eighteenth century, I suppose. To match her furniture. (*Hans Karl is silent*) Her boudoir is charming. That small *chaise-longue* of hers! It's a signed piece.

HANS KARL

Yes, the small *chaise-longue*. Riesener.

STANI

Yes, Riesener it is. What a good memory for names you have! The signature's underneath.

HANS KARL

Underneath at the foot.

STANI

She's always dropping little combs out of her hair, and when one bends to pick them up one can see the inscription. (*Hans Karl crosses right and shuts the library door*) Do you feel a draught? Are you susceptible?

[669]

Hugo von Hofmannsthal

HANS KARL

Yes, at the front my gunners and I got as full of rheumatism as old hounds.

STANI

Do you know, she thinks the world of you, does Antoinette.

HANS KARL

lights up and smokes

Ah!

STANI

But truly, beyond compare. It was only because she thinks me wonderfully like you that I had any chance with her in the beginning. For instance, our hands. She goes into ecstasies about your hands. (*He spreads out his own hand and gazes at it*) But not a word of all this to Mamma, please. It's just a thoroughgoing flirtation, not by any means a *liaison*. But Mamma exaggerates everything to herself.

HANS KARL

My dear Stani, is it likely that I should ever mention such a thing?

STANI

Bit by bit, of course, she's been finding out the differences between us. *Ça va sans dire.*

HANS KARL

Antoinette?

[670]

STANI

She told me all about the beginning of her friendship with you.

HANS KARL

But I've known her for ages.

STANI

No, I mean what happened two years ago. In the second year of the war. When you were on leave after your first wound, and spent some days at Grünleiten.

HANS KARL

Does she date our friendship from then?

STANI

Of course. Since then you've been her greatest friend. As counsellor, as confidant, as anything you please, simply *hors ligne*. You've been an angel to her, she says.

HANS KARL

She's inclined to exaggerate, our Antoinette.

STANI

But she gave me all the particulars, about how she was terrified to be left alone at Grünleiten with her husband, who happened to be on leave too, and how she had sent a message to Feri Uhlfeldt, who was chasing after her at that time like the devil, asking him to come next day, and how she caught sight of you in the theatre that very evening and it came over her like an inspiration so that she begged you to drive back with her and spend the evening with her *à trois* with Adolf.

HANS KARL

I hardly knew him in those days.

STANI

Yes, by the way, that's something she can't understand. How you could have become so friendly with him later on. Such a dull pedantic fool, such a blockhead.

HANS KARL

There she's unfair to her husband, very!

STANI

Well, I'm not going to take sides. But she has a delightful way of telling it all.

HANS KARL

That's her strong point, these little confidences.

STANI

Yes, that's how she leads one on. The whole of that evening, I can see it all before me, how she showed you the garden after supper, the charming terraces beside the river, how the moon rose—

HANS KARL

She went into so much detail, did she?

STANI

And how in that one evening's conversation with her you were able to talk her out of having anything to do with Feri Uhlfeldt. (*Hans Karl smokes and says nothing*) That's what I admire so much in you; you have little to say, you are so absent-minded, yet you have such a strong

[672]

influence. That's why I find it quite natural, though so many people never stop talking about it, that you've been a year and a half in the Upper House without ever rising to speak. Absolutely right for someone like you! A great gentleman like you makes himself felt by his mere presence! Oh, I'm taking you as a model to study. Give me a year or two and I'll get there. At the moment I'm still too full of passion. You never go out for anything and never try to talk people into anything, that's just what's so elegant in you. Any other man in your shoes that evening would have become her lover.

HANS KARL

with a twinkle in his eye

Do you think so?

STANI

Positively. But of course I understand well enough that at your time of life you're too serious for that. It's no longer a temptation to you: that's how I explain it to myself. You know, that's me all over: I do like to account for everything. If I'd had time to stay at the University—science, that would have been my subject. I should have hit on themes, on problems, on questions that simply don't occur to other people. A life without reflection is no life for me. For instance, now: when a man realizes that he's no longer young, does it come over him all of a sudden?—That must be a most unpleasant moment.

HANS KARL

Well, you know, I think it comes on quite gradually. When someone lets you precede him one day through a doorway and you say to yourself: of course, he's much younger than I am, although he's a full-grown man.

STANI

Very interesting. How closely you observe things. You're altogether like me in that. And then do you just get used to being old?

HANS KARL

Well, there are still moments that give you a shock. For instance, when you suddenly realize you have stopped believing that there are people who can explain everything to you.

STANI

But there's one thing I don't understand, Uncle Kari, that, as experienced and well preserved as you are, you don't get married.

HANS KARL

Now!

STANI

Yes, now. For you're past the stage of looking for little adventures. You know, I could quite well understand that any woman would still be inclined to take an interest in you. But Toinette has made it clear to me why no woman's interest in you ever becomes serious.

HANS KARL

Ah!

STANI

Yes, she's given a lot of thought to it. She says you don't hold a woman because you haven't enough heart.

HANS KARL

Ah!

STANI

Yes, you lack the essential quality. That, she says, is the enormous difference between you and me. She says your hand is always loose on its wrist, ready to let go, and a woman feels that, and even if she were on the point of falling in love with you it would prevent the crystallization.

HANS KARL

Is that how she puts it?

STANI

Indeed, that's her great charm, she makes good conversation. You know, I demand that absolutely: any woman who is to hold me must be able to make conversation as well as being absolutely devoted.

HANS KARL

She does it enchantingly.

STANI

Absolutely. She has charm and spirit and temperament, but there's one thing she doesn't have: breeding.

HANS KARL

Do you think so?

STANI

You know, Uncle Kari, I'm a very fair-minded man; a woman can have given me, a hundred times over, the utmost proofs of her good will towards me—I'll grant her good points yet remain firmly aware of her bad ones. You understand, I think everything out and always make a division into two categories. So I put women into two main categories: these made for love-affairs and those for marriage. Antoinette belongs to the first category. Let her be Adolf Hechingen's wife a hundred times over, for me she's not a wife but—the other kind.

HANS KARL

That's where she belongs, of course. If one likes to divide people into such categories.

STANI

Absolutely. That's why, by the way, it's utterly stupid to try reconciling her to her husband.

HANS KARL

But if he is her husband after all? Forgive me, perhaps that's a very bourgeois notion.

STANI

You know, if I may go on, I make my categories and stick to them absolutely, affairs of gallantry on one side, marriage on the other. Marriage is not an experiment. It's the result of coming to a right decision.

HANS KARL

From which you are of course far removed.

STANI

Not at all. Ready to take the decision at any moment.

HANS KARL

At this very moment?

STANI

I find myself extraordinarily well qualified to make a woman happy, but please don't tell Mamma that, I want to keep complete freedom of action. I'm exactly like you in that. I can't bear being driven into a corner. (*Hans Karl smokes*) The decision must be instantaneous. At once or not at all, that's my motto!

HANS KARL

Nothing in the world interests me so much as how a man can move from one situation into another. So you would never postpone a decision?

STANI

Never, that's absolute weakness.

HANS KARL

But there's such a thing as complications?

STANI

I refuse to admit them.

HANS KARL

Suppose there were contradictory obligations interfering with each other?

STANI

In that case one chooses which are the ones to honour.

[677]

HANS KARL

But in making this choice one can be sometimes rather at a loss.

STANI

How so?

HANS KARL

Well, let us say hampered by self-reproach.

STANI

That's for hypochondriacs. I'm a very sound specimen. At the front I hadn't a single day's illness.

HANS KARL

Ah, you're always absolutely satisfied that you've done the right thing?

STANI

Yes, if it weren't the right thing I should have behaved differently.

HANS KARL

I don't just mean correct behaviour—but, to put it briefly, you let blind chance, or shall we say destiny, guide you?

STANI

How so? I always keep things well in hand.

HANS KARL

Yet sometimes in such decisive moments one is tempted to let a fantastic notion intervene: the notion of a Higher Necessity.

STANI

What I do is simply necessary, or I shouldn't do it.

HANS KARL *showing interest*

Forgive me if I take an example from actual life—that's not really the thing to do—

STANI

But please do—

HANS KARL

Let us suppose that a certain situation brought you close to the decision to get married.

STANI

Today or tomorrow.

HANS KARL

But then you're already more or less tied up with Antoinette.

STANI

I should break with her at once!

HANS KARL

Ah! Without any occasion for it?

STANI

But the occasion for it is at hand all the time. Look, our affair has been going on since the spring. Yet for the last six or seven weeks there's been something about Antoinette, I don't know what—to say I suspect her would be

[679]

to say too much—but the mere idea that she might be preoccupied with someone else besides me, you know, I'm absolutely against that.

HANS KARL

I see.

STANI

You know, I can't help it. I shouldn't like to call it jealousy, it's rather a not being able to understand how a woman attached to me could be interested in someone else at the same time—do you follow me?

HANS KARL

But Antoinette's so innocent whenever she's up to mischief. It makes her almost more endearing than ever.

STANI

There I simply don't understand you.

SCENE IX

NEUGEBAUER

has come in quietly

Here are the letters, your lordship. I found them in the first place I looked—

HANS KARL

Thank you. Please give me them. (*Neugebauer hands over the letters*) Thank you.

Neugebauer goes out.

[680]

SCENE X

HANS KARL

after a short pause

Do you know whom I think of as a born husband?

STANI

Well?

HANS KARL

Adolf Hechingen.

STANI

Antoinette's husband? Ha ha ha!—

HANS KARL

I say it in all seriousness.

STANI

But Uncle Kari!

HANS KARL

In his attachment to his wife there is a Higher Necessity.

STANI

He's a born—I won't say what!

HANS KARL

What happens to him matters to me.

STANI

For me he comes into the category of men lacking instincts. Do you know whom he hangs on to when you're not in the Club? Me. Me, of all people! He has a flair!

Hugo von Hofmannsthal

HANS KARL

I'm fond of him.

STANI

But he's inelegant from top to toe.

HANS KARL

But he has a kind of inward grace.

STANI

An inelegant, long-winded bore.

HANS KARL

He needs a bottle of champagne to quicken his blood.

STANI

Don't let him hear that, he'll take it literally. I can't stand a man of no elegance when he's been drinking.

HANS KARL

I'm fond of him.

STANI

He takes everything literally, including your friendship for him.

HANS KARL

He's entitled to take that literally.

STANI

Forgive me, Uncle Kari, you're not a man to be taken literally; anyone who does that falls into the category of men lacking instincts.

[682]

HANS KARL

But he's such a good, decent fellow.

STANI

He may be, if you say so, but that's no reason for his continually harping on your kindness. That gets on my nerves. An elegant man can show *bonhomie,* but he can't be a kind man. Excuse me, I say to him, Uncle Kari is a great gentleman and therefore of course a great egotist. You forgive me?

HANS KARL

It's no use, I'm fond of him.

STANI

That's so eccentric of you! But you have no need to be eccentric. You have the wonderful quality of presenting yourself as you are, without the slightest effort—as a great gentleman. Without any effort! That's the great thing. Second-rate men are always making efforts. Take that Theophilus Neuhoff who's been cropping up everywhere this last year. What kind of existence has such a creature except a continuous wretched effort to copy a way of life that simply isn't his?

SCENE XI

LUKAS

comes in hastily

May I ask—has your lordship given instructions that visitors from outside are to be shown in?

HANS KARL

Absolutely not. What's all this?

LUKAS

Then the new footman must have mixed things up. The porter's lodge has just telephoned to say that Herr Baron Neuhoff is on his way up. Please tell me what to do with him.

STANI

You see, just when we were speaking about him. That's no accident. Uncle Kari, that man is my *guignon,* and I conjure him up. A week ago at Helen's, just when I was going to tell her what I thought of Herr von Neuhoff, in that very moment he appeared in the doorway. Three days ago I was just leaving Antoinette—who should be in the anteroom but Herr von Neuhoff? Yesterday morning at my mother's I had something urgent to discuss with her, and as soon as I reached the anteroom what I found was Herr von Neuhoff.

VINCENT

comes in, announces

Herr Baron Neuhoff is in the anteroom.

HANS KARL

Now of course I'll have to receive him.

Lukas makes a gesture that the visitor is to be admitted.

Vincent opens the folding-doors and shows him in.

Vincent and Lukas go out.

[684]

SCENE XII

NEUHOFF

comes in

Good evening, Count Bühl. I made so bold as to enquire if you were at home.

HANS KARL

Do you know my nephew Freudenberg?

STANI

We have met before.

They sit down.

NEUHOFF

I was to have had the pleasure of meeting you tonight at the Altenwyls'. Countess Helen had promised herself some small satisfaction in bringing us together. My disappointment was all the more grievous when I learned from Countess Helen this afternoon that you had begged to be excused.

HANS KARL

You have known my cousin, have you, since last winter?

NEUHOFF

Known, yes—if one dare use such a word in reference to her. There are moments when one suddenly realizes how ambiguous the word is; it describes the most superficial relationship in the world and at the same time the deepest mystery of communion between person and person. (*Hans Karl and Stani exchange a look*) I have the good fortune

[685]

to see Countess Helen frequently and to be bound to her by ties of devotion. (*A short, somewhat embarrassed pause*) This afternoon—we were both in Bohuslawsky's studio—Bohuslawsky is painting my portrait, that's to say, he's tormenting himself unreasonably about catching the expression of my eyes; he says there's a certain something in them that can be seen only at rare moments—it was he who begged Countess Helen to come and see the portrait and give him her opinion about the eyes—well, she said to me: Count Bühl isn't coming, you should go to see him. Just pay him a visit, quite simply. He is a man with whom natural lack of affectation achieves everything and calculated behaviour nothing at all. A wonderful man in our calculating world, was my answer—but that's what I thought he was like, that's what I guessed him to be, at our very first meeting.

STANI

Did you meet my uncle at the front?

NEUHOFF

On the Staff.

HANS KARL

Not the most congenial company to be found in.

NEUHOFF

One could tell how you felt about it, for you said extremely little.

HANS KARL *smiling*

I'm no great conversationalist, am I, Stani?

The Difficult Man

STANI

Among close friends you are!

NEUHOFF

You've put your finger on it, Count Freudenberg, your uncle likes to make his payments in gold; he can't demean himself to accept the paper currency of ordinary inter-course. His words can give away nothing less than intimate friendship, and that is beyond price.

HANS KARL

You are extremely kind, Baron Neuhoff.

NEUHOFF

You should have your portrait painted by Bohuslawsky, Count Bühl. He would catch your essence in three sittings. You know that he's renowned for his portraits of children. Your smile has just a suggestion in it of a child's laughter. Don't misunderstand me. What is it makes real dignity so inimitable? Because there is a residue of the childlike in it. By way of this childlike quality Bohuslawsky would get round to imbuing your portrait with something which is ex-tremely rare in our world and distinguishes you in the high-est degree: dignity. For we live in a world that lacks dignity.

HANS KARL

I hardly know what world you're referring to: at the front we met with human dignity in plenty, all of us—

NEUHOFF

That's why a man like you was in his element at the front. How great were your achievements, Count Bühl! I have in mind the noncommissioned officer in hospital who was buried in the same trench with you and thirty of your riflemen.

HANS KARL

My brave sergeant, Franz Hütter! Did my cousin tell you about him?

NEUHOFF

She permitted me to accompany her when she visited the hospital. I shall never forget the dying man's expression and what he said. (*Hans Karl is silent*) He spoke only about you. And in what a tone! He knew that the lady he was speaking to was a relative of his captain's.

HANS KARL

Poor Franz Hütter!

NEUHOFF

Perhaps Countess Helen wished to let me have an impression of you such as a thousand social encounters could not have provided.

STANI *a little sharply*

Perhaps she wished above all to see the man himself and to hear about Uncle Kari.

NEUHOFF

For a being like Helen Altenwyl it takes a situation of that kind to bring out her true self. Beneath her perfect simplicity, her pride of race, there lies hidden a stream of loving feeling, a sympathy that radiates through every pore: to anyone whom she loves and respects she is bound by inexpressible ties that nothing can disrupt and nothing disconcert. Woe to the husband who fails to respect this unutterable sense of affinities in her, who would be narrow-hearted enough to wish to monopolize for himself all these radiations of sympathy. (*A short pause. Hans Karl smokes*) She is like you, one of these people whom one cannot win, who must bestow themselves upon one. (*Again a short pause. Continues with great, perhaps not wholly genuine, assurance*) I am a wanderer, my curiosity has driven me half round the world. I am fascinated by what is difficult to know; I am drawn to whatever hides itself. A proud and precious creature like Countess Helen I should like to see in your company, Count Bühl. She would become a different being, she would blossom out; for I don't know anyone who is so responsive to human quality.

HANS KARL

We're all a little that way inclined here. Perhaps my cousin is not so unusual in that respect.

NEUHOFF

The social circle which ought to surround a creature like Helen Altenwyl should consist, I think, of men like you. Every culture puts out its own flowers: substance without pretension, nobility mellowed by infinite grace, is what the culture of this ancient society produces, which has succeeded in doing what the ruins of Luxor and the forests of the Caucasus could not do, to hold an inconstant creature like myself spellbound in its magic circle. But do explain one thing to me, Count Bühl. It is precisely the men of your stamp—to whom society owes its true character—that one meets all too seldom in it. You seem to avoid society.

STANI

Oh, not at all. You will meet Uncle Kari this very evening at the Altenwyls', and I'm even afraid that, pleasant as this little talk has been, we must soon give him the opportunity of dressing.

He has risen from his chair.

NEUHOFF *rising*

If we must, then I shall say adieu for the present, Count Bühl. If ever, in any circumstances whatsoever, you need a knight-errant (*already making for the door*), who is willing to enter, unconditionally and reverently, into the service of the noble and the good wherever he finds it, please call upon me. (*Hans Karl and Stani behind him escort him. As they reach the door the telephone rings*) Do stay where you are, you are wanted on the telephone.

STANI

May I escort you to the stairway?

HANS KARL *at the door*

I thank you very much for your friendly visit, Baron Neuhoff. (*Neuhoff and Stani go out. Hans Karl left alone with the loudly ringing telephone goes to the wall and presses the button of the house telephone, calling*) Lukas, switch off the telephone! I can't stand that indiscreet machine! Lukas!

The telephone stops ringing.

SCENE XIII

STANI

comes back

Only for a moment, Uncle Kari. I must hear what you think of this gentleman!

HANS KARL

What you think of him seems to be already cut and dried.

STANI

Oh, I find him simply impossible. I simply don't understand a type like that. And yet he comes of quite a good family!

HANS KARL

So you think he's utterly unacceptable?

STANI

But, I ask you: every word he speaks is a gaffe.

HANS KARL

He wants to be very amiable, he wants to win people over.

STANI

But a gentleman keeps his countenance, he doesn't crawl into the bosom of an utter stranger.

HANS KARL

And, besides, he believes that a man can make something of himself—now, I should regard that as naïve or the result of a faulty upbringing.

STANI

walking to and fro in agitation

All these tirades about Helen!

HANS KARL

That a girl like Helen should discuss one of us with him doesn't particularly amuse me either.

[691]

STANI

I'm sure there's not a word of truth in it. A fellow who blows hot and cold at the same time.

HANS KARL

Something like it must have happened as he said. But there are people who can't help distorting every *nuance*.

STANI

You're so tolerant!

HANS KARL

I'm simply growing old, Stani.

STANI

It infuriates me, anyhow; his whole tone is an affront, the false assurance, the oily glibness, that twiddling with his odious little pointed beard.

HANS KARL

He has intelligence, but it's of a kind to make one feel queasy.

STANI

These unspeakable indiscretions. I ask you, what business of his is the expression on your face?

HANS KARL

Au fond, perhaps one should be sorry for a man like that.

STANI

I call him an odious creature. But I must go up to Mamma now. I'll be seeing you anyhow in the Club tonight, Uncle

Kari. (*Agathe peeps through the door right, thinking Hans Karl is alone. Stani turns and comes forward again. Hans Karl waves Agathe back*) You know, I just can't simmer down. First, the vulgarity of flattering a man like you to your face.

HANS KARL

No, that wasn't very elegant.

STANI

Secondly, the parading of God knows how thick a friendship with Helen. Thirdly, the probing to see if you were interested in her.

HANS KARL *smiling*

Do you think he wanted to spy out the ground?

STANI

Fourthly, his unbounded indiscretion in hinting at his future situation. He practically announced himself as her husband-to-be. Fifthly, his odious perorations, which make any retort quite impossible. Sixthly, his impossible exit lines. He delivered himself of a regular birthday oration, a whole leading article. But I'm keeping you, Uncle Kari. (*Agathe has peeped again through the door; the same business as before. Stani is already nearly through the door but comes forward again*) Just a word more, if I may? There's one thing I can't understand, that this affair with Helen doesn't affect you more.

HANS KARL

Why me?

STANI

Well, Helen's too close to me for these impossible phrases about "devotion" and "being bound to her" not to stick in my throat. I've known Helen all her life, like a sister!

HANS KARL

The moment comes when sisters leave their brothers.

STANI

But not for a Neuhoff! No, no!

HANS KARL

A small modicum of insincerity goes down well with women.

STANI

A fellow like that shouldn't be allowed anywhere near Helen.

HANS KARL

We shan't be able to prevent it.

STANI

We'll see about that! Not anywhere near her!

HANS KARL

He has announced our coming relationship.

STANI

What state of mind must Helen be in to get involved with this creature!

HANS KARL

You know, I've learned not to draw conclusions about a woman's state of mind from anything she does.

STANI

Not that I'm jealous; but to think of a person like Helen as the wife of this Neuhoff—it's so sheerly incredible— the idea is simply beyond my grasp—I must talk it over with Mamma at once.

HANS KARL *smiling*

Yes, do that, Stani.

Stani goes out.

SCENE XIV

LUKAS

comes in

I'm afraid the telephone was switched on here.

HANS KARL

I don't want it to be.

LUKAS

Very well, your lordship. The new footman must have turned the switch without my noticing him. He has his fingers and his ears everywhere he has no business to have them.

HANS KARL

Pack him off tomorrow morning at seven o'clock.

[695]

LUKAS

Very good. It was Count Hechingen's man who was ringing up. The Count would like to speak to you himself
about whether your lordship is going to Count Altenwyl's
soirée or not this evening. Because Countess Hechingen
will be there.

HANS KARL

Ring up Count Altenwyl's now and say I have had a previ-
ous engagement cancelled and beg to be allowed to come to
the soirée after all. And then put me on to Count Hechingen; I'll speak to him myself. And meanwhile ask the lady's
maid to come in.

LUKAS

Very good.

Goes out. Agathe comes in.

SCENE XV

HANS KARL

takes the packet of letters

Here are the letters. Tell the Countess that I can part with
these letters because of the beautiful memories I have that
nothing can destroy; I shall have them always with me not
in a letter, but everywhere.

AGATHE

Oh, I kiss your hand! You make me so happy. For now I
know that my lady will soon meet our Count again.

HANS KARL

She will meet me tonight. I'm going to the party.

[696]

AGATHE

And dare we hope that she—that the man who meets her will be the same as ever?

HANS KARL

She has no better friend.

AGATHE

Oh, I kiss your hand.

HANS KARL

She has only two sincere friends in the world, myself and her husband.

AGATHE

Oh, goodness, I don't want to hear that. Oh my goodness, what bad luck that our Count has grown so friendly with Count Hechingen. My poor lady has indeed been spared nothing.

HANS KARL

nervously moving away a step or two

Do women really have so little intuition of what a man is like? And of who is really fond of them?

AGATHE

Oh, anything but that. We'll believe anything your lordship tells us, but not that—that's too much!

HANS KARL

pacing up and down

So not that. Not to be able to help! Not even so little!

Pause

[697]

Hugo von Hofmannsthal

AGATHE

shyly, coming nearer to him

Or you might try, all the same. But not through me: I'm not clever enough to be a go-between. I shouldn't find the right words. And not in writing, either. That only causes misunderstandings. But face to face: yes, surely! Then you might persuade her. What couldn't you persuade my lady to! Not perhaps at the first try. But time and again—if you make an appeal to her better feelings—how could she resist you?

The telephone rings again.

HANS KARL

goes to the telephone and speaks into it

Yes, speaking. Here. Yes, I'm listening. I'll wait. Count Bühl. Yes, in person.

AGATHE

I kiss your hand.

She goes out quickly through the middle doors.

HANS KARL *at the telephone*

Hechingen, good evening to you. Yes, I've thought better of it. I've agreed to go. I'll find an opportunity. Certainly. Yes, that was partly why I made up my mind to go. A soirée's the very thing, since I don't play bridge and I don't think your wife does either. There's no need. No need for that either. For your pessimism! Pessimism, I said! There's no need for you to be cast down. Throw it off absolutely! All alone? Then try the old bottle of champagne. I'll certainly report the result to you before midnight. Don't be too hopeful either, of course. You know that I'll do my utmost. It suits with my own feeling, too. Suits with my own feeling! What? The connection bad? I said: it suits with my own feeling. Feeling! A word that doesn't matter. No, not absurd, a word. I said: a word that doesn't matter. What word? Feeling! No, I only said it didn't matter because you didn't catch it for so long. Yes. Yes. Yes! Adieu. Over! (*He rings off*) There are people who make everything complicated, and yet he's such a decent fellow!

SCENE XVI

STANI

once more in the middle doors

Am I presuming too much, Uncle Kari?

HANS KARL

Not at all, I'm at your disposal.

STANI

coming forward beside him

I must tell you, Uncle Kari, that meanwhile I've had a talk with Mamma and come to a decision. (*Hans Karl looks at him*) I'm going to get engaged to Helen Altenwyl.

HANS KARL

You're going to—

STANI

Yes, I've made up my mind to marry Helen. Not today and not tomorrow, but fairly soon. I've thought it all out. On the stairs, as I was going up to the second landing. By the

[699]

time I reached Mamma on the second floor I had it all cut and dried. The idea struck me in a flash, you know, when I saw that you weren't really interested in Helen.

HANS KARL

Aha.

STANI

Do you understand? That was just one of Mamma's notions. She always says that one never knows where one is with you—possibly, she says, you did, after all, toy with the idea of marrying Helen—and you're still the head of the family for Mamma, she's altogether a Bühl at heart.

HANS KARL

half turned away

Dear Crescence!

STANI

But I contradicted everything she said. After all, I know you through and through. I've always felt that there wasn't anything in the idea of your being interested in Helen.

HANS KARL

suddenly turning round

And your mother?

STANI

Mamma?

HANS KARL

Yes, how did she take it?

[700]

STANI

All for it, of course, delighted. She went quite red in the face with joy. Does that surprise you, Uncle Kari?

HANS KARL

Just a little, just a shade—I've always had the impression that your mother always thought of Helen in a particular way.

STANI

An aversion?

HANS KARL

Not at all. Just an intention. A supposition.

STANI

An earlier one? Some time ago?

HANS KARL

No, half an hour ago.

STANI

Pointing in what direction? But Mamma is such a weather-cock! She forgets such things in no time. Any decision that I come to brings her to her knees at once. She yields to the man in me. She adores the *fait accompli*.

HANS KARL

So you have decided?

STANI

Yes, I have decided.

HANS KARL

In a twinkling, like that!

STANI

That's the whole point. That's what impresses women so much in me. And that's just how I always keep the initiative. (*Hans Karl smokes*) You see, perhaps you did once think of marrying Helen—

HANS KARL

Goodness, years ago maybe. In an idle moment, as one thinks of so many things.

STANI

Do you see? I never thought of it at all! And yet, in the very moment when I do think of it, I put it into execution. —Is something disturbing you?

HANS KARL

I couldn't help thinking about Antoinette for a moment.

STANI

But everything in the world has to come to an end sometime.

HANS KARL

Of course. And you're not bothering at all about whether Helen's free or not? She seems, for instance, to have given this Neuhoff grounds for hope.

STANI

That's exactly what I'm depending on. The hopes of a Herr von Neuhoff I can merely ignore. But that Helen should consider for a moment a Theophilus Neuhoff proves only that she has no serious preoccupation at all. Complications of that nature aren't worth thinking about. They're freaks of caprice, or shall we say, aberrations.

HANS KARL

She's not easy to fathom.

STANI

But I know her *genre*. When it comes to the point, she couldn't take an interest in any type of man except our own kind: anything else is an aberration. You're so quiet, do you have one of your headaches?

HANS KARL

Not at all. I'm admiring your courage.

STANI

You, admiring courage!

HANS KARL

This is a different courage from the kind in the trenches.

STANI

I do understand you so well, Uncle Kari. You're thinking of the other chances I may be missing. You feel that perhaps I'm disposing of myself too easily. But, you see, there again I have quite a different outlook: I'm all for common sense and definite conclusions. Forgive me for saying so, Uncle Kari, but *au fond* you're an idealist: your thoughts fly off to the absolute, to some ideal of perfection. That's a very elegant way of thinking, but it can't be realized. *Au fond* you're like Mamma; you think nothing's good enough for me. Now I've thought this matter out as it is. Helen is a year younger than I am.

HANS KARL

A year?

STANI

She's of an excellent family.

HANS KARL

One could not be better born.

STANI

She's elegant.

HANS KARL

Very elegant.

STANI

She's rich.

HANS KARL

And above all, so lovely.

STANI

She's well-bred.

HANS KARL

Incomparably so.

STANI

And in my opinion, above all she has the two qualities most essential in marriage. First: she cannot tell a lie; second: she has the best manners in the world.

[704]

HANS KARL

She is charmingly considerate, as only old women usually are.

STANI

Her mind lights up everything.

HANS KARL

You needn't tell me that. I love talking to her.

STANI

And in time she'll adore me.

HANS KARL

to himself, involuntarily

That's possible, too.

STANI

Not only possible. Quite certain. Marriage does that for women of her *genre*. In a *liaison* everything depends on chance and circumstance, so that fantastic things may happen, deceptions and God knows what. In marriage all is based on a permanent relationship; in the long run each partner absorbs the quality of the other to such an extent that no real difference can arise: always provided that the marriage is based on a right decision. That's the meaning of marriage.

SCENE XVII

LUKAS *entering*

Her ladyship Countess Freudenberg.

[705]

CRESCENCE

comes past Lukas, moving rapidly

Well, what does my Kari say to the boy now? I'm more than delighted. Let us have congratulations!

HANS KARL

a little absently

My dear Crescence, I wish him the greatest success.

Stani silently takes leave.

CRESCENCE

Send the car back for me.

STANI

It's at your disposal. I'm going on foot.

Exit

SCENE XVIII

CRESCENCE

His success will depend very much on you.

HANS KARL

On me? But it's written on his forehead that he'll always get what he wants.

CRESCENCE

Helen will go by your judgment.

HANS KARL

How so, Crescence, in what way?

CRESCENCE

And her father Altenwyl of course even more. Stani's an eligible young man but not a brilliant match. I'm under no illusions about that. But if my Kari backs him up, a word from him has tremendous weight with the older people. I'm sure I don't know why.

HANS KARL

Simply because I'm almost one of them myself.

CRESCENCE

None of this airiness about old age! You and I are neither old nor young. I do hate half-and-between situations. I'd rather be quite on the shelf with grey hair and horn-rimmed spectacles.

HANS KARL

That's why my sister has begun match-making so early.

CRESCENCE

I've always wanted to do it for my Kari, as long as twelve years ago. But he always put up a dumb, obstinate resistance.

HANS KARL

My dear Crescence!

CRESCENCE

Haven't I said a hundred times: let my Kari tell me what he wants and I'll take it in hand.

HANS KARL

Often enough, God knows, Crescence.

Hugo von Hofmannsthal

CRESCENCE

But one never knew where one stood with Kari. (*Hans Karl nods*) And now Stani's simply going to do what Kari never would. I can hardly wait to see little children running about again in Hohenbühl and Göllersdorf.

HANS KARL

And falling into the lake! Do you remember how they fished me out half-drowned? Do you know—I sometimes have the idea that nothing new happens in the world.

CRESCENCE

What's in the back of your mind?

HANS KARL

That whatever happens has been long ready, waiting some-where, and only comes to light suddenly. You know, like the lake at Hohenbühl, when the water's been drawn off in autumn and suddenly the carp and the tails of the stone Tritons are all there which one could hardly see before. A grotesque idea, what!

CRESCENCE

Has something suddenly upset you, Kari?

HANS KARL

pulls himself together

On the contrary, Crescence. I thank you as warmly as I can, you and Stani, for the way you have quickened my life with your vitality and your decisiveness.

He kisses her hand.

[708]

CRESCENCE

Does my Kari find that it does him good to have us beside him?

HANS KARL

Haven't I a very fine evening ahead of me? First, a serious talk with Toinette—

CRESCENCE

But there's surely no need for that now!

HANS KARL

Oh, I might as well talk to her, I had my mind made up to it in any case, and then as Stani's uncle I have those various important conversations to take in hand.

CRESCENCE

The most important thing is to present Stani to Helen in a good light.

HANS KARL

So I have a regular programme. Does Crescence see how she is reforming me? But do you know—I have an idea— first I'll go for an hour to the circus, they have a clown there—a kind of simple Simon.

CRESCENCE

Furlani, it is. Nanni's quite crazy about him. It's not the kind of thing that amuses me.

HANS KARL

I find him enchanting. He delights me much more than the wittiest talk of anybody on earth. I shall enjoy myself enormously. I'll go to the circus, then have something to eat in a restaurant, and then turn up in a very good mood at the soirée and carry out my programme.

CRESCENCE

Yes, my Kari will come and prepare Helen to hear what Stani has to say, you can do that kind of thing so well. You would have made such a wonderful ambassador if you had stuck to your career.

HANS KARL

It's rather late now for that too.

CRESCENCE

Well, have a good time and don't be too long in following us.

Hans Karl escorts her to the door. Crescence goes out.

SCENE XIX

Hans Karl comes forward again. Lukas has come in with him.

HANS KARL

I'm going to wear my tails. I'll ring in a minute.

LUKAS

Very good, your lordship.

Hans Karl goes out left.

SCENE XX

VINCENT

comes in right

What are you doing now?

The Difficult Man

LUKAS

I'm waiting for the dressing-room bell to ring, then I'm going in to help.

VINCENT

I'll come with you. It's quite good for me to get in the way of it.

LUKAS

You haven't been asked for, so you will keep out.

VINCENT

helping himself to a cigar

Well, he's an easy-going, amenable kind of creature, his relations do what they like with him. In a month's time I'll be winding him round my little finger. (*Lukas locks the cigar cabinet. A bell is heard. Lukas hurries*) Don't go yet. Let him ring twice. (*He sinks into an armchair. Lukas goes out behind him. Vincent to himself*) He's sending his love letters back, he's marrying off his nephew, and he himself has made up his mind to an old bachelor's life with me. That's just what I thought would happen. (*Over his shoulder, without turning round*) Well, my *dear* sir, I'm very pleased with everything, I'm going to stay!

Curtain

Act Two

At the Altenwyls'. A small drawing-room in eighteenth-century style. Doors left, right, and in the middle. Altenwyl with Hans Karl entering from the right. Crescence with Helen and Neuhoff standing in conversation left.

SCENE I

ALTENWYL

My dear Kari, I am doubly obliged to you for coming, since you don't play bridge and are therefore willing to put up with the modest odds and ends of entertainment one can still provide in a drawing-room. You know already that you will find here only the same familiar faces, no artists or other celebrities—indeed, Edine Merenberg is extremely scornful of such old-fashioned hospitality, but neither Helen nor I relish the kind of social intercourse Edine rates so highly, where with the first mouthful of soup she asks her neighbour whether he believes in the transmigration of souls or has ever sworn brotherhood with a fakir.

CRESCENCE

I must give you the lie there, Count Altenwyl, for I met an entirely new face at my bridge-table, and Mariette Stradonitz whispered to me that he's a world-famous scholar we've never heard of simply because we're all illiterate.

ALTENWYL

Professor Brücke is a great celebrity in his subject and a welcome political colleague of mine. He enjoys enormously being in a drawing-room where he meets with no colleagues from the academic world, so that he is, as it were, the sole representative of learning in a purely social circle, and since my house can offer him this modest indulgence—

CRESCENCE

Is he married?

ALTENWYL

At any rate I have never had the honour of meeting Madame Brücke.

CRESCENCE

I find famous men odious, but their wives are still worse. Kari agrees with me there. We're all for trivial people and trivial conversations, aren't we, Kari?

ALTENWYL

I have my own old-fashioned predilections, Helen knows what they are.

CRESCENCE

You should back me up, Kari. I find that nine-tenths of what passes for intellectual conversation is just twaddle.

NEUHOFF *to Helen*

Are you equally severe, Countess Helen?

HELEN

We have every reason, we of the younger generation, to feel that if anything in the world makes our flesh creep it's the art of conversation: words that flatten everything real under a dead layer of soothing syrup.

[713]

Hugo von Hofmannsthal

CRESCENCE

Do back me up, Kari!

HANS KARL

Let me off this time. Furlani doesn't put one in the frame of mind to be brilliant.

ALTENWYL

In my opinion, the art of conversation is a lost art nowadays: it consists not in pouring out words oneself like a waterfall but in stimulating others. In my time one used to say: with my guest I must manage the conversation so that when his hand is on the door-latch he'll feel that he has been brilliant, then on the way downstairs he'll think me brilliant. Nowadays, if you'll excuse my rudeness, no one understands how to make conversation or how to keep silent—oh, allow me to present Baron Neuhoff to you, my cousin Count Bühl.

NEUHOFF

I already have the honour of Count Bühl's acquaintance.

CRESCENCE *to Altenwyl*

It's to Edine you should be saying all these clever things— she drives her cult of important people and printed books to ridiculous lengths. I begin to hate the very words: important people—they sound so domineering!

ALTENWYL

Edine is a very clever woman but she's always trying to kill two birds with one stone: to improve her education and also make something on the side for her charities.

[714]

HELEN

Forgive me, Papa, she's not really a clever woman, rather a silly one, for she would give her eyes to have clever people round her but always picks the wrong ones.

CRESCENCE

It surprises me that her wild wool-gathering doesn't cause more confusion.

ALTENWYL

People like her have guardian angels.

EDINE

arriving through the middle door

I see that you're speaking about me, please go on doing it, don't be embarrassed.

CRESCENCE

Well, Edine, have you met the famous man yet?

EDINE

I'm furious, Count Altenwyl, that you gave him to her as a partner and not to me. (*Sits down near Crescence*) You have no idea how much I'm interested in him. After all, I read these people's books. Only a week or two ago I read a thick book by this Brückner.

NEUHOFF

He's called Brücke. He's the second President of the Academy of Sciences.

EDINE

In Paris?

NEUHOFF

No, here in Vienna.

EDINE

But on the book it said: Brückner.

CRESCENCE

Perhaps a printer's mistake.

EDINE

The book was called *On the Origin of All Religions*. What learning was in it, what depth! And such a fine style!

HELEN

I'll bring him to you, Aunt Edine.

NEUHOFF

If you allow me, I'll find him and bring him here as soon as he's disengaged.

EDINE

Please do, Baron Neuhoff. Tell him I've been longing to meet him for years.

Neuhoff goes out left.

CRESCENCE

He'll ask for nothing better, I should think, he's a fairly thorough—

EDINE

Don't be in such a hurry to call people snobs; didn't Goethe too think every duchess and countess a—dear me, I'd better be careful what I say.

The Difficult Man

CRESCENCE

She's got on to Goethe again, our Edine.

Looks round for Hans Karl, who has moved right with
Helen.

HELEN *to Hans Karl*

You like Furlani so much, do you?

HANS KARL

A man like him is a real recreation to me.

HELEN

Does he have such clever tricks?

She sits down right, Hans Karl beside her.

Crescence goes out through the middle door.

Altenwyl and Edine have sat down left.

HANS KARL

He has no tricks at all. He's just the zany, the simple
Simon.

HELEN

A kind of buffoon, then?

HANS KARL

No, that would be overdoing it. He never does that, nor
does he do caricatures either. He plays his role: the man
who wants to understand everybody and help everybody
and yet brings everything into the utmost confusion. He
makes the silliest blunders, the gallery rocks with laughter,
and yet he does it with such elegance, such discretion, that

[717]

one realizes how much he respects himself and everything in the world. He makes a hash of everything; wherever he intervenes there's a complete mess, and yet one wants to cry out: "He's right, all the same!"

EDINE *to Altenwyl*

But a cultivated mind gives us women much more to hold on to! Antoinette, for instance, lacks that completely. I keep telling her she should cultivate her mind, it gives one other things to think of.

ALTENWYL

In my time conversation had quite a different set of values. We thought highly of a witty repartee: we used to lay ourselves out to be brilliant.

EDINE

What I say is: when I make conversation I want to be taken out of myself. I want to get away from the everyday round. I want to find myself in a different world!

HANS KARL

to Helen, continuing his conversation

You see, Helen, all these feats are difficult enough—these balancing tricks and juggling and the rest of it—they all need a fabulous concentration of will power and even intelligence. More intelligence, I fancy, than most conversations—

HELEN

I'm sure of that.

[718]

The Difficult Man

HANS KARL

Absolutely. But what Furlani does is on a much higher
level than what all the others do. All the others are following a purposeful line and look neither right nor left,
they hardly even breathe till they have achieved their purpose: that's the whole content of their trick. But he apparently has no purpose of his own at all—he only enters
into the purposes of others. He wants to join in everything
the others are doing, he's so full of good will, he's so fascinated by every single bit of their performance: when he
balances a flowerpot on his nose he's balancing it only out
of politeness, so to speak.

HELEN

But doesn't he let it drop?

HANS KARL

Yes, but the point lies in the way he lets it drop. He lets
it drop out of sheer ecstasy and bliss, because he's managed
to balance it so well! He believes that once you are doing
a thing well it should go on happily of itself.

HELEN *to herself*

And that's usually more than the flowerpot can bear and
so it falls down.

ALTENWYL *to Edine*

This business-like tone that's so prevalent today! And, I
ask you, even between men and women: a kind of open
pursuit of conscious purpose in social intercourse!

EDINE

Yes, I detest that too. One needs a little artistic manoeu-
vring, a touch of hide-and-seek—

Hugo von Hofmannsthal

ALTENWYL

Young people today have forgotten that to travel hopefully is better than to arrive—they're so headlong, so direct!

EDINE

Because they haven't read enough! Because they don't cultivate their minds enough!

During this exchange they have risen and go off together left.

HANS KARL *to Helen*

When one is watching Furlani, the cleverest clowns strike one as vulgar. He's wonderful to watch in his lovely nonchalance—but his very nonchalance of course needs twice as much skill as the tension of the others.

HELEN

I can understand why you find him sympathetic. Anything that betrays a purpose lurking behind it seems a little vulgar to me too.

HANS KARL

Oho, tonight I myself am laden with purposes, and these purposes concern you, Countess Helen.

HELEN

drawing her brows together

Countess Helen! Do you say "Countess Helen" to me?

Huberta appears in the middle door and darts a swift but knowing glance at Hans Karl and Helen.

The Difficult Man

HANS KARL

without noticing Huberta

No, but seriously, I must beg you to have five minutes' talk with me—later on, sometime or other—we neither of us play bridge.

HELEN

a little uneasy but very self-controlled

You make me feel apprehensive. What can you have to say to me? It sounds unpromising.

HANS KARL

If it's going to bother you, then for goodness' sake we'll call it off.

Huberta has vanished.

HELEN *after a short pause*

Very well, then, if you like, but later on. I see Huberta, she seems to be bored. I must look after her.
She rises.

HANS KARL

You're so delightfully considerate.

Has also risen.

HELEN

Now you must say good evening to Antoinette and the other ladies. (*She leaves him but pauses in the middle door*) I'm not considerate: I'm only aware of what's going on inside people and get worried about it—and then I react by showing people the regard I have for them. My good manners are just a kind of nervous defence, to keep people at arm's length.

She goes out. Hans Karl follows her slowly.

SCENE II

Neuhoff and the Famous Man appear together in the door-way left.

THE FAMOUS MAN

now in the middle of the room, looks through the doorway right

Over there, in the group beside the fireplace, is the lady whose name I wanted to ask you.

NEUHOFF

The one in grey? That's the Duchess of Pergen.

THE FAMOUS MAN

No, I've known her a long time. The lady in black.

NEUHOFF

The Spanish Ambassadress. Have you been introduced to her? Or may I—

THE FAMOUS MAN

I should very much like an introduction. But perhaps we'd better arrange it in this way—

NEUHOFF

with barely perceptible irony

I am entirely at your service.

The Difficult Man

THE FAMOUS MAN

If you would perhaps be so good as to mention me first to the lady, explaining my reputation to her, since she's a foreigner, and my standing in the world of science and in society—then I could follow it up at once by getting Count Altenwyl to introduce me.

NEUHOFF

But with the greatest pleasure.

THE FAMOUS MAN

A scholar of my standing is not concerned merely to increase his acquaintance, but to be known and recognized for what he is.

NEUHOFF

No doubt about it. Here comes Countess Merenberg, who is particularly looking forward to meeting you. May I—

EDINE *coming forward*

This is a great pleasure. With such an eminent man, Baron Neuhoff, I beg you not to introduce him to me but to present me to him.

THE FAMOUS MAN *bowing*

I am very happy, Countess.

EDINE

I don't need to tell you, do I, that I am one of the most enthusiastic readers of your famous books. I'm always transported by your deep philosophy, your immense learning, and your beautiful prose style.

[723]

THE FAMOUS MAN

You astound me, Countess. My books are hardly light reading. True, they are not intended exclusively for professional scholars but the public they envisage must have a rather unusual depth of understanding.

EDINE

No, no, not at all! Any woman could benefit from reading such fine, profound books which lift her into a higher sphere: that's what I never tire of telling Toinette Hechingen.

THE FAMOUS MAN

May I ask which of my works has had the privilege of attracting your attention?

EDINE

But of course that wonderful book *On the Origin of All Religions*! That has such depth, and such uplift, it's an education in itself—

THE FAMOUS MAN *icily*

Hm. It is certainly a book much talked about.

EDINE

But not nearly enough. I've just been saying to Toinette that we ought all of us to have it for bedside reading.

THE FAMOUS MAN

The press in especial has gone beyond all bounds in staging publicity for this opus.

[724]

The Difficult Man

EDINE

How can you say such a thing! Such a book is surely one of the greatest—

THE FAMOUS MAN

It has interested me considerably, Countess, to find you one of the enthusiasts for this production. I myself am quite unacquainted with the book and could only with difficulty bring myself to add one to the circle of those who read such compilations.

EDINE

What? Are you not the author?

THE FAMOUS MAN

The author of this journalistic potpourri is my colleague Brückner. There is certainly a fatal similarity in our names, but the likeness ends there.

EDINE

It shouldn't be allowed for two famous philosophers to have names so like each other.

THE FAMOUS MAN

It is certainly regrettable, especially for me. In any case, Herr Brückner is far from being a philosopher. He's a philologist, or rather a drawing-room philologist, or, better still, a philological journalist.

EDINE

I'm terribly sorry to have got so mixed up. But I'm sure I must have some of your famous works in my house, Professor. I read everything that helps one along a bit. I've just got a very interesting book about Semi-Pelagianism lying on my table, and another called *The Soul of Radium.* If you would come to see me some time in the Heugasse—

THE FAMOUS MAN *coldly*

I should be honoured, Countess. But I am already over-whelmed with engagements.

EDINE

is on the point of going but stands still again

But I'm terribly sorry that you're not the author! For now I can't ask you the question I wanted to ask. And I would have wagered anything that you were the one man who could answer it so that my mind is set at rest.

NEUHOFF

Won't you put your question to the Professor, all the same?

EDINE

You're certainly a man of even more profound learning than the other one. (*To Neuhoff*) Should I really? It's something that matters a great deal to me. I would give my eyes to have my mind set at rest.

THE FAMOUS MAN

Won't you sit down, Countess?

EDINE

looking anxiously around in case some one should come in, says quickly

What do you imagine Nirvana would be like?

[726]

THE FAMOUS MAN

Hm. For an extempore answer to that question you had much better apply to Herr Brückner.

A short pause

EDINE

And now I must go back to my bridge-table. Good evening for the present, Professor.

She goes out.

THE FAMOUS MAN
obviously upset

Hm.—

NEUHOFF

Poor, dear Countess Edine. You shouldn't take her too seriously.

THE FAMOUS MAN *coldly*

This is not the first time a member of the lay public has mistaken me for that other—I almost begin to believe that the charlatan Brückner is deliberately working to that end. You can hardly conceive how painful is the inward impression left by a grotesque and false misunderstanding such as we have just experienced. To see a trumpery pretence of sham knowledge, heralded by the fanfares of a rascally press, in full sail on the broad stream of popularity— to see oneself mistaken for that, against which one believed oneself inviolably shielded behind the icy silence of indifference—

[727]

Hugo von Hofmannsthal

NEUHOFF

But you don't need to tell me all that, my dear Professor!
I can feel for you and with you down to the smallest detail.
To see oneself misunderstood in one's best qualities, all
one's life—that is the destiny—

THE FAMOUS MAN

In one's best qualities.

NEUHOFF

To see precisely that side of oneself misjudged which is
what chiefly matters—

THE FAMOUS MAN

One's whole lifework confounded with a piece of journalistic—

NEUHOFF

That is the destiny—

THE FAMOUS MAN

Which in a rascally press—

NEUHOFF

—of the unusual man, as soon as he lets himself down to
the level of trivial people, of women who cannot tell the
fundamental difference between an empty mask and a man
of weight and standing!

THE FAMOUS MAN

To find even in a drawing-room the hateful signs of mob
rule—

The Difficult Man

NEUHOFF

Don't be so upset. How can a man of your eminence—
nothing that an Edine Merenberg and all the nobodies may
say can come anywhere near you.

THE FAMOUS MAN

It's the fault of the press, that witches' brew of this, that
and everything. But here I should have thought I might be
safe from it. I see that I have overestimated the exclusive-
ness of this circle, at least where the intellectual life is concerned.

NEUHOFF

Intellect and these people! Life—and these people! All the
people you see here ceased to exist long ago. They're nothing but shadows now. Nobody who circulates in these rooms
belongs to the real world in which the intellectual crises of
this century are resolved. Just look around you: consider
that figure in the next room, from his hair-parting to the
soles of his feet balancing himself in the complete assurance
of unlimited triviality—besieged by women and girls—Kari
Bühl.

THE FAMOUS MAN

Is that Count Bühl?

NEUHOFF

In person, the renowned Kari.

THE FAMOUS MAN

I've had no opportunity to make his acquaintance so far.
Are you a friend of his?

Hugo von Hofmannsthal

NEUHOFF

Not particularly, but enough to sum him up for you in a couple of words: absolute, arrogant nonentity.

THE FAMOUS MAN

He has an extraordinary pre-eminence in the highest society. He's regarded as a personality.

NEUHOFF

There's nothing in him that could stand up to examination. In a purely social sense I appreciate him half out of habit; but you lose less than nothing in not knowing him.

THE FAMOUS MAN

keeps on staring in that direction

I should be very interested to make his acquaintance. Do you think it would compromise me to make the first approach?

NEUHOFF

You would be wasting your time, as with all these people here.

THE FAMOUS MAN

I should be very pleased to be properly introduced to Count Bühl, by one of his intimate friends, say.

NEUHOFF

I have no wish to pass for one of these, but I'll arrange it for you.

THE FAMOUS MAN

I am much obliged to you. Or do you think it wouldn't be compromising for me to accost him of my own accord?

NEUHOFF

In either case you do dear Kari too much honour if you
take him so seriously.

THE FAMOUS MAN

I don't deny that I attach much importance to obtaining
the discriminating and incorruptible approval of high society to add to the plaudits my learning has already brought
me from a wide international public, and which I may
regard as the sunset glow of a far-from-commonplace day
spent in the service of knowledge.

They go out.

SCENE III

*Antoinette with Edine. Nanni and Huberta meanwhile
have appeared in the middle door and are coming forward.*

ANTOINETTE *to them all*

Do say something, do give me some advice, for you see how
upset I am. I'll make a hopeless mess of everything if you
don't help me.

EDINE

I'm all for leaving her by herself. She must meet him as if
by chance. If we act as a convoy we'll simply frighten him
off.

HUBERTA

He's not so shy. If he wanted to speak to her by herself
he would just look through us.

ANTOINETTE

So let's sit down here, anyhow. Stay beside me, all of you, but not as if on purpose.

They all sit down.

NANNI

We can just go on talking comfortably: the chief thing is, it mustn't look as if you're running after him.

ANTOINETTE

If only one had Helen's *raffinement,* she runs after him at every step and makes it look as if she were keeping out of his way.

EDINE

I'm all for leaving her alone. She should simply go to meet him as if nothing had happened.

HUBERTA

How can she meet him as if nothing had happened, in the state she's in?

ANTOINETTE *nearly in tears*

Don't tell me that I'm in a state! Try to take my mind off myself! Or else I'll lose all my self-possession. If only I had someone to flirt with!

NANNI *beginning to rise*

I'll bring Stani along.

ANTOINETTE

Stani would be less than no good to me. As soon as I know that Kari's in the same house, the others simply don't exist for me any longer.

HUBERTA

Maybe Feri Uhlfeldt would still exist.

ANTOINETTE

If Helen were in my shoes, she'd know what to do. Without turning a hair she would make a screen out of Theophilus and operate from behind him.

HUBERTA

But she hasn't even looked at Theophilus, she's been shadowing Kari all the evening.

ANTOINETTE

Must you tell me that too, so that I can go as white as a sheet? (*Rises*) Is he talking to her?

HUBERTA

Of course he's talking to her.

ANTOINETTE

All the time?

HUBERTA

As often as I've peeped in.

ANTOINETTE

Oh my goodness, if you keep on telling me horrid things I won't be fit to look at!

She sits down again.

NANNI

making to rise

If your three friends are too much for you, we can go away. I'd as soon be playing bridge.

ANTOINETTE

Do stay with me, do give me some advice, do tell me what I'm to do.

HUBERTA

Since she sent her maid to see him only an hour ago, she can hardly meet him now with her nose in the air.

NANNI

I see it the other way about. She must behave as if he didn't matter to her. I know that from playing cards: it's when you play your hand lightly that you have luck. You must always keep inside yourself the feeling of being on top.

ANTOINETTE

Being on top is exactly what I feel like, isn't it!

HUBERTA

But you'll handle him quite wrongly if you give yourself away like that.

EDINE

If she would only let us give her a line to follow! I know what men are like.

HUBERTA

Let me tell you, Edine, men aren't all as like as peas.

ANTOINETTE

The most sensible thing would be for me to go home.

NANNI

Who would throw in a hand so long as there was a chance left?

EDINE

If she would only listen to sensible advice. I have such a good instinct for these psychological situations. There's absolutely no reason why her marriage shouldn't be annulled, it's been like a prison for her all these years, and when it's annulled Kari will marry her if the affair is only half reasonably managed.

HUBERTA

who has glanced right

Hush!

ANTOINETTE

starts

Is he coming? Oh God, how my knees are trembling.

HUBERTA

It's Crescence coming. Pull yourself together.

ANTOINETTE *to herself*

My God, I can't stand her, nor she me either, but I'll commit every sort of *bassesse* before her because she's his sister.

SCENE IV

CRESCENCE

comes in from right

Good evening, how are you all? Toinette looks quite out of sorts. Not a word among you? So many young women! Stani shouldn't have gone off to the Club, should he?

Hugo von Hofmannsthal

ANTOINETTE *with an effort*

We're getting on very well for the present without gentle-men.

CRESCENCE *still standing*

What do you think of Helen tonight, isn't she looking won-derful? When she's a young married woman she'll be so imposing that nobody will stand a chance against her!

HUBERTA

Is Helen so much in your good graces of a sudden?

CRESCENCE

You're all very charming too. But Antoinette should take more care of herself. She looks as if she hadn't slept for three whole nights. (*Going*) I must tell Poldo Altenwyl how brilliant I find Helen tonight.

Goes out.

SCENE V

ANTOINETTE

My God, now I have proof positive that Kari's going to marry Helen.

EDINE

How do you make that out?

ANTOINETTE

Didn't you sense that she's beginning to cry up her future sister-in-law?

NANNI

Nonsense, don't be so despairing about nothing and less than nothing. He'll be coming through the door in a minute.

ANTOINETTE

If he comes in when I'm like this I'll be quite—(*puts her little handkerchief to her eyes*)—done for.

HUBERTA

We'd better go. She'll calm down meanwhile.

ANTOINETTE

No, you two go and see whether he's still talking to Helen and interrupt him if he is. You've often enough interrupted me when I wanted to be alone with him. And Edine can stay here.

They have all risen. Huberta and Nanni go out.

SCENE VI

Antoinette and Edine sit down again left, at the back.

EDINE

My dear child, you've handled this whole affair with Kari quite wrongly from the first.

ANTOINETTE

How can you tell that?

EDINE

Because Mademoiselle Feydeau gave me all the details, so I know how you bungled the whole situation even at Grünleiten.

ANTOINETTE

That malicious gossip, what does she know about it!

EDINE

It's not her fault if she heard you running barefoot down the stairs and saw you wandering with him in the moonlight with your hair down your back.—You've simply taken the whole affair much too *terre à terre* from the beginning. Of course men are very *terre à terre*, but that's just why on our side we must bring in some higher element. A man like Kari Bühl has never in all his life met anyone who could have instilled a bit of idealism into him. And so he himself is incapable of introducing anything finer into a love-affair, and so it goes on, ad infinitum. If you had only asked some advice from me in the beginning, if you had let me prescribe a line for you to follow, and recommend you a book or two—you would have been his wife at this moment!

ANTOINETTE

Please, Edine, don't exasperate me.

SCENE VII

HUBERTA *appears in the doorway*

Well, Kari's coming. He's looking for you.

ANTOINETTE

Holy Mother of God!

They have risen.

NANNI

who has been peeping out right

And Helen's on her way here from the other drawing-room.

ANTOINETTE

My God, at the very moment when everything's in the balance she has to come here and ruin it all. Stop her somehow. Go and meet her. Keep her away from here!

HUBERTA

Do put some kind of a good face on it.

NANNI

We can just slip away quietly.

SCENE VIII

HELEN

comes in right

You look as though you've just been talking about me. Have you? (*Silence*) Are you enjoying yourselves? Shall I collect some gentlemen for you?

ANTOINETTE

going up to her, almost losing her self-control

We're enjoying ourselves enormously and you're an angel, my dear, to bother about us. I haven't said as much as good evening to you yet. You're looking lovelier than ever. (*Kisses her*) But just leave us and go away again.

Hugo von Hofmannsthal

HELEN

Am I disturbing you? Then I shall just go away again.

Goes.

SCENE IX

ANTOINETTE

draws her fingers over her face as if to wipe off the kiss

What am I doing? Why should I let her kiss me? That viper, that false creature!

HUBERTA

Do pull yourself together a bit.

SCENE X

Hans Karl has come in right.

Edine, Nanni, and Huberta slip away.

ANTOINETTE

after standing silent a moment with bent head, goes quickly up to him, quite close

I've taken the letters and burnt them. I'm not a sentimental goose, as my Agathe makes out, to cry my eyes out over old letters. The only thing that's real to me is what I have at any one moment, and what I don't have I want to forget. I don't live in the past, I'm not old enough for that.

HANS KARL

Shall we sit down?

Leads her to the armchairs.

ANTOINETTE

I'm simply not one of the artful kind. If a woman isn't sly and subtle, she can't hold a man like you. For you're the same sort as your nephew Stani. Let me tell you that, once and for all. I know you both. Monsters of selfishness and utterly without delicacy. (*After a little pause*) Do say something!

HANS KARL

If you would allow me, I should like to remind you of our time together—

ANTOINETTE

Oh, I'm not going to let myself be ill-used—not even by someone who was once not indifferent to me.

HANS KARL

At that time, I mean two years ago, you were temporarily estranged from your husband. You were in great danger of falling into the wrong hands. Then some one came along— who happened to be me. I wanted to—to comfort you— that was my sole intention—to save you from the danger —that I knew—or felt—to be threatening you. That was a chain of fortuitous events—or a piece of clumsiness— I don't know which to call it—

ANTOINETTE

These few days at Grünleiten are the only truly precious thing in all my life. These I won't let you—the memory of them I won't let anyone degrade for me.

Rises.

[741]

HANS KARL *in a low voice*

But it all means so much to me. It was so beautiful. (*Antoinette sits down, with a troubled glance at him*) It was so beautiful!

ANTOINETTE

"Who happened to be me." Putting it like that is an insult to me. You've grown cynical out at the front. A cynic, that's the right word for you. You've lost all feeling for what's possible and what impossible. What did you say? It was "a piece of clumsiness" on your part? You're doing nothing but insult me.

HANS KARL

At the front many things came to look different to me. But I did not become a cynic. The very opposite, Antoinette. When I think of what happened between us at the beginning it seems so delicate, so mysterious, I can hardly trust myself to think of it. I feel like asking myself: how did I fall heir to that? How did I have the right? But (*lowering his voice*) I regret nothing.

ANTOINETTE

lowering her eyes

All beginnings are beautiful.

HANS KARL

Every beginning holds an eternity.

ANTOINETTE

without looking at him

Au fond you think that everything's possible and everything permissible. You don't want to see how helpless a creature is that you tread underfoot—how utterly at your mercy, for that would perhaps stir up your conscience.

HANS KARL

I have none. (*Antoinette looks at him*) Not where we are concerned.

ANTOINETTE

I have been this and that to you—and at this moment I know as little how I stand with you as if there had never been anything between us. You are simply frightening!

HANS KARL

Nothing is evil in itself. The moment is not evil, only holding on to it is forbidden. Only the clutching at what may not be held fast—

ANTOINETTE

Oh, we're not simply like those midges that live only from sunrise to sunset. We're still there next day. That doesn't suit you, of course, a man of your kind.

HANS KARL

Everything that happens depends on chance. It doesn't bear thinking of, how much we are creatures of chance, and how chance brings us together and drives us apart, and how anyone could set up house with anyone if chance willed it.

ANTOINETTE

I won't have—

HANS KARL

goes on talking, paying no heed to her protest

And that's so gruesome a thought that men had to find something to haul them out of the morass, by the hair of their own heads. And so they found the institution that binds chance and promiscuity into what is necessary and permanent and valid: the institution of marriage.

ANTOINETTE

I'm aware that you want to palm me off on my husband. There's not a moment since you sat down here that I haven't been aware of it, and haven't let myself be fooled. You really do feel you're entitled to everything, first seduce a woman and then insult her.

HANS KARL

I'm no seducer, Toinette, I don't go chasing women.

ANTOINETTE

Yes, that's your masterpiece, that's what you won me round with, that you're no seducer, no ladies' man, only a friend, but a real friend. You make play with that, as you make play with everything you have and everything you lack. According to you, a woman shouldn't only fall in love with you but love you beyond reason, and for your own sake, and not even just as a man—but—I don't know how to put it, oh my God, why must one and the same man be so charming and at the same time so monstrously vain and selfish and heartless!

HANS KARL

Do you know what a heart is, do you know that? A man who has given his heart to a woman can show it only through one thing, one only thing in the world: through constancy, through permanence. Through that only: that is the proof, the one and only.

The Difficult Man

ANTOINETTE

You can leave Ado out of it—I can't live with Ado.

HANS KARL

He loves you. Once and for all time. He chose you among
all the women in the world and he has loved you and
will love you for ever, do you know what that means?
For ever, whatever happens to you. It means having a
friend who loves the whole of you; for whom you will
always be lovely, not only today and tomorrow, but later
on, much later on; for whom the veils that the years, or
whatever comes upon you, may throw over your face—
for his eyes they won't be there, you remain always what
you are, the loveliest, the dearest, the one and only one.

ANTOINETTE

He never chose me like that. He simply married me. I
know nothing about all the rest.

HANS KARL

But he knows about it.

ANTOINETTE

All that fine talk is make-believe, it isn't real. He makes
himself believe it—he makes you believe it—you're all
alike, you men, you and Ado and Stani, you're all cut out
of the same block and that's why you understand each
other so well and can play so well into each other's hands.

HANS KARL

He doesn't make me believe it, this is something I know
myself, Toinette, this is a sacred truth which I know—
I must always have known it, but it was only at the front

that it first became clear to me: there is the accident of chance, which apparently does with us what it will—but in the middle of being thrown hither and thither, dazed and in fear of death, we are also aware of, and we know, that there is also a Necessity which chooses us from one moment to the next, which comes, so quietly, so close to our hearts and yet cuts keen as a sword. Without that there would have been nothing you could call a life at the front but only men dying in heaps like brute beasts. And the same Necessity runs between men and women as well— where that exists, there is a having-to-come-together, and forgiveness and reconciliation and a standing-by-one-another. And here is a place for children, and here is a marriage and a sacrament, in spite of everything—

ANTOINETTE

rises.

And all this means nothing else than that you want to get married and that you're going to marry Helen.

HANS KARL

still sitting, catches hold of her

But I'm not thinking of Helen at all! I'm speaking about you. I swear that it's you I'm speaking about.

ANTOINETTE

But all your thoughts are revolving round Helen.

HANS KARL

I swear to you: I've been charged with a message for Helen. Quite the reverse of what you think. I have to tell her tonight—

[746]

ANTOINETTE

What are you going to tell her tonight—a secret?

HANS KARL

Not one that concerns me.

ANTOINETTE

But something that makes a bond between you?

HANS KARL

The very opposite, rather.

ANTOINETTE

The opposite? A farewell—are you to tell her something that comes to a farewell between you and her?

HANS KARL

There's no need of a farewell, for there has never been anything between us. But if it gives you any satisfaction, Toinette, it is almost like a farewell.

ANTOINETTE

A lifelong farewell?

HANS KARL

Yes, lifelong, Toinette.

ANTOINETTE

turning her eyes full upon him

Lifelong? (*Thoughtfully*) Yes, she's a secretive creature and does nothing twice and says nothing twice. She takes back nothing—she has herself well in hand: a single word is

decisive for her. If you say farewell to her—then it will be
a farewell and for ever. For her, it will be. (*After a little
pause*) I won't let you talk me into having Ado. I don't like
his hands. Nor his face. Nor his ears. (*Very low*) But
your hands I love.—What are you, then? Yes, who are you?
A cynic, an egoist, a devil, that's what you are! To leave
me in the lurch, that's too ordinary for you. To keep me,
you're too heartless for that. To hand me over to someone
else, you're too subtle for that. So you want to be rid of
me and yet keep me in your power, and for that Ado seems
to be the right man.—Go and marry Helen, do. Marry
whenever you like! I could perhaps have some use for your
love, but none at all for your good advice. (*Makes to go
away. Hans Karl takes a step towards her*) Let me go. (*She
takes a few steps away from him, then half turns towards
him*) What's to become of me now? Go on and talk me out
of Feri Uhlfeldt, then, for Feri has such strength when he
wants something. I've told Feri I don't want him, he re-
plied that I can't tell what he's like as a friend, since I've
never had him for a friend. These arguments muddle one
up so. (*Half in tears, tenderly*) Whatever happens to me
will be your fault now.

HANS KARL

You need one thing in the world—a friend. A good friend.
(*He kisses her hand*) Do be good to Ado.

ANTOINETTE

To him I can't be good.

HANS KARL

You can be good to anyone.

ANTOINETTE *gently*

Kari, don't insult me like that.

HANS KARL

Understand it as it is meant.

ANTOINETTE

I usually do understand you well enough.

HANS KARL

Can't you try it?

ANTOINETTE

For your sake I could try. But you'd have to stand by me and help me.

HANS KARL

Now you've given me a half-promise.

SCENE XI

The Famous Man has come in right and advances towards Hans Karl; the other two do not notice him.

ANTOINETTE

You promised me something once.

HANS KARL

To help in the beginning.

ANTOINETTE *close to him*

To be fond of me!

[749]

Hugo von Hofmannsthal

THE FAMOUS MAN

Pardon, I seem to be intruding.

Goes out quickly.

HANS KARL *close to her*

So I am.

ANTOINETTE

Say something sweet to me, just for the moment. The moment is all that matters. I can live only in the moment. I have such a bad memory.

HANS KARL

I'm not in love with you, but I'm fond of you.

ANTOINETTE

And what you're going to say to Helen is a farewell?

HANS KARL

A farewell.

ANTOINETTE

So Kari bargains me away and hands me over!

HANS KARL

But you were never so close to me as now.

ANTOINETTE

You will come to me often, to support me? You can persuade me to anything.

Hans Karl kisses her on the brow, almost without being aware of doing so.

[750]

ANTOINETTE

Thank you.

She runs off through the middle door.

HANS KARL

discomposed, collects himself

Poor little Antoinette.

SCENE XII

CRESCENCE

comes through the middle door, very quickly

Well, you've done that brilliantly! You're simply first-rate at managing these things.

HANS KARL

What? But you don't know anything about it.

CRESCENCE

What else do I need to know? I know all of it. Antoinette comes rushing along with tears in her eyes and runs right past me, but as soon as she notices who I am she flings her arms round my neck and rushes off again like the wind; that tells me everything. You've roused her conscience, you've appealed to her better self, you've made it clear to her that she has to give up all hopes of Stani, and you've shown her the only way out of her entanglements, that she should go back to her husband and try to lead a quiet, respectable life.

[751]

HANS KARL

Yes, well, something like that. But it didn't work out in detail quite like that. I haven't got your purposeful approach. I'm too easily deflected from a line, I must admit.

CRESCENCE

But that doesn't matter. Now that you've made such a brilliant success of this, I can't wait, now that you're in the vein, for you to tackle Helen and Poldo Altenwyl. Please just go and do it now, I'm crossing my fingers for you, only keep in mind that Stani's happiness depends on your persuasions.

HANS KARL

You needn't worry, Crescence, while I was talking to Antoinette Hechingen I suddenly saw the line I must take with Helen. I'm quite in the mood for it. You know, that's my weakness, that I so rarely see a clear issue ahead of me; but this time I do see it.

CRESCENCE

There you are, what a good thing it is to have a programme. It pulls everything together so that it makes sense. Come along, then: we'll go and look for Helen, she must be in one of the drawing-rooms, and whenever we find her I'll leave you alone with her. And as soon as we know the result, I'll rush to the telephone and summon Stani here.

SCENE XIII

Crescence and Hans Karl go out left.

Helen and Neuhoff come in right. One hears faint music from a distant room.

[752]

NEUHOFF *behind Helen*

Do stand still for a moment. That trifling empty saccharine music and this half-light set you off wonderfully.

HELEN

has stood still, but now moves on towards the armchairs left

I don't like posing as a model, Baron Neuhoff.

NEUHOFF

Not even if I shut my eyes? (*Helen says nothing, she stands left.*) What a creature you are, Helen! No one ever was what you are. Your simplicity is the result of colossal tension. Motionless as a statue, you are yet vibrating within yourself, no one divines it, but he who does divine it vibrates in sympathy. (*Helen looks at him, sits down. Neuhoff, at a little distance, goes on*) You are in every way wonderful. And like everything high, almost frighteningly matter-of-course.

HELEN

Do you find what is high a matter of course? A noble thought.

NEUHOFF

Perhaps one could marry him—that's what your lips wanted to say, Helen!

HELEN

Are you a lip-reader like deaf and dumb people?

NEUHOFF *a step nearer*

You *will marry me,* because you feel the force of my will in a weak-willed world.

[753]

Hugo von Hofmannsthal

HELEN *to herself*

Must one? Is it a commandment to which a woman must submit: when she is chosen and desired?

NEUHOFF

There are desires that haven't much of a past. These one can well tread under one's fine, aristocratic feet. But mine has a past. It has travelled half round the world. Here it has found its fulfilment. You have been found, Helen Altenwyl, by the most forceful will on the most roundabout journey in the most ineffectual of all worlds.

HELEN

I was born in it and I am not ineffectual.

NEUHOFF

You people have sacrificed everything to fine appearances, your strength too. We, in our northern corner of the world, where the centuries pass over our heads, we have kept our strength. So we meet as equals and yet as less than equal, and out of this inequality has grown my right to you.

HELEN

Your right?

NEUHOFF

The right of the spiritually stronger over the woman he can infuse his spirit into.

HELEN

I don't care for these mystical turns of phrase.

[754]

The Difficult Man

NEUHOFF

There must be a mystical bond between two people who have recognized each other at first sight. Your pride should not deny it.

HELEN *standing up*

It denies it again and again.

NEUHOFF

Helen, you would be my salvation—you would make me whole, draw out my full potentiality!

HELEN

I have no interest in anyone whose life is subject to such conditions!

She takes a few steps past him: her eyes are fixed on the open door right by which she came in.

NEUHOFF

How your expression has changed! What is it, Helen? (*Helen is silent, keeps looking right. Neuhoff has come up behind her, follows her glance with his own*) Oh! Count Bühl has come into the picture! (*He steps back from the door*) His nearness draws you like a magnet—why, you incomprehensible creature, can't you feel that you don't exist for him?

HELEN

I do exist for him, somehow I do exist!

NEUHOFF

Spendthrift that you are! You bestow everything upon him, even the strength with which he holds you.

[755]

HELEN

The strength with which a man holds one—surely that's bestowed on him by God.

NEUHOFF

You astound me. What is it in a Kari Bühl that can exert this fascination over you? Undeserving, not even making an effort of any kind, without will power, without dignity—

HELEN

Without dignity!

NEUHOFF

That boneless equivocal creature has no dignity.

HELEN

What words these are to use!

NEUHOFF

My northern style sounds rather harsh in your pretty ears. But I stand by its harshness. Equivocal is what I call a man who half gives himself and half holds back—who keeps a reserve in all things—calculates in all things—

HELEN

Calculation and Kari Bühl! Do you really see such a short way into him? Certainly it's impossible to plumb his words to the bottom, as is so easily done with other people. The awkward diffidence that makes him so amiable, his shy pride, his meeting you on your own level, certainly that's a kind of hide-and-seek he plays, and just as certainly eludes the grasp of coarse hands.—He's never made rigid by vanity which turns all other people into stiff wooden images—he's never debased by prudence, which makes most people so commonplace—he belongs only to himself—nobody knows him, so it's not to be wondered at if you don't know him!

NEUHOFF

I've never seen you like this before, Helen. I do delight in this unique moment! For once I see you as God made you, body and soul. A spectacle for the gods. I abominate sentimental weakness in men as in women. But severity that relents is glorious! (*Helen is silent*) You must admit that it shows some superiority in a man when he can appreciate in a woman the way she's admiring another man. But I can do that, since I snap my fingers at your infatuation for Kari Bühl.

HELEN

You mistake your feelings. You're bitter, where bitterness is out of place.

NEUHOFF

How can I be bitter about what I tread underfoot?

HELEN

You don't know him! You've hardly spoken to him.

NEUHOFF

I went to visit him—(*Helen looks at him*) It's beyond words how cheap this man holds you—you mean nothing to him. It's you he treads underfoot.

HELEN *quietly*

No.

Hugo von Hofmannsthal

NEUHOFF

It was a duel between me and him, a duel for you—and I was not defeated.

HELEN

No, it was no duel. It deserves no such heroic name. You went there to do exactly what I'm doing now! (*Laughs*) I take no end of trouble to watch Count Bühl without his seeing me. But I do it with no hidden intent.

NEUHOFF

Helen!

HELEN

I'm not thinking all the time of what I can get out of it!

NEUHOFF

But you're grinding me into the dust, Helen—and I am letting you do it! (*Helen is silent*) And nothing brings me any nearer?

HELEN

Nothing.

She takes a step towards the door right.

NEUHOFF

Everything about you is lovely, Helen. When you sit down it is as if you are reposing after a great sorrow—and when you walk across a room it is as if you go to meet a momentous decision.

Hans Karl has appeared in the doorway right.

Helen makes no answer to Neuhoff.

[758]

The Difficult Man

She moves slowly and silently towards the door right.

Neuhoff goes out quickly left.

SCENE XIV

HANS KARL

Yes, I have something to say to you.

HELEN

Something very serious?

HANS KARL

That's the assumption with which one is sometimes expected to comply. For everything in the world is set a-going by words. (*They sit down*) It's rather ridiculous, I admit, for a man to imagine that by stringing words together skilfully he can exert God knows how great an influence in this life of ours, where in the long run everything depends on what is essentially inexpressible. Speech is based on an indecent excess of self-esteem.

HELEN

If people only knew how little they matter not one of them would utter a word.

HANS KARL

You have such a clear mind, Helen. You always know at any moment exactly what's in question.

HELEN

Do I?

[759]

HANS KARL

You're a wonderfully understanding person. So one has to be very careful.

HELEN

looks at him

To be careful?

HANS KARL

Certainly. Sympathy's a good thing, but to use it as a vehicle, and sit back in it, would be shockingly indiscreet. That's why one must be particularly on guard when one has a feeling of being well understood.

HELEN

You must, of course. That's your nature. Any woman who thought of pinning you down would be lost from the start. Yet anyone who believes that you have said a final farewell might well get a greeting from you another day. —Tonight you found Antoinette charming again.

HANS KARL

You see everything!

HELEN

You use up these poor women in your own way, but you don't really care much for them. One needs to be very self-assured or else a little common to go on being a sweetheart of yours.

HANS KARL

If that's how you see me, you must find me quite repulsive!

[760]

The Difficult Man

HELEN

Not at all. You are charming. In these affairs you behave just like a child.

HANS KARL

Like a child? And yet I'm nearly an old man. But that's monstrous. To be thirty-nine and not to know what one's up to is disgraceful.

HELEN

I've never needed to worry about what I was up to. I'm never really up to anything, there's nothing in me but quiet, respectable good behaviour.

HANS KARL

Your good behaviour is enchanting!

HELEN

I don't want to be sentimental, that bores me. I'd rather be *terre à terre,* like anybody at all, than sentimental. And I don't want to be moody and I don't want to be a coquette. So there's nothing for me but to be as well-behaved as possible. (*Hans Karl is silent*) Au fond, whatever we women do, singing sol-fa, let us say, or going in for politics, we always mean something else by it.—To sing sol-fa is more indiscreet, to be well-behaved is discreeter, it expresses the deliberate intention of committing no indiscretions. Neither against oneself nor against anyone else.

HANS KARL

Everything in you is special and lovely. Nothing can ever go wrong with you. Marry anyone at all, marry Neuhoff, no, not Neuhoff, if that can be avoided, but any lively

[761]

young man, say a man like my nephew Stani, yes, indeed, Helen, you should marry Stani, he so much wants to, and anyhow nothing bad can ever happen to you. For you are indestructible, that is clearly written in your face. I'm always fascinated by a really lovely face, but yours—

HELEN

I'd rather you didn't say such things to me, Count Bühl.

HANS KARL

But no, it isn't your loveliness that strikes one most, it's something quite different: in you one can read Necessity. Of course you don't understand what I mean, I understand myself much worse when I'm talking than when I'm silent. I can't even try to explain it to you, it's simply something I learned when I was at the front: that there is something written in people's faces. You see, even in a face like Antoinette's I can read—

HELEN

with a fleeting smile

But I'm well aware of that.

HANS KARL *earnestly*

Yes, it's a charming, attractive face, but one and the same dumb reproach is stamped on it all the time: Why have you all left me to the frightful accidents of Chance? And that gives her little mask such a helpless, desperate look that one can't help feeling anxious about her.

HELEN

But, all the same, Antoinette is *there*. She is wholly absorbed in the moment, that's what women should be like, since the moment is everything. But what is the world to make of a person like me? For me the moment simply doesn't exist, I stand there and see the lights shining and in me they have already gone out. And I am talking to you, we are quite alone together in a room, but in me that is already over: as if some outside person had come in and interrupted us, Huberta or Theophilus Neuhoff or anyone, and it is all already at an end, that I was ever sitting alone with you, aware of this music that couldn't be more unsuited to either of us—and you already somewhere else among other people. And I too somewhere else among people.

HANS KARL *in a low voice*

Anyone must be happy who is allowed to live with you, and should thank God for it to the end of his life, Helen, to the very end of his life, whoever he may be. Don't take Neuhoff, Helen—rather take a man like Stani, or not even Stani, anyone else as long as he's a fine and noble creature—and a man: all the things that I am not.

He stands up.

HELEN

also stands up, she feels that he is on the point of going away

But you're saying farewell! (*Hans Karl makes no answer*) And even this is something I have known beforehand. That a moment would come when you'd suddenly bid me farewell and make an end—although there was nothing at all to put an end to. But the others, where there really was something, to them you can never say farewell.

Hugo von Hofmannsthal

HANS KARL

Helen, there are good reasons.

HELEN

I think I've already gone over in my mind everything in the world that concerns us two. We have already stood together like this, with insipid music in the air, while you bid me farewell like this, once and for all.

HANS KARL

It's not just an impulse of the moment, Helen, that makes me bid you farewell. Oh no, you mustn't think that. For when one has to say farewell to someone there's always something behind it.

HELEN

And what is that?

HANS KARL

One must belong very closely to someone and yet not be allowed to belong completely.

HELEN

flinches

What do you mean by that?

HANS KARL

Out at the front, there was often a time—my God, who could possibly mention such things!

HELEN

Yes, you, to me. Now.

[764]

The Difficult Man

HANS KARL

There were such hours, towards evening or in the night, at early dawn with the morning star in the sky—Helen, you were very near to me then. And then the trench caved in and buried us, you've heard about that—

HELEN

Yes, I've heard about it.

HANS KARL

It lasted only a moment, thirty seconds, they said, but the inner life has a different measure of time. For me it was a whole lifetime that I lived through, and in that span of time you were my wife. Isn't that amusing?

HELEN

I was your wife?

HANS KARL

Not my future wife. That's the queer thing about it. My wife, quite simply. A *fait accompli*. The whole thing was more like something in the past than something in the future. (*Helen is silent*) My God, I'm an impossible person, as I keep telling Crescence! Here I am beside you at a soirée and I start reminiscing like old Millesimo, God bless him, who used to be left sitting alone in the end with his pointless anecdotes and never noticed that he was telling them only to himself.

HELEN

But I'm not leaving you to yourself, Count Kari, I'm listening. You had something to say to me: was that it?

Hugo von Hofmannsthal

HANS KARL

This was it, a very subtle lecture that some Higher Power read me. I'll tell you, Helen, what the gist of it was. (*Helen has sat down again; he sits down too. The music has stopped playing*) It had to be impressed on me, at a specially selected moment, just what the happiness looks like that I have thrown away. How I have thrown it away, you know as well as I do.

HELEN

I know as well as you do?

HANS KARL

Simply because I did not recognize, while there was still time, what the one thing necessary consisted in, what really mattered. And I did not recognize it because of the weakness of my own nature. And so I did not stand the test. Later on, in the field hospital, in the many quiet days and nights, I was able to see it all with indescribable clearness and certainty.

HELEN

Was this what you wanted to say to me, just this?

HANS KARL

Convalescence is such a queer state. The whole world came back to me again like something clean and new and yet so natural. I was suddenly able to realize what it is to be human. And what it must be like for two human beings to join their lives together and become *one*. I was able—in imagination at least—to picture to myself—what it implies, how sacred it is and how wonderful. And strangely enough it was not my own marriage that, in a way quite uncalled for, occupied the central place in all this speculation—although it's possible enough that I might marry some day—but it was your marriage.

HELEN

My marriage! My marriage—to whom, then?

HANS KARL

That I don't know. But I was able to imagine to myself in exact detail how it all would be, and how it would run its course, with few people about and everything sacred and ceremonious, and how it would all be as is only fitting for your eyes and your forehead, and your lips which cannot say a superfluous word, and your hands which cannot subscribe to a dishonourable deed—and I even heard your pure, clear voice saying Yes, purely and clearly—all from a distance, since of course I was not there, I was not there at all!—How could an outsider like myself attend such a ceremony?—But it has been a delight to me to tell you for once what I feel for you.—And of course one can do that only in a specific moment, like the present one, in a definitive moment, so to speak—(*Helen nearly breaks down, but controls herself. Hans Karl goes on, with tears in his eyes*) My God, now I've quite upset you, that's what's so impossible in me, I'm moved to tears as soon as I say or hear anything that isn't utterly banal—it's my nerves since the shell-shock, but that of course must infect sensitive people like you—I shouldn't be let out among people —I keep telling Crescence that—I beg your pardon a thousand times, please forget all the nonsense I've been pouring out—there are so many memories that rise up in confusion at a moment of parting—(*Quickly, because he feels that they are no longer alone*)—but anyone in his senses naturally keeps them to himself—Adieu, Helen, Adieu.

The Famous Man has come in right.

HELEN

hardly able to command herself

Adieu!

They want to clasp hands—neither's hand finds the other's. Hans Karl makes to go out right. The Famous Man intercepts him. Hans Karl looks round left. Crescence is just coming in left.

THE FAMOUS MAN

It has long been my earnest desire, your lordship—

HANS KARL

quickly makes for the door right

Excuse me, sir.

Pushes past the Famous Man.

Crescence goes up to Helen, who is standing there as pale as death.

The Famous Man has gone away disconcerted.

Hans Karl appears once more in the doorway right, looks in, as if undecided, and disappears again at once when he sees Crescence with Helen.

HELEN

to Crescence, almost in a dazed state

Is that you, Crescence? He did come in again. Did he say something else?

The Difficult Man

She totters, Crescence supports her.

CRESCENCE

But I'm so happy! You're so deeply moved, and that makes me so happy!

HELEN

Excuse me, Crescence, don't be angry with me.

Frees herself and hurries out left.

CRESCENCE

You're much more devoted to each other than you know, Stani and you!

She wipes her eyes.

Curtain

Act Three

Entrance hall in the Altenwyls' house. Right, the outside door leading into the drive. In the middle a staircase rising to a gallery from which, left and right, double doors open into the living rooms. Below, near the staircase, low divans or benches. A conservatory off the back of the hall, right.

SCENE I

THE ALTENWYLS' BUTLER, WENZEL

stands right, beside the exit door. There are other footmen outside in the porch, visible through the glass screens of the door. Wenzel calls to the footmen

Councillor Professor Brücke!

The Famous Man comes down the staircase. A footman comes from right with his fur coat, inside which are hanging two mufflers and a pair of galoshes.

WENZEL

while the Famous Man is being helped into his coat

Does the Councillor wish for a car?

THE FAMOUS MAN

Thank you, no. Hasn't his lordship Count Bühl just gone in front of me?

WENZEL

Just this very moment.

THE FAMOUS MAN

Did he drive off?

WENZEL

No, his lordship sent his car away; he saw two gentlemen driving in and stepped into the porter's lodge till they were past. He must be barely out of the gates now.

THE FAMOUS MAN *hurrying*

I'll overtake him.

He goes out; at the same time Stani and Hechingen are visible, entering together.

SCENE II

Stani and Hechingen come in, behind each of them a foot-man takes his overcoat and hat.

STANI

after nodding to the Famous Man in passing

Good evening, Wenzel, is my mother here?

WENZEL

Yes, her ladyship is in the card-room.

He goes out, so do the footmen.

Stani makes for the stairs. Hechingen takes a side-glance at himself in a looking-glass; obviously he is nervous.

[771]

Hugo von Hofmannsthal

Another of the Altenwyls' footmen comes down the stair-
case.

STANI *stopping him*

You know who I am, don't you?

FOOTMAN

Yes indeed, your lordship.

STANI

Go through the reception-rooms and look for Count Bühl
until you find him. Then go up to him quietly and tell
him I'd like to have a word with him, either in the corner
room off the picture-gallery or in the Chinese smoking-
room. Have you got that? Well, what is it you've to say
to him?

FOOTMAN

I have to announce that Count Freudenberg wishes to have
a private word with his lordship, either in the corner
room—

STANI

All right.

Footman returns upstairs.

HECHINGEN

Pst, footman!

The footman does not hear him, goes on his way upstairs.

Stani has sat down. Hechingen looks at him.

STANI

Perhaps you'd better go on without me? I've sent up a
message and I'll wait here a moment for the answer.

HECHINGEN

I'll keep you company.

STANI

No, don't let me detain you. You were in a great hurry
to come here—

HECHINGEN

My dear Stani, you see me in a very strange predicament.
Once I cross the threshold of that reception-room my fate
will be decided.

STANI

irritated by Hechingen's nervous pacing up and down

Hadn't you better sit down? I'm only waiting for the footman, as I told you.

HECHINGEN

I can't sit down, I'm too distracted.

STANI

Perhaps you drank up your champagne a little too fast.

HECHINGEN

At the risk of boring you, my dear Stani, I must confess
that something of great importance to me is at stake.

STANI

*while Hechingen once more walks away in nervous agita-
tion*

But something serious is often at stake. The only thing
that matters is not to betray the fact.

[773]

Hugo von Hofmannsthal

HECHINGEN

again coming nearer

Your Uncle Kari, my very good friend, has undertaken to
have a talk with Antoinette, with my wife, the outcome of
which, as I said—

STANI

Uncle Kari?

HECHINGEN

I must say that I couldn't entrust my fate to the hands of
a nobler, a more unselfish friend—

STANI

But of course.—If he has only been able to find the time
for it.

HECHINGEN

What?

STANI

He sometimes takes on a little too much, my Uncle Kari.
When anyone asks him to do something—he can never
say no.

HECHINGEN

We arranged that I should wait in the Club until he telephoned to tell me whether to come here or put off my
arrival till a more opportune moment.

STANI

Ah. In your shoes I should certainly have waited.

[774]

HECHINGEN

I simply wasn't in a state to wait any longer. Just think what's at stake for me!

STANI

In these critical decisions one should show a certain detachment.—Aha!

Sees the footman coming out above and descending the stairs. Stani goes to meet him, leaving Hechingen standing.

FOOTMAN

No, I think his lordship must have gone.

STANI

You think? Didn't I tell you to look round till you found him?

FOOTMAN

Several gentlemen have also been asking for him. His lordship must have slipped out without being noticed.

STANI

Sapristi! Then go to my mother and tell her that I urgently beg her to come to me for a moment in the first anteroom. I must have a word with my uncle or with her before I go in.

FOOTMAN

Very good.

Goes upstairs again.

[775]

Hugo von Hofmannsthal

HECHINGEN

My instinct tells me that Kari will appear in a minute to report the result, and that it will be a good result.

STANI

You have such a reliable instinct, have you? My congratulations.

HECHINGEN

Something has kept him from telephoning, but he has really drawn me to come here. I feel myself continuously in touch with him.

STANI

Wonderful!

HECHINGEN

That works both ways with us. He often puts into words what I've just been thinking.

STANI

You're clearly a marvellous medium.

HECHINGEN

My dear friend, when I was a gay young dog like you I shouldn't have thought these things possible either, but by the time one's thirty-five one's eyes are opened to a great deal. It's as if one had been deaf and blind earlier.

STANI

You don't say so!

HECHINGEN

I have Kari to thank for my second education. I lay great stress on the fact that without him I should simply never have got my feet clear of the entanglements in my life.

STANI

That's saying a lot.

HECHINGEN

A person like Antoinette, even though one is her husband, that doesn't mean a thing, one has no idea of her inner fineness. One should never forget that such a being is a butterfly whose bloom shouldn't be brushed from her wings. If you only knew her, I mean, if you knew her well enough—(*Stani makes a courteous bow*) I can now see my relationship to her like this, that it's simply my duty to let her have the freedom her bizarre, fantastic nature requires. Her nature is that of a *grande dame* of the eighteenth century. Only by allowing her full freedom can one attach her to oneself.

STANI

Ah.

HECHINGEN

One must be generous, that's what I owe to Kari. I shouldn't think it at all out of the question to be friendly in a generous way with any admirer of hers.

STANI

I see what you mean.

[777]

Hugo von Hofmannsthal

HECHINGEN

I should try to make him a friend of mine, not out of policy, but quite without forethought. I should meet him warmly more than halfway: that's how Kari has taught me to take people, with a supple wrist.

STANI

But all that Uncle Kari says is not to be taken *au pied de la lettre*.

HECHINGEN

Of course not *au pied de la lettre*. But let me beg you not to forget that I have a fine feeling for what's in question. It all depends on a certain something, an inner grace— I mean to say, it must all be a continuous impromptu.

He paces nervously up and down.

STANI

But first and foremost one must know how to preserve one's *tenue*. For instance, if Uncle Kari had to wait for a decision about anything whatever, no one would be able to guess it from his demeanour.

HECHINGEN

But of course. Behind this statue, or behind the big azalea there, he would stand chatting with the utmost nonchalance—I can just see him! At the risk of boring you, I must tell you that I am aware of what would be going on inside him—down to the finest nuances.

STANI

But since we can't both stand behind the azalea, and this idiot of a footman is apparently never coming back, perhaps we should go up.

[778]

HECHINGEN

Yes, let's both go. It's a comfort to me not to be quite alone at such a moment. My dear Stani, I have the greatest sympathy for you!

Takes his arm.

STANI *freeing his arm*

But not arm-in-arm like débutantes in their first year, but perhaps each of us separately.

HECHINGEN

Yes, yes, just as you please.

STANI

Let me suggest that you go first. I'll come close behind you.

Hechingen goes first and disappears above. Stani follows him.

SCENE III

HELEN

comes through a small hidden door in the left wall. She waits until Stani has disappeared. Then she calls to the butler in a low voice

Wenzel, Wenzel, I want to ask you something.

WENZEL

coming quickly out of his room and moving towards her

Yes, my lady?

Hugo von Hofmannsthal

HELEN

in a very casual voice

Did you notice whether Count Bühl has gone?

WENZEL

Yes, he went five minutes ago.

HELEN

Did he leave anything?

WENZEL

What does my lady mean?

HELEN

A letter, or a verbal message.

WENZEL

Not with me, but I'll ask the others. (*He goes over to the footmen. Helen stands still, waiting. Stani is visible for a moment on the upstairs landing. He tries to see with whom Helen is speaking and then disappears again. Wenzel comes back to Helen*) No, nothing at all. He sent his car away, lit a cigar and just walked out. (*Helen says nothing. Wenzel, after a little pause*) Is there anything else, my lady?

HELEN

Yes, Wenzel, I'll come back in a few minutes and then I shall be going out.

WENZEL

In the car, so late in the evening?

HELEN

No, I shall go on foot.

WENZEL

Is someone ill?

HELEN

No, there's no one ill. I only want to speak to somebody.

WENZEL

Does my lady want anyone with her as well as the Miss?

HELEN

No, I shall go quite alone, Miss Jekyll won't be with me. I'll slip out here at a moment when none of the guests is about. And I'll give you a letter for Papa.

WENZEL

Am I to give it to him at once?

HELEN

No, give it to Papa when he has seen the last of the guests off.

WENZEL

When everybody's gone?

HELEN

Yes, at the moment when he orders the lights to be turned out. But then, stay beside him. I'd like you to—

She falters.

WENZEL

What, my lady?

HELEN

How old was I, Wenzel, when you first came here?

WENZEL

A little girl five years old, my lady was.

HELEN

That's all right, Wenzel, thank you. I'll come out by this door and you'll give me a signal when the hall is clear.

Gives him her hand to kiss.

WENZEL

Yes, my lady.

Kisses her hand.

Helen disappears through the little door.

Wenzel goes out.

SCENE IV

Antoinette and Neuhoff come from beside the staircase, right, out of the conservatory.

ANTOINETTE

That was Helen. Was she alone? Did she see me?

NEUHOFF

I don't think so. But what does it matter? You don't need to be afraid of meeting her eyes, at least.

ANTOINETTE

But I am afraid of her. Every time I think of her I feel as if someone has been telling me lies. Let's go somewhere else, we can't sit about here in the hall.

NEUHOFF

Calm yourself. Kari Bühl has gone. I saw him going away just a moment ago.

ANTOINETTE

Just at this very moment?

NEUHOFF

understanding her thoughts

He went out all by himself, without anyone else seeing him.

ANTOINETTE

What?

NEUHOFF

A certain person did *not* accompany him here and did *not* exchange a single word with him during the last half-hour he was in the house. I took note of that. You can relax.

They sit down.

ANTOINETTE

He swore to me he was going to bid her farewell for ever. If I could see her face, then I should know—

NEUHOFF

That face of hers is hard as stone. Better stay here with me.

ANTOINETTE

I—

[783]

Hugo von Hofmannsthal

NEUHOFF

Your face is enchanting. Other people's faces conceal everything. But yours is a continuous avowal. One could read in your face everything that has ever happened to you.

ANTOINETTE

Could one? Perhaps—if one had only the shadow of a right to do so.

NEUHOFF

That right arises out of the moment and one just takes it. You are a woman, a real, bewitching woman. You belong to no one and to everyone! No, you haven't belonged to anyone yet, you're still waiting.

ANTOINETTE

with a nervous little laugh

Not for you!

NEUHOFF

Yes, precisely for me; that's to say, for a man such as you have never known, a real man, with chivalry and kindness rooted in strength. The Karis of this world have only ill-used you and betrayed you from first to last, the sort of men who have no kindness, no core of strength, no nerve and no loyalty! These playboys, who catch a creature like you again and again in their nets, leave you unrewarded, unthanked, unhappy, humiliated in your tenderest femininity!

Tries to seize her hand.

[784]

ANTOINETTE

How you do work yourself up! But I'm safe from you, for your cold cast-iron intellect shows through every word you say. I'm not even afraid of you. I don't want you!

NEUHOFF

As for my intellect, I hate it! I want to be set free from it, I desire only to lose it in you, sweet little Antoinette!

He makes to seize her hand. Hechingen comes into sight upstairs, but at once draws back. Neuhoff has seen him, takes his hand away, alters his attitude and his facial expression.

ANTOINETTE

Ah, now I've seen through and through you! How suddenly your whole face can change! I'll tell you what has happened: you saw Helen passing by upstairs, and at that moment I could read *you* like an open book. Resentment and impotence, anger, shame, and the determination to get me —*faute de mieux*—all that was in your face. Edine scolds me for not being able to read complicated books. But that was complicated enough, and yet I read it all in a flash. Don't waste your time on me. I don't want you.

NEUHOFF *bending over her*

You shall want me, Antoinette!

ANTOINETTE

rises

No! I don't! I don't! For what shoots out of your eyes is the will to have me in your power, only the will—and it may be very manly—but I don't care for it. And if that's the best you can do, every single one of us, even the most ordinary of women, has something that's better than your best, and is proof against your best through a touch of fear. But not the kind of fear that turns one's head, only a quite banal, prosaic fear. (*She moves towards the staircase, but pauses again*) Do you understand? Have I made myself quite clear? I'm afraid of you, but not afraid enough, that's your bad luck. Adieu, Baron Neuhoff.

Neuhoff has gone off quickly to the conservatory.

SCENE V

Hechingen appears upstairs and comes running quickly downstairs. Antoinette is disconcerted and recoils.

HECHINGEN

Toinette!

ANTOINETTE *involuntarily*

The last straw!

HECHINGEN

What did you say?

ANTOINETTE

I'm taken by surprise—you must understand that.

HECHINGEN

And I'm delighted. I thank God, I thank my lucky stars, I thank this moment!

ANTOINETTE

You look somehow different. Your expression is different, I don't know how. Don't you feel well?

HECHINGEN

Isn't it only because these dark eyes of yours haven't looked at me for a long time?

ANTOINETTE

But it's not so long since we saw each other.

HECHINGEN

Seeing and looking at are two different things, Toinette. (*He has come closer to her. Antoinette retreats*) But perhaps it's something different that's changed me, if I may be so presumptuous as to talk about myself.

ANTOINETTE

What's changed you, then? Has something happened? Have you begun to take an interest in someone?

HECHINGEN

To see your charm and your pride in action, suddenly to see before one's eyes the whole woman one loves, to see her living and breathing!

ANTOINETTE

Oh, so you're speaking of me!

HECHINGEN

Yes, you. I was lucky enough to see you for once as you are, since for once I wasn't there to intimidate you. Oh, what thoughts I had as I stood up there! This wife of

Hugo von Hofmannsthal

mine, desired by all and denying herself to all! My destiny, your destiny, for it's our common destiny. Do sit down here beside me!

He has sat down, stretches a hand out to her.

ANTOINETTE

We can talk just as well standing, since we're such old acquaintances.

HECHINGEN

standing up again

I've never known you before. I've had to get new eyes for that. The man who comes to you now is a different man, a changed man.

ANTOINETTE

There's a new ring in the kind of things you say. Where have you been learning it?

HECHINGEN

The man speaking to you now is a man you don't know, Toinette, just as he hasn't known you! A man who wishes for nothing else, dreams of nothing else, but to become known to you and to know you.

ANTOINETTE

Ado, I do implore you not to speak to me as if I were someone you'd just picked up in the dining-car of an express train.

HECHINGEN

With whom I'd like to travel right to the end of the world!

Wants to kiss her hand, she draws it away from him.

ANTOINETTE

Please do believe that this rubs me up the wrong way. Old married couples are used to taking a certain tone with each other. One doesn't change that all at once, it's enough to make one's head go round.

HECHINGEN

I don't know anything about old married couples, I don't know anything about our situation.

ANTOINETTE

But it's the given situation.

HECHINGEN

Given? There's no such thing. Here you are, and here am I, and everything's starting new from the beginning.

ANTOINETTE

Nonsense, nothing is starting new from the beginning.

HECHINGEN

Life is made up of perpetual new beginnings.

ANTOINETTE

No, no, for goodness' sake get back to your old way of talking. I can't stand much more of this. Don't be cross with me, I have a bit of a migraine, I was thinking of going home earlier on, before I knew I was going to meet you —how could I possibly tell?

HECHINGEN

You couldn't possibly tell who it would be that would come to meet you, and that it wouldn't be your husband but a new ardent admirer, as ardent as a boy of twenty! That's what troubles you, that makes you light-headed.

Tries to clasp her hand.

ANTOINETTE

No, it doesn't make me light-headed at all, it makes me stone-cold sober. It makes me so *terre à terre* that everything seems flat and stale, myself included. I've had a miserable evening, I ask only one favour of you, do let me go home.

HECHINGEN

Oh, Antoinette!

ANTOINETTE

That's to say, if you have something definite to tell me, then tell me, I'll be glad to listen, but one thing I do implore you! Tell me in your ordinary style, your usual style.

Hechingen, disconcerted and sobered, is silent.

ANTOINETTE

Well, what is it you want to say to me?

HECHINGEN

I'm upset to see that my presence seems to take you by surprise on the one hand and to be a burden to you on the other. I had allowed myself to hope that a dear friend of mine would have found the opportunity of speaking to you about myself and my unchanging feelings for you. I had persuaded myself that on this basis an improvised explanation between us might possibly find an altered situation in being or could at least produce one.—Let me beg you not to forget that until now you've never given me a chance to speak to you about my own inner life—I regard our relationship as one, Antoinette—am I boring you very much?

ANTOINETTE

But do go on, please. I suppose there's something you want to tell me. I can't think of any other reason for your coming here.

HECHINGEN

I regard our relationship as one that binds me, only me, Antoinette, and lays on me, only on me, a testing time, a trial, the duration of which is for you to determine.

ANTOINETTE

But what's the point of that, what should it lead to?

HECHINGEN

Indeed, if I turn to look inside myself, Toinette—

ANTOINETTE

Well, what's there, when you turn to look?

She puts her hands to her temples.

HECHINGEN

—it seems that the testing time needn't last for long. Over and over again in the sight of the world I shall endeavour to adopt your standpoint, I shall go on defending your charm and your freedom. And if anyone deliberately misrepresents you, I shall refer him in triumph to the experience of the last few minutes, to that eloquent proof of how well you are equipped to keep within bounds the men who admire and besiege you.

ANTOINETTE *nervously*

What do you mean?

HECHINGEN

You are much desired. Your type is the *grande dame* of the eighteenth century. I see no manner of cause for regret in that. One's judgment should be based on the nuance of behaviour, not on the fact. I lay great stress on making it clear that whatever you do, your motives are elevated for me beyond all suspicion.

ANTOINETTE *nearly in tears*

My dear Ado, you mean very well, but my migraine is getting worse with every word you say.

HECHINGEN

Oh, I'm very sorry. All the more as these moments are infinitely precious to me.

ANTOINETTE

Please, have the goodness—

She totters.

HECHINGEN

I understand. A car?

ANTOINETTE

Yes. Edine has offered me hers.

HECHINGEN

At once. (*He goes and gives the order. Comes back with her cloak. While he helps her into it*) Is that all I can do for you?

ANTOINETTE

Yes, that's all.

WENZEL

at the glass door, announces

Her ladyship's car.

Antoinette goes out very quickly. Hechingen makes to follow her, then checks himself.

SCENE VI

STANI

comes from behind out of the conservatory. He seems to be looking for someone

Oh, it's you, have you seen my mother anywhere?

HECHINGEN

No, I haven't been in the drawing-rooms. I've just been seeing my wife to her car. It was a situation without parallel.

STANI

preoccupied with his own affairs

I can't understand it. Mamma first sends me a message to meet her in the conservatory, and then another to wait for her here by the stairs—

[793]

HECHINGEN

I absolutely must have a good talk with Kari now.

STANI

Then you'll have to go out and look for him.

HECHINGEN

My instinct tells me he went out only to find me at the Club and will soon come back.

Goes upstairs.

STANI

What it is to have an instinct that tells one everything! Oh, here's Mamma!

SCENE VII

CRESCENCE

comes through the hidden little door left at the side of the main staircase

I've come down the service stairs, these footmen do nothing but muddle one up. First he tells me you beg me to come to the conservatory, then he says in the gallery—

STANI

Mamma, this is an evening of general confusion without end. I had really got to the point, if it hadn't been for you, of turning on my heel, going home, taking a shower, and crawling into bed. I can endure much, but to be put in a false position is so odious to me that it jars on my nerves. I implore you urgently to put me *au courant* in our affairs.

CRESCENCE

But I simply don't understand how your Uncle Kari could go away without giving me so much as a hint. That's his usual absent-mindedness, it drives me to despair, my dear boy.

STANI

Please do explain the situation a little. Please tell me in outline what has been happening, never mind the details.

CRESCENCE

But everything went exactly according to programme. First your Uncle Kari had a very agitated interview with Antoinette—

STANI

That was the first mistake. I knew it would be, for it was much too complicated. Well, go on, what else?

CRESCENCE

What else can I say? Antoinette comes rushing past me, completely upset, then immediately afterwards your Uncle Kari sits down with Helen—

STANI

It really is too complicated to manage two such conversations in one evening. Then Uncle Kari—

CRESCENCE

His talk with Helen goes on and on for a long time, I come to the door—Helen sinks into my arms, I am in raptures, she runs away in confusion, as one might expect, I rush to the telephone and summon you here!

STANI

Yes, well, I know that, but please explain what has been happening since!

CRESCENCE

I rush full tilt through the rooms looking for Kari and don't find him. I have to go back to my cards, you can imagine what my game was like. Mariette Stradonitz declares hearts, I play diamonds, meanwhile I pray to all the saints in the calendar. On top of that I revoke in clubs. At long last I can get up, I look for Kari again, he's not to be found! I go through the whole flight of half-dark rooms till I come to Helen's door, I hear her sobbing inside. I knock and tell her who I am, she gives me no answer. I slip back to the card-table again, Mariette asks me three times if I'm not well, Louis Castaldo looks at me as if I were a ghost—

STANI

Now I understand it all.

CRESCENCE

How? What? I don't understand anything.

STANI

All of it, all of it. The whole thing's clear to me.

CRESCENCE

How can my boy explain that?

STANI

Clear as two and two makes four. Antoinette in her despair must have been telling tales, having understood from Uncle Kari that she's lost me for ever. A woman when she's desperate loses all her *tenue,* so she went slinking up to Helen and poured out such scandalous tittle-tattle that Helen, flying up in the air with her colossal sensitivity, decided to give me up even if it should break her heart.

CRESCENCE

And that's why she wouldn't open her door to me!

STANI

And Uncle Kari, when he saw what he'd done, cleared out of the mess as fast as he could.

CRESCENCE

But that would be simply dreadful! My dear boy, what do you say to that?

STANI

My dear Mamma, I say only one thing, the only thing that a gentleman can say to himself in a false position: one remains what one is, and no prospect, good or bad, can make any difference to that.

CRESCENCE

Stani's a dear boy, and I adore the way he's taking it, but still one shouldn't throw up the game at this point.

STANI

But whatever you do, spare me a false position.

CRESCENCE

For a man who carries himself so well as you do, there's no such thing as a false position. I'll go now and look for

[797]

Helen and ask her just what did happen between a quarter to ten and now.

STANI

I implore you urgently—

CRESCENCE

But my dear boy's a thousand times too precious for me to foist him on any family, even if it were the Emperor of China's. On the other hand, I'm too fond of Helen to let her happiness be sacrificed because of the tittle-tattle of a jealous goose like Antoinette. So let Stani do me the favour of staying here and then taking me home, for he can see how upset I am.

She goes up the staircase. Stani follows her.

SCENE VIII

Helen has come through the hidden little door in the wall left, in her fur cloak, ready to go out. She waits till Crescence and Stani are far enough up the stairs not to see her. At the same moment Hans Karl is visible through the glass door right; he sheds his hat, coat, and stick and comes in. Helen has seen Hans Karl before he has caught sight of her. In a twinkling her expression alters completely. She lets her cloak drop from her shoulders so that it lies behind the staircase and comes forward to meet him.

HANS KARL *discomposed*

Helen, are you still here?

HELEN

now and later in a firm, decided attitude and with a light, almost assured tone

This is where I belong: this is my home.

HANS KARL

You look quite different. Something has happened!

HELEN

Yes, something has happened.

HANS KARL

When, so suddenly?

HELEN

About an hour ago, I think.

HANS KARL

in an uncertain voice

Something unpleasant?

HELEN

What?

HANS KARL

Something upsetting?

HELEN

Oh yes, that, certainly.

HANS KARL

Something that can't be made good?

HELEN

That remains to be seen. Do you see what's lying there?

HANS KARL

Over there? A fur. A lady's cloak, it looks like.

HELEN

Yes, that's my cloak. I was just on the point of going out.

HANS KARL

Going out?

HELEN

Yes, and I'll tell you why in a minute. But first you'll tell me why you've come back. That's not a usual way of behaving.

HANS KARL *hesitating*

It always makes me rather embarrassed when someone asks me a straight question.

HELEN

But I do ask you a straight question.

HANS KARL

I can't explain it very easily.

HELEN

We can sit down.

They sit down.

HANS KARL

Earlier on, in our conversation—upstairs, in the small drawing-room—

[800]

HELEN

Ah, upstairs in the small drawing-room.

HANS KARL

discomposed by her tone

Yes, indeed, in the small drawing-room. I made a great mistake then, a very great mistake.

HELEN

Oh?

HANS KARL

I referred to something out of my past.

HELEN

Something out of your past?

HANS KARL

To certain preposterous, entirely personal notions that ran through my mind out at the front and later in hospital. Purely personal fancies, hallucinations, so to speak. Many things that were absolutely out of place.

HELEN

Yes, I understand. Well?

HANS KARL

That was the wrong thing to do.

HELEN

In what way?

HANS KARL

One can't call the past to witness like the police summoning evidence. What's past is past. No one has the right, in a conversation about present affairs, to bring the past into it. I'm putting it very badly, but I'm quite clear in my mind about it.

HELEN

I hope so.

HANS KARL

It was very painful for me to remember, as soon as I was alone, how little, at my age, I have myself in hand—and so I have come back to give you your full freedom—I beg your pardon, that was a clumsy slip of the tongue—to give you the reassurance that it has nothing to do with you.

HELEN

Nothing to do with me? Reassurance? (*Hans Karl, uncertain, makes to rise. Helen keeps her seat*) So that's what you wanted to tell me—about why you went away?

HANS KARL

Yes, why I went away and of course also why I came back. The one explains the other.

HELEN

Aha. Thank you very much. And now I'll tell you why you came back.

HANS KARL

You'll tell me?

HELEN

turning her eyes full upon him

You came back because—yes, there is such a thing, praise be to God! (*She laughs*) Yet it's perhaps a pity that you came back. For this is perhaps not the right place to say what must be said—perhaps it would have been better —but now it simply must be said, here.

HANS KARL

Oh my God, you find me incomprehensible. Say it straight out!

HELEN

I understand everything well enough. I understand what drove you away and what has brought you back again.

HANS KARL

You understand it all? I don't understand it myself.

HELEN

We can speak even more softly, if you like. What drove you away was your lack of confidence, your fear of your own self—you're not offended?

HANS KARL

Fear of my own self?

HELEN

Fear of your own underlying will. Yes, it's inconvenient, that will, it doesn't lead one in the pleasantest paths. But it brought you back here.

HANS KARL

I don't understand you, Helen!

HELEN

without looking at him

Running away like that isn't difficult for you, but you often have difficult moments afterwards when you're alone with yourself.

HANS KARL

You know all that?

HELEN

Because I know all that, I could have had the strength to do the impossible for your sake.

HANS KARL

What impossible thing would you have done for my sake?

HELEN

I should have run after you.

HANS KARL

How "run after"? What do you mean?

HELEN

Run after you here, through that door, into the street. Haven't I shown you my cloak lying over there behind the stair?

HANS KARL

You would have—? But where to?

HELEN

Into the Club, or anywhere—how do I know, simply until I found you.

HANS KARL

Would you have, Helen—? Would you have looked for me? Without thinking about—

HELEN

Yes, without thinking about anything else at all. I am running after you—I want you to—

HANS KARL

his voice faltering

You, my dear, you want me to—? (*To himself*) These impossible tears again! (*To her*) I can't hear you very well. You speak so low.

HELEN

You hear me quite well. And now you are in tears— but that rather helps me to speak out—

HANS KARL

My dear—what did you say?

HELEN

Your underlying will, your deepest self; do understand me. It turned you right round when you were alone and brought you back to me. And now—

HANS KARL

Now?

HELEN

Now I don't really know whether you can truly love any-one—but I'm in love with you, and I want—but it's mon-strous that you leave me to say it!

Hugo von Hofmannsthal

HANS KARL *faltering*

You want from me—

HELEN

her voice faltering as much as his

My share—of your life, of your soul, of everything—my share!

A short pause

HANS KARL

Helen, all that you are saying agitates me beyond measure, for your own sake, Helen, for your sake, of course. You're mistaken in me, I have an impossible character.

HELEN

You are as you are, and I want to know you as you are.

HANS KARL

It's an unspeakable danger for you. (*Helen shakes her head*) I'm a man who has nothing but misunderstandings on his conscience.

HELEN *smiling*

Yes, so it seems.

HANS KARL

I've hurt so many women.

HELEN

Love isn't a soothing syrup.

HANS KARL

I'm a boundless egoist.

HELEN

Are you? I don't think so.

HANS KARL

I'm so unstable, nothing can hold me firm.

HELEN

Yes, you can—what's the word?—seduce and be seduced.
You genuinely loved them all and left them all in the
lurch again. Poor women! None of them simply had the
strength for both of you.

HANS KARL

How?

HELEN

It's in your nature to desire, to reach out in longing. But
not for this—or that—what you long for is everything—
from one woman—for ever! One of these women should
have had the strength to keep you expecting more and
more from her. Then you would never have left her.

HANS KARL

How well you know me!

HELEN

After a little while you felt indifferent to all of them, and
were wildly sorry for them, but had no great friendship for
any of them: that was my comfort.

HANS KARL

How you do know everything!

HELEN

That was my sole interest in life. The only thing I have understood.

HANS KARL

I must feel ashamed before you, my dear.

HELEN

But am I ashamed before you? No, no. Love cuts deep into the living flesh.

HANS KARL

All that you knew and endured—

HELEN

I wouldn't have lifted my little finger to draw one of these women away from you. I couldn't have brought myself to do it.

HANS KARL

What magic there is in you. Not at all like other women. You make one so serene inside oneself.

HELEN

Of course you can't yet realize the friendship I have for you. That will take a long time—if you can give it me.

HANS KARL

How you said that!

HELEN

Now go, so that no one sees you. And come soon again. Come tomorrow, early in the afternoon. It's no business of other people's, but Papa should be told at once—Papa, certainly!—Or don't you think so?

HANS KARL *embarrassed*

It's just this—my good friend Poldo Altenwyl for days past has had an undertaking, a wish—that he wants to foist on me officially: he wants me, quite superfluously, to make a speech in the Upper House—

HELEN

Aha—

HANS KARL

And so for weeks I've been keeping out of his way very carefully—I've avoided being left alone with him—in the Club, on the street, or anywhere—

HELEN

Don't worry—there will be only the one main topic—I guarantee that.—Here's someone coming already: I must go.

HANS KARL

Helen!

HELEN

already on the way out, pauses for a moment

My dear! Good night!

Picks up her cloak and disappears through the hidden door left.

[809]

SCENE IX

CRESCENCE

at the top of the stairs

Kari! (*She comes quickly down the stairs. Hans Karl is
standing with his back to the staircase*) Kari! Have I found
you at last! What an evening of confusion this has been!

She comes round and sees his face

Kari! Something has happened! Tell me, what is it?

HANS KARL

Something has happened to me, but we're not going to pick
it to pieces.

CRESCENCE

But, please, won't you explain—

SCENE X

HECHINGEN

*Comes downstairs, stands still, and calls to Hans Karl in a
low voice*

Kari, if you could spare me a second—

HANS KARL

I'm at your disposal. (*To Crescence*) I must really be excused.

Stani begins to walk down the stairs.

CRESCENCE *to Hans Karl*

But the boy! What am I to say to the boy? The boy is in a
false position!

STANI

comes right down, to Hechingen

Excuse me, I absolutely must speak to Uncle Kari for a
minute.

He greets Hans Karl.

HANS KARL

Just a moment, my dear Ado!

Leaves Hechingen standing, turns to Crescence

Come over here by yourself: I have something to tell you.
But we're not going to discuss it at all.

CRESCENCE

But I'm not an indiscreet person!

HANS KARL

You're an angel of goodness. But, listen! Helen has got engaged.

CRESCENCE

To Stani? She's accepted him?

HANS KARL

Not so fast. Don't start wiping your eyes just yet, you don't
know yet.

Hugo von Hofmannsthal

CRESCENCE

It's your goodness that makes me want to cry. The boy owes everything to you.

HANS KARL

Wait, Crescence!—Not to Stani.

CRESCENCE

Not to Stani? Well, to whom, then?

HANS KARL

in great embarrassment

Congratulate me, Crescence!

CRESCENCE

You?

HANS KARL

But then leave, at once, and don't mention it in conversation. She has—I have—we have got engaged to each other.

CRESCENCE

You have! Oh, I'm in raptures!

HANS KARL

Please, keep in mind above all that you've promised to spare me the odious confusions that a man exposes himself to when he mixes with people.

CRESCENCE

Of course I'll do nothing—

Turns her eyes on Stani.

HANS KARL

As I have said, I won't explain anything to anyone and I beg to be spared the usual misunderstandings!

CRESCENCE

Kari, you shouldn't be so obstinate! When you were a little boy you had exactly that face when anyone crossed you. I never could bear it even then! I'll do exactly as you wish.

HANS KARL

You're the best sister in the world, and now let me be excused, Ado needs to have a talk with me—another talk to be gone through, in God's name.

Kisses her hand.

CRESCENCE

I'll wait!

Crescence and Stani draw to one side, at a distance, but now and then visible.

SCENE XI

HECHINGEN

You have such a serious look! There's reproach in your face!

HANS KARL

Not in the least: I beg you not to start weighing my looks too scrupulously, at least not tonight.

[813]

HECHINGEN

Has something happened to alter your opinion of me? Or your opinion of my situation?

HANS KARL *lost in thought*

Your situation?

HECHINGEN

My situation with respect to Antoinette, of course! May I ask you what conclusions you have come to about my wife?

HANS KARL *nervously*

I do beg your pardon, but I'd rather not speak about women tonight. Once one begins analyzing, one falls into the most odious misunderstandings. So I beg you to let me off!

HECHINGEN

I understand. I comprehend entirely. From what you say, or rather from what you are indicating in the most delicate manner, the only conclusion I can draw is that you regard my situation as hopeless.

SCENE XII

Hans Karl says nothing, looks distractedly right.

Vincent has come in, right, in the same suit as in Act I, a small bowler hat in his hand.

Crescence has gone up to Vincent.

HECHINGEN

very cast down by Hans Karl's silence

This is the critical moment of my life, and I did see it coming. Now I need your support, my dear Kari, if my whole world isn't to collapse.

HANS KARL

But my dear Ado—(*To himself, looking at Vincent*) What's going on here?

HECHINGEN

I shall, if you allow me, recapitulate the premises on which I based my hopes—

HANS KARL

Excuse me for one second, I see that something has gone wrong.

He goes over to Crescence and Vincent. Hechingen is left standing alone. Stani has withdrawn to one side, showing some signs of impatience.

CRESCENCE *to Hans Karl*

Now he tells me you're going off tomorrow morning early —what does this mean?

HANS KARL

What's this? I've given no such order—

CRESCENCE

Kari, with you one never gets away from shilly-shallying. And just when I had got myself into the right frame of mind for your engagement!

HANS KARL

May I remind you—

[815]

Hugo von Hofmannsthal

CRESCENCE

Oh my goodness, it just slipped out!

HANS KARL *to Vincent*

Who sent you here? What does this mean?

VINCENT

Your lordship gave the order yourself, half an hour ago, by telephone.

HANS KARL

To you? I gave no order to you.

VINCENT

Your lordship instructed the porter's lodge that at seven o'clock tomorrow morning you would be going off to your hunting-lodge at Gebhardtskirchen—or, rather, this morning, since it's now a quarter past midnight.

CRESCENCE

But, Kari, what does it all mean?

HANS KARL

If people would only stop expecting me to give an account of every breath I draw.

VINCENT *to Crescence*

But it's quite easily explained. The portress ran up to the house with the message, Lukas wasn't anywhere about at the moment, so I took the matter in hand. I warned the chauffeur, I had the suitcases brought down from the box-room, I had the secretary Neugebauer stirred up in case he was needed—why should he sleep when the whole house is

awake?—and now here I am at your service, ready for
further instructions.

HANS KARL

Go back to the house at once, cancel the car, have the
suitcases unpacked again, beg Herr Neugebauer to go back
to bed, and take yourself off so that I never see your face
again! You are no longer in my service. Lukas already
knows what is to be done with you. Now go!

VINCENT

I must say, this is a great surprise to me.

Goes out.

SCENE XIII

CRESCENCE

But do let me have only a word or two! Do explain—

HANS KARL

There's nothing to explain. When I left the Club I was
quite determined, for various reasons, to go off in the morning early. That was at the corner of the Freyung and the
Herrengasse. There's a café at that corner, and I went in
and telephoned home from there; then, when I came out
of the café, instead of turning into the Freyung as I had intended, I came down the Herrengasse and arrived in here
again—and then Helen—

He draws his hand over his forehead.

CRESCENCE

But you should be left to yourself.

[817]

She goes over to Stani, who is hanging about in the background.

HANS KARL

gives himself a shake and returns to Hechingen, very cordially

I do beg you to forgive me for all that has happened, I've done nothing but make mistakes and I ask you to forgive me for all of them. I can't give you any detailed report about this evening's doings. I beg you, all the same, to think kindly of me.

Holds out his hand.

HECHINGEN *overcome*

But now you're taking leave of me, my dear friend! You have tears in your eyes. But I do understand you, Kari. You are a true, good friend; people like me are simply not able to extricate ourselves from the meshes of the destiny prepared for us by the smiles or frowns of women, but you have lifted yourself once for all far above that atmosphere —(*Hans Karl gestures him to stop*) You can't deny it, you have that aura of superiority around you, and as in the long run life never stands still but must always progress or regress, you simply can't help having round you from day to day the increasing loneliness of the superior man.

HANS KARL

And that's just another colossal misunderstanding!

He looks anxiously right, where Altenwyl with one of his guests is now visible in the door of the conservatory.

HECHINGEN

How so? How am I to understand your words?

HANS KARL

My dear Ado, please excuse me for the moment from trying to explain them or anything else. Be so good as to step
over here with me, for there's something approaching from
over there that I don't feel equal to meeting.

HECHINGEN

What is it, what is it?

HANS KARL

There, in the door, behind me.

HECHINGEN

looks over at the door

That's only our host, Poldo Altenwyl—

HANS KARL

—Who thinks that the tail-end of his soirée is the very
moment for swooping down on me with horrid intent; since
what does one go to a soirée for, if not to let every man
with something or other on his mind pounce on one in the
most ruthless manner!

HECHINGEN

I don't understand—

HANS KARL

The idea is that I should make my début as an orator in
the Upper House the day after tomorrow. Our Club has

[819]

Here

---

entrusted him with this charming mission, and since I've been avoiding him everywhere he's lurking here in his own house to catch me when I'm alone and unprotected. Please do fall into lively talk with me, even a little agitated, as if we were settling some important matter.

HECHINGEN

And you're going to refuse again?

HANS KARL

Am I supposed to stand up and make a speech about peace among peoples and the unitedness of nations—I, a man whose sole conviction is that it's impossible to open one's mouth without causing the most ineradicable confusion? I'd rather give up my hereditary seat and crawl into a barrel for the rest of my life. Am I to let loose a flood of words every one of which will seem positively indecent to me?

HECHINGEN

That's putting it a bit strongly.

HANS KARL

with great intensity, but without raising his voice

But everything one utters is indecent. Merely to put anything into words is an indecency. And when one looks at it closely, my dear Ado, except that men never look closely at anything in the world, there's something positively shameless in our daring even to experience some things! To go through some experiences and not consider oneself indecent needs an insane self-complacency and a measure of fatuousness which a grown man may well keep in some hidden corner of himself but can never admit the existence of, even to himself! (*Looks right*) He's gone.

Makes for the street door. Altenwyl is no longer visible.

CRESCENCE

intercepting Kari

No making an escape just yet! Kari must explain the whole situation to Stani! (*Hans Karl looks at her*) But the boy can't simply be left standing! The boy has shown such forbearance, such self-restraint, that I'm struck with admiration. A word can surely be said to him.

She beckons Stani to approach. Stani comes a step nearer.

HANS KARL

All right, one more word. But this is the last soirée I'll ever be seen at. (*To Stani, going up to him*) It was a mistake, my dear Stani, to trust me as an advocate for anything.

Clasps his hand.

CRESCENCE

Kari should at least embrace the boy! The boy has carried himself with the most unexampled self-control throughout. (*Hans Karl stands looking rather absently into the distance*) Well, if Kari won't embrace the boy, I must at least embrace him because of the way he has carried himself.

HANS KARL

Perhaps you'd be good enough to wait till I'm gone.

Reaches the front door quickly and disappears.

[821]

SCENE XIV

CRESCENCE

Well, I don't care, I must embrace somebody! Too much has happened for a woman with a feeling heart like mine simply to go home without more ado and get into bed!

STANI

takes a step back

Please, Mamma! In my opinion there are two categories of demonstrative behaviour. One of them is most strictly reserved for private life: that includes all gestures of tenderness between blood relations. The other has, so to speak, a practical and social function: it is the pantomimic expression of any unusual situation which belongs as it were to family history.

CRESCENCE

Well, that's the situation we're in!

Altenwyl with some guests has come out of the living rooms upstairs and is beginning to descend the stairs.

STANI

And for this kind of situation, the right and proper forms have existed for a thousand years. What we have experienced here tonight was, for good or for ill, if we are to call things by their right names, a betrothal. A betrothal culminates in an embrace between the betrothed parties.—In our case the betrothed couple are too eccentric to recognize these formalities. Mamma, you're the nearest relation to Uncle Kari, and there is Poldo Altenwyl, the father of the bride. Let my Mamma go without saying a word and embrace him, and then the whole affair will have taken on its proper, official aspect.

Altenwyl with his guests has come downstairs. Crescence rushes up to him and embraces him. The guests stand in astonishment.

Curtain

NOTES

Biographical Note

Hugo von Hofmannsthal was born in Vienna on February 1, 1874, the only child of a family of Austrian, south German-Jewish, and Lombard antecedents. When he entered the University of Vienna, in 1892, he was already famous as a poet—as "Loris," his *nom de plume*. Hofmannsthal first studied law; after military service, in 1894–95, he turned to romance philology and took the Ph.D. in 1898. Nearly all of his lyrical poetry was written during the nineties, as well as most of the short lyrical plays later collected as "little dramas" (the most famous is *Death and the Fool,* 1893) and a few tales and essays. He married in 1901 and settled in Rodaun, a village near Vienna. He had three children. Occasionally he travelled—the Continent; England twice, briefly; Greece, Morocco, Sicily once. In 1899, Hofmannsthal had begun to write for the stage. From about 1908 until his death, he collaborated with both the composer Richard Strauss and the producer Max Reinhardt. His drama *Elektra* (1904), an adaptation from Sophocles, became the libretto in 1909 of an opera of Strauss. There followed the operas *Der Rosenkavalier* (1911), *Ariadne in Naxos* (1912), *The Woman without a Shadow* (1919), *The Egyptian Helen* (1928), and *Arabella* (staged in 1933). Reinhardt produced Hofmannsthal's rendering of *Oedipus Rex* (1909), his morality play *Everyman* (1911), and his comedy *The Difficult Man* (1918). During all these years, Hofmannsthal continued to write essays. He began two works of prose fiction: *Andreas* (1912–13) and *The Woman without a Shadow* (1919); only the latter was completed. During the first World War, he dedicated his efforts to his country, imperial Austria, and after the war to the new Austrian republic and to the idea of the European community. He was the guiding spirit behind the Salzburg Festival; his *Everyman* became one of its central pieces. For the Festival he wrote *The Salzburg Great Theatre of the World* (1922); that and his last tragedy, *The Tower* (1925, second version, 1927), had their starting-points in plays of Calderón. Hofmannsthal died suddenly on July 15, 1929, at Rodaun.

H. S.

Textual Notes

Introduction

Except where other references are given, all quotations from Hofmannsthal's works are based on the fifteen-volume *Gesammelte Werke,* edited by Herbert Steiner, published by S. Fischer Verlag, Frankfurt a/M. The two volumes of translations preceding the present one (*Selected Prose,* 1952; *Poems and Verse Plays,* 1961) are referred to by their titles.

x. *Nietzsche:* "As you see, I am essentially antitheatrical by nature; for the theatre, that mass art *par excellence,* I have that scorn deep down in my soul that every artist has today. *Success* in the theatre—with that a man goes down in my esteem to the point of no recall; *failure*—there I prick up my ears and begin to respect." *Nietzsche contra Wagner* (1888).

Stefan George: See *Briefwechsel zwischen George und Hofmannsthal* (Munich, 1953), pp. 133–34.

George's attitude to music, and that of his followers, is the subject of G. R. Urban's study *Kinesis and Stasis* (The Hague, 1962). The Circle's antipathy to music, too, was anticipated by Nietzsche in his later writings, especially the polemics against Wagner, though Nietzsche's antipathy was neither wholehearted nor all-inclusive.

xi. *Karl Wolfskehl:* Born at Darmstadt in 1869, first met Stefan George in 1893 and became one of his closest associates. He collaborated with George as joint editor of a series of selections from German writers admired by the Circle. In later life he emerged as a poet of original vision, and though always loyal to George's example and

[829]

memory, became closely identified with the Jewish tradition after 1933. He died at Auckland, New Zealand, in 1948.

See *The Correspondence between Richard Strauss and Hugo von Hofmannsthal,* with an introduction by Edward Sackville-West (London and New York, 1961; American edn.: *A Working Friendship*). The passages quoted are from pp. xx, 12, 49, 58, 77, 81, 108, and 109.

Harry Graf Kessler: See his *Tagebücher 1918–1937* (Frankfurt a/M, 1961), p. 589. Count Kessler, born in Paris in 1868, was active as a diplomat, patron of the arts, publisher, and lecturer in the cause of democracy. Together with his friend Aristide Maillol, the sculptor, he accompanied Hofmannsthal on his journey to Greece in 1908. Six years later he collaborated with Hofmannsthal in writing the dance scenario *Josephslegende* for Richard Strauss and Diaghilev. Kessler had to leave Germany after 1933 and died in a French village in 1937.

Bodenhausen: See *Hugo von Hofmannsthal, Eberhard von Bodenhausen: Briefe der Freundschaft* (Düsseldorf, 1953), p. 161. E. von Bodenhausen (1868–1918) was a lawyer, art critic, and industrialist. He was one of the founders of the literary periodical *Pan,* to which Hofmannsthal contributed, and became one of Hofmannsthal's closest friends.

xv.   *The Letter of Lord Chandos:* See the English version in *Selected Prose,* pp. 129–41. See also Donald Davie's comment on the Letter in his *Articulate Energy* (London, 1955), pp. 1–5.

xvi.   *Essay on Paul Bourget:* See *Prosa I* (1956), p. 9.

Eleonora Duse: For Hofmannsthal's tribute to her, see *Prosa I,* p. 70.

The sense, not the words: Hofmannsthal, *Briefe 1890–1901* (Berlin, 1935), p. 42. The letter is to Felix Baron Oppenheimer.

xvii.   *Between the fleeting fame:* From the *Book of Friends.* See *Selected Prose,* p. 352.

Poems on the deaths of actors: See *Poems and Verse Plays,* pp. 66–71 and 560. The translation of the poem on Mitterwurzer is by Stephen Spender.

xix.   *The stage as dream image:* For Hofmannsthal's note for his essay "Die Bühne als Traumbild" (1903), see my "Hofmannsthals Bibliothek," *Euphorion* (Heidelberg), LV (1961), 43.

xx.   *Space between characters:* See *Selected Prose,* p. 266.

Textual Notes

Prologue to the "Antigone": See *Poems and Verse Plays,* pp. 545 and 541. The translator is Christopher Middleton.

xxii.   *Kainz:* For the poem on this actor, see *Gedichte und lyrische Dramen* (1946), pp. 51–52.

xxiii.   *To have genius . . . :* See *Aufzeichnungen* (1959), p. 209. It has been suggested that the word "Unvernunft" (unreason) here is a misreading for "Urvernunft" (primal reason or *logos*), in which case the sense intended would be the opposite of the sense conveyed in the printed text. Because of a·basic conflict in Hofmannsthal's own nature, either word seems plausible and in character.

xxiv.   *The shaped work . . . :* See Hofmannsthal's lecture (1922) on Grillparzer, *Prosa IV* (1955), p. 126.

"I"-suppression: See *Selected Prose,* p. xl.

xxv.   *The Triumph of Time:* Though Strauss rejected this ballet libretto, it was eventually performed with music by Alexander von Zemlinsky (1872–1942), Austrian conductor and composer, and Schönberg's teacher, active in Vienna, Mannheim, Prague and Berlin. He emigrated in 1938 to New York.

Hofmannsthal also collaborated with the Austrian composer Egon Wellesz (born 1885), who composed the music for Hofmannsthal's ballet scenario *Achilles auf Skyros* in 1922 and for the opera *Alkestis,* based on Hofmannsthal's early adaptation of the play by Euripides. Part of the operatic version of this text (1923) was prepared by the composer.

Frank Kermode: See his essay "Poet and Dancer before Diaghilev" in his *Puzzles and Epiphanies* (London, 1962). The passage quoted is from p. 4, but the whole essay is relevant.

xxvi.   *Fear:* See *Selected Prose,* pp. 155–64. The translation is by Tania and James Stern.

xxvii.   *Oscar Wilde:* See Hofmannsthal's essay in *Prosa II* (1951), pp. 133–38. The passage quoted is on p. 138.

xxviii.   See *Hugo von Hofmannsthal–Carl J. Burckhardt: Briefwechsel* (Frankfurt a/M, 1957), p. 298.

xxx.   *Postcard to Marie Herzfeld:* Unpublished; in the British Museum, Egerton MS. 3150. The card is undated, but the blurred postmark appears to read March 3, 1893.

xxxi.   *Song is marvellous . . . :* See *Aufzeichnungen,* p. 28.

xxxiii.   *Mabel Collins:* Hofmannsthal's library contains a copy of

[831]

the third edition (London, 1910) of her *The Idyll of the White Lotus,* but he had previously read the work in an earlier edition. The allegory involves two "mysterious Queen" figures, one of whom is called the "spirit of light" or "Queen mother"; it is the other, associated with darkness and evil, whom Hofmannsthal mainly had in mind both in *The Mine at Falun* and in the sketches for *Jupiter and Semele.* Not only is Hofmannsthal's Queen of the Mountain more closely akin to Mabel Collins's dark Queen, but it is her evil High Priest Agmahd whose name Hofmannsthal borrowed for the attendant spirit in *The Mine at Falun.* (The source is dealt with in "Hofmannsthals Bibliothek," p. 59.)

E. M. Butler: See her article "Hofmannsthal's 'Elektra': A Graeco-Freudian Myth," *Journal of the Warburg Institute* (London), II:2 (1938). The passage quoted from Hermann Bahr is from his *Dialog vom Tragischen* (Berlin, 1904); in fact the book appeared in 1903, as *Electra* did also.

xxxiv. Hofmannsthal's comments on *Electra:* See *Aufzeichnungen,* pp. 217, 201, 131, and 237.

Ad me Ipsum: See *Aufzeichnungen,* pp. 211–44.

William H. Rey: See his *Weltentzweiung und Weltversöhnung in Hofmannsthals Griechischen Dramen* (Philadelphia, 1962), p. 36.

xli. *In action, in deeds* . . . : From Hofmannsthal's notes for a lecture *The Idea of Europe* (1916) in *Prosa III* (1952), p. 378. Other remarks on *Electra* occur in the same volume, pp. 138, 139, 335, 353–55, and 365.

xlii. *Else Lasker-Schüler:* See her *Briefe an Karl Kraus* (Cologne and Berlin, n. d.), p. 82; and *Dichtungen und Dokumente* (Munich, n. d.), pp. 517–18.

xliii. Hofmannsthal on his *Everyman:* "Das Spiel vor der Menge," *Prosa III,* pp. 60–65; "Das Alte Spiel von Jedermann," ibid., pp. 114–32.

xliv. *The powerful imagination is conservative* . . . : See *Aufzeichnungen,* p. 41.

xlv. For details of Hofmannsthal's reading and annotation of these books, see "Hofmannsthals Bibliothek," pp. 31–35.

xlvii. *Neo-Platonism:* Cf. introduction to *Poems and Verse Plays,* pp. xxxix–xl.

xlviii. *The poet's starting point:* From a letter by Hofmannsthal to Fritz Setz, in *Corona* (Munich), X (1940), 6.

xlix.　It was by Grimmelshausen's *Simplicissimus,* too, that Hofmannsthal's attention was drawn to the Spanish moralist Antonio de Guevara (1480–1545). Grimmelshausen's novel concludes with a long passage from Guevara that comprises the passages quoted in *The Tower;* but Hofmannsthal adapted Grimmelshausen's German translation.

liv.　*Bertolt Brecht:* A specific and curious parallel between the two dramatists can be found in Brecht's *Im Dickicht der Städte* (*In the Jungle of Cities*), written at about the same time as the early version of *The Tower* and first performed in Munich on May 9, 1923, and again in Berlin in 1924. A passage in Brecht's play (Scene 6)—"Now the crayfishes mate, the love-cry of the stags is in the thicket, and the badger can be hunted"—is extraordinarily like the opening of Basilius's speech about his past prowess in Act II of *The Tower.* Since Hofmannsthal does not appear to have seen Brecht's play performed, and since the play was not published until 1927—four years after the first publication of Hofmannsthal's passage—the borrowing, if any, must have been Brecht's.

The social side of his nature: In his retrospective postscript of 1927 to *Der Rosenkavalier,* in *Prosa IV,* pp. 426–30, Hofmannsthal remarks on the "social genesis" of this work in conversations with his friend Count Harry Kessler. These conversations seem to have taken the place of literary sources, and it is likely that Kessler helped Hofmannsthal to invent a plot. Hofmannsthal wrote another short comment on the libretto in 1911: "Ungeschriebenes Nachwort zum Rosenkavalier," *Prosa III,* pp. 43–45.

lv.　The original version of the second act of *Der Rosenkavalier* was published in *Die Neue Rundschau* (Frankfurt a/M), LXIV: 3 (1953), with a commentary by Willi Schuh.

lvii.　*Maria Theresia:* See Hofmannsthal's essay in *Prosa III,* pp. 387–400. Hofmannsthal's notes on Maria Theresia in his copy of La Bruyère are transcribed in "Hofmannsthals Bibliothek," p. 46.

lviii.　*Adam Müller:* (1779–1829) German Romantic political economist.

lx.　*Franz Tumler:* See his "Rosenkavalier und Arabella," *Neue Deutsche Hefte* (Gütersloh), No. 29 (September 1956).

lxiii.　*Anton Wildgans:* See *Der Briefwechsel Hofmannsthal–Wildgans* (Zurich, Munich, Paris, 1935), p. 52.

lxv.　*Prussian and Austrian:* In *Prosa III,* pp. 407–9.

Textual Notes

lxviii.   *Emil Staiger:* "Hugo von Hofmannsthal: 'Der Schwierige' " in *Meisterwerke Deutscher Sprache* (3rd edn., Zurich, 1957).

lxx.   *Kafka:* See Gustav Janouch, *Conversations with Kafka* (London, 1953), pp. 99–100.

T. S. Eliot: A Note on "The Tower"

The aptness of Mr. Eliot's comparison with Valéry's *La Crise de l'esprit* is borne out by the evidence of Hofmannsthal's library. This contains a copy of Valéry's *Variété* (new edn., Paris, 1924) in which Hofmannsthal marked several passages of *La Crise de l'esprit*. What is more, Hofmannsthal took over two of these passages for his lecture "Das Vermächtnis der Antike" (1926). There Valéry's words *"L'Esprit est en vérité cruellement atteint"* are quoted in translation and ascribed to "a Frenchman," and Valéry's *"Nous espérons vaguement, nous redoutons précisément; nos craintes sont infiniment plus précises que nos espérances"* is paraphrased without quotation marks or reference to the source.

Hofmannsthal's library, his borrowings from other writers, and his marginalia in books still extant are dealt with in "Hofmannsthals Bibliothek."

Electra

First performed as a play on October 30, 1903, at the Kleines Theater, Berlin, with Gertrud Eysoldt in the title role. Published in book form in 1903 (dated 1904). Opera composed in 1906–1908; first performed at the Royal Opera House, Dresden, on January 25, 1909, with Ernestine Schumann-Heink as Klytämnestra. Libretto published in 1908 with a cover drawing by Lovis Corinth.

The first English translation, by Arthur Symons, was undertaken at the request of the actress Mrs. Patrick Campbell and first performed in Edinburgh on September 19, 1908.

The Salzburg Great Theatre of the World

Written for the annual Salzburg Festival, which Hofmannsthal helped to institute, and first produced there by Max Reinhardt at the Col-

[834]

legienkirche on August 12, 1922, with music by Einar Nilson and décor by Alfred Roller. The cast included Alexander Moissi as the Beggar and Helene Thimig as Wisdom.

The play is based on Calderón's *El Gran Teatro del Mundo* (1642). The characters in Calderón's allegory include the Rich Man, Peasant, Beggar, Wisdom, and Beauty, and also the Soul of an Unborn Child and the Law of Grace. The motto in Hofmannsthal's play, "Do Right: Under God!" is adapted from Calderón. The differences between the two works are crucial and numerous; and there is a great deal more overt moralizing in Calderón's play.

84.   *A O U:* Vowels in various combinations played an important role in late antique magical practices and in particular were part of the prophecies of the sibyls. Hofmannsthal may intend an allusion to the characterization of Christ in the Apocalypse of St. John as Alpha and Omega; certainly here he intends a reference to the banishment of superstitious abracadabra which has called up so many evil spirits.

The Tower

There are two wholly distinct versions of this play, of which the earlier is translated here. Both versions were first performed on February 4, 1928: the earlier version at the Prinzregententheater, Munich, the later at the Hamburg Schauspielhaus.

The earlier version was first published in two issues of Hofmannsthal's periodical *Neue Deutsche Beiträge* (February 1923 and January 1925), and in a single volume by the same press (Bremer Presse, Munich) in 1925. In its revised form—on which the translation is based—it was first published posthumously in the three-volume edition of Hofmannsthal's *Gesammelte Werke* (1934). The later version, undertaken mainly with the stage in mind and incorporating changes suggested by Max Reinhardt, was first published as a separate volume in 1927.

Hofmannsthal's correspondence with Martin Buber, recently published in *Die Neue Rundschau* (Frankfurt a/M), LXXIII: 4 (1962), sheds new light on Hofmannsthal's revision of the earlier version of *The Tower*. Martin Buber, in his letter of May 14, 1926, informed Hofmannsthal of his objections to the last act and the introduction in it of two new dimensions—the "spirit world" of the Gipsy episode and the "new generation" represented by the Children's King and his followers—pointing out that both served to break the unity of the play and to strain the reader's credulity. Announcing the revised version to Buber in his letter of December 19 of the same year, Hofmannsthal wrote that it would not "include those things which disturbed you—and about which you were right."

Both versions are now available in *Dramen IV* (1958). The school edition referred to in Mr. Eliot's *Note* reproduces the text of the earlier version as printed in 1925.

There are interesting thematic links between *The Tower* and Hofmannsthal's projected Semiramis dramas, also based on a play by Calderón.

200. *But the faculty opposes you:* In Central Europe, the university faculty of medicine controls medical theory and practice generally, and so the term "faculty" becomes an equivalent for the modern "professional code."

201. *Schwenkfeldian:* Kaspar von Schwenkfeld (1489–1561) was a Silesian nobleman and mystic, mainly remembered for his refutation of Luther's defence of the doctrine of justification by faith and for his glorification of the human aspect of Christ. The Doctor's practical mysticism is suspected of having a similar heretical basis; and Sigismund's own *imitatio Christi* could be seen in this light.

266. *And his afflictions are not too many:* These words are a paraphrase of those reported to have been spoken by Georg Büchner on his deathbed. Hofmannsthal's knowledge of Büchner's works is attested by books in his library, and the influence of Büchner's prose style is very marked in several of Hofmannsthal's works. It is especially significant that the words of this revolutionary writer should have been put in the mouth of Hofmannsthal's Sigismund at this point in the play. For an English rendering of Büchner's words and a discussion of their relevance to his works, see my *Reason and Energy* (New York and London, 1957), pp. 202–3.

333. *Speak to us . . . Call him by his name:* There are distinct similarities between this scene and the scene in Paul Claudel's *Tête d'or* in which the hero reveals himself to the people. Hofmannsthal read Claudel's play in 1919, 1920, and 1923, and marked several passages.

345. *Dear friend, my place is a dreadful place:* Cf. Paul Claudel's

Textual Notes

La Ville in *L'Arbre* (2nd edn., Paris, 1901), p. 393, where Cœuvre says: *"Ma considération est adequate à ce qui est. Rien n'a pu ou ne peut/Etre, qui ne soit à ce moment même; toutes choses sont présentes pour moi."* Hofmannsthal re-read this work in September 1919 and heavily marked the passage in question.

376. *I ask you nothing but that which you cannot say:* Cf. Claudel's *Tête d'or* in *L'Arbre*, p. 21, where Cèbès says: *"Eh bien! autre chose que tu peux dire, c'est cela que je te demande."* The passage is marked in Hofmannsthal's copy.

The Cavalier of the Rose

The opera was first performed at the Royal Opera House, Dresden, on January 26, 1911, with décor and costumes designed by Alfred Roller. In the same year the text was published in book form with the subtitle *A Comedy for Music.* A film version was made in 1926.

The name Faninal may well be an anagram of Fainall in Congreve's *The Way of the World,* a copy of which (in the Mermaid Series Congreve, n. d.) is extant in Hofmannsthal's library.

397. *Platz am Hof:* Largest square in the "Inner City" of Vienna; it contains many town houses and palaces of the nobility.

504. *Graben:* This broad promenade in the "Inner City" was a fashionable centre of imperial Vienna.

Arabella

This was Hofmannsthal's last libretto for Strauss, and it was first performed at the Staatsoper, Dresden, on July 1, 1933, after his death. Hofmannsthal wrote the text in 1927 and 1928. The basic situation and plot, which were partly derived from Molière's *Le Dépit Amoureux* (1654), had occupied Hofmannsthal for many years. His story *Lucidor* (1909) dealt with them more psychologically, but without the social setting and implications of the libretto. *Lucidor* bore the subtitle *Figures for an Unwritten Comedy.*

The present translation was begun by the late Nora Wydenbruck and left unfinished when she died in 1959. She had translated the whole of the first act and part of the second, up to the entrance of Fiacre-Milli. Christopher Middleton took over at this point, also revising Countess Wydenbruck's version so as to make the whole consistent in diction and cadence.

For the circumstances of the writing and composition of *Arabella*, see the Strauss-Hofmannsthal *Correspondence*, pp. 422–46 and 470–536.

540.   *The Ring:* The Ringstrasse, a broad boulevard built in the mid-nineteenth century on the site of the old ramparts that encircled the "Inner City." It is an outstanding example of street architecture.

553.   *Prater:* A park in eastern Vienna, one of the largest in Europe; frequented by all social classes.

597.   *Lenau:* Pseudonym of Nicolaus Franz Niembsch von Strehlenau (1802–50), Austrian Romantic poet. His *Don Juan* is the basis of the programme for Richard Strauss's tone poem.

The Difficult Man

First performed at the Residenztheater, Munich, on November 8, 1921, with Gustav Waldau in the title role and Elisabeth Bergner as Helen. The comedy was completed in 1918 and published in the periodical *Neue Freie Presse* in 1920. It appeared in book form in 1921.

Hofmannsthal's free adaptation of Molière's comedy *Les Fâcheux*, so unlike Molière's play and so close to *The Difficult Man* as to be in some ways a preliminary study for it, was written in 1915 and first produced by Max Reinhardt at the Deutsches Theater, Berlin, on April 26, 1916, under the title *Die Lästigen*.

Hofmannsthal jotted down preliminary drafts and notes for this comedy on the fly-leaves of two works by Kierkegaard, *Stadien auf dem Lebenswege* (Leipzig, 1886) and *Tagebuch des Verführers* (Leipzig, 1903). Antoinette's bad memory owes something to Kierkegaard's distinction in the former work between "the erotic understanding of recollection" and "mere memory." Stani's insistence (p. 677) that "the decision must be instantaneous" is a borrowing from the same work ("Whatever is to be good, must be at once, for 'at once' is the most divine of all categories and deserves to be honoured like *ex templo* in the language of the Romans . . . what does not happen at once is no good.") Stani's words (p. 675) "She says your hand is always loose on its wrist, ready to let go" are another borrowing, though less direct, and Kierkegaard's work is pervaded by a fear of fine words akin to Hans Karl's. The religious and theological question "Guilty? Not Guilty" in Kierkegaard's book is also posed in Hofmannsthal's early notes for the play, but he concealed it in the final version, only taking over the antinomy between chance and necessity, and Hans Karl's identification of necessity with the sacrament of marriage.

669. *Riesener:* Jean Henri Riesener (1734–1806), French cabinetmaker of the Louis XVI period, largely responsible for the famous "Bureau du Roi," now in the Louvre.

817. *Freyung and Herrengasse:* The Freyung is a square in the "Inner City"; the Herrengasse, a street of aristocratic houses running from the Freyung to the Hofburg, the palace of the Habsburgs.